ECHOES AND EVIDENCES
OF THE BOOK OF MORMON

ECHOES AND EVIDENCES
OF THE BOOK OF MORMON

Edited by
Donald W. Parry, Daniel C. Peterson, and John W. Welch

FOUNDATION FOR ANCIENT RESEARCH AND MORMON STUDIES (FARMS)
BRIGHAM YOUNG UNIVERSITY
PROVO, UTAH

Cover design: Andrew Livingston
Cover painting: *Cave of Records,* by Robert T. Barrett. Oil on Canvas. Copyright Institute for the Study and Preservation of Ancient Religious Texts.

Foundation for Ancient Research and Mormon Studies (FARMS)
  farms.byu.edu
Institute for the Study and Preservation of Ancient Religious Texts
  ispart.byu.edu
Brigham Young University
  www.byu.edu
P.O. Box 7113
University Station
Provo, Utah 84602

© 2002 FARMS
All rights reserved
Printed in the United States of America
10 09 08 07 06 05 04 03 02   10 9 8 7 6 5 4 3 2 1

Library of Congress Cataloging-in-Publication Data

Echoes and evidences of the Book of Mormon / edited by Donald W. Parry, Daniel C. Peterson, John W. Welch.
  p. cm.
Includes bibliographical references and index.
ISBN 0-934893-72-1 (alk. paper)
1. Book of Mormon—Evidences, authority, etc. I. Parry, Donald W. II. Peterson, Daniel C. III. Welch, John W. (John Woodland)
BX8627 .E24 2002
289.3'22—dc21
                    2002014235

Contents

List of Illustrations vii

Introduction ix

"By the Gift and Power of God" 1
   Elder Neal A. Maxwell

The Power of Evidence in the Nurturing of Faith 17
   John W. Welch

New Light from Arabia on Lehi's Trail 55
   S. Kent Brown

By Objective Measures: Old Wine into Old Bottles 127
   Noel B. Reynolds

Hebraisms and Other Ancient Peculiarities in the
Book of Mormon 155
   Donald W. Parry

Not Joseph's, and Not Modern 191
   Daniel C. Peterson

Ancient Texts in Support of the Book of Mormon 231
   John A. Tvedtnes

How Could Joseph Smith Write So Accurately
about Ancient American Civilization? 261
   John L. Sorenson

The Wrong Type of Book 307
   John Gee

A Steady Stream of Significant Recognitions 331
 John W. Welch

Converging Paths: Language and Cultural Notes on
the Ancient Near Eastern Background
of the Book of Mormon 389
 Stephen D. Ricks

From a Convert's Viewpoint 421
 Alison V. P. Coutts

Appendix: Echoes and Evidences from the
Writings of Hugh Nibley 453

Scripture Citation Index 489

Alphabetical Listing of Hits 497

Contributors 501

About the Institute 507

List of Illustrations

Events Surrounding the Translation of the
Book of Mormon, 1829–1830 6

Testimony of the Three Witnesses
in Oliver Cowdery's Hand 10

Lehi's Possible Routes to Bountiful 58

Wordprints and the Book of Mormon 133

Simile Curses 157

Cognate Accusatives 177

Tenochtitlán, the Aztec Capital 263

Ceramic Figurine 289

How Do You Say "Law" in Hebrew? 355

Doubled Documents 376

Golden Plates 408

La Gran Tenochtitlán 424

Introduction

As we stand at the threshold of the twenty-first century, the achievements of the last hundred years stand out in bold relief. Just as many astonishing and incredibly useful discoveries have been made in numerous areas of research—from technology to medical science—surprising advances have similarly been made in the field of Book of Mormon studies. In 1909, when B. H. Roberts published the first two volumes of his *New Witnesses for God,* drawing together his favorite evidences in support of the Book of Mormon, no one could have dreamed of or anticipated the outpouring of discoveries in that book that would follow in the twentieth century. *Echoes and Evidences of the Book of Mormon* takes inventory of many of the most striking of those discoveries that support the claim that the Book of Mormon was translated by Joseph Smith from bona fide ancient records.

During the twentieth century, many writers contributed to Book of Mormon research. Among the most important yields of evidences were those set forth in the three volumes of Roberts's

New Witnesses for God (1909, 1911), in which Roberts focused mainly on the theology of the Nephite prophets but also wrestled with the historical, geographical, and cultural implications of their records. Janne Sjodahl produced a significant one-volume commentary, the first of its kind, *An Introduction to the Study of the Book of Mormon* (1927), which examined a variety of cultural and linguistic dimensions of the book. In 1942, Francis Kirkham published a two-volume work, *A New Witness for Christ in America*, focusing on the coming forth of the Book of Mormon in the 1820s.

It was not until the late 1940s and 1950s that Sidney B. Sperry and Hugh W. Nibley began examining the Book of Mormon extensively in the context of ancient cultures. Sperry, ultimately in his *Book of Mormon Compendium* (1968), looked to ancient Israel for background information behind the words of Lehi, Nephi, and their descendants.

Nibley, in his groundbreaking volumes *Lehi in the Desert* (1952), *An Approach to the Book of Mormon* (1964), and *Since Cumorah* (1967), widened the scope of inquiry and looked throughout the ancient Near East, Egypt, Arabia, Israel, and the Mediterranean world for answers to such questions as, "Does [the Book of Mormon] correctly reflect 'the cultural horizon and religious and social ideas and practices of the time'? Does it have authentic historical and geographical background? Is the *mise-en-scène* mythical, highly imaginative, or extravagantly improbable? Is its local color correct, and are its proper names convincing?"[1]

Occasionally, Nibley likened Joseph Smith's translation of the Book of Mormon to shooting arrows and being right on target, scoring "hits" or "bull's-eyes."[2] For Nibley, such dead aim in the Book of Mormon occurs whenever a certain detail has significant and astonishing parallels to the ancient world, especially when those parallels were unknown to the world at the time of Joseph Smith. At times, Joseph hit not only the broadside of the ancient cultural barn but the bull's-eye as well, and with his eyes blindfolded to boot. Referring to the book of Ether alone, Nibley wrote, "The list of bull's-eyes is a long one," and the "percentage of hits is not less staggering."[3]

Nibley explained further:

> Even if every parallel were the purest coincidence, we would still have to explain how the Prophet contrived to pack such a dense succession of happy accidents into the scriptures he gave us. Where the world has a perfect right to expect a great potpourri of the most outrageous nonsense, and in anticipation has indeed rushed to judgment with all manner of premature accusations, we discover whenever ancient texts turn up to offer the necessary checks and controls that the man was astonishingly on target in his depiction of general situations, in the almost casual mention of peculiar oddities, in the strange proper names, and countless other unaccountable details. . . . As the evidence accumulates, it is not the Prophet but his critics who find themselves with a lot of explaining to do.[4]

In this work, Nibley was not alone. Dozens of other scholars, trained in biblical studies, archaeology, classics, history, law, linguistics, anthropology, political science, philosophy, Near Eastern studies, literature, and numerous other fields, began noticing similar hits arising out of their own fields of study. Books and articles in the field of Book of Mormon studies blossomed.[5] In the 1980s and 1990s, research updates were published monthly in the newsletter of the Foundation for Ancient Research and Mormon Studies, and those cutting-edge reports were collected and published in *Reexploring the Book of Mormon* (1992) and *Pressing Forward with the Book of Mormon* (1999). Also during those two decades, the Religious Studies Center at Brigham Young University produced a series of volumes containing scores of additional essays on various features of the Book of Mormon.[6] Scattered among all these publications were so many further hits that it became difficult for new readers to get up to speed in studying the Book of Mormon.

In order to help people find access to this substantial body of research, the editors of the present volume set out to identify, collect, catalog, and publish as many such hits and other Book of Mormon parallels to the ancient world as possible. With the help of other colleagues, we scanned the entire scope of Book of Mormon research and collected many impressive findings from the last part of the twentieth century. We then invited several of the most active Book of Mormon researchers to select and summarize a number of these discoveries, as well as those from previous generations of scholars. The result is a rich array of keen observations, mainly uncovering details that Joseph Smith, in all likelihood, had no possible knowledge of in 1829 while he was translating the Book of Mormon. The present collection does not exhaust all of the possibilities, but it will help readers, especially those not fully conversant with the research literature, to skim the cream of this extensive and sometimes hard-to-find academic literature.

Echoes and Evidences of the Book of Mormon comprises twelve chapters with more than one hundred hits or other evidences and ancient parallels. The opening chapter holds special significance because it was authored by Elder Neal A. Maxwell, a member of the Quorum of the Twelve Apostles. All of the contributors add distinct perspectives of knowledge to Book of Mormon studies because they represent a wide variety of professional fields, including Hebrew, Arabic, Egyptology, biblical law, political science, education, the Dead Sea Scrolls, Mesoamerica, and Jewish studies. The appendix contains hits culled from Dr. Nibley's writings.

Not all of the points presented in this volume carry equal weight. Some are obvious bull's-eyes, and others simply hit the outer edges of the target. Some of these echoes from the ancient world reverberate loudly, others faintly. Some are stronger, some are weaker, but all are of significant probative interest. In collecting and selecting these items, we have tried to include

- points that are clearly present in ancient sources,
- items that are clearly reflected in the text of the Book of Mormon,
- details that are relatively obscure or subtle,
- patterns or practices that are complex or intricate,
- features that are unusual or distinctive,
- information that was little known in the 1820s,
- scholarship that was unavailable to Joseph Smith, and
- insights that require considerable training to detect or appreciate even today.

Although many questions remain to be explored in the world of Book of Mormon research, important advances have been made in the twentieth century, and those strides are becoming more widely recognized.

Astute readers will notice few areas of overlap between the points selected and discussed by the various contributors to this volume. This is not coincidental, for the participants have met together and coordinated coverage. Over the years, these researchers have openly shared, critiqued, appreciated, and benefited from one another's work. The editors have deliberately sought to minimize areas of overlap by assigning or shifting the discussion of particular topics among the authors, always with the consent of those asked to defer.

Readers should understand that the points discussed in this volume are only brief summaries. Behind each one stand various scholarly sources, both ancient and modern, as well as the analyses of several scholars, who are frequently but not always Latter-day Saints. Thus, the selections in this book serve especially as points of entry into the ongoing world of scholarship concerning ancient civilizations.

We hope this book will be easy to use. For readers' convenience, each hit has been identified in the margin and listed alphabetically at the end of the book.

We express great appreciation to Don Brugger, associate director of publications at FARMS, for his tireless assistance in helping to bring this volume together and to completion. Daniel McKinlay extracted the hits from the works of Hugh Nibley. Many others in the FARMS editorial and research departments also contributed significantly to this volume.

Now we invite readers to enjoy a survey of echoes and evidences of the Book of Mormon as an ancient book, as Book of Mormon research moves forward into the twenty-first century.

Donald W. Parry
Daniel C. Peterson
John W. Welch

NOTES

1. Hugh W. Nibley, *Lehi in the Desert; The World of the Jaredites; There Were Jaredites,* ed. John W. Welch, Darrell L. Matthews, and Stephen R. Callister (Salt Lake City: Deseret Book and FARMS, 1988), 4.

2. See, for example, ibid., 255, 263.

3. Ibid., 255.

4. Hugh Nibley, *The Prophetic Book of Mormon,* ed. John W. Welch (Salt Lake City: Deseret Book and FARMS, 1989), 325–26.

5. A good summary of this scholarship is found in Terryl L. Givens, *By the Hand of Mormon: The American Scripture That Launched a New World Religion* (Oxford: Oxford University Press, 2002).

6. See, for example, Monte S. Nyman and Charles D. Tate Jr., eds., *The Book of Mormon: Alma, the Testimony of the Word* (Provo, Utah: BYU Religious Studies Center, 1992).

"By the Gift and Power of God"

Elder Neal A. Maxwell

The coming forth of the Book of Mormon is a marvelous episode not only in Church history but also in human history. You and I owe many people for their roles in bringing us the Book of Mormon, a book filled with plain and precious salvational truths which came forth by "the gift and power of God" (Book of Mormon title page). Through the labors and sacrifices of many, the "marvellous work and a wonder" foreseen by Isaiah (Isaiah 29:14) restored vital truths which had been lost to mankind for centuries! We can best express our gratitude by reading and applying the teachings of the Book of Mormon.

A Divine Gift

After all, the Book of Mormon's stated purpose is for "the convincing of the Jew and Gentile that Jesus is the

---

This article is reprinted from the *Ensign* magazine, January 1997, 36–41.

Christ" (title page), making it a divine gift to the entire human family.

In fact, Nephi tells us that God "doeth not anything save it be for the benefit of the world" (2 Nephi 26:24). The knowledge concerning God's plan of salvation, repeatedly and carefully set forth in the Book of Mormon, can counter the hopelessness and despair of some who lament the human predicament in which they feel mortals are "conceived without consent" and "wrenched whimpering into an alien universe."[1] So many mortals desperately need to know there is divine design. No wonder the Lord told Joseph Smith that the Restoration came to increase faith in the earth! (see Doctrine and Covenants 1:21).

Originally translated from reformed Egyptian into English, the words of the Book of Mormon are now available in eighty-eight languages. Reaching one hundred languages is likely within the next several years. From its first edition of 5,000 copies in 1830 and on through 1995, nearly 78,000,000 copies are estimated to have been distributed.

We know the book's influence will continue to grow. "Wherefore, these things shall go from generation to generation as long as the earth shall stand; and they shall go according to the will and pleasure of God; and the nations who shall possess them shall be judged of them according to the words which are written" (2 Nephi 25:22). Among other words foretelling the book's growing influence are these: "The day cometh that the words of the book which were sealed shall be read upon the house tops" (2 Nephi 27:11). Hence the Book of Mormon's best days still lie ahead!

Perspective on the Translation Process

The Prophet Joseph Smith worked by the gift and power of God amid numerous interruptions, bitter persecutions, and even the "most strenuous exertions" to wrest the actual plates from him (Joseph Smith—History 1:60). His was not the tranquil life of a detached scholar in some sheltered sanctuary where he could work at his uninterrupted leisure. Chores had to be done. His family had to be cared for. Joseph was so conscientious that the Lord counseled him: "Do not run faster or labor more than you have strength and means provided to enable you to translate; but be diligent unto the end" (Doctrine and Covenants 10:4).

TRANSLATION PROCESS

Many who read the Book of Mormon understandably desire to know more about its coming forth, including the actual process of translation. This was certainly so with faithful and loyal Hyrum Smith. Upon inquiring, Hyrum was told by the Prophet Joseph that "it was not intended to tell the world all the particulars of the coming forth of the Book of Mormon" and that "it was not expedient for him to relate these things."[2] Thus what we do know about the actual coming forth of the Book of Mormon is adequate, but it is not comprehensive.

Our primary focus in studying the Book of Mormon should be on the principles of the gospel anyway, not on the process by which the book came forth. Yet because its coming so amply fulfilled Isaiah's prophecy of a "marvellous work and a wonder," we may find strengthened faith in considering how marvelous and wondrous the translation really was.

MARVELOUS
POWER TO
TRANSLATE

"Sight and Power to Translate"

The Prophet Joseph alone knew the full process, and he was deliberately reluctant to describe details. We take passing notice of the words of David Whitmer, Joseph Knight, and Martin Harris, who were observers, not translators. David Whitmer indicated that as the Prophet used the divine instrumentalities provided to help him, "the hieroglyphics would appear, and also the translation in the English language . . . in bright luminous letters." Then Joseph would read the words to Oliver.[3] Martin Harris related of the seer stone: "Sentences would appear and were read by the Prophet and written by Martin."[4] Joseph Knight made similar observations.[5]

Oliver Cowdery is reported to have testified in court that the Urim and Thummim enabled Joseph "to read in English, the reformed Egyptian characters, which were engraved on the plates."[6] If these reports are accurate, they suggest a process indicative of God's having given Joseph "sight and power to translate" (Doctrine and Covenants 3:12).

If by means of these divine instrumentalities the Prophet was seeing ancient words rendered in English and then dictating, he was not necessarily and constantly scrutinizing the characters on the plates—the usual translation process of going back and forth between pondering an ancient text and providing a modern rendering.

The revelatory process apparently did not require the Prophet to become expert in the ancient language. The constancy of revelation was more crucial than the constant presence of opened plates, which, by instruction, were to be kept from the view of unauthorized eyes anyway.

While the use of divine instrumentalities might also account for the rapid rate of translation, the Prophet sometimes may have used a less mechanical procedure. We simply do not know the details.

We do know that this faith-filled process was not easy, however. This fact was clearly demonstrated in Oliver Cowdery's own attempt at translation. Oliver failed because he "did not continue as [he] commenced," and because, lacking faith and works, he "took no thought save it was to ask" (Doctrine and Covenants 9:5, 7). He was not properly prepared to do it. Even so, we owe so much to Oliver Cowdery for his special service as a scribe.

Whatever the details of the process, it required Joseph's intense, personal efforts along with the aid of the revelatory instruments. The process may have varied as Joseph's capabilities grew, involving the Urim and Thummim but perhaps with less reliance upon such instrumentalities in the Prophet's later work of translation. Elder Orson Pratt of the Quorum of the Twelve Apostles said Joseph Smith told him that he used the Urim and Thummim when he was inexperienced at translation but that later he did not need it, which was the case in Joseph's translation of many verses of the Bible.[7]

Some additional things we know about the process of translation further qualify the Book of Mormon as a "marvellous work and a wonder."

A Marvelous Feat of Inspiration

One marvel is the very rapidity with which Joseph was translating—at an estimated average rate of eight of our printed pages per day! The total translation time was about sixty-five working days.[8] By comparison, one able LDS translator in Japan, surrounded by reference books, language dictionaries, and translator colleagues ready to

SHORT TRANSLATION TIME

Events Surrounding the Translation of the Book of Mormon, 1829–1830

Jan.

Feb. — Joseph receives D&C 4 in Harmony, Pennsylvania
The Lord appears to Oliver Cowdery

Mar. — Joseph translates a few pages of the Book of Mormon
Martin Harris of Palmyra visits Joseph in Harmony

Apr. — Oliver arrives in Harmony to meet Joseph

May

Book of Mormon Translated
April 7–End of June

June

July — E. B. Grandin and T. Weed decline to print Book of Mormon

Aug. — Grandin agrees to print; typesetting begins
Martin Harris mortgages his farm

Sept.

Oct.

Nov. — Printer's manuscript is prepared through Alma 36

Dec.

Jan.

Feb.

Mar. — Printing is finished

Apr. — Restored Church of Christ officially organized

help if needed, indicated that he considered an output of one careful, final page a day to be productive. And he is retranslating from earlier Japanese to modern Japanese! More than fifty able English scholars labored for seven years, using previous translations, to produce the King James Version of the Bible, averaging about one precious page per day. The Prophet Joseph Smith would sometimes produce ten pages per day![9]

A second marvel of the Book of Mormon translation process is that from what we know, rarely would Joseph go back, review, or revise what had already been done. There was a steady flow in the translation. The Prophet's dictating resulted—just as the compositor, John H. Gilbert, remembered—in no paragraphing.

Emma Smith said of the inspired process: "After meals, or after interruptions, [Joseph] would at once begin where he had left off, without either seeing the manuscript or having any portion of it read to him."[10] One who has dictated and been interrupted must usually resume by inquiring, "Now, where were we?" Not so with the Prophet!

If one were manufacturing a text, he would constantly need to cross-check himself, to edit, and to revise for consistency. Had the Prophet dictated and revised extensively, there would be more evidence of it. But there was no need to revise divinely supplied text. Whatever the details of the translation process, we are discussing a process that was truly astonishing!

With regard to the physical circumstances of the Prophet Joseph Smith and his scribe, Martin Harris was quoted as saying there was a blanket or curtain hung between himself and Joseph during the translation process. If Martin is accurately quoted, perhaps this occurred when the

Prophet was copying characters directly from the plates in the sample to be taken to Professor Charles Anthon, since the dates mentioned are several months before Martin Harris's brief scribal duties began. I say this because although David Whitmer mentions a blanket being used, it was only to partition off the living area in order to keep both the translator and scribe from the eyes of visitors.[11]

In fact, Elizabeth Anne Whitmer Cowdery, Oliver's wife, said, "Joseph never had a curtain drawn between him and his scribe."[12] Emma likewise said of her days as scribe, early on, that Joseph dictated "hour after hour with nothing between us."[13]

Of course, the real revelatory process involved Joseph's mind and faith, which could not be seen by others in any case.

A third marvel of the translation process is that although he was intensely involved in translating an ancient record, the Prophet Joseph himself was clearly unschooled in things ancient. For example, early in the work he came across words concerning a wall around Jerusalem and asked Emma if the city indeed had walls. She affirmed what Joseph simply hadn't known.[14]

He knew nothing, either, of the literary form called chiasmus, which appears in the Bible at various places and, significantly, also appears in the Book of Mormon.

Emma does mention, however, and so does David Whitmer, the Prophet's spelling out of unfamiliar names, letter by letter, especially if asked by the scribe. For instance, Oliver Cowdery first wrote the name *Coriantumr* phonetically. He then immediately crossed out his phonetic spelling and spelled the name as we now have it in the Book of Mormon. *Coriantumr* with its "-mr" ending clearly would have required a letter-by-letter spelling out by the Prophet.

Fourth, we marvel that the Prophet Joseph Smith worked completely without referring to any other sources. None of the twelve people who either participated or merely observed mentioned Joseph's having any reference materials present. (The twelve people were Emma Smith, Martin Harris, Oliver Cowdery, Elizabeth Ann Whitmer Cowdery, David Whitmer, William Smith, Lucy Mack Smith, Michael Morse, Sarah Hellor Conrad, Isaac Hale, Reuben Hale, and Joseph Knight Sr.) Since the Prophet dictated openly, these individuals would have been aware of any suspicious behavior or procedures. Emma was emphatic on this very point: "He had neither manuscript nor book to read from, [and] if he had anything of the kind he could not have concealed it from me."[15]

Thus the Book of Mormon came *through,* but not *from,* Joseph Smith!

There is need for caution in assuming or suggesting that the Prophet had great flexibility as to doctrine and as to the substance of the language he used. This may be gauged by his emphatic words about the title page of the Book of Mormon. On one occasion he said that "the title page of the Book of Mormon is a literal translation, taken from the very last leaf, on the left hand side of the collection or book of plates, which contained the record which has been translated; the language of the whole running the same as all Hebrew writing in general; and that, said *title page is not by any means a modern composition either of mine or of any other man's who has lived or does live in this generation.*"[16]

Our observation that the Prophet was not shaping the doctrine is no discredit to Joseph Smith. On the contrary, some of King Benjamin's words were not solely his either,

The Testimony of three witnesses

Be it known unto all nations kindreds tongues & people unto whom this work shall come that we through the grace of God the Father & our Lord Jesus Christ have seen the plates which contain this record which is a record of the people of Nephi & also of the Lamanites his brethren & also of the people of Jared which came from the tower of which hath been spoken & we also know that they have been translated by the gift & power of God for his voice hath declared it unto us wherefore we know of a surety that the work is true & we also testify that we have seen the engravings which are upon the plates & they have been shewn unto us by the power of God & not of man & we declare with words of soberness that an angel of God came down from Heaven & he brought & laid before our eyes that we beheld & saw the plates & the engravings thereon & we know that it is by the grace of God the Father & our Lord Jesus Christ that we beheld & bear record that these things are true & it is marvellous in our eyes nevertheless the voice of the Lord commanded us that we should bear record of it wherefore to be obedient unto the commandments of God we bear testimony of these things & we know that if we are faithful in Christ we shall rid our garments of the blood of all men & be found spotless before the Judgement seat of Christ & shall dwell with him Eternally in the Heavens & the honor be to the Father & to the Son & to the Holy Ghost which is one God. Amen.

Oliver Cowdery
David Whitmer
Martin Harris

Testimony of the Three Witnesses
in Oliver Cowdery's hand

but "had been delivered unto him by the angel of the Lord" (Mosiah 4:1). Similarly, Nephi said his words "are the words of Christ, and he hath given them unto me" (2 Nephi 33:10).

Oliver Cowdery, the most constant and involved witness to the miraculous translation, always affirmed the divinity of the process. Though later disaffected for a time from the Church, he nevertheless came humbly back. He spoke forthrightly about how he "wrote with my own pen the intire book of Mormon (save a few pages) as it fell from the Lips of the prophet."[17] Oliver would not have humbly returned to the Church at all, especially seeking no station, had there been any kind of fraud!

OLIVER'S FIRM TESTIMONY

Instead, at the approach of death, Oliver could not have been more dramatic about his testimony concerning the Book of Mormon. Oliver's half-sister, Lucy P. Young, reported: "Just before he breathed his last he asked to be raised up in bed so he could talk to the family and friends and he told them to live according to the teachings in the [B]ook of Mormon and they would meet him in Heaven then he said lay me down and let me fall asleep in the arms of Jesus, and he fell asleep without a struggle."[18]

What an exit endorsement!

The book's spiritual significance, of course, lies in its capacity for "convincing . . . the Jew and Gentile that Jesus is the Christ." This is the very same reason given by the Apostle John concerning some text he wrote: "But these are written, *that ye might believe* that Jesus is the Christ, the Son of God; and that believing ye might have life through his name" (John 20:31; emphasis added). This is why prophets write, whether John, Nephi, Mormon, or Moroni.

Why do we not have more disclosure concerning the process of translation of the Book of Mormon? Perhaps the full process was not disclosed because we would not be ready to understand it, even if given. Perhaps, too, the Lord wanted to leave the Book of Mormon in the realm of faith, though it is drenched with intrinsic evidence. After all, Christ instructed Mormon, who was reviewing the Savior's own teachings among the Nephites, not to record all of them on the plates because "I will try the faith of my people" (3 Nephi 26:11). Perhaps the details of translation are withheld also because we are intended to immerse ourselves in the substance of the book rather than becoming unduly concerned with the process by which we received it.

"No Error in the Revelations Which I Have Taught"

In any case, as soon as the translation process was completed, it was necessary for the Prophet Joseph to move on quickly in what would be a very busy and highly compressed ministry. This ministry included retranslating hundreds of verses in the Bible; fully establishing the Church; receiving various priesthood keys, with each of which came new duties and new concerns, from heavenly messengers; leading the winnowing Zion's Camp march; and calling and training many of the Church leaders, including the Quorum of the Twelve Apostles and others, as in the School of the Prophets. (Notably, the Prophet sent nine of the Twelve to England when he could least afford to send them.) He also continued receiving revelations; he oversaw large gatherings of Church members in Kirtland, Jackson County, and Nauvoo. He experienced awful and severe apostasy among members, especially in the Kirtland period and in Nauvoo. On one illustrative occasion, when Wilford Woodruff met Joseph in Kirtland, the Prophet scrutinized him for a moment, then said: "Brother Woodruff, I am glad to see you. I hardly know when I meet those who have been my brethren in the Lord, who of them are my friends. They have become so scarce."[19] As his ministry progressed, he focused on temple building and temple ordinances—in many ways, the crowning achievement of his life.

The Prophet Joseph did all of these and so much more while serving simultaneously as father and husband. He and Emma lost six of their children to early death.

Finally, of course, came the engulfing events leading up to the Martyrdom.

So many large undertakings were compressed into such a small period of time! The Prophet's ministry almost defies description. No wonder Joseph once said that if he hadn't experienced his own life, he would not have believed it himself.[20]

Near the end of his ministry, with so much betrayal about him, the Prophet Joseph said to the members, "I never told you I was perfect; but there is no error in the revelations which I have taught."[21] His summational statement includes the marvelous Book of Mormon, the coming forth of which we have examined briefly. Though it was not his book, Joseph was its remarkable translator. It was actually the book of prophets who had long preceded him. His intensive labors of translation let these prophets speak so eloquently for themselves—to millions of us! In fact, more printed pages of scripture have come through Joseph Smith than from any other human.

Mine is an apostolic witness of Jesus, the great Redeemer of mankind. It was He who called the Prophet Joseph

Smith, tutored him, and nurtured him through his adversities, which were to be "but a small moment" (Doctrine and Covenants 121:7). Once the Prophet Joseph hoped aloud that he might so live amid his own suffering that one day he could take his place among Abraham and the "ancients," hoping to "hold an even w[e]ight in the balances with them."[22] I testify that Joseph so triumphed, which is why we rightly sing of his being "crowned in the midst of the prophets of old."[23]

Notes

1. Morris L. West, *The Tower of Babel* (New York: Morrow, 1968), 183.

2. Joseph Smith, *History of the Church of Jesus Christ of Latter-day Saints,* ed. B. H. Roberts (Salt Lake City: Deseret News, 1946), 4:220.

3. Quoted in James H. Hart, "About the Book of Mormon," *Deseret Evening News,* 25 March 1884, 2.

4. Quoted in Edward Stevenson, "One of the Three Witnesses: Incidents in the Life of Martin Harris," *The Latter-day Saints' Millennial Star,* 6 February 1882, 86–87.

5. See Dean Jessee, "Joseph Knight's Recollection of Early Mormon History," *BYU Studies* 17/1 (1976): 35.

6. "Mormonites," *Evangelical Magazine and Gospel Advocate,* 9 April 1831.

7. See *The Latter-day Saints' Millennial Star,* 11 August 1874, 498–99.

8. See "How long did it take Joseph Smith to translate the Book of Mormon?" I Have a Question, *Ensign,* January 1988, 47.

9. See the bulletin *Insights: An Ancient Window* (Provo, Utah: Foundation for Ancient Research and Mormon Studies), February 1986, 1.

10. Joseph Smith III, "Last Testimony of Sister Emma," *The Saints' Herald*, 1 October 1879, 290.

11. See Lyndon W. Cook, ed., *David Whitmer Interviews: A Restoration Witness* (Orem, Utah: Grandin Book, 1991), 173.

12. Quoted in John W. Welch and Tim Rathbone, "The Translation of the Book of Mormon: Basic Historical Information," FARMS report WRR–86, 25.

13. Joseph Smith III, "Last Testimony of Sister Emma," 289.

14. See E. C. Briggs, "Interview with David Whitmer," *The Saints' Herald*, 21 June 1884, 396.

15. Joseph Smith III, "Last Testimony of Sister Emma," 289, 290.

16. *Times and Seasons*, 15 October 1842, 943; emphasis added.

17. Journal of Reuben Miller, October 1848, Archives of The Church of Jesus Christ of Latter-day Saints.

18. Letter of Lucy Cowdery Young, 7 March 1887, Archives of The Church of Jesus Christ of Latter-day Saints.

19. Quoted in Matthias F. Cowley, ed., *Wilford Woodruff, fourth president of the Church of Jesus Christ of Latter-day Saints: history of his life and labors as recorded in his daily journals* (Salt Lake City: Bookcraft, 1964), 68.

20. See Joseph Smith, *History of the Church*, 6:317.

21. Joseph Fielding Smith, ed., *Teachings of the Prophet Joseph Smith* (Salt Lake City: Deseret Book, 1976), 368.

22. Dean C. Jessee, ed., *The Personal Writings of Joseph Smith* (Salt Lake City: Deseret Book, 1984), 395.

23. *Hymns* (Salt Lake City: The Church of Jesus Christ of Latter-day Saints, 1985), no. 27.

The Power of Evidence in the Nurturing of Faith

John W. Welch

Since the publication of the Book of Mormon in 1830, its adherents have sought, found, and enjoyed publishing evidences in its support. What spiritual value do such evidences have? How do bits of knowledge contribute to an increase of faith? How do reason and revelation work together? What is evidence, and how is it related to faith? Without diminishing the essential power of the Holy Ghost in bearing testimony, and knowing that we cannot prove anything in absolute terms, I still speak favorably about the power of evidence. It is an important ingredient in Heavenly Father's plan of happiness.

Both Reason and Revelation

Basic to the discussion of evidence and faith is the relationship between reason and revelation. One of my favorite scriptures is Doctrine and Covenants 88:118, a text that

---

This chapter is adapted from *Nurturing Faith through the Book of Mormon: The Twenty-Fourth Annual Sidney B. Sperry Symposium* (Salt Lake City: Deseret Book, 1995), 149–86.

is posted conspicuously on a plaque in the old stairwell between the third and fourth floors of the Harold B. Lee Library: "As all have not faith, seek ye diligently and teach one another words of wisdom; yea, seek ye out of the best books words of wisdom; seek learning, even by study and also by faith." We would do well to post this verse in our own libraries. This passage gives significant place to the role of scholarship in the restored church. It commands us to "seek" (which would include doing research) and to seek "diligently" (we must do it thoroughly and carefully); it obligates us to teach one another (to share our findings generously) and to draw out of "the best books" (which cautions us that some books will be better than others); and it tells us to do all this "even by study and also by faith" (in other words, both are required). Nothing is more fundamental for a Latter-day Saint scholar than to maintain a proper balance between the intellectual and spiritual pursuits of life.

Many church leaders and authors have written about study and faith, and everyone agrees that we should have both.[1] President Gordon B. Hinckley has said: "There is incumbent upon each of us . . . the responsibility to observe the commandment to study and to learn. . . . None of us can assume that we have learned enough."[2] Elder Neal A. Maxwell has affirmed: "If there is sometimes too little respect for the life of the mind, it is a localized condition and is not institutional in character."[3] "The Lord sees no conflict between faith and learning in a broad curriculum. . . . The scriptures see faith and learning as mutually facilitating, not separate processes."[4] Elder Boyd K. Packer has said: "Each of us must accommodate the mixture of reason and revelation in our lives. The gospel not only permits but *requires* it."[5]

The difficult problem is not whether to have both study and faith but how to get these two together and in what order of priority or in what type of combination. In attempting to describe or prescribe the proper coordination of study with faith, LDS thinkers have turned or may turn to various analogies, as we often must when we are confronted with our deepest intellectual or religious concepts. Each of these metaphors is potentially quite powerful. Some work better than others, but each may offer insight into the roles of scholarly evidence in nurturing or strengthening faith.

Some analogies emphasize that both study and faith are necessary. In the bicycle-built-for-two metaphor, the relationship between reason and revelation is likened to two riders on a tandem bicycle. When both riders pedal together, the bicycle (the search for truth) moves ahead more rapidly. Each rider must work, or the other must bear a heavy and perhaps exhausting burden; but only one (that is faith) can steer and determine where the bicycle will go, although the other (reason) can do some backseat driving.

In another metaphor, these two necessary elements are brought together as in a marriage, with "all the tension, adjustments, frustration, joys, and ecstasy one finds in a marriage between man and woman."[6]

Similarly, the apostle Paul used the human body as a strong metaphor to show the need for many parts in an organic whole. It would be unseemly for "the head [to say] to the feet, I have no need of you"; they are "many members, yet but one body" (1 Corinthians 12:20–21). As B. H. Roberts has cautioned, let us not have "the heart breathing defiance to the intellect."⁷ And one might equally add, let us also not have the intellect pounding submission to the heart.

Specific Ways Evidence Nurtures Faith

Although we should not expect to find a sign somewhere that says "Nephi slept here" or a drop of blood on the Mount of Olives that establishes the truth of Christ's ordeal in Gethsemane,⁸ the world has been told to expect circumstantial evidences of the truth. An 1842 editorial announcing some archaeological discoveries in Central America that was published in the *Times and Seasons* when Joseph Smith was editor boldly asserts: "We can not but think the Lord has a hand in bringing to pass his strange act, and proving the Book of Mormon true in the eyes of all the people. . . . It will be as it ever has been, the world will prove Joseph Smith a true prophet by circumstantial evidence, in experiments, as they did Moses and Elijah."⁹

Without overstating the value of these factors, evidence plays several specific roles in the cultivation of faith. Comments by General Authorities and personal experiences by many people are instructive and have affirmed various functions.

Elder John A. Widtsoe taught that evidence can remove honest doubt and give assurances that build faith. "After proper inquiries, using all the powers at our command," he said, "the weight of evidence is on one side or the other. Doubt is removed."¹⁰ "Doubt of the right kind—that is, honest questioning—leads to faith" and "opens the door to truth,"¹¹ for where there is doubt, faith cannot thrive. Elder Joseph Fielding Smith likewise affirmed that evidence, as convincing as in any court in the land, proves "beyond the possibility of doubt that Joseph Smith and Oliver Cowdery spoke the truth."[12]

Over and over, I have found that solid research confirms the revelations of God. As Elder Maxwell has stated, "That a truth is given by God and then is confirmed through scholarship makes it no less true."[13] President Hinckley has said that in a world prone to demand evidence, it is good that archaeology, anthropology, or historical research can "be helpful to some" and "confirmatory."[14]

Evidence also makes the truth plain and plausible. In 1976 Elder Maxwell predicted: "There will be a convergence of discoveries (never enough, mind you, to remove the need for faith) to make plain and plausible what the modern prophets have been saying all along."[15] I believe that this prophecy has been amply fulfilled in the last twenty years. Literally hundreds of newly discovered insights converge on the same supporting conclusion. Certain things that might at first have appeared outrageous, on closer inspection have turned out to be right on target. The ancient Jaredite transoceanic migration that lasted 344 days (see Ether 6:11) ceases to seem so fantastic when that turns out to be exactly the length of time it takes the Pacific current to go from Asia to Mexico.[16] The oddity of Nephi's making new arrows when only his bow had broken suddenly becomes plausible when one realizes that arrows and bows must match each other in weight, length, and stiffness,[17] again making "plain and plausible" what the Book of Mormon has said all along.

In an important sense, evidence makes belief possible. I am very impressed by the words of Austin Farrar in speaking about C. S. Lewis and quoted by Elder Maxwell on several occasions: "Though argument does not create conviction, lack of it destroys belief. What seems to be proved may not be embraced; but what no one shows that ability to defend is quickly abandoned. Rational argument does not create belief, but it maintains a climate in which belief may flourish."[18]

Thus, evidence in a sense brings people toward belief. Some people have the gift to believe quite readily (see D&C 46:13–14), but most people need evidence, clues, and inducements to believe because they are by nature stubborn. Alma told the poor in Antionum that it was blessed to believe in the word of God "without stubbornness of heart, yea, without being brought to know the word, or even compelled to know" (Alma 32:16); but being "brought to know" is better than never coming to know at all. I have been "brought to know" many things by means of evidence, even though that evidence has fallen short of compelling me to know.

Evidence is also useful in articulating knowledge and defending against error and misrepresentation. Scholars can serve important roles "as articulators" of evidence, and when combined with "submissiveness and consecration," solid academic research can be useful "to protect and to build up the Kingdom."[19] If people misunderstand the thoroughly Christian character of the Book of Mormon, I would hope that statistical evidence about the pervasive references to Christ in the book would be quite arresting and informative.[20] I would hope that evidence about the distinctively personal testimonies of Christ uniquely borne by ten Book of Mormon prophets would be deeply impressive and convincing.[21]

Evidence helps to keep pace in the give-and-take of competing alternatives: Do you expect "incontrovertible proof to come in this way? No, but neither will the Church be outdone by hostile or pseudo-scholars."[22] The historical facts in support of Joseph's testimony, to quote Elder Jeffrey R. Holland, leave one "speechless absolutely, totally, and bewilderingly incredulous," at the bald suggestion that Joseph Smith simply wrote the Book of Mormon.[23]

Perhaps most of all, evidence promotes understanding and enhances meaning. In all our study, we should seek understanding.[24] Just as traveling to the Holy Land has richly enhanced my understanding of the world of the Bible, as it has for many people, evidence provides essential building blocks in understanding the full character of the Book of Mormon. Many factors, like the doubled, sealed documents, help me understand this record better as a powerful and ancient testament, for to be understood, our facts must be placed "in their proper context."[25] Evidence helps to put many parts of the Book of Mormon in context.

A clear delineation of evidence also strengthens the impression left by any text on the mind and soul. Evidence has a way of drawing my attention to subtle details that otherwise escape notice on casual reading. With evidence about ancient Israelite festivals in mind, I read with heightened attention and gratitude the text in Mosiah 3:11 about Christ's blood atoning for those who have "ignorantly sinned," because it was of primary concern on ancient holy days to purify the people from all their iniquities (see Leviticus 16:21–22), with special reference being made to sins committed in ignorance (see Numbers 15:22–29).[26]

Marshalling evidence builds respect for the truth. I have been amazed and pleased to watch the Book of Mormon win respect for itself and for the gospel of Jesus Christ. I had long appreciated and valued the Book of Mormon, but it was not until I began to see it speaking for itself before sophisticated audiences, especially in connection with such things as chiasmus and law in the Book of Mormon, that I began to sense the high level of respect that the book really can command. On many grounds, the Book of Mormon is intellectually respectable.[27] The more I learn about the Book of Mormon, the more amazed I become at its precision, consistency, validity, vitality, insightfulness, and purposefulness. I believe that the flow of additional evidence nourishes and enlarges faith.[28]

Finally, the presentation of evidence impels people to ask the ultimate question raised by that evidence. Once a person realizes that no one can explain how all this got into the Book of Mormon, the honest person is at last at the point where he or she must turn to God to find out if these things are indeed true. Elder Bruce R. McConkie advised readers to ask themselves over and over, a thousand times, "Could any man have written this book?"[29] By asking this question again and again, one invites all kinds of ideas that may bear one way or the other on the answer to that question. As ideas surface, evidence can help the reader explore those possibilities and inevitably return with increased intensity to the question, "Could any man have written this book?" If one will ponder the great miracle of the Book of Mormon, Elder McConkie promises, "the genuine truth seeker will come to know," again and again, "by the power of the Spirit, that the book is true."[30]

Moroni 10:3–4 promises this testimony but on several prerequisites: one must "read these things" (one must study it); one must "remember how merciful the Lord hath been"; and one must "ponder" this record. Then "if ye shall ask with a sincere heart, with real intent, having faith in Christ," the answer will be revealed. Many people have told me how evidences have helped to impel them through this process of reading, studying, pondering, and asking.

The Holy Ghost bears record of the Father and of the Son (see 3 Nephi 11:32, 36). Scripturally, this truth is beyond question. Elder B. H. Roberts wrote in 1909: "The power of the Holy Ghost . . . must ever be the chief source of evidence for the truth of the Book of Mormon. All other evidence is secondary. . . . No arrangement of evidence, however skillfully ordered; no argument, however adroitly made, can ever take its place."[31] It would certainly be an abuse to supplant testimony and faith with evidence, or with anything else, but scrutinizing evidence can help. Elder Roberts continued: "Evidence and argument . . . in support of truth, like secondary causes in natural phenomena, may be of first rate importance, and mighty factors in the achievement of God's purposes."[32] Indeed, the careful presentation of evidence clarifies the truth and enhances the power of testimony. Elder Roberts concluded: "To be known, the truth must be stated and the clearer and more complete the statement is, the better opportunity will the Holy Spirit have for testifying to the souls of men that the work is true."[33]

Study and Faith Working Together

In all of these faith-promoting functions, it is not enough just to have one's mind and one's spirit both alive and functioning; the two must work together, each contributing in its own proper way. To turn to another metaphor, the correlation of faith and reason works like our two eyes (representing mind and spirit); working together they give depth to our sight, and with the aid of a pair of binoculars (representing scholarship and revelation), we see close up and in bold relief many marvelous things. For this process to work, however, both eyes must be healthy and both lenses in the binoculars must be clean and in focus.

I also like to think of faith and reason as two arms working together to play a violin. One hand fingers the strings and the other draws the bow. When these two distinct functions are brought together with skill and purpose, they produce expressions that ontologically transcend the physics of either part individually. According to this view, for an LDS scholar to proceed on either spirit or intellect alone is like trying to play a violin with only one arm.

Gaining Faith in General

Nurturing faith in the Book of Mormon is just a specialized case of nurturing faith in general. Faith is increased by purposeful study, diligent prayer, attending church, rendering service, experimenting with the word, and feeling the Spirit. Evidence can play a role in this process in several ways.

First, Paul declared: "So then faith cometh by hearing, and hearing by the word of God" (Romans 10:17). The presentation of evidence can help people to hear the word, to pay attention, to listen more closely, to hear what is really being said. King Benjamin admonished his people to "open your ears that ye may hear, and your hearts that ye may understand, and your minds that the mysteries of God may be unfolded to your view" (Mosiah 2:9). I have seen evidence, when it is presented modestly and accurately, help people listen to the Book of Mormon who otherwise would not give it the time of day. I have seen it soften hearts and prepare the way for testimony to be borne and received.

Second, faith comes by prayerful study. In the words of President Hinckley: "It will take study of the word of God. It will take prayer and anxious seeking of the source of all truth."[34] The study of scriptural evidence can be a vital aid in this process, for faith is only faith if it is in things "which are true" (Alma 32:21). The intelligent use of evidence helps people sort out propositions that are clear, true, or plausible from those that are muddled, false, or bogus.

Third, faith also comes from sacrifice. For Elder McConkie, "faith and sacrifice go hand in hand. Those who have faith sacrifice freely for the Lord's work, and their acts of sacrifice increase their faith."[35] "The tests and trials of mortality are designed to determine whether men will use their time and talents in worldly or spiritual pursuits."[36] These tests include tests of the mind as much as any other tests. And the quest for rigorous scriptural evidence demands the dedication of time, the consecration of talents, and the willingness to be swallowed up in the Lord's purposes.

Some Problems with Evidence

Evidence may perform several useful functions, but this is not to say that evidence is some kind of panacea or elixir of pure knowledge. Evidence can even raise certain problems if it is not kept in proper balance.

Some people place too much weight on evidence. The scriptures caution against becoming overconfident or too secular. But such abuses are no different from anything else in life: riches may be abused, but that does not mean we stop working for a living; an artist runs the risk of pride, but that does not mean we cease improving our talents. As with all tools, the mind must be carefully used. Like a hammer, the intellect can be used either to build up or to tear down. Jesus gave us another analogy, that of a fruit tree, to help us determine the right balance: "By their fruits ye shall know them" (Matthew 7:20).

Other people go the opposite extreme and give too little attention to evidence and latch on to answers too readily. Sidney Sperry once commented, "Too many persons in every generation, including our own, hope for things—fantastic things—in the name of faith and religion, but give little thought as to whether or not they are based on truth."[37]

Others halt between the two and become consumed by questions. It is a fact of life that we can ask more questions than can ever be answered. It takes skill and wisdom even to ask a good question. Sperry is a good example of a scholar who willingly addressed the so-called Isaiah question or the problem of the Sermon on the Mount in 3 Nephi. My work on these topics has not only satisfied all of my honest inquiries but has opened many unexpected insights. My study of the Sermon on the Mount as a temple text embedded in 3 Nephi 11–18 has elucidated the Book of Mormon beyond my most remote expectation and has turned what I saw as a potential problem into a great strength.[38]

The "Problem" of Proof

Of course, we cannot "prove" that the Book of Mormon or any other ultimate tenet of religious faith is true. Hugh Nibley has said, "The evidence that will prove or disprove the Book of Mormon does not exist."[39] Our desire is not to become some grand inquisitor, wanting to put other people over a barrel by producing undeniable reasons for belief that will convince the whole world and compel everyone to believe.[40] Since this is so, why should one bother to gather evidence or to do religious research at all?

In an ideal world, evidence would not be necessary. Things would be known directly, immediately, and certainly. The only problem is, we do not live in an ideal world, and it was not intended by God that we should so live. We are surrounded in this probationary state by possibilities, choices, and the need to seek and to work out our salvation with fear and trembling.

Moreover, in working with evidence, we must not forget what or who is really on trial. To quote President Benson: "The Book of Mormon is not on trial—the people of the world, including the members of the Church, are on trial as to what they will do with this second witness for Christ."[41] In the same way, when the world presumed to judge its Messiah to be a thing of naught, in reality the world was being judged: "He that believeth not is condemned already," says the Gospel of John, "and this is the condemnation, that light is come into the world, and men loved darkness rather than light" (John 3:18–19). As so often occurs, the gospel stands things on their heads: the weak are strong, the rich are poor, and the losers are the finders. And likewise, the testers are being tested. In dealing with and reacting to evidence, we actually reveal more about ourselves than we do about the subjects being tested, and we sharpen the sword not of human discernment but of divine judgment.

For this reason also we can understand why evidence does not affect all people in the same way. Not everyone will need evidences, and not all people will need them at every stage of their lives. Individuals see data differently, and "God made us free so to do."[42] In the end, it will always come down to the choice each person must make between believing the good or rejecting it. Abundant miraculous and physical evidence was given to Pharaoh, but he still rejected Jehovah. Evidence is the vehicle that makes the plan of choice and accountability viable. Without evidence both for and against two alternatives, no bona fide choice could ever be possible. Paraphrasing Lehi, we might add, Adam fell that men might choose; and evidence is that they might have a basis on which to choose.

Faith, Choice, and the Nature of Evidence

These theological observations about evidence invite a closer look at evidence itself. The better we understand both faith and evidence and the subjective elements that bridge the two, the better we will be able to bring them both beneficially together. Having seen how evidence contributes to faith, consider the elements of faith and the roles of personal choice in the nature of evidence and how evidence works.

People often misjudge the nature of evidence because, à la Perry Mason, they may take an overly simplistic view of evidence. The concept of evidence is complex. The power of evidence is shaped by metaphysical assumptions (such as causation) and cultural conditions (such as the value placed on proof), and it combines wide fields of human experience (including such philosophical concerns as epistemology, the reliability of sensory experience, the adequacy of language, the nature of history, and the psychology of persuasion).

The word *evidence* derives from the Latin *ex videns*, meaning anything that comes from *seeing* and also from *seeming*. Evidence is literally what meets the eye and, more than that, what seems to be from what we see. Evidence is based on hard facts, but even under the best of circumstances it works less automatically and more subjectively than many people realize. If evidence were not such a complicated matter, many things would be much simpler in our courtrooms, legislative sessions, and corporate board rooms as well as in our lecture halls and Gospel Doctrine classrooms.

Though this complexity may present problems in many cases, it also allows evidence to combine with faith, because in its complexity evidence is both a product of empirical data attractive to the mind amenable to study and the result of personal choices generated by the Spirit in faith. Not only is seeing believing but believing is seeing, as has been often said. Philosophical worldviews that would have it only one of these two ways offer us a model that limps on one leg.

In exploring the workings of evidence, I have found that the practice and study of law is a valuable experimental laboratory. Every legal case requires judges, lawyers, jurors, witnesses, and parties to define the issues, to organize evidence relevant to those issues, and to reach conclusions about the relative persuasiveness of the evidence.[43] This wrenching world of legal experience—as problematic as it may seem to the general population after the advent of public television in the courtroom—is a furnace of realities that can teach us many things about the use and abuse of evidence. From these experiences, several operational rules emerge that illustrate the combination of objective and subjective elements in evidence, opening the way for one to add reason to one's faith and to engage faith in one's reason.

1. *Any piece of evidence is deeply intertwined with a question.* No real evidence exists until an issue is raised which that evidence tends to prove or disprove. By choosing what questions we will ask, we introduce a subjective element into the inquiry—seeking and asking begin in faith. At the same time, our questions in turn determine what will become evidence—faith begins with asking and seeking.

Some questions are relatively simple and mostly objective: Where was Tom on the day of the crime? Other questions are more difficult and intermediate: What was Tom thinking? Ultimate questions frame the crux of the case and are largely subjective: Did Tom commit murder? Evidence may answer the simpler questions, but it rarely settles the ultimate issues. Judges and jurors adopt "findings of fact" and "conclusions of law" that are based on evidence, but those findings do not emerge spontaneously. They are separate, subjective formulations made by them in response to the evidence.

Similarly, we approach religious matters by asking different levels of questions. Certain queries ask ultimate questions: Did Joseph Smith tell the truth? Did Jesus appear to the Nephites? Such questions are usually tackled by breaking the question down and asking intermediate and easier questions: Is it reasonable to think that Lehi came from Jerusalem around 600 B.C.? Does it appear that many authors contributed to the writing of the Book of Mormon? To answer the intermediate questions, we start looking for specific bits of data. Was there timber in Arabia suitable for shipbuilding? (Indeed there was.) In what style did the Jews write around 600 B.C.? (They used many varieties of parallelism.) In response to such evidence, we then voluntarily form our own "findings of fact," or opinions relative to the questions we have asked.

The study of chiasmus in the Book of Mormon illustrates in more detail this interaction of questions and data in the operation of evidence. One might ask: What does the presence of chiasmus in a text prove?[44] Chiasmus is usually thought of as evidence of Hebrew style, which it is, but it may be evidence of many other things as well, depending fundamentally on what question a person asks. For example, is the English text of the Book of Mormon orderly, complex, precise, and interestingly composed in purposeful units, or is it dull, chaotic, and redundant (as some have suggested)? Chiasmus gives evidence to answer that question. What is the meaning of a text? Form is often linked with content,[45] as in Alma 36, in which Alma meaningfully places the turning point in his life at the chiastic turning point of his beautiful chapter.[46] Were Book of Mormon authors well trained and careful in using their skills? Did they revise and rework their own earlier texts? The abrupt antithetical parallelisms in Mosiah 27:29–30 that were reworked into the chiastic pattern of Alma 36 offer internal evidence of the skill and care of these authors. Because all authors did not use chiasmus in the same ways, this literary element also provides evidence of multiple authorship and historical development in the Book of

Mormon. King Benjamin is quite classical in his use of chiasmus. Alma the Younger is more creative and personal in his use of chiasmus.[47] Chiasmus also provides evidence that the Book of Mormon was translated from an underlying Hebrew text, as is seen especially in Helaman 6:10. Chiasmus may further prove something about the precise nature of Joseph Smith's work as translator. Each time a word appears within these given frameworks, it seems to have been rendered by the same English word.

Each of these bits of evidence is interesting in its own right, but these points do not begin to function as evidence until we have provided the question we seek to answer. Thus, we are involved in the inception and conception of evidence by the questions we choose to raise.

Some of the questions are simple, and objective answers to those questions from the realm of evidence may, to a large extent, confirm faith or make faith plausible. But the ultimate questions are more subjective, and although influenced by reason, their answers remain predominantly in the realm of belief.

2. *Just about anything can serve potentially as evidence, depending on what a person wishes to emphasize.* Some have viewed violent opposition to the Book of Mormon as evidence of its divinity.[48] Others see evidence of the same in its acceptance worldwide. Some rightly find evidence for the spiritual truthfulness of the Book of Mormon in its clarity, plainness, and expansiveness.[49] Others rightly find evidence for its miraculous origins in its complexity, subtlety, and precision. Some properly find persuasiveness in its uniformity and its conformity with eternal truths, whereas others appropriately find confirmation in its variety and cultural idiosyncrasies.

When we seek evidence of something, we are prospecting, looking around at just about anything to see what we can find. Of course, not everything we find will ultimately amount to useful evidence, but just because some people may go overboard and wish to see every hole in the ground in South America as evidence of pre-Columbian baptismal fonts, that does not mean we should reject all evidence as worthless. Thomas Edison had several silly ideas before coming up with his many inventions.

3. *For this reason, evidence can almost always be found or generated for and against just about any proposition.* Only a very impoverished mind cannot find evidence for just about anything he or she wants. Once again, this points out that evidence is not only discovered but also created. That creation is not arbitrarily *ex nihilo,* but neither is it impersonally predestined.

4. *Different kinds of legal evidence evoke different kinds of responses.* The law allows physical evidence, written documents, oral testimony, and so on. But at the same time, different people or legal situations may require or prefer to favor one kind of evidence over another. No rules automatically determine how one kind of evidence stacks up against another or what kind of evidence is best.

Many different types of evidence likewise exist for the Book of Mormon: internal and external, comparative and analytic, philological and doctrinal, statistical and thematic, chronological and cyclical, source critical (the seams between the texts abridged by Moroni in the book of Ether are still evident)[50] and literary. Its historical complexity and plausibility are supported by the study of warfare in the Book of Mormon (including remarkable coherence in its martial law, sacral ideology of war, and campaign strategy, buttressed by archaeological evidence regarding weaponry, armor, fortifications, and seasonality).[51] Evidence is found to enrich the prophetic allegory of Zenos by researching the horticulture of olives (it is evident that whoever wrote Jacob 5 had a high degree of knowledge about olives, which do not grow in New York).[52] Numerous legal practices in the Book of Mormon presuppose or make the best sense when understood against an ancient Israelite background. And so on, many times over. It objectively boggles the mind: How could any author keep all of these potential lines of evidence concurrently in his head while dictating the Book of Mormon without notes or a rough draft? It also subjectively engages the Spirit: How should all these different kinds of evidence be received, assessed, and evaluated?

5. *Legal evidence is often circumstantial.* The more direct the evidence, the more probative it usually is, and in some courts "circumstantial evidence only raises a probability."[53] But on the other hand, people may also choose to view circumstantial evidence as desirable and even necessary in certain situations. Indeed, the circumstances surrounding a particular event or statement are usually essential to understanding the matter. To quote Henry David Thoreau, "Some circumstantial evidence is very strong, as when you find a trout in the milk."[54] A dictum from the United States Supreme Court explains the power of circumstantial evidence: "Circumstantial evidence is often as convincing to the mind as direct testimony, and often more so. A number of concurrent facts, like rays of light, all converging to the same center, may throw not only a clear light but a burning conviction; a conviction of truth more infallible than the testimony even of two witnesses directly to a fact."[55] Accordingly, the

convergence of huge amounts of circumstantial evidence, such as in the astonishingly short time in which the Book of Mormon was translated,[56] may be viewed quite favorably, if a person's spiritual disposition inclines one to receive and value such evidence.

6. *Another fascinating and crucial question is, How are we to evaluate the cumulative weight of evidence?* Some compilations of evidence are strong; other collections are weak. Yet once again, in most settings, no scale for evaluating the cumulative weight of evidence is readily available. No canons of method answer the question, How much evidence do we need in order to draw a certain conclusion? Answering this question is another choice that combines and bridges faith and evidence.

An interesting scale has developed in the law that prescribes specific levels of proof that are required to support certain legal results. The world of evidence is not black and white; there are many shades of gray. Ranging from a high degree of certitude on down, standards of proof on this spectrum include:

1. Beyond a reasonable doubt, dispositive, practically certain
2. Clear and convincing evidence, nearly certain
3. Competent and substantial evidence, well over half
4. Preponderance of evidence, more than half, more likely than not
5. Probable, as in probable cause, substantial possibility
6. Plausible, reasonably suspected
7. Material, relevant, merely possible.

Thus, for example, a person cannot be convicted of a first-degree murder unless the prosecution can prove its case "beyond a reasonable doubt." A civil case, however, between two contesting parties to a contract will be decided by a simple preponderance of the evidence. A grand jury can indict a person on probable cause.

But even within this spectrum, as helpful and sophisticated as it is, no precise definitions for these terms exist. Lawyers and judges still have only a feeling for what these legal terms mean, and their applications may vary from judge to judge. For example, a survey conducted in the Eastern District of New York among ten federal judges determined that the phrase "beyond a reasonable doubt" ranged from 76 percent to 95 percent certainty (although most were on the high end of this range). "Clear and convincing evidence" covered from 60 percent to 75 percent.[57] Obviously, a degree of subjectivity is again involved in deciding what level of certitude should be required or has been achieved in a given case.

In a religious setting, no arbiter prescribes or defines the level of evidence that will sustain a healthy faith. All individuals must set for themselves the levels of proof that they will require.[58] Yet how does one privately determine what burden of proof the Book of Mormon should bear? Should investigators require that it be proved beyond a reasonable doubt before experimenting with its words to learn of its truth or goodness? Should believers expect to have at least a preponderance of the evidence on their side in order to maintain their faith? Or is faith borne out sufficiently by a merely reasonable or plausible position, perhaps even in spite of all evidence? Few people realize how much rides on their personal choice in these matters and that their answer necessarily originates in the domain of faith.

7. *Different legal cases call for different configurations of evidence.* Some matters of common law or statute are what one might call single-factor cases: the presence or absence of a single factor is dispositive of the matter. More often, however, legal rules call for a number of elements that must be proved in order for a claim to be established. In such cases, every element is crucial, and each must be satisfied for the legal test to be met. In other cases, however, several criteria are recognized by law, none of which is absolutely essential but, given the facts and circumstances of the particular case, may be an indicative factor. Thus, for example, in determining whether a person is either an independent contractor or an employee, more than twenty factors have been recognized by law as being potentially significant in resolving the issue, but none of them is absolutely essential.[59] Similarly, Book of Mormon evidences may come in all three of these configurations.

In ultimate matters of faith, however, the individual must decide what configuration of evidence to require. Is the ultimate issue of Book of Mormon origins to be answered by a single-factor test, by satisfying the requirements of a multiple-element set (and if so, who defines what the essential elements are to be?), or by drawing on various facts and circumstances accumulated through spiritual experience and research? Individual choice on this matter will again affect how the objective evidence works in any given individual's mind and spirit.

8. *In certain cases, the sum of the evidence may be greater than the total of its individual parts.* "Pieces of evidence, each by itself insufficient, may together constitute a

significant whole, and justify by their combined effect a conclusion."⁶⁰ The cumulative effect of evidence is in some ways perplexing, but again reflects the role of the observer's preference in how evidence works. Individual pieces of evidence, each of which standing alone is relatively insignificant and uninteresting, may take on vast importance in a person's mind as they combine to form a consistent pattern or coherent picture. It is in some senses ironic that a few strong single facts can be overwhelmed and defeated by a horde of true but less significant facts, a strategy I used in winning several tax cases. But should one give greater credence to a wide-ranging accumulation of assorted details or to a few single strong factors? Only personal judgment will answer that question.

9. *Another interesting effect occurs when a good case is actually weakened by piling on a few weak additional points.* A bad argument may be worse in some minds than no argument at all if the weak arguments tend to undermine confidence in the strong points. But who can tell what will work or not work for one person or another? The degree of confidence a person is willing to place in any evidence is another manifestation of faith or personal response.

10. *Similarly, advocacy and rhetoric are virtually part of the evidence.* The techniques of presenting evidence are often as important as the evidence itself, and the subjective decision to feature certain points in favor of others can be the turning point of a case. Important facts forcefully presented take on added significance; crucial evidence overlooked and underused will not always even be noticed by the judge or jury.

Again, it is a sobering reality that the apparent victory in debates often goes to the witty, the clever, the articulate, and the overconfident. Hopefully, good arguments will always be presented in a clear manner so as not to obscure their true value; but because this does not always happen, prudent observers need to be careful to separate kernels of truth from the husks they are packaged in.

11. *Not all evidence ultimately counts.* In a court of law, the judge and jury will eventually decide to ignore some of the evidence, especially hearsay, mere opinions, or statistical probabilities. Similarly, in evaluating Book of Mormon evidence, one needs to be meticulous in separating fact from opinion. Likewise, fantastic statistics can be generated by either friends or foes of the book. This does not mean that statistical presentations should be ruled out of Book of Mormon discussions; some wordprinting studies, for example, have achieved noteworthy results.[61] But such evidence must not be exaggerated and must be approached with sophistication.

12. *Constraints on time and the availability of witnesses or documentary evidence may be completely fortuitous yet also very important.* If a witness is unavailable to testify in court, the case may be lost. Documentary evidence known or presumed once to have existed is scarcely helpful. To reach a legal decision, time limitations are imposed on all parties; and in most cases, evidence discovered after a decision has become final is simply ignored.

In much the same way, important evidence relevant to religious matters will often be perpetually lacking. Thus, a person must subjectively choose at what point enough has been heard. Further historical or archaeological discoveries may eventually surface, but in the meantime, one must choose. In this regard, Elder Richard L. Evans counseled, "And when we find ourselves in conflict and confusion, we can well learn to wait awhile for all the evidence and all the answers that now evade us."[62] And President Hugh B. Brown recommended: "With respect to some things that now seem difficult to understand, we can afford to wait until we have all the facts, until all the evidence is in . . . . If there seems to be conflict, it is because men, fallible men, are unable properly to interpret God's revelations or man's discoveries."[63]

The Need for Caution

Clearly, the matter of evidence is complex. While certain evidences will be demonstrably stronger and more objective than others, the processing of evidence is not simply a matter of feeding the data in one end of a machine and catching a conclusion as it falls out the other. Even in the law we read: "Absolute certainty and accuracy in fact-finding is an ideal, rather than an achievable goal."[64] Caution and care are in order.

Caution on the side of reason tells us that the power and value of evidence may be overrated in the world. Although evidence is certainly required to prevent our legal system of justice from degenerating into the Salem witch trials, even under the best of circumstances evidence is often ambiguous, incomplete, or nonexistent.

Caution is also advised on the side of faith. Revealed knowledge must be understood and interpreted correctly. What has actually been revealed? Do we know by revelation where the final battles in the Book of Mormon were fought? Do we know that because twenty-one chapters of Isaiah are quoted in the Book of Mormon that all sixty-six were on the plates of brass? Moreover, the implications of revelation are not always clear. Does the revealed fact that God is a God of order require us to reject the Heisenberg principle of uncertainty? Elder Widtsoe thought so. Perhaps that principle is only an expression of incomplete information, which will "disappear with increasing knowledge,"[65] but until we have further knowledge we must walk with caution in both spheres.

A Puzzle

Maybe another metaphor will help—that of an old jigsaw puzzle. The picture on the box is a broad, or holistic, view of some reality given by revelation; but the picture on our box is incomplete (see Article of Faith 9) and unclear in spots (see 1 Corinthians 13:12). Moreover, we are also missing several pieces of the puzzle, and we are not even sure how many are gone. Some of the pieces in our box do not appear to belong to our puzzle at first, and others quite definitely are strays. The picture on the box becomes clearer to us, however, with greater study of its details. The more closely we examine the available pieces and the more use we make of our minds, the more we are able to put together a few pieces of solid truth here and there. We may, of course, put some of the pieces in the wrong place initially, but as other pieces are put into position and as we continually refer to the picture on the lid, we are able to correct those errors. As our understanding of both the picture and the pieces progresses, we gain greater respect for what we know, for how it all fits together, and for what we yet do not know.

Redeeming the Mind

In the end, what we need is not a metaphor, but a metamorphosis. Metaphors strongly depict the paradigm, but only a shift of heart will make the difference if we are going to learn wisdom even by study and also by faith. How are we to foster both spirit and intellect? I have five suggestions.

First, be competent but resist pride. Joseph F. Smith firmly declared, "Of those who speak in his name, the Lord requires humility, not ignorance."[66] All are susceptible to the pervasive curse of pride, but scholars are above average in the pride category. We know by sad experience that when people get a little power, their natural disposition is to exercise unrighteous dominion, and clearly, knowledge is a form of power. Competence facilitates intellect, just as humility facilitates the Spirit.

Second, never oversimplify and never overcomplicate. Truth is both simple and complex. The scriptures affirm both. The message of the gospel is simple, the way is clear, the path is straight; but the content of the gospel is also imponderable, inscrutable, and unfathomable.

Third, learn with a purpose, and then give purpose to your learning. The bridge between faith and reason is purposeful activity. Study gives us facts, truth, and knowledge; faith gives us values, goodness, and objectives. Both are necessary. Knowledge, in and of itself, is morally neutral until it is put to work in support of some chosen purpose. There is a trouble with truth: Satan knows a lot of truth. He knows the laws of physics, physiology, psychology, and social behavior. What he lacks is the willingness to do what is good. That conviction comes through the Light of Christ and with faith in Jesus. Without the love of Christ, truth is dangerous. No one, scholars included, operates above the moral law. I continue to be impressed in Alma 32 that what we learn when we plant the seed is not that the seed is true but that it is good. We should know that the gospel is both good and true, for our knowledge will "operate toward [our] salvation or condemnation as it is used or misused."[67]

Fourth, not only must we cultivate and listen to both intellect and spirit but we must apply the steps of repentance in overcoming our rebellious thoughts every bit as much as in rectifying our disobedient actions.[68] I find in the gospel a remarkable ability to harmonize and transcend such stubborn dichotomies as spirit and matter, rights and duties, and human and divine.[69] In no case is that power to unify more significant than in harmonizing the mind and the spirit. The only power that can achieve such unities is the power that truly makes one, the atonement of Jesus Christ. Our minds and our spirits both have need of the atonement. A clean engine runs better, and so do a cleansed spirit and mind.

Perhaps it strikes you as odd to think of redeeming your mind. But is the human intellect any less or any more in need of redemption than any other part of the soul? Is a mortal's mind any less subject to the fall than the body? Mind and spirit are polarized only when both are unredeemed. The natural mind is an enemy to God, but through the redeeming powers of the atonement of Christ, the human spirit and the human intellect both become mutually cooperative counterparts as they work in harmony with the mind and will of God.

So, the question becomes, Has our thinking been redeemed? Have our mind and spirit both been sanctified by the atoning blood of Christ? Has the finger of the Lord touched our inert cerebral stones and made them into light-giving gems? Have you been "transformed by the renewing of your mind"? (Romans 12:2). Has your mind yielded "to the enticings of the Holy Spirit, and . . . [become] as a child, submissive, meek, humble, patient, full of love, willing to submit to all things which the Lord seeth fit to inflict"? (Mosiah 3:19). Elder Maxwell has said, "Absolute truth calls for absolute love and absolute patience."[70] The qualities mentioned by King Benjamin in Mosiah apply as much to the mind as to anything else. The basic meaning of the word *atonement* in Greek is to reconcile two alienated parties.[71] The atonement can fully reconcile the tensions between reason and revelation not by obliterating the distinctiveness between reasoned thought and heartfelt spiritual experience but by bringing both into oneness in Christ.

Finally, seek the fulness. What we seek in the dispensation of the fulness of times is the fulness of the everlasting gospel, not just one half or the other of the loaf of the bread of life. Longing to pour out upon the Saints more of what he knew, Joseph Smith once remarked, "It is my meditation all the day, and more than my meat and drink, to know how I shall make the Saints of God comprehend the visions that roll like an overflowing surge before my mind."[72] Hugh Nibley has similarly said, "Our search for knowledge should be ceaseless, which means that it is open-ended. . . . True knowledge never shuts the door on more knowledge, but zeal often does"; Adam and Abraham had "far greater and more truth than what we have, and yet the particular genius of each was that he was constantly 'seeking for *greater* light and knowledge.'"[73] We are not likely to have the kind of faith it will take to receive all that the Father has if we have not served him with all that we do have, that is, with all our heart, might, mind, and strength.

The Choice Is Ours

"Of all our needs," President Gordon B. Hinckley has said, "the greatest is an increase in faith."[74] Anything that truly helps in that process, even a little bit, should be useful to us.

As a young man and still today, I have always felt very satisfied in my testimony of the Book of Mormon. At first, I believed that the book was true with little or no evidence of any kind at all. Never expecting to find great proofs or evidence for the book, I have been astonished by what the Lord has done. In all of this, I have not been disappointed but richly satisfied.

It seems clear enough that the Lord does not intend for the Book of Mormon to be an open-and-shut case intellectually, either pro or con. If God had intended that, he could have left more concrete evidences one way or the other. Instead, it seems that the Lord has maintained a careful balance between requiring us to exercise faith and allowing us to find reasons that affirm the stated origins of this record. The choice is then entirely ours. Ultimately, evidences may not be that important, but then it is easy to say that the airplane or the parachute has become irrelevant after you are safely on the ground.

We are blessed to have the Book of Mormon. It is the word of God. It would be ideal if all could accept it without suspicion and then, upon humble prayer, receive the witness of the Holy Ghost that it is true, but in this less than ideal world, it is good that so much evidence can bring us to believe and help us to nurture faith in this extraordinary book.

NOTES

1. See, for example, Henry B. Eyring, ed., *On Being a Disciple-Scholar* (Salt Lake City: Bookcraft, 1995); and Robert L. Millet, ed., *"To Be Learned Is Good If..."* (Salt Lake City: Bookcraft, 1987).

2. Gordon B. Hinckley, *Faith: The Essence of True Religion* (Salt Lake City: Deseret Book, 1989), 73.

3. Neal A. Maxwell, *Deposition of a Disciple* (Salt Lake City: Deseret Book, 1976), 15.

4. Neal A. Maxwell, "The Disciple-Scholar," in *On Being a Disciple-Scholar,* ed. Eyring, 3.

5. Boyd K. Packer, "'I Say unto You, Be One' (D&C 38:27)," *Brigham Young University 1990–91 Devotionals and Fireside Speeches* (Provo, Utah: Brigham Young University, 1991), 89.

6. Used by Lowell L. Bennion, "The Uses of the Mind in Religion," *BYU Studies* 14/1 (1973): 47–55, arguing that one cannot turn one's back on either the religious (biblical) or the rational (Greek) tradition, 48.

7. Truman G. Madsen, "Philosophy," in B. H. Roberts, *The Truth, the Way, the Life,* ed. John W. Welch (Provo, Utah: BYU Studies, 1994), lxxiii.

8. "The Lord does not convince men of his truth by placing before their eyes and in their hands tangible evidence, as a lawyer may do before the court, marking it exhibit A and exhibit B, and then expect it to be accepted. The Lord expects the searcher

after truth to approach him with a contrite spirit and with sincerity of purpose, if he will do this and keep the commandments of the Lord, he shall receive the witness through the Holy Spirit and shall know the truth." Joseph Fielding Smith, *Doctrines of Salvation* (Salt Lake City: Bookcraft, 1954–56), 3:228.

9. Joseph Smith, *Teachings of the Prophet Joseph Smith,* sel. Joseph Fielding Smith (Salt Lake City: Deseret Book, 1938), 267.

10. John A. Widtsoe, *Evidences and Reconciliations,* 3rd ed. (Salt Lake City: Bookcraft, 1943), 28.

11. Ibid., 29.

12. Smith, *Doctrines of Salvation,* 2:124.

13. Maxwell, *Deposition of a Disciple,* 16.

14. Hinckley, *Faith,* 10.

15. Maxwell, *Deposition of a Disciple,* 49.

16. See John L. Sorenson, *An Ancient American Setting for the Book of Mormon* (Salt Lake City: Deseret Book and FARMS, 1985), 111, 368 n. 16.

17. See John W. Welch, ed., *Reexploring the Book of Mormon* (Salt Lake City: Deseret Book and FARMS, 1992), 41–43.

18. Austin Farrar, "Grete Clerk," in *Light on C. S. Lewis,* comp. Jocelyn Gibb (New York: Harcourt and Brace, 1965), 26; cited in Neal A. Maxwell, "Discipleship and Scholarship," *BYU Studies* 32/3 (summer 1992): 5.

19. Maxwell, "Discipleship and Scholarship," 5.

20. See Susan Easton Black, *Finding Christ through the Book of Mormon* (Salt Lake City: Deseret Book, 1987).

21. See John W. Welch, "Ten Testimonies of Jesus Christ from the Book of Mormon," in *Doctrines of the Book of Mormon,* ed. Bruce A. Van Orden and Brent L. Top (Salt Lake City: Deseret Book, 1992), 223–42.

22. Maxwell, *Deposition of a Disciple,* 49. Elder Maxwell has enumerated a lengthy list of evidences that raise "vexing challenges for disbelievers and critics who reject the true account but remain surrounded by increasing incredibilia." Neal A. Maxwell, "The Ends of the Earth Shall Inquire after Thy Name,"

address delivered at the Missionary Training Center, Provo, Utah, 23 August 1994.

23. Jeffrey R. Holland, "A Standard unto My People," address delivered at CES Symposium, Brigham Young University, Provo, Utah, 9 August 1994 (Provo, Utah: FARMS, 1994), 7.

24. See Stephen L Richards, in Conference Report of the Church of Jesus Christ of Latter-day Saints (hereafter Conference Report), October 1954, 96.

25. Hinckley, *Faith,* 78.

26. John W. Welch, "The Temple in the Book of Mormon," in *Temples of the Ancient World,* ed. Donald W. Parry (Salt Lake City: Deseret Book and FARMS, 1994), 353–55.

27. See John W. Welch, "A Book You Can Respect," *Ensign,* September 1977, 45–48.

28. See B. H. Roberts, *Deseret News,* 11 October 1930.

29. Bruce R. McConkie, *A New Witness for the Articles of Faith* (Salt Lake City: Deseret Book, 1985), 466.

30. Ibid., 466.

31. B. H. Roberts, *New Witnesses for God* (Salt Lake City: Deseret Book, 1909), 2:vi–vii.

32. Ibid., 2:vii; cited by Ted E. Brewerton, "The Book of Mormon: A Sacred Ancient Record," in Conference Report, October 1995, 39; or *Ensign,* November 1995, 31.

33. Roberts, *New Witnesses for God,* 2:vii.

34. Hinckley, *Faith,* 5.

35. McConkie, *New Witness,* 189.

36. Ibid., 188.

37. Sidney B. Sperry, "Some Universals in the Book of Mormon," *Journal of Book of Mormon Studies* 4/1 (1995): 232.

38. John W. Welch, *Illuminating the Sermon at the Temple and the Sermon on the Mount* (Provo, Utah: FARMS, 1999).

39. Hugh W. Nibley, *Since Cumorah* (Salt Lake City: Deseret Book and FARMS, 1987), xiv.

40. See Richard L. Bushman, "My Belief," *BYU Studies* 25/2 (1985): 23–30. Bushman rightly learned that such expectations

are unrealistic (pp. 28–29), but there are other alternatives besides discarding all evidence as "essentially irrelevant" (p. 30).

41. Ezra Taft Benson, "A New Witness for Christ," in Conference Report, October 1984, 7; or *Ensign,* November 1984, 8.

42. Maxwell, *Deposition of a Disciple,* 18.

43. For an excellent précis of the legal science of evidence and proof, see Peter W. Murphy, "Teaching Evidence, Proof, and Facts: Providing a Background in Factual Analysis and Case Evaluation," *Journal of Legal Education* 51/4 (2001): 568–98.

44. See John W. Welch, "What Does Chiasmus in the Book of Mormon Prove?" in *Book of Mormon Authorship Revisited: The Evidence for Ancient Origins,* ed. Noel B. Reynolds (Provo, Utah: FARMS, 1997), 199–224.

45. In Mosiah 5:10–12, for example, King Benjamin is interested in contrasting those who remember the covenantal name and those who do not. The structure of the chiasm in this text accentuates this sharp contrast, the *either/or* separating the two options. In Alma 41:13–15, the balanced sense of divine justice, which will reward good for that which is good, and righteous for that which is righteous, is conveyed subtly by the balance implicit in its literary structure. A similar effect is achieved in Leviticus 24, where the "bruise for bruise, eye for eye" sense of talionic justice is reflected perfectly in the chiastic structure that embraces that content. John W. Welch, "Chiasmus in Biblical Law," in *Jewish Law Association Studies IV: The Boston Conference Volume,* ed. Bernard Jackson (Atlanta: Scholars, 1990), 5–22, esp. 7–11.

46. See John W. Welch, "Alma 36: A Masterpiece," in *Rediscovering the Book of Mormon,* ed. John L. Sorenson and Melvin J. Thorne (Salt Lake City: Deseret Book and FARMS, 1991), 114–31.

47. The pair of lists that is inverted to become a list of pairs in the opposite order in Alma 41:13–15 is brilliantly creative.

48. See McConkie, *New Witness,* 462.

49. Ibid., 467.

50. See John W. Welch, "Preliminary Comments on the Sources behind the Book of Ether" (Provo, Utah: FARMS, 1986).

51. See William J. Hamblin and Stephen D. Ricks, eds., *Warfare in the Book of Mormon* (Salt Lake City: Deseret Book, 1990).

52. Steven D. Ricks and John W. Welch, *Allegory of the Olive Tree* (Salt Lake City: Deseret Book and FARMS, 1994), 484–562.

53. *Reg. v Rowton* (1865), 13 W.R. 437; cited in Norton-Kyshe, *Dictionary of Legal Quotations,* 88.

54. Henry David Thoreau, *Journal,* 11 November 1850; cited in Angela Partington, ed., *The Oxford Dictionary of Quotations* (Oxford: Oxford University Press, 1992), 696.

55. *Thompson v Bowie,* 71 U.S. (4 Wall.) 463, 473 (1867); cited in Eugene C. Gerhart, ed., *Quote It! Memorable Legal Quotations* (New York: Boardman, 1969), 205.

56. See "How Long Did It Take to Translate the Book of Mormon?" in Welch, ed., *Reexploring,* 1–8.

57. *United States v Fatico,* 458 Federal Supplement 388, 410 (Eastern District of New York, 1978). See Timothy J. Martens, "The Standard of Proof for Preliminary Questions of Fact under the Fourth and Fifth Amendments," *Arizona Law Review* 30 (1988): 33.

58. Elder Widtsoe felt that "the weight of evidence" on one side or the other was sufficient to remove all doubt (Widtsoe, *Evidences and Reconciliations,* 28). Joseph Fielding Smith asserted that the highest standard of proof could be met, that evidence "prove[d] beyond the possibility of doubt that Joseph Smith and Oliver Cowdery spoke the truth" (Smith, *Doctrines of Salvation,* 2:124).

59. See Revenue Ruling 87–41, 1987–1 Cumulative Bulletin 296.

60. Lord Wright, in *Grant v Australian Knitting Mills, Ltd.,* A. C. (1936) 85, 96; cited in M. Frances McNamara, ed., *2,000 Classic Legal Quotations* (Rochester, N.Y.: Lawyers Cooperative, 1992), 207.

61. See John L. Hilton, "On Verifying Wordprint Studies: Book of Mormon Authorship," *BYU Studies* 30/3 (1990): 89–108.

62. Richard L. Evans, in Conference Report, October 1952, 96.

63. Hugh B. Brown, in Conference Report, April 1955, 82.

64. Perry Meyer, "Evidence in the Future," *Canadian Bar Journal* 51 (1973): 118.

65. Widtsoe, *Evidences and Reconciliations,* 13. Widtsoe also stated, "Chance, disorder, chaos are ruled out of the physical universe" (ibid., 19).

66. Joseph F. Smith, *Gospel Doctrine* (Salt Lake City: Deseret Book, 1919), 206.

67. Ibid., 206, citing *Juvenile Instructor* 41 (August 1906): 465.

68. Indeed, the word for *repentance* in Greek, *metanoia,* means literally to change one's mind.

69. See John W. Welch, "BYU Studies: Into the 1990s," *BYU Studies* 31/4 (1991): 25.

70. Maxwell, *Deposition of a Disciple,* 17.

71. See Gerhard Kittel, ed., *Theological Dictionary of the New Testament* (Grand Rapids, Mich.: Eerdmans, 1964), 1:255, 258. See also Hugh W. Nibley, "The Meaning of the Atonement," in *Approaching Zion,* ed. Don E. Norton (Salt Lake City: Deseret Book and FARMS, 1989), 556, 560–61.

72. Smith, *Teachings of the Prophet Joseph Smith,* 296.

73. Nibley, *Approaching Zion,* 70–71.

74. Gordon B. Hinckley, "Lord, Increase Our Faith," in Conference Report, October 1987, 68; or *Ensign,* November 1987, 54.

New Light from Arabia on Lehi's Trail

S. Kent Brown

Nudged firmly by the Lord, Lehi and Sariah led their family out of Jerusalem and into the desert of Arabia, beginning an exodus that would be celebrated in story and song for a thousand years. Yet, until the translation of the Book of Mormon, their saga would not be known to the wider world for almost two and one-half millennia. While spending months, perhaps years, at a base camp near the northeastern arm of the Red Sea, the family maintained occasional contact with their estate at Jerusalem through the four sons, Laman, Lemuel, Sam, and Nephi. Twice these sons went back the approximately 250 miles to the city at the behest of the Lord, the first time to obtain a scriptural record inscribed on plates of brass and the second time to persuade another family, that of a man named Ishmael, to join them at the camp in their quest for a promised land. Then, after the Lord directed the party to move deeper into the desert, they packed up their tents and provisions and crossed the "river Laman," never to return again to Jerusalem, effectively cutting themselves off from hearth and home. The question is, Could Joseph Smith have made up the story of this journey based on literary and historical sources available to him during his early years? As we shall see, the answer is no.

Routes from Jerusalem to First Camp

Lehi's Route to First Camp

The mild surprise in the early part of the narrative is that anyone fleeing Jerusalem or its environs would head for Arabia, camping near the Red Sea. Almost all flights into exile that are recorded in the Bible show people going southwest to Egypt, not southeast into Arabia.[1] To be sure, hundreds of years later Jews would flee the Roman siege of Jerusalem by traveling into Arabia (A.D. 68–70). But unless a reader knew the unfamiliar names of Arabian cities and peoples noted in the Bible, there are few hints of meaningful connections in that direction as early as the seventh century B.C., when Lehi and Sariah were on the move.[2] Now there is a growing body of evidence, made available long after Joseph Smith's day, for extensive contacts between Arabia and Jerusalem in antiquity, most commercial and military.[3]

Lehi, Sariah, and their four sons could have followed a number of routes from Jerusalem to the Red Sea. None of them would have run north and south along the shoreline of the Dead Sea, except along the western shoreline from the Ein Gedi oasis southward. On both the east and west sides of the Dead Sea the terrain slopes steeply from cliffs to water's edge and would not have allowed them to pass. The challenges of negotiating such terrain would have escalated, of course, for pack animals.[4]

The Route South

If family members traveled south from Jerusalem, starting toward Bethlehem, at least two routes were available. One was the trade route that led south to Hebron, then to Arad and down through the Zohar Valley into the Arabah Valley, which continues the Jordan Valley southward.[5] This trail would have been the most direct and would have led them toward the tip of the eastern arm of the Red Sea where Aqaba and Eilat are now located. In this connection one should not discount the possibility that the family generally followed a trade route not only for this segment of the journey but for later segments too. Even though Nephi's narrative of the journey does not specifically mention meeting other people, the party surely would have done so. And Nephi offers hints that family members ran into others as they traveled.[6]

A second southward trail open to them would have carried them down into the Arabah Valley next to the Dead Sea. It was the so-called ascent of Ziz (see 2 Chronicles 20:16 Revised Standard Version), which connected the area near Tekoa, birthplace of the prophet Amos, and Ein Gedi, which lay on the west shore of the Dead Sea. Tekoa lies south and slightly east of Jerusalem, and the party could have reached the neighborhood by traveling through or near Bethlehem. From here the trail descends eastward through rugged country to the oasis of Ein Gedi. At that point the party would have turned south toward the Red Sea, keeping at first to the west shore of the Dead Sea.[7]

The Route East, Then South

Two other trails would have led the family to the east, taking them down into the Jordan Valley a few miles south

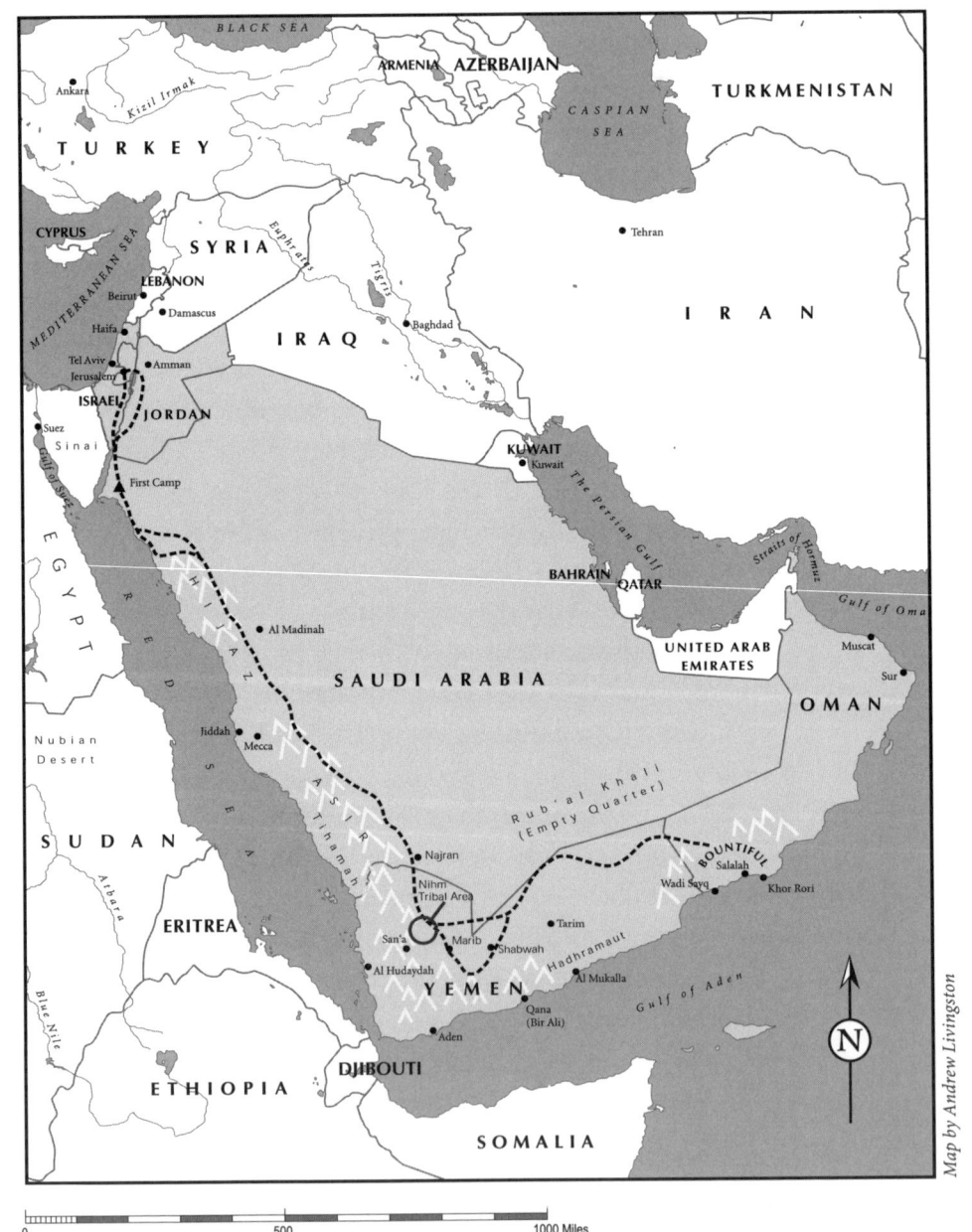

of Jericho. From either trail the party would then have ascended into the highlands of Moab, where they would have turned south and followed either the King's Highway or a road that ran farther east through Edomite territory toward the Red Sea. Of the two routes, the first departed from the east side of Jerusalem and skirted southward around the Mount of Olives, then turned eastward and followed the trade route that connected with the northwest shore of the Dead Sea through Wadi Mukallik (Nahal Og). This trail was known in antiquity as the "Route of Salt" because caravans carried salt extracted from the Dead Sea from its northwest shore up to Jerusalem.[8] The family could have broken off from following this trail at any point after descending into the Jordan Valley and then aimed for the mountains of Moab, perhaps reaching the King's Highway near Mount Nebo.

The second or more northerly route would also have taken the family from the east side of Jerusalem, but on an eastward track up over the Mount of Olives near the modern village of At-Tur and eventually down through Wadi Kelt. This path, too, carried trade and travelers between the Jordan Valley and Jerusalem. The family would have exited Wadi Kelt just south of Jericho. From there it was an easy trek across the Jordan Valley to the base of the mountains of Moab.

What does all this mean? The fact that the Book of Mormon narrative follows the family of Lehi and Sariah from Jerusalem to the tip of the Red Sea and beyond, seeing them set up camp in northwest Arabia (see 1 Nephi 2:4–6), fits what is now known about commercial travel in the late seventh and early sixth centuries B.C. In addition, though the direction of travel—generally southeast—is unexpected because most known flights of people seeking refuge from Jerusalem went into Egypt, not Arabia, the Lord was leading Lehi and Sariah to a promised land in the New World, not into exile.

Location of First Camp

LOCATION OF FIRST CAMP

There are four factors to remember about the camp of Lehi and Sariah in northwest Arabia. First, this area, also known as Midian, was rather heavily populated in antiquity.[9] Hence, it may be incorrect to think that the family was completely isolated in this region. Second, they camped about three days' journey south or southeast of modern Aqaba, a distance of between forty-five and seventy-five miles, depending on their speed and endurance (see 1 Nephi 2:6).[10] Third, the camp lay next to a "river of water" (v. 6) that "emptied into the Red Sea" (v. 8). Lehi described this stream as "continually running" (v. 9). Fourth, the evident impressive character of the valley where they located their camp led Lehi to term the valley "firm and steadfast, and immovable" (v. 10).

Nephi's narrative thus offers a few clues about the camping place. The most astonishing is the claim that there was a "continually running" stream of water in that part of Arabia. After all, students of geography believe that Arabia has been largely a desert for thousands of years and that water flows only after heavy rains.[11] But there is an unforeseen surprise in the mountains south of Aqaba, a surprise that Joseph Smith could not have learned about.

In 1952 Hugh Nibley pointed out that the camp had to lie near "the Gulf of Aqaba at a point not far above the Straits of Tiran" where Lehi, "perhaps from the sides of Mt. Musafa or Mt. Mendisha," beheld that the stream of water ran into the Red Sea.¹² In 1976 Lynn and Hope Hilton visited the area and proposed that the likely location of the camp was at the oasis Al-Bad⁽ in Wadi al-Ifal, about seventy-five miles south and east of Aqaba. Although any running water at the oasis was seasonal, flowing only after heavy seasonal rains, there were springs. Besides, the distant hills were impressive to behold. Thus, the Al-Bad⁽ oasis seemed to be a good fit with Nephi's narrative.¹³ More recently, George Potter has come upon a deep valley that cuts through the granite mountains that border the Gulf of Aqaba on its east shore. Known locally as Wadi Tayyib al-Ism ("Valley of the Good Name") and lying almost seventy-five miles south of Aqaba by foot, the valley holds a stream that flows year-round. Moreover, even though the amount of water flowing in the stream has diminished in recent years because of pumping, it still reaches almost to the shore of the Red Sea. Further, the valley itself is characterized by narrow passages and steep sides that rise about two thousand feet, features that would fit Lehi's description of an impressive valley.¹⁴ Hence, Wadi Tayyib al-Ism is a very attractive candidate for the party's first camp in a desert region that features no other known "continually running" stream.

There is actually a fifth consideration that Joseph Smith could not have known. It concerns the custom of a newcomer's naming a place and its geographical features. That is exactly what Lehi did when he camped next to a desert stream in an impressive valley. He called the stream by the name of his oldest son, Laman, and the valley by the name of his second son, Lemuel (see 1 Nephi 2:8–10; 16:12). Such actions seem odd in light of the fact that people lived in this part of Arabia and therefore the valley where the family camped probably had already received a name.

It was Hugh Nibley who first drew attention to this aspect of the narrative and also pointed out what was obvious, that the names conferred by Lehi did not stick.[15] Charles Doughty, an Englishman who traveled in Arabia during the nineteenth century, made a similar point. During his journey in Arabia, Doughty observed that "every desert stead" had received a name. In fact, many had two or more names. Why? Because landmarks and important places received names from both local residents and from traveling caravanners. These names were never the same because the places in question meant different things to these individuals, depending on the function and importance of the landmarks or depending on an event that occurred there. Perhaps oddly, a person cannot predict which name will stick to a locale, that of the local people or that of the caravanners who visited places again and again.[16] In any event, the constant passing through a region by local herdsmen or by caravanners contrasts with the journey of Lehi and Sariah's party only once through Arabia.

Lehi's Sacrifices

The chief question concerning Lehi's sacrifices in the wilderness is how Joseph Smith knew the proper sacrifices that travelers were to offer according to the Mosaic law. The answer is that he did not. But Lehi did. And he offered sacrifices suitable for the occasions noted in Nephi's narrative, including burnt offerings for atonement.[17]

Nephi's account highlights three occasions on which his father, Lehi, offered sacrifices (to be distinguished from burnt offerings). These occasions were when the family arrived at their first campsite (see 1 Nephi 2:7), when the sons of Lehi returned with the plates of brass (see 5:9), and

Lehi's
Appropriate
Sacrifices

when the sons returned with the family of Ishmael (see 7:22). In each instance, Nephi specifically connects the offering of sacrifices with thanksgiving. Such a detail allows us to know that these sacrifices were the so-called peace offerings that are mandated in the law of Moses (see Leviticus 3).[18] According to Psalm 107, a person was to "sacrifice the sacrifices of *thanksgiving*" for safety in journeying (v. 22, emphasis added), whether through the desert or on water (see vv. 4–6, 19–30).

The burnt offerings are a different matter entirely. They are for atonement rather than thanksgiving (see Leviticus 1:2–4). This type of offering presumes that someone has sinned and therefore the relationship between God and his people has been ruptured, requiring restoration.[19] The priests offered this sort of sacrifice twice daily in the sanctuary of ancient Israel on the chance that someone in Israel had sinned. While the priests could not know that some Israelite had sinned, the Lord obliged them to make the offering anyway. In this sense it was a just-in-case sacrifice.[20]

Lehi offered burnt offerings on two occasions. The second occurred after the sons had returned from Jerusalem with the family of Ishmael in tow (see 1 Nephi 7:22). Had there been sin? Yes. The older sons had sought to bind Nephi and leave him in the desert to die (see 7:6–16). Even though they repented and sought Nephi's forgiveness (see 7:20–21), Lehi felt the need to offer burnt offerings for atonement. In the earlier instance, Lehi offered such sacrifices after the return of his sons from Jerusalem with the plates of brass (see 1 Nephi 5:9). Had there been sin? Again, the answer is yes. The two older brothers had beaten the younger two, drawing the attention of an angel (see 3:28–30). There was also the matter of the unforeseen death of Laban (see 4:5–18; 5:14, 16). Even though Nephi knew through the Holy Spirit that the Lord had commanded him to kill Laban and thus justified Laban's death (see 4:11–13),[21] Lehi was evidently unwilling to take any chances that the relationship between God and his family had not been securely reconciled. So he offered burnt offerings, exactly the right sacrifice for the occasion.

Cultural and Geographical Dimensions of Lehi's Dream

Lehi's Dream in Ancient Context

Lehi's dream, perhaps more than any other segment of Nephi's narrative, takes us into the ancient Near East. For as soon as we focus on certain aspects of Lehi's dream, we find ourselves staring into the world of ancient Arabia. Lehi's dream is not at home in Joseph Smith's world but is at home in a world preserved both by archaeological remains and in the customs and manners of Arabia's inhabitants. Moreover, from all appearances, the dream was prophetic—and I emphasize this aspect—for what the family would yet experience in Arabia. To be sure, the dream was highly symbolic. Yet it also corresponds in some of its prophetic dimensions to historical and geographical realities. The test is in the details.

Wealth

One of the dominant images in Lehi's dream is the "great and spacious building" whose occupants wear "exceedingly fine" clothing (1 Nephi 8:26, 27). Such expressions point to obvious wealth. On a symbolic level the building and its inhabitants represented "the world and the wisdom thereof," as Nephi reminds us (11:35). But the wealthy occupants of the building were also at home in

Arabia. Most probably, Lehi's party saw some of this opulence in travels farther south.

All recent commentators, from Ahmed Fakhry (1947) to Nigel Groom (1981), note the extraordinary wealth of the ancient kingdoms that arose in the southwestern sector of the Arabian Peninsula, in what is modern Yemen.[22] A chief source of that wealth was incense, which camel trains carried into the Mediterranean and Mesopotamian areas from a time beginning long before Lehi and Sariah.[23] The wealth derived not only from the sale of incense but also from taxing the goods, from transporting them, and from offering services in the form of food and so on to the men and animals that made up the caravans. The wealth led to massive public works programs, which included dams for irrigation and temples for the deities worshipped by people there.[24]

Geography

The scenes in the dream alternate between long, lonely stretches of desert crossed at night (see 1 Nephi 8:4–8) and regions of dense population (see vv. 21, 24, 27, 30, 33). Lehi also wrote of deep canyons—known as wadis—that were almost impossible to traverse (compare "a great and a terrible gulf" in 12:18 and "an awful gulf" in 15:28). After rains, the seasonal streams in the wadis fill with mud and debris (called "filthy water" in 12:16 and "filthiness" in 15:26–27).[25] In contrast, Lehi described occasional green fields next to the desert graced not only by abundant water (there were already extensive irrigation works in south Arabia that supported a larger population than the one living there now) but also by lush vegetation represented by the tree full of delicious fruit (see 8:9–13).[26] He saw heavily traveled paths leading to the green areas (see vv. 20–21) as well as "forbidden paths" and "strange roads" of the surrounding desert where the unwary would become "lost" (vv. 23, 28, 32). Further, Lehi's mention of "a mist of darkness" (v. 23) reminds one of the heavy mists and fogs that blanket the coasts of Arabia, especially during the monsoon season, including the place where the family most likely emerged from the desert.[27]

The dream is also true to other cultural and geographical dimensions of the family's world. For example, Lehi's dream began in "a dark and dreary wilderness" wherein Lehi and a guide walked "in darkness" for "many hours" (1 Nephi 8:4, 8). Plainly, they were walking at night, the preferred time for traveling through the hot desert. Further, when Lehi reached the tree that grew in "a large and spacious field"—which field is different from the wilderness—he partook of the fruit of the tree and then looked for his family, apparently expecting to see them (see vv. 9, 12–14). This sort of detail meshes with the custom of family travel in the Near East, with the father going as a vanguard to look for danger and for food while the mother and younger children follow. When there are other adult members in a clan or family, the males form a rear guard, as did Laman and Lemuel in this set of scenes (vv. 17–18). Hence, in the dream Lehi was evidently not alone with the guide as they traveled. His family members were following him, but at a safe distance as custom required.[28]

Multitudes of People

The dream of Lehi teems with people. Although the dream begins with a desert journey undertaken only by Lehi, his family members, and a guide (see 1 Nephi 8:5–7,

14, 17–18), it quickly fills with others. In his own words, Lehi "saw numberless concourses of people" who "did come forth, and commence in the path which led to the tree" (vv. 21, 22). Soon he "beheld others pressing forward" to take "hold of the end of the rod of iron," which also would bring them to the tree (v. 24). In the next scene, he "beheld . . . a great and spacious building" that "was filled with people, both old and young, both male and female" (vv. 26, 27). Moreover, in another setting Lehi "saw other multitudes," some of whom came to the tree and others of whom began "feeling their way towards that great and spacious building," each group proceeding cautiously and purposefully because of the murky mists (vv. 30, 31). Where did all of these people come from? Was not Arabia basically an empty place?

The answer is yes and no. There are vast regions where no human inhabitant lives. The problem in those areas, of course, is a lack of water. But anciently both the northwest and southwest sections of the Arabian Peninsula supported large populations, as well as large numbers of animals.[29] It was through these very areas that Lehi's party passed. Though animals do not appear in Lehi's dream—the lone exception is a lamb (see 1 Nephi 10:10)—people do. And lots of them, matching the images in the dream. Although it is possible for a modern author to make up parts of a story that are unrealistic, the story will not gain credibility in the eyes of readers unless the author carefully masks the unrealistic elements with a heavy dose of reality in the other parts. In the case of Lehi's dream, it is impressive that even this detail of large numbers of people fits the ancient context of the family's journey into Arabia.

No source that Joseph Smith had access to would have told him this fact.

Architecture

The "great and spacious building" of Lehi's dream appeared unusual enough to his eye that he called it "strange" (1 Nephi 8:33). He also wrote that this building in his dream "stood as it were in the air, high above the earth" (1 Nephi 8:26). Why would Lehi, who had evidently traveled a good deal during his life (he possessed "tents," 1 Nephi 2:4), call a building strange? And does the word *strange* fit with the fact that the building soared into "the air, high above the earth"? Evidently, Lehi's descriptions of this building point to architecture unfamiliar to him. Furthermore, his words prophetically anticipate architecture that he and his party would see in south Arabia.

Recent studies have shown that the so-called skyscraper architecture of modern Yemen, featured most vividly by the towering buildings in the town named Shibam in the Hadhramaut Valley, has been common since at least the eighth century B.C. and is apparently unique in the ancient world. The French excavations of the buildings at ancient Shabwah in the 1970s, including homes, indicate that the foundations of these buildings supported multistoried structures. In addition, "many ancient South Arabian building inscriptions indicate the number of floors within houses as three or four, with up to six in [the town of] Ẓafār." Adding to the known details, "these inscriptions also provide the name of the owners" of these buildings.[30]

In this light, it seems evident that Lehi was seeing the architecture of ancient south Arabia in his dream. For contemporary buildings there "stood as it were in the air," rising to five or six stories in height. Such structures would naturally give the appearance of standing "high above the earth" (1 Nephi 8:26). Could Joseph Smith have known that any of these architectural features existed in the days of Lehi and Sariah? The answer has to be no.

Ancient and Modern Writings on Arabia

At issue are, first, whether Joseph Smith or any of his family or neighbors could have gained access before 1830 to written works that spoke about ancient Arabia and, second, whether such works were available in libraries near his home. The year 1830, of course, saw the publication of the Book of Mormon. The libraries that Joseph Smith could have visited include that of Dartmouth College in Hanover, New Hampshire (which was close to where his family lived from 1811 to 1813, when he was between five and seven years old), and John H. Pratt's Manchester lending library (which was in the neighborhood of Palmyra, New York, where Joseph Smith spent his teenage years, from 1816 on).[31]

WRITINGS ON ARABIA

Classical Authors

Sources for information on Arabia include the classical writings of Strabo (ca. 64 B.C.–A.D. 19), Diodorus Siculus (fl. ca. 60–30 B.C.), and Pliny the Elder (ca. A.D. 23–79), as well as the anonymous sailor who authored the account in Greek titled *The Periplus of the Erythraean Sea* (ca. A.D. 100).[32] We can set aside most classical works as possible sources of information about ancient Arabia for Joseph Smith. Strabo's *Geography* did not appear in English translation until 1854. The *Bibliothēkē* of Diodorus Siculus appeared in English translation as early as 1814, but a copy was not in the Dartmouth library until 1927. Although *The Periplus of the Erythraean Sea* was published in an English translation in 1807, the Dartmouth library did not acquire its copy until 1908, and John Pratt's library in New York never owned a copy. Pliny's *Natural History* appeared in an English translation in 1635. But again, evidence does not confirm that his writings were available to readers in English either at Dartmouth before 1924 or in John Pratt's library at any time. The only classical work available in English translation from Pratt's library before 1830, for example, was that of Josephus.[33]

Comparing Interests

An important dimension of the classical sources consists of the authors' distinctive interests. Except for the anonymous *Periplus of the Erythraean Sea,* which featured information almost exclusively about the coastal areas of Arabia, no firsthand information comes to us from classical authors. They featured descriptions of the land and peoples—some inaccurate—that were based chiefly on reports of others. In contrast, 1 Nephi rehearses personal difficulties in the wilderness of Arabia as well as God's deliverance from such troubles. As an example of classical authors' interests, Diodorus Siculus writes about animals not generally found in the Mediterranean region, about gold mining and smelting by slaves in Arabia, and about the sweet smell of the land because of its aromatic plants. Pliny also devotes page after page to aromatic plants in Arabia.[34] Nothing like these interests appears in the narrative of 1 Nephi. Why not? Because 1 Nephi rests on the personal experiences of people who traveled through Arabia, whereas the classical authors selected their information out of curiosity, some of which is inaccurate and even fanciful. On this basis alone, we conclude that Joseph Smith did not fall under the influence of such works.

Naturally, ancient authors writing about Arabia will exhibit some overlapping. That would include 1 Nephi and Pliny's *Natural History,* the latter circulating in English by Joseph Smith's time, although not in libraries where he lived.[35] But the points of overlap are few, and the concerns that underlie such points differ significantly. For instance, Pliny notes that a people called "Minaei have land that is fertile in palm groves and timber." Nephi also mentions that he and his brothers harvested "timbers" to build their ship (see 1 Nephi 18:1–2). But any hypothetical link between the two accounts cannot be sustained. The interest of Pliny's secondhand report is to point out the sources of the Minaean people's wealth. By comparison, Nephi's minor concern is to tell us about how he and others built a seaworthy ship. Another point of overlap is Pliny's report that "the Sabaei" people of south Arabia "irrigated agricultural land" and produced "honey and wax."[36] On his part, Nephi reports on irrigated land of sorts from the dream of his father, Lehi, who saw a "field" next to "a river of water" that was evidently irrigating the field as well as the most prominent plant in it, a tree (see 1 Nephi 8:9–13). Moreover, Nephi writes of "wild honey" in the coastal area that he and others called Bountiful (17:5; 18:6). But Pliny, as in his description of the Minaeans, is writing about the source of the Sabaeans' wealth. By contrast, the irrigated field of Lehi's dream supports a tree that represents the tree of life, whose fruit is "desirable to make one happy" (8:10). In addition, Nephi's note about "wild honey," a delicacy that one can still find in the cliffs that overlook the sea in southern Oman, does not mirror Pliny's economic interest in domestic honey and its by-product of wax.[37] Again, we conclude that the interests of Pliny's secondhand description differ markedly from the firsthand, vivid record of 1 Nephi.

There is one final distinction that concerns the purpose for which these ancient authors wrote. Diodorus Siculus sums up rather neatly his purpose when, after his long description of Arabia, he declares that he had "reported many things to delight lovers of reading."[38] In comparison, Nephi writes that he intends to "show unto [his readers] that the tender mercies of the Lord are over all those whom he hath chosen, because of their faith, to make them mighty unto the power of deliverance" (1 Nephi 1:20). Such purposes influenced how ancient authors selected the information that they would report. In the cases of Diodorus and Nephi, the differences could hardly be sharper.

Contemporary Authors

From Joseph Smith's era we need to review the published works of contemporary authors. Why? Because, some might suggest, Joseph Smith could have gained access to the information reported by classical authors about Arabia by consulting sources that relied on them and that had been written in or near Joseph Smith's era. The first two volumes of Carsten Niebuhr's *Reisebeschreibung nach Arabien und andern umliegenden Ländern,* dealing with Niebuhr's ill-fated expedition to Arabia from 1761 to 1767, were published in 1774 and 1778. Robert Heron translated and published these volumes in English in 1792 under the title *Niebuhr's Travels through Arabia and Other Countries in the East.* This work was reissued in 1799. We note that the only ancient tie to Arabia that Niebuhr discusses concerns the incense trade and the trees that produced the resin. The rest of his work consists of observations about Arabia of his day.[39] But Niebuhr's map of south Arabia raises an important question, for it shows the area of the "Nehhm" tribe. This identification becomes an issue in light of recent studies because the Nehhm tribal area most probably links to "the place that was called Nahom" of Nephi's narrative (1 Nephi 16:34).[40] Could Joseph Smith have obtained information from Niebuhr's map? No, because the English translation of Niebuhr's book and accompanying map were unavailable to him either at the Dartmouth library, which did not acquire a copy of the English translation until December 1937,[41] or from John Pratt's library, which did not own it. Besides, there are problems with the geography of Niebuhr's map. He pictures the Nehhm tribal area as north of both the Hadramaut region and its main water course, the Wadi Masilah (mistakenly spelled Wadi Meidam by Niebuhr). Thus, according to Niebuhr's map, a traveler would go south from Nehhm to reach the Hadramaut area. But in fact a traveler would have to go eastward almost 150 miles across the Ramlat Sabᶜatayn desert. This eastward direction, incidentally, is preserved in Nephi's narrative, not in Niebuhr's map (see 1 Nephi 17:1). (For further discussion about Nahom, see the sections below titled "Adopting the Name *Nahom*" and "Journey from Nahom to Bountiful.")

A second set of key works includes Jean-Baptiste d'Anville's geographical description of Arabia in his three-volume *Géographie ancienne abrégée*, which appeared in 1768. His map *Prémièr Partie de la Carte d'Asie* was printed in 1751 and notes for the first time in a Western publication the approximate location of the Nehem tribe in south Arabia.⁴² Before 1830 d'Anville's work appeared twice in English translations. John Horsley translated d'Anville's volumes, publishing them in 1814 as *Compendium of Ancient Geography.* The maps that appeared with this rendition are the most complete and are based on d'Anville's maps. Another translation of d'Anville's French work was Robert Mayo's *An Epitome of Ancient Geography,* which first appeared in 1818. The map of Arabia is much simpler than that which accompanied Horsley's translation. But neither of these English translations reached the Dartmouth library before Joseph Smith's family moved from the area. Likewise, d'Anville's map that notes the tribal area of Nehem was never part of the collections of either the Dartmouth library or John Pratt's library while Joseph Smith lived in these areas.⁴³

The same can be said about Edward Gibbon's *History of the Decline and Fall of the Roman Empire.* Volume 5 of his original six-volume work came off the press in 1788. In this volume he devoted chapter 50 to a brief description of Arabia and the rise of Islam under Mohammed. Gibbon repeats straightforwardly what he has learned about Arabia from his sources, sometimes uncritically including the fantastic as if it were fact. As an example, he recalls the story of Agatharchides, alluded to by Diodorus Siculus, to the effect that "the soil was impregnated with gold and gems."⁴⁴ In sum, his description of Arabia focuses on places and products of the region, showing topographical and economic interests. Such are foreign to Nephi's account.

The Libraries

A review of the holdings of John Pratt's Manchester lending library and those of Dartmouth College has yielded no evidence that any of the aforementioned works dealing with Arabia—classical or contemporary—existed in these two collections in Joseph Smith's day. They are simply absent from the accession lists of John Pratt's library. In the case of Dartmouth College, the library did not acquire any of these works until after 1830, except volume 2 of Horsley's English translation of d'Anville's work, which came to the library in 1823. Apparently only one of d'Anville's maps came with the translation, but which one is unknown; copies of forty maps came to the library in 1936. Dartmouth College acquired Edward Gibbon's famous historical work only in 1944 and the English translation of Niebuhr's volumes in 1937, much too late for Joseph Smith to have consulted them.[45] Furthermore, the books in John Pratt's library that claimed to treat the ancient world deal with Arabia only in a general way, focusing almost exclusively on the northern area near the Persian Gulf.[46] In this light it is safe to conclude that Joseph Smith did not enjoy access to works on Arabia in either of the libraries that lay near his home at one point or another in his youth. In a similar vein, any hypothesis that Joseph Smith had access to a private library that contained works on ancient Arabia is impossible to sustain.

Conclusion

The narrative of 1 Nephi focuses on a traveling party's attempts to follow God's commandments and thereby stay alive in a harsh clime. We sense no interest in unusual features for the sake of the unusual. On the other hand, except for the *Periplus*, the accounts by classical writers, and by the contemporary authors who based their works on those writers, are all secondhand reports that explore chiefly the unusual dimensions of Arabia that they had learned from others, all the while ignoring everyday living conditions. One thinks, for instance, of Diodorus's wild tale about the fantastic wealth of the city of Sabae wherein the king of this city was not allowed to leave the palace and the inhabitants lived their lives surrounded by objects of gold and silver and precious stones.[47] None of this sort of interest appears in the Book of Mormon text of 1 Nephi.

One further observation is worth making. Carsten Niebuhr's books contrast with the works of d'Anville and Gibbon in the sense that they highlight the personal experiences of the author, who had spent time in Arabia. Even so, Niebuhr's interests do not coincide with those of 1 Nephi. For example, he shows little interest in ancient Arabia and the kind of life that archaeological remains might illuminate. Instead, almost all of his concern focuses on describing people whom he met and places that he visited. This sort of material does not appear in the pages of 1 Nephi. In fact, one of the unusual but persistent characteristics of Nephi's narrative is that Nephi mentions no one whom party members met on their trek. Evidently, he purposely omits mention of all persons and preexisting places, except for Nahom (see 1 Nephi 16:34).

Journey from the First Camp to Nahom

Journey to Nahom

How long was the journey from the first camp to Nahom, and at what point did the party cross from the west side of the Al-Sarāt mountain range to the east? The first question can be answered from clues in Nephi's narrative, plus an appeal to an account in Strabo (ca. 64 B.C.–A.D. 19). The second is more elusive because hints about passing through the mountains are indirect. Even so, there are enough clues to indicate that the family crossed a natural barrier, such as a mountain range, which would fit with their trip through this part of Arabia. Let us take them up in reverse order.

Mountains

A range of mountains, called Al-Sarāt, runs almost the entire length of the west coast of Arabia and separates the coastal lowlands from the uplands of the interior. The peaks in the north rise to heights of five thousand feet while those in the south reach much higher. A limited number of passes and valleys offer access from one side of the range to the other.[48] At some point the party had to cross the mountains before reaching "the place which was called Nahom," where the group turned "nearly eastward" (1 Nephi 16:34; 17:1). Otherwise, the mountains would have formed a major barrier to their eastward trek. Nephi's narrative offers hints that the family went into the mountains not long after leaving the camp.

The first hint is the amazing initial success of the hunters in the party.[49] For after leaving a place they called Shazer, which lay four days' journey from their first camp (see 1 Nephi 16:13), they traveled "for the space of many days, slaying food by the way" (v. 15). This expression indicates abundant cover for hunters that one finds in mountainous terrain rather than in the open, flat region of the maritime plain that runs along the shore of the Red Sea.

A second clue has to do with the possible location of Shazer. Nephi reported that the party had stopped specifically to rest and hunt at Shazer after traveling for only "four days." Shazer lay in "nearly a south-southeast direction" from the first camp (vv. 13–14). Traveling this general direction would have kept the group near the shore of the Red Sea, at least initially. But after the family departed from Shazer, Nephi's account mentions the Red Sea for the last time, a significant point (v. 14). In this light, we can theorize two possible locations for Shazer. Both point to the family's leaving the Red Sea coast soon and traveling into the mountains. First, Shazer may have lain next to the coast a few miles from the mountains and may have been the party's last stop before they entered mountainous terrain, which would explain Nephi's last mention of the Red Sea. Second, it is also possible that Shazer lay inside a mountain valley not far from the Red Sea, a valley that led into and across the mountains.[50] There are not enough hints in the narrative to determine which alternative may be correct.

The third clue has to do with the word *borders*. This term seems to mark a mountainous zone. Early in his narrative, Nephi had apparently used the term *borders* in connection with the mountainous region that runs along the Gulf of Aqaba farther to the north (see 1 Nephi 2:5, 8).[51] Then, as the party moved south from the first camp, Nephi wrote that party members traveled "in the most fertile parts of the wilderness, which were in the borders near the Red Sea" (16:14). In this context, the term *borders* may well point to mountainous areas.[52]

A fourth clue has to do with "the most fertile parts of the wilderness." Such areas did not lie along the coastal plain immediately south of the base camp, because that territory has been known for centuries as a region that does not support much plant life.[53] Hence, one would not expect to find large numbers of wild animals there either. Such "fertile parts," as Nephi described them, either lay in the mountains, perhaps in a season when there was rain,[54] or consisted of the oases that lay on the eastern side of the mountain range.[55] The oases were already populated but often lay a good distance from hunting grounds.

In sum, from hints in Nephi's narrative, it seems that the family went into the mountains not long after leaving Shazer.[56] Importantly, Joseph Smith does not seem to have known of this natural barrier even though the Book of Mormon narrative offers clear hints that it exists. Joseph Smith's only known statement about the geography of Arabia and the route of Lehi's family shows no knowledge of the mountain chain, or other geographical features for that matter. He simply said that the party traveled from "the Red Sea to the great Southern Ocean," a rather simple statement when compared to Nephi's complex narrative.[57]

Length of Trip

Because it was from Nahom that the party "did travel nearly eastward," two questions arise. How far had the group come, and how long had the trip taken to this point? If our conclusion about the general location of Nahom is correct (see next section), Lehi's extended family traveled altogether approximately 1,400 miles to reach this area. The first 250 or so miles brought them to the first camp, their valley of Lemuel. The remaining 1,150 or so miles lay between the first camp and Nahom. There remained approximately 700 miles to traverse to their Bountiful, where they would build their ship (see 1 Nephi 17:5, 8). The total length of their land journey would be at least 2,100 miles from Jerusalem.⁵⁸

The time spent to reach Nahom from the first camp concerns us here. The answer is quite simple. Indicators in the narrative tell us that the trip from the first camp to Nahom took less than a year (see section below). As a comparison, we know of other groups—chiefly caravanners—who traveled between south Arabia and destinations either on the northeast coast of the Red Sea or on the southeast coast of the Mediterranean, the reverse of the party's journey. Such groups required only months to traverse those long distances. For example, it took six months for a Roman military force of ten thousand to venture down the west side of Arabia in 25–24 B.C. The soldiers started from a small port called Lucē Comē (most probably modern ʿAynūnah),⁵⁹ crossed the mountains, and finally reached a city called Marsiaba (perhaps ancient Marib). Then, because the army had lost many soldiers due to unhealthful water and food, they retreated hastily, taking only two months to travel between 1,000 and 1,100 miles one way.⁶⁰ If the starting point for the Roman army was Lucē Comē, which lies not far from the Straits of Tiran, and if the army reached the area of Marib in the south, then the Romans' trek almost matches that of the party of Lehi and Sariah from the first camp both in terms of distance and in terms of the general route that they followed.⁶¹

Clues in Nephi's narrative indicate that Lehi's party likewise took no longer than a year to reach Nahom, evidently not far from where the Roman army would later stop. How do we know that? The answer comes from Nephi's placement of details in his narrative. We start with observations about the marriages that took place in the camp before everyone departed (see 1 Nephi 16:7). While we cannot be entirely certain how long after the marriages the party left the camp, we would expect that one or more of the new brides became pregnant within the first months of marriage. Thus, they may have been pregnant when they set out from the camp. So we should expect a report of childbirths. And we find it. What may be significant is that Nephi noted the first births of children only as he finished his record of later events at Nahom, not before (see 1 Nephi 17:1). We naturally conclude that the women gave birth to their first children at Nahom and that the journey from the camp to Nahom took a year or less, the length of the new brides' pregnancies. This length of time more or less matches the time required for the later Roman expedition, though it is longer because of the possible pregnancies of some of the brides in Lehi's party. Thus, the Book of Mormon narrative approximates what we know from an ancient account of soldiers traveling in Arabia.

Adopting the Name *Nahom*

The issue of where Nahom was located is basically settled. From the first camp the family journeyed to "the place which was called Nahom," whence they turned "nearly eastward" (1 Nephi 16:34; 17:1). Nephi's statement about Nahom reveals that the name was already attached to this spot. Members of the party must have learned it from natives of the area. Incidentally, Nephi's statement forms the first firm evidence that they had met others while traveling.⁶²

On the basis of three inscriptions dated to the time of Lehi and Sariah, the location of Nahom almost certainly lay in the area near Wadi Jawf, a large valley in northwest

Location of Nahom

Yemen.⁶³ The inscriptions appear on small votive altars given to the Bar'an Temple near Marib by a certain Biʿathar of the tribe of Nihm.⁶⁴ This tribe is known from Islamic sources that date to the ninth century A.D., fifteen hundred years after Lehi and Sariah.⁶⁵ In this later period the tribe dwelt south of the Wadi Jawf, near Jebel (or Mount) Nihm, where it currently resides.⁶⁶ The inscriptions, which date to the seventh and sixth centuries B.C., certify that the Nihm/Nehem/Nahom area lay in the same general region, almost fourteen hundred miles south-southeast of Jerusalem.⁶⁷ In the world of archaeology, written materials are valued above all other evidence, and these inscriptions secure the general location of Nahom.⁶⁸

The important ingredient in the name *Nahom* is *NHM*, consonants shared by the name *Nihm*. Although the sound of the middle letter, *h,* may be different in the two names,⁶⁹ it is reasonable that when the party of Lehi heard the Arabian name *Nihm* (however it was then pronounced), the term *Nahom* came to their minds, a term that is familiar from the Old Testament.⁷⁰ As others have noted, *Nahom* derives from the Hebrew verb meaning "to comfort" or "to console."⁷¹ Even though the meaning was quite different in Old South Arabian—it referred to masonry dressed by chipping⁷²—the meaning in Hebrew may connect with the consolation that members of the party sought at Nahom after they buried Ishmael, father of one of the two families in the party. Except for the name Shazer (see 1 Nephi 16:13), each place-name that Nephi records in his narrative—Valley of Lemuel, River of Laman, Bountiful, Irreantum—bears a meaning for members of the party. On this basis, it is reasonable to presume that the name *Nahom* was also significant to them, perhaps reminding them of God's comfort.

The Incense Trail

There are hints in the narrative that those in Lehi's party knew of the incense trail, an aspect of ancient Arabia that Joseph Smith could not have known (see the section "Ancient and Modern Writings on Arabia" above).[73] This route, already well established by the era of Lehi and Sariah, had already developed an infrastructure that would support desert travel, including wells and food sources for humans and animals.

INCENSE TRAIL

The Route

It is not really possible to speak of a single trail. At times this trail was only a few yards wide when it traversed mountain passes. At others, it was several miles across. In places the trail split into two or more branches that, at a point farther on, would reunite into one main road. Essentially, the trail carried caravan traffic, loaded with frankincense and myrrh, from southern Arabia into the Mediterranean and Mesopotamian regions. Until late antiquity, the trail ran along the east side of the mountain range in western Arabia rather than along the west or coastal side.[74] In addition, its caravans carried exotic goods that had come to Arabia by ship from India and China. Indeed, it was one of the most important economic highways of the ancient world, and therefore competition and disruption were not tolerated.[75]

The party of Lehi and Sariah could easily have followed, or traveled parallel to, the trail as they moved deeper into Arabia, except in areas where rugged hills or extensive boulder fields at the sides of the trail prevented a person from leaving the main road. The trail and its spurs kept to the main wells and grasslands where caravanners could obtain water and food for their animals and themselves. It is apparent that Lehi's party had met people who knew and used this trail because some in the group threatened to return home from Nahom, even though they were by then approximately fourteen hundred miles south of Jerusalem (see 1 Nephi 16:36) and even though twice between the first camp and Nahom they had faced the terrifying prospect of starvation (see 1 Nephi 16:17–32, 39).

As we might expect, the terrain through which the trail ran differed from place to place. In the south, where inhabitants harvested and packed the incense, the trail ran from populated area to populated area where cultivation was extensive because of irrigation works. Farther north, past Nahom, the trail passed through a vast, sparsely settled area that was inhabited largely by unruly nomads who had to be controlled and cajoled by the governments and merchants that profited from the incense trade. It was evidently in this area that the party of Lehi and Sariah came to rely heavily on their compass to lead them to the "fertile parts of the wilderness" where they could find fodder for their animals and food for themselves (see 1 Nephi 16:14, 16). Joseph Smith, of course, would not have been acquainted with such a huge desert region lying between two rather fruitful areas, one in the south and one in the north, for northwest Arabia, the location of the first camp, also offered regions of rather high fertility and settlement where a person could find oases and, in antiquity, large areas of cultivation.[76]

From northwest Arabia the northward trail split, one spur turning west toward Egypt and the other continuing north toward such destinations as Jerusalem, Gaza, and Damascus. Even though the terrain was rough and dry along this part of the trail, towns and cities sprang up at regular intervals and their citizens made much of their living by servicing the incense caravans.

Afflictions

It is important to add a few words about the kinds of vicissitudes that the party met along the way. Nephi said of their troubles that "we did . . . wade through much affliction," afterward characterizing the hardships less vividly as "afflictions and much difficulty" (1 Nephi 17:1, 6). Later Book of Mormon authors who had consulted the full set of records added important details, speaking of the family's suffering from both "famine" and "all manner of diseases" while crossing the desert (Mosiah 1:17; Alma 9:22). Joseph Smith would not necessarily have known about either kind of difficulty.[77]

Modern knowledge of Arabia shows it to be a land of harsh deserts with agriculture only in certain spots. Charles Doughty calls northwest Arabia "this land of famine," adding that "famine is ever in the desert."[78] In contrast, beginning with Theophrastus (372–287 B.C.), authors of the classical age, whose writings only savants in Joseph Smith's day would have had some access to, uniformly but incorrectly portrayed the region as one of agricultural abundance and natural, luxuriant growth, giving rise to the name *Arabia Felix*—Arabia the Blessed.[79] Thus, Nephi's narrative agrees with what is now known of the Arabian Peninsula rather than with what was seemingly true about Arabia from ancient classical sources.

What about disease? To be sure, in both Strabo's account of the Roman military force that met disaster in Arabia in 25–24 B.C. and in a brief note in the *Periplus of the Erythraean Sea* there is information about illness.[80] But none of this information about the general climate of health was available to Joseph Smith. It is chiefly modern explorers who have documented the awful conditions that meet travelers. For example, Ahmed Fakhry speaks of a cultivated valley that only descendants of African slaves live in because of the high risk of malaria. Doughty writes of wells filled "with corrupt water" and "infected with camel urine," a common phenomenon. He adds that he and his fellow travelers had to strain out "wiggling white vermin . . . through . . . our kerchiefs."[81] Hence, the Book of Mormon offers a portrait of difficulties compatible both with what has recently become known about desert travel in Arabia and with the ancient situation that has continued roughly the same into modern times because of unchanging travel and climatic conditions.[82]

Peoples and Kingdoms of Arabia

PEOPLES OF ARABIA

This topic connects back to the section on Lehi's dream. The issue has partly to do with the wealth of ancient Arabia. In the nineteenth century some of the best guides to Arabia in the Western world were the studies produced by the German explorer Carsten Niebuhr, who had traveled there in the mid-eighteenth century. The only problem with his explorations is that he hardly touched on the issue of ancient wealth, focusing instead on the then current situation. What he found were modest towns and villages, rulers of moderate means, and independent bedouins. There were only the smallest hints of former glory.[83] Of course, there is more than the fabulous wealth that Joseph Smith would not have known about. It concerns writing. But first we will touch on wealth.

Wealth

We merely remind ourselves of the abundant riches that came to the people of southern Arabia in large part because they controlled the growing and harvesting of the world's best incense. In the dream of Lehi, this feature appears connected most directly to the people whom he saw wearing "exceedingly fine" clothing and, less directly, to the verdant, irrigated fields that supported a very large population in antiquity (see 1 Nephi 8:27, 9–10, 13).[84] Joseph Smith could not have known about these dimensions of life in Arabia that existed about 600 B.C.

Writing on Metal Plates

The Book of Mormon came to Joseph Smith on plates of gold. While it is possible to find in the Near East many examples of ancient writing on metal plates, including seals, which confirm a precedent for writing on metals, those found in south Arabia are also relevant for our comparative purposes. Recent decades have seen a number of discoveries of writing on hard surfaces from south Arabia.[85] Examples come from ancient temples, indicating perhaps that people understood such writing to be connected in some way to the realm of the divine. Moreover, they apparently chose hard surfaces—metal and stone—for writing because of durability. Significant for this study, skilled Arabian artisans had adopted and developed the skills to inscribe important records on metal surfaces. Of course, the record on the plates of brass would have served as the chief model for Nephi's later efforts to keep records on metal plates. Even so, the artisans and scribes who created records on stone and metal in all the major centers of south Arabia may also have impressed Nephi, who wrote his narrative on metal plates only after passing through Arabia[86] (there are indications that the party kept a diary of the Arabian trek, but on a perishable material, not on metal plates).[87]

Alphabet

Perhaps even more remarkable are the possible connections between the ancient alphabet of people in Arabia and that which appears on the so-called Anthon Transcript of the Book of Mormon, a one-page document in possession of the RLDS Church (now known as the Community of Christ).[88] A preliminary review has shown that twenty-five of the characters reproduced in the Anthon Transcript (some are duplicates of one another) are at home in Old North Arabian, a dialect of ancient Arabic spoken and written in northwest Arabia, where Lehi and Sariah set up their first camp. In addition, twelve of the characters on the transcript (again, some are duplicates) are the same as those known from Old South Arabian. This latter dialect was spoken and written in an area south and east of Nahom through which Lehi and Sariah would have passed.[89] Since the party of Lehi and Sariah spent no less than "eight years" in the Arabian Peninsula (1 Nephi 17:4), it may be possible to see a connection coming through these travelers.

Journey to Bountiful

Journey from Nahom to Bountiful

The most important piece in this section concerns Nephi's note that "we did travel nearly eastward from that time forth," after events at Nahom (1 Nephi 17:1). This geographical notice is one of the few in Nephi's narrative, and it begs us to examine it. We first observe that, northwest of Marib, the ancient capital of the Sabean kingdom of south Arabia, almost all roads turn east, veering from the general north-south direction of the incense trail. Moreover—and we emphasize this point—the eastward bend occurs in the general area inhabited by the Nihm tribe. Joseph Smith could not have known about this eastward turn in the main incense trail. No source, ancient or contemporary, mentions it.[90] Only a person who had traveled either near or along the trail would know that it turned eastward in this area. To be sure, the longest leg of the incense trail ran basically north-south along the upland side of the mountains of western Arabia (actually, from the north the trail held in a south-southeast direction, as Nephi said). But after passing south of Najran (modern Ukhdūd, Saudi Arabia), both the main trail and several shortcuts turned eastward, all leading to Shabwah, the chief staging center for caravans in south Arabia.[91] One spur of the trail continued farther southward to Aden. But the traffic along this section was very much less than that which went to and from Shabwah. The main trail and its spurs ran eastward, matching Nephi's description. Wells were there, and authorities at Shabwah controlled the finest incense of the region that was coming westward from Oman, both overland and by sea. It is the only place along the incense trail where traffic ran east-west. Further, ancient laws mandated where caravans were to carry incense and other goods, keeping traffic to this east-west corridor.[92] Neither Joseph Smith nor anyone else in his society knew these facts. But Nephi did.

In a different vein, there are hints that this stage of the journey required the longest time and was the most difficult. Even though the distance from Nahom eastward to the seacoast—the party's Bountiful—was seven hundred miles or less, about half the distance that the party had already traveled from Jerusalem to Nahom, it seems that the party spent the bulk of its "eight years in the wilderness" on this leg of the journey (1 Nephi 17:4).[93] This observation should not surprise us. There is no clear evidence that, during the era of Lehi and Sariah, an established incense trail ran east of Shabwah, the major south Arabian city where caravans stopped to allow grading and taxing of incense coming from that general area. Instead, almost all goods reached Shabwah from the ancient seaport of Qana, which lay to the south.[94] Hence, Lehi and Sariah could not even travel parallel to a route taken by camel drivers and their cargoes. Presumably their party followed a course that snaked eastward between the sands of the "Empty Quarter" on the north and the craggy landscape on the south.[95] In addition, it is now known that the tribes in the region east of Shabwah were in a constant state of tension with one another and that a person could not cross tribal boundaries without having to negotiate afresh the terms of safe conduct. Such negotiations could and often did lead to temporary servility for the traveler among local tribes.[96] Moreover, there were no assured sources of food in the region east of Shabwah except flocks and herds that belonged to tribesmen. Agriculture was little practiced.[97]

Severe Challenges

Such challenges fit the vivid reminiscences of the party's troubles preserved by writers other than Nephi. These later Book of Mormon authors, who enjoyed access to the fuller account of the party's journey, preserve recollections of troubles that differ markedly from details in Nephi's rather full narrative of the trip from Jerusalem to Nahom. For instance, King Benjamin recalls that at certain points along the way party members "were smitten with famine" (Mosiah 1:17). To be sure, the family had suffered from lack of food during the trip from the first camp to Nahom (see 1 Nephi 16:17–32, 39). But the word *famine* sounds a more ominous note. Moreover, Alma also writes of Lehi's party suffering "from famine" as well as "from sickness, and all manner of diseases" (Alma 9:22). In addition, Alma records that party members "did not travel a direct course, and were afflicted with hunger and thirst" (Alma 37:42). In contrast, according to Nephi's account, experiencing famine and disease, and not traveling a direct course, had not occurred to the party before arriving at Nahom. Hence, we should probably understand that the difficulties noted by Benjamin and Alma befell the group only after they turned "nearly eastward" at Nahom (1 Nephi 17:1).

Enemies

In almost identical language, both Amaron and Alma write of God's preserving Lehi's party from "the hands of their enemies" (Omni 1:6; Alma 9:10). Who were these enemies? According to the fuller part of Nephi's narrative, it was not anyone whom party members met between the first camp and Nahom. The most attractive possibility is that the group met such people on the leg of the journey between Nahom and the seacoast, even though Nephi himself does not mention enemies.[98] (Nephi's abbreviated account of crossing south Arabia from Nahom consists of only four verses, 1 Nephi 17:1–4.) Such a view strengthens the impression that the toughest and longest period of the trip came between Nahom and the sea. Another piece that fits into this part of the trip is Nephi's note that party members had not made "much fire, as [they] journeyed," an evident attempt to avoid drawing the attention of marauding raiders (1 Nephi 17:12).[99] As a final addition to the portrait, Alma seems to tie a recollection of ancestors who were "strong in battle" to Lehi's party, whom God "delivered . . . out of the land of Jerusalem" (Alma 9:22). If so, then we are to think that the party struggled against more than the harsh realities of the desert as they forged on toward the seacoast. That is, one of their biggest challenges may have come in dealing with tribesmen whom they met. This impression, too, matches what we know of tribal troubles in this part of Arabia.[100]

Such a scene of desperate difficulties consisting of disease, famine, and enemies—difficulties that find expression chiefly in sources other than Nephi's narrative—resonates with the situations that one would certainly encounter in south Arabia.[101] What is the likelihood that Joseph Smith knew such details of life there? The answer is zero.

Bountiful

DETAILS
ABOUT
BOUNTIFUL

There is only one area along the southern coast of the Arabian Peninsula that matches botanically Nephi's description of Bountiful as a place of abundant fruit, wild honey,[102] and timbers (see 1 Nephi 17:5–6; 18:1–2, 6). It is the Dhofar region of southern Oman. The summer monsoon rains turn the area into a green garden. In addition, one finds small deposits of iron ore there from which Nephi could have made his tools for building the ship that would carry the party to the New World. There is no way that Joseph Smith could have known these facts.

Although one must view attempts to tie Bountiful to a specific locale in Dhofar with deep caution, Latter-day Saint writers have rightly pointed to this area as the probable general region where the party of Lehi and Sariah emerged from the desert.[103] It is almost as if one can hear party members singing in Nephi's narrative when he writes of their escape from the harsh desert into an area teeming with fruit: "We did come to the land which we called Bountiful, because of its much fruit and also wild honey; and . . . we were exceedingly rejoiced when we came to the seashore" (1 Nephi 17:5–6).[104] At long last, the group had escaped the grasp of the living death of desert famine.

Fruit

Wendell Phillips calls "the narrow half-moon shaped coastal plain of Dhofar . . . the only major fertile region between Muscat and Aden."[105] Jörg Janzen adds the note that "the hothouse climate which prevails in the oasis plantations for most of the year permits the cultivation of many sorts of fruit, particularly bananas and papayas, and of vegetables, cereals and fodder. At least two and sometimes even three harvests a year could be achieved."[106] Clearly, Dhofar has been a fruitful area.

Honey

The wide availability of domesticated bees and honey in certain regions of Arabia has been known since Eratosthenes of Cyrene wrote about the subject (ca. 275–194 B.C.) and Strabo quoted him.[107] But it is impossible that Joseph Smith would have had access to this source because Strabo's *Geography* did not appear in English translation until 1854. Only recent years have seen biologists take a firm interest in the bees of the Arabian Peninsula.¹⁰⁸ Terry Ball and others of the faculty of Brigham Young University reported that wild honeybees—to be distinguished from Eratosthenes' domesticated bees—live in the rock cliffs of the escarpment that rises above the maritime plain near Salalah, making the retrieval of honey an interesting challenge.¹⁰⁹ Thus, wild bees and their honey are still in this part of Arabia.

Timbers

Trees form part of the luxuriant, tropical growth in Dhofar, Oman. One question, of course, is which of the species Nephi shaped for his ship (see 1 Nephi 18:1–2, 6). We do not know. It is possible that Nephi somehow acquired teak logs floated from India, because sources earlier than Lehi speak of this kind of import for the work of shipwrights in the area of the Persian Gulf, hundreds of miles to the north. It is the judgment of George Hourani that "Arabia does not . . . produce wood suitable for building strong seagoing ships," and thus "the materials for building strong vessels had to be brought from India."¹¹⁰ On the other hand, it seems more likely that Nephi secured timbers that were nearby, because he relates that he and his brothers "did go forth" to obtain timbers (1 Nephi 18:1).

Although we do not know the species of tree that Nephi may have used—he may have cut different trees for different parts of his ship—trees have been growing in the Dhofar region for millennia. To be sure, most trees grow on the escarpment above the maritime plain and coastal waters of the sea. But there is evidence that trees once grew closer to the sea before people stripped them from the lower lands, most recently in the 1960s. In fact, Jörg Janzen writes that apparently the coastal plain of southern Oman was once "thickly wooded," at least in the vicinity of the wadis.[111] Before him, Bertram Thomas had seen in 1928 the "the seaward slopes [of the foothills] velvety with waving jungle."[112]

The heavy vegetation of southern Oman is something of an oddity. Why? Because the rather scantly vegetated mountains of northern Oman, hundreds of miles away, actually receive on average 10 percent more rain per year. Janzen explains that the vegetation of Dhofar is far richer because of the relatively slow rate of rainfall during the summer monsoon—it comes in the form of mist and drizzle—and thus the ground absorbs the water better. In addition, the monsoon cloud cover slows evaporation.[113] As a result, the vegetation remains rich and diverse and supports a wide variety of life forms.[114]

Mists

The mention of mists brings us back to Lehi's dream, noted earlier. To be sure, inhabitants experienced mists in desert regions, a mixture of dust and fog. And it may be these that Lehi envisioned in his dream.[115] On the other hand, the mists of Lehi's dream could certainly anticipate the mists that build along the coasts, particularly in Dhofar during the monsoon season, an aspect that Joseph Smith could not have known about. In this connection, Janzen writes of a "coastal mist during the summer months" in Dhofar. Against the middle altitudes of the mountains, "the clouds most frequently stack up, giving rise to thick fog near the summits." Because of the weather patterns, Janzen calls the area "a tropical 'mist oasis.'" The increased moisture, as one might expect, means that much more dew forms in the desert areas north of the mountains.¹¹⁶ The main point is that the notation about mists in the Book of Mormon narrative fits an Arabian coastal context.

Ore

Where could Nephi have found ore to make his tools? (see 1 Nephi 17:9–10, 16). We know that there were copper mines at ancient Magan near the Persian Gulf that had been worked as early as the Sumerian period (third millennium B.C.). But the mines were more than six hundred miles to the north of where the party of Lehi and Sariah reached the coast.¹¹⁷ And because Nephi offers no hint that he had to travel far to find ore, particularly a trip that would have taken him back into the desert, it seems out of the question that he traveled to the distant Persian Gulf region in order to obtain copper. Moreover, concerning iron ore, Hourani observes that "Arabia does not . . . contain iron for nailing [ships], nor is it near to any iron-producing country."¹¹⁸

For the record, Nephi did not need a large deposit of copper or iron ore for his tools. Fifty pounds or so would have met his needs. In February 2000, geologists from Brigham Young University discovered two large deposits of iron ore in the Dhofar region of Oman. And they both lie within a few days' walk of any campsite along the seacoast.¹¹⁹ Although iron ore in the amounts that make mining profitable do not occur in southern Oman, ore does occur in sufficient quantities that Nephi could easily have traveled to a substantial deposit and extracted enough to smelt for his tools. Thus, the natural occurrence of iron ore in the Dhofar area offered a clear solution to Nephi's need for tools.

Conclusion

The entire thrust of these remarks underscores the observation that Joseph Smith could have known almost nothing about ancient Arabia when he began translating the Book of Mormon. Yet the narrative of the journey of the party of Lehi and Sariah through ancient Arabia, written by their son Nephi, fits with what we know about the Arabian Peninsula literally from one end to the other, for their journey began in the northwest and ended in the southeast sector. Nephi's narrative faithfully reflects the intertwining of long stretches of barren wilderness with pockets of verdant, lifesaving vegetation. Recent discoveries have illumined segments of the account, tying events to known regions (e.g., Nahom) and climatic characteristics (e.g., mists along the coastal mountains). People in Joseph Smith's world may have possessed accurate information about one or two aspects of Arabia through classical sources (e.g., incense trade, honey production). But those same sources offered inaccurate caricatures of Arabia that Nephi's narrative does not mirror (e.g., that the peninsula was graced by large forests, etc.). Hence, on both fronts—modern discoveries and more accurate information—the Book of Mormon account shines as a radiant beam across the centuries, inviting us to adopt its more important message of spiritual truths as our own.[120]

NOTES

1. See 1 Kings 11:26–40 (Jeroboam); Jeremiah 43:1–7 (Jeremiah and others); compare the journeys of Abraham and Jacob into Egypt (Abraham 2:21; Genesis 12:10; 46:1–7). According to the annals of Sargon II, king of Assyria (721–705 B.C.), Greek

rulers of Ashdod fled twice to Upper Egypt to avoid Sargon's army (see James B. Pritchard, ed., *Ancient Near Eastern Texts Relating to the Old Testament*, 3rd ed. with supplement [Princeton: Princeton University Press, 1969], 285, 286).

2. Although Yemenite Jews recount traditions that a few Israelites under Moses turned into Arabia rather than going to the promised land and, more to the point, that generations later thousands of Jerusalemites fled to Arabia because of the dire prophecies of Jeremiah, none of these traditions hold up to literary and archaeological scrutiny. See, for instance, Reuben Ahroni, *Yemenite Jewry: Origins, Culture, and Literature* (Bloomington, Ind.: Indiana University Press, 1986), 24–37; and Tudor V. Parfitt, *The Road to Redemption: The Jews of the Yemen 1900–1950* (Leiden: Brill, 1996), 3–7. In the Bible, Ezekiel mentions Arabia in general terms (see Ezekiel 27:21). Other passages note cities in Arabia by name, most unfamiliar to Western readers, as well as goods that came from them. We read of Dedan and its citizens (Isaiah 21:13; Ezekiel 27:20); Sheba (1 Kings 10:1; Job 6:19; Psalm 72:10, 15; Isaiah 60:6; Jeremiah 6:20; Ezekiel 27:22; 27:23; 38:13); the Kedar tribe of northwest Arabia (Isaiah 21:16–17); and Tema (also Teyma; Job 2:11; 4:1; 6:19; 15:1; 22:1; 42:9; Isaiah 21:14; Jeremiah 25:23–24).

3. This observation about commercial ties may indicate why Lehi turned to Arabia when taking flight. The pottery record of Midianite ware as early as the thirteenth and twelfth centuries B.C. indicates extensive, old contacts between northwest Arabia and areas as far north as Hebron. But scholars cannot determine whether the spread of Midianite ware came by commerce or by migration. See Beno Rothenberg and Jonathan Glass, "The Midianite Pottery," in *Midian, Moab and Edom: The History and Archaeology of Late Bronze and Iron Age Jordan and North-West Arabia*, Journal for the Study of the Old Testament Supplement Series 24, ed. John F. A. Sawyer and David J. A. Clines (Sheffield: JSOT Press, 1983), 65–124, esp. 113–16. For a summary of evidence for commercial contacts between people

of Jerusalem and those of Arabia in the seventh century B.C., see Yigal Shiloh, "South Arabian Inscriptions from the City of David, Jerusalem," *Palestine Exploration Quarterly* 119/1 (1987): 9–18.

4. The family must have taken pack animals—very possibly camels—to carry tents and other essentials (1 Nephi 2:4). The sections of the tents would have weighed more than one hundred pounds each. But even camels cannot carry such burdens if they are underfed and tired (see Bertram Thomas, *Arabia Felix* [New York: Charles Scribner's Sons, 1932], 164–65). That camels were more suited to desert travel than other animals can be seen in the offhanded remark of Ahmed Fakhry, who traveled through southwestern Arabia with camels and mules: "It is impossible for laden mules to walk in that loose sand, and so we had to ride camels" (*An Archaeological Journey to Yemen [March–May 1947]* [Cairo: Government Press, 1952], 1:12). Charles Doughty adds that donkeys "must drink every second day" (*Travels in Arabia Deserta* [New York: Random House, 1936], 1:325).

5. For information on the three trade routes that brought goods to Jerusalem from the south and the east, see M. Har-El, "The Route of Salt, Sugar, and Balsam Caravans in the Judean Desert," *GeoJournal* 2/6 (1978): 549–56.

6. The expression "the place which was called Nahom" indicates that the family learned the name *Nahom* from others (1 Nephi 16:34). In addition, when family members were some fourteen hundred miles from home at Nahom, some knew that it was possible to return (v. 36), even though they had run out of food twice (vv. 17–19, 39). Further, Doctrine and Covenants 33:8 hints that Nephi may have preached to people in Arabia. See also S. Kent Brown, "A Case for Lehi's Bondage in Arabia," *Journal of Book of Mormon Studies* 6/2 (1997): 205–17.

7. This route is favored by D. Kelly Ogden in "Answering the Lord's Call (1 Nephi 1–7)," in *Studies in Scripture, Volume Seven: 1 Nephi to Alma 29,* ed. Kent P. Jackson (Salt Lake City: Deseret

Book, 1987), 17–33, especially 23. Har-El also draws attention to this route that ascends from Ein Gedi ("The Route of Salt," 555; also "Israelite and Roman Roads in the Judean Desert," *Israel Exploration Journal* 17/1 [1967]: 18–25, esp. 19 [map], 21, 25). The first mapping effort was undertaken by Claude R. Conder and Horatio Herbert Kitchener (*Survey of Western Palestine: Memoirs of the Topography, Orography, Hydrography, and Archaeology* [London: Palestine Exploration Fund, 1883], 58).

8. For the routes running east from Jerusalem, see Har-El, "The Route of Salt," 549–56. Nelson Glueck describes a series of forts that would have protected travelers on the eastern road, though they were not in use in Lehi's era (*The Other Side of the Jordan* [New Haven, Conn.: American Schools of Oriental Research, 1940], 128–34). For the route of the King's Highway, see Barry J. Beitzel, "Roads and Highways (Pre-Roman)," *Anchor Bible Dictionary*, ed. David Noel Freedman et al. (New York: Doubleday, 1992), 5:779 and accompanying maps.

9. "From the late second millennium, parts of the Hejaz and Tabuk region in the north were intensively settled" (M. C. A. MacDonald, "Along the Red Sea," in *Civilizations of the Ancient Near East*, ed. Jack Sasson et al. [New York: Charles Scribner's Sons, 1995], 2:1350).

10. The speed of daily travel depends on the speed of the pack animals, most likely camels in this case. Nigel Groom notes that a loaded camel travels "slightly less than $2\frac{1}{2}$ miles an hour" and "rarely exceed[s] 25 miles" per day (*Frankincense and Myrrh: A Study of the Arabian Incense Trade* [London: Longman Group, 1981], 173, 211). Rather offhandedly, Wendell Phillips notes that loaded camels travel "three m.p.h. (the proper pace)" (*Unknown Oman* [New York: David McKay Co., 1966], 222). On the required three days of travel from Jerusalem before offering sacrifice, see David R. Seely, "Lehi's Altar and Sacrifice in the Wilderness," *Journal of Book of Mormon Studies* 10/1 (2001): 62–69.

11. See, for example, Rushdi Said's statement that "the Red Sea . . . is left without a single flowing river. In this respect the

Red Sea is unique and without rival" (*The River Nile: Geology, Hydrology and Utilization* [New York: Pergamon, 1993], 7). George Rentz also writes that "Arabia contains no large perennial rivers" ("Al-ᶜArab, Djazīrat," *The Encyclopaedia of Islam* [Leiden: Brill, 1960–], 1:537).

12. Hugh W. Nibley, *Lehi in the Desert; The World of the Jaredites; There Were Jaredites* (Salt Lake City: Deseret Book and FARMS, 1988 [originally published as three separate books in 1952]), 85.

13. See Lynn M. and Hope Hilton, *In Search of Lehi's Trail* (Salt Lake City: Deseret Book, 1976), 63–68; also "In Search of Lehi's Trail, Part 2: The Journey," *Ensign*, October 1976, 43–45.

14. See George D. Potter, "A New Candidate in Arabia for the Valley of Lemuel," *Journal of Book of Mormon Studies* 8/1 (1999): 54–63.

15. See Nibley, *Lehi in the Desert*, 75–76.

16. Doughty, *Travels in Arabia Deserta*, 1:88. As an illustration that this practice continued in Nephite society, the fleeing people of Alma named the valley of their first encampment "the valley of Alma." Even though the group spent only a few hours in the valley, it remained memorable as the spot of their first taste of freedom after a bitter bondage and as the place where the Lord promised to "stop" their pursuers (see Mosiah 24:20–23).

17. The main study so far is that of the author, "What Were Those Sacrifices Offered by Lehi?" in his *From Jerusalem to Zarahemla* (Provo, Utah: BYU Religious Studies Center, 1998), 1–8.

18. See Jacob Milgrom, *Leviticus 1–16*, Anchor Bible 3 (New York: Doubleday, 1991), 218–19.

19. See ibid., 175–77, 267–68, 858.

20. As an example, Job 1:5 records that Job "offered burnt offerings" just in case his "sons [had] sinned."

21. John W. Welch and John A. Tvedtnes have discussed ancient legal dimensions of Nephi's act. See Welch, "Legal Perspectives on the Slaying of Laban," *Journal of Book of Mormon Studies* 1/1 (1992): 119–41; and Tvedtnes, *The Most Correct*

Book: Insights from a Book of Mormon Scholar (Salt Lake City: Cornerstone, 1999), 110–12.

22. See Fakhry, *Archaeological Journey to Yemen;* and Groom, *Frankincense and Myrrh*. As a measure of wealth, ancient inscriptions from southern Arabia mention the dedication of gold and other precious objects to various deities. See the dedicatory inscriptions in Jacqueline Pirenne, *Corpus des Inscriptions et Antiquités sud-Arabes*, Académie des Inscriptions et Belles-lettres, Tome I, Section 1 (Louvain: Peeters, 1977), translated on pp. 42, 48, 68, 72, 76, 79, 84, 131–32, 148, 160, 176, 182, 183, and 220. Ancient reports of wealth, some fantastic and all unavailable to Joseph Smith, occur in Pliny's *Natural History* 6.32 (§§160–61); Strabo's *Geography*, 16.4.3, 19; and Diodorus Siculus's *Bibliothēkē* 3.47.4–8.

23. Inscriptions show that frankincense trade with Egyptians began in the third millennium B.C. See Groom, *Frankincense and Myrrh*, 22–37.

24. See Pliny, *Natural History* 12.32 (§§63–65); and J. G. T. Shipman, "The Hadhramaut," *Asian Affairs* 71/2 (1984): 155; Jean-François Breton, "Architecture," in *Queen of Sheba: Treasures from Ancient Yemen,* ed. St. John Simpson (London: The British Museum Press, 2002), 142–48.

25. Reuben Aharoni reports that the flooding in and around Aden after downpours used to turn the streets of Aden into rushing streams that swept people and animals out to sea (*The Jews of the British Crown Colony of Aden* [Leiden: Brill, 1994], 35). Jörg Janzen writes that in cyclonic downpours along the Dhofar coast of Oman "great masses of water then turn the wadis into torrents (sing. *sayl*) and lead to extensive flooding. . . . Some livestock is almost invariably drowned and even human lives are sometimes lost." Further, "in June 1977 . . . in South-East Dhofar . . . hundreds of goats, cattle and camels, and many people, were taken unaware and drowned" (*Nomads in the Sultanate of Oman* [Boulder, Colo.: Westview, 1986], 29–30). Again, after rains in southwest

Arabia there are "huge 'sayls' [in] Bayhān, which sometimes flow through the length of the valley and far out into the desert for days on end" (Groom, *Frankincense and Myrrh*, 182).

26. For example, Wendell Phillips (*Unknown Oman*, 189–90) observes that the water captured behind the Marib dam "was distributed to create mile upon mile of green fields" at the edge of the desert. Robert W. Stookey (*Yemen—the Politics of the Yemen Arab Republic* [Boulder, Colo.: Westview, 1978], 9) states that early inhabitants of southern Arabia "built some of the most imposing hydrological works of the ancient world, sustaining dense, prosperous populations in regions which now support merely a few nomadic herdsmen." This is in a region, significantly, "where terraced fields and palm groves house today over half of the people living in the [Arabian] peninsula" (Maurizio Tosi, "The Emerging Picture of Prehistoric Arabia," *Annual Review of Anthropology* 15 [1986]: 463–64). Such observations rest firmly on archaeological and geomorphological studies and on the recovery of inscriptions. For archaeological research, see, for example, George R. H. Wright, "Some Preliminary Observations on the Masonry Work at Mārib," *Archäologische Berichte aus dem Yemen*, Band 4 (Mainz am Rhein: Verlag Philipp von Zabern, 1987), 63–78. For geomorphological work, see Ueli Brunner, *Die Erforschung der Antiken Oase von Mārib mit Hilfe geomorphologischer Untersuchungsmethoden, Archäologische Bericht aus dem Yemen*, Band 2 (Mainz am Rhein: Verlag Philipp von Zabern, 1983). For a list of publications of inscriptions, see "Références et Orientations bibliographiques," in Pierre Robert Baduel, ed., *L'Arabie antique de Karib'îl à Mahomet: Nouvelles données sur l'histoire des Arabes grâce aux inscriptions, La Revue du Monde Musulman et de la Méditerranée* 61 (1991–93): 162–63.

27. George Rentz writes that "fogs and dews are common in the humid regions [of Arabia]" (article "Al-ʿArab, Djazīrat"), and Adolf Grohmann and Emeri van Donzel observe that a "particularity of the climate of the western slopes [of the al-Sarāt mountain chain]

are the Tihāma fogs" (article "Al-Sarāt"); both articles appear in *The Encyclopaedia of Islam*, 1:537 and 9:39, respectively.

28. For an observation about how a desert-dwelling family moves with its baggage animals and also the reasons for traveling at night, see Doughty, *Travels in Arabia Deserta*, 1:86 and 257, as well as Strabo (ca. 64 B.C.–A.D. 19), who writes that "in earlier times the camel-merchants traveled only by night" *(Geography,* 17.1.45). The order of march and encampment for the Israelites mandated in the Bible is probably modeled on that of family travel, placing the most precious items in the middle for maximum protection (see Numbers 1:47–53; 2:34; 10:14–28, 33; also Nehemiah 9:19).

29. Inscriptions include notices of the large numbers of people taken hostage and the huge numbers of animals captured in battles as early as the seventh century B.C. Even though the numbers may be exaggerated, they bespeak a flourishing set of societies in south Arabia. See Christian Robin, "Quelques Épisodes marquants de l'Histoire sudarabique," in Baduel, ed., *L'Arabie antique de Karib'îl à Mahomet*, 55–57. Juris Zarins reports that an inscription dating to about 50 B.C. from Marid, a site near Najrān (JA577), "mentions an attack on Najrān with the ravaging of 68 townships, 60,000 field plots and 97 wells" (Juris Zarins et al., "Preliminary Report on the Najrān /Ukhdūd Survey and Excavation, 1982/1402 A.H.," *Atlal: The Journal of Saudi Arabian Archaeology* 7 [1403 A.H.–A.D. 1983]: 22. Zarins is citing the earlier works by Albert W. F. Jamme, *Sabaean Inscriptions from Māḥrām Bilqīs* [Baltimore: Johns Hopkins, 1962], 79, 323; and Alfred Felix Landon Beeston, *Warfare in Ancient South Arabia*, Qahtan: Studies in Old South Arabian Epigraphy, Fasc. 3 [London: Suzac, 1976], 39–40).

30. See J.-F. Breton, "Architecture," *Queen of Sheba*, ed. Simpson, 142–48; the quotations are from p. 143.

31. For a review of these years, see Richard L. Bushman, *Joseph Smith and the Beginnings of Mormonism* (Urbana, Ill.: University of Illinois Press, 1984), 31–42.

32. Consult Edward Gibbon's summarizing list of classical authors who wrote on Arabia in his *History of the Decline and Fall of the Roman Empire*, chap. 50 in any edition, note 2.

33. See the listing of the books available near Joseph Smith's New York home by Robert Paul in "Joseph Smith and the Manchester (New York) Library," *BYU Studies* 22/3 (1982): 333–56. The works of Josephus bear the accession numbers 181–86. The information about the holdings of the Dartmouth library was in a communiqué from Patricia A. Crossett, a former employee of Dartmouth College and the current LDS institute instructor there, dated 22 March 2001.

34. On aromatic plants, see Diodorus Siculus, *Bibliothēkē*, 2.49, 53; 3.46; Pliny, *Natural History* 12.24, 29–41 (§§41, 50–84); on gold mining, see Diodorus, *Bibliothēkē*, 2.50.1; 3.12–14; and on strange animals, see Diodorus, *Bibliothēkē*, 2.50–52.

35. The Dartmouth College library did not acquire an English translation of Pliny's *Natural History* until 1924.

36. Pliny treats both the Minaei and the Sabaei in *Natural History*, 6.32 (§161).

37. Strabo, citing Eratosthenes, also reports on honey, an account unavailable to Joseph Smith. Strabo writes that in south Arabia "the country is in general fertile, and abounds in particular with places for making honey" (*Geography*, 16.4.2).

38. Diodorus Siculus, *Bibliothēkē*, 3.54.7.

39. A handy account of Niebuhr's efforts to publish his papers appears in Thorkild Hansen, *Arabia Felix: The Danish Expedition of 1761–1767*, translated from the Danish *Det Lykkelige Arabien* by James and Kathleen McFarlane (London: Collins, 1964), 356–63; see also 202–301 for a helpful summary of Niebuhr's experiences in Arabia. Also see Carsten Niebuhr, *Reisebeschreibung nach Arabien und andern umliegenden Ländern* (Kopenhagen: Nicolaus Möller, 1774), 1:255–469; and consult his *Beschreibung von Arabien* (1772; reprint, Graz, Austria: Akademische Druck- und Verlagsanstalt, 1969), 143–50. Niebuhr was inspired in part to travel to Arabia because of the works of d'Anville; see Gerald

R. Tibbets, *Arabia in Early Maps* (New York: Oleander Press, 1978), 30.

40. Consult Ross T. Christensen, "The Place Called Nahom," *Ensign,* August 1978, 73; Warren P. and Michaela K. Aston, *In the Footsteps of Lehi* (Salt Lake City: Deseret Book, 1994), 3–25; S. Kent Brown, "'The Place Which Was Called Nahom': New Light on Nahom from Ancient Yemen," *Journal of Book of Mormon Studies* 8/1 (1999): 66–68; and Warren P. Aston, "Newly Found Altars from Nahom," *Journal of Book of Mormon Studies* 10/2 (2001): 56–61.

41. This date comes from a message dated 9 February 2001, from Ann Mehugo, a librarian at Dartmouth College, and in the message from Patricia A. Crossett of 22 March 2001 (see n. 33 above).

42. Jean Baptiste Bourguignon d'Anville, *Géographie ancienne abrégée,* 3 vols. (Paris: Merlin, 1768). This work was the basis for the two English translations. D'Anville's map of the world, which shows Arabia and was titled "Orbis Veteribus Notus," was published in 1761. See Raymond Lister, *Antique Maps and Their Cartographers* (Hamden, Conn.: Archon Books, 1970), 49. This map shows few details about Arabia and does not include the Nehem tribal area. For d'Anville's map titled *Prémièr Partie de la Carte d'Asie,* which does include the Nehem tribal area, published in 1751, see Tibbets, *Arabia in Early Maps,* 29–31, 165–66. Consult also the critique of the accuracy of d'Anville's maps of Arabia, especially for the interior areas, in David George Hogarth, *The Penetration of Arabia* (London: Lawrence and Bullen, Ltd., 1904), 35–37.

43. See John Horsley, trans., *Compendium of Ancient Geography, by Monsieur d'Anville,* 2 vols. (New York: R. M'Dermut and D. D. Arden, 1814). The chapter on Arabia appears in volume 2, pages 3–20. Ten maps drawn by d'Anville accompanied these volumes and were offered for sale separately. But they did not include d'Anville's map *Prémièr Partie de la Carte d'Asie.* See also Robert Mayo, *An Epitome of Ancient Geography,* Sa-

cred and Profane, Being an Abridgement of D'Anville and Wells (Philadelphia: A. Finley, 1818). The pages that deal with Arabia are 203–14. The map of Arabia, which the author has simplified from d'Anville's original, shows few of Arabia's geographical features. Volume 2 of Horsley's translation was acquired by the Dartmouth College library in 1823, apparently without a map that shows Arabia. A collection of forty of d'Anville's maps was acquired in 1936, one of which is *Prémièr Partie de la Carte d'Asie*. Mayo's translation has never been part of the Dartmouth collection. John Pratt's library in New York never owned anything by d'Anville. The dates for the Dartmouth library collection come from Patricia A. Crossett (see n. 33 above).

44. Edward Gibbon, *The History of the Decline and Fall of the Roman Empire* (London: Strahan and Cadell, 1776–88), 5:173; Diodorus Siculus, *Bibliothēkē*, 2.50.1; consult the references to wealth in classical sources in note 22 above.

45. See notes 41 and 43 for the dates. One of the important dimensions of both Niebuhr's map and d'Anville's map of Arabia is that they each note the existence of an area called Nehhm or Nehem in the general region that "the place which was called Nahom" would have lain (1 Nephi 16:34). Information about d'Anville's works comes from *A Catalogue of the Books in the Library of Dartmouth College*, Published by Order of the Trustees, November 1825 (Concord, N.H.: Hough, 1825). Importantly, during April 2001, I searched the John Hay Library of Brown University as a further test. The results were similar to those at the library of Dartmouth College. The earliest contemporary work acquired by the Brown Library was a multivolume copy of Gibbon's *History* published in 1781. It came to the library before 1793. But it was incomplete and is missing the important chapter 50 wherein Gibbon deals with Arabia. The Brown Library did not acquire Niebuhr's work in English until 1854. Further, it acquired d'Anville's geographical study in Horsley's English translation only in 1846. The earliest acquisition of a classical source in English was that of Pliny's *Natural History* in 1793.

The Brown Library acquired none of the other classical sources that discuss Arabia before 1846 when it came into possession of a translation of the *Periplus of the Erythrean Sea*. See the further discussion in the sections of this chapter titled "Adopting the Name *Nahom*" and "Journey from Nahom to Bountiful."

46. See, for example, the works that bore the accession numbers 52–59, 85, 166–167, and 225–29 in John Pratt's library (in Paul, "Manchester [New York] Library," 345–50; see n. 33 above). Actually, none of these books address ancient Arabia. Their only geographical or economic interest in Arabia lies in the area of the Persian Gulf, many hundred miles from where Lehi and Sariah traveled. My student assistant, Levi R. Smylie, has also examined another work that appeared before 1830 and claims to discuss Arabia. But it shows interest only in the area of the Persian Gulf. See William Heude, *A Voyage up the Persian Gulf and a Journey Overland from India to England in 1817* (London: Longman, Hurst, Rees, Orme, and Brown, 1819). An Italian work that dealt with western Arabia appeared in 1510 but was not translated into English until 1863. See John Winter Jones, trans., *The Travels of Ludovico di Varthema in Egypt, Syria, Arabia Deserta and Arabia Felix, in Persia, India, and Ethiopia* (London: Hakluyt Society, 1863).

Eugene England has examined geographical works that appeared before the publication of the Book of Mormon in "Through the Arabian Desert to a Bountiful Land: Could Joseph Smith Have Known the Way?" in *Book of Mormon Authorship: New Light on Ancient Origins*, ed. Noel B. Reynolds (Provo, Utah: BYU Religious Studies Center, 1982), 145 and note 2. None of those works have any connection to ancient Arabia. Lynn M. and Hope A. Hilton have also examined a number of works and come to the same conclusion (*Discovering Lehi* [Springville, Utah: CFI Publishing, 1996], 183–89).

47. See Diodorus Siculus, *Bibliothēkē*, 3.47.4–9.

48. George Rentz says that the average elevation of the peaks in the mountain chain is less than 2,000 meters (approximately

6,500 feet) and that the highest peak in the south is about 3,760 meters (approximately 12,300 feet). He also writes that "passes across al-Sarāt . . . are few and far between, and are usually difficult of transit" (see his article "Al-ʿArab, Djazīrat," in *Encyclopaedia of Islam*, 1:536). Grohmann and van Donzel note that "there are only a few gaps in the al-Sarāt chain [of mountains]" ("Al-Sarāt," *Encyclopaedia of Islam*, 9:39).

49. Doughty notes that he accompanied some Arabs on a hunting trip but that they were unable to bag any of the eleven wild goats that they ran across, even with rifles (*Travels in Arabia Deserta*, 1:173).

50. The Hiltons suggest that Shazer was an oasis at Wadi al-Azlan near the Red Sea, which lay about one hundred miles south of the al-Badʿ oasis (*In Search of Lehi's Trail*, 77). This site is about midway between the modern coastal towns al-Muwaylih and al-Wajh, which serve Muslim pilgrims traveling from Egypt to Mecca and Medina. From our reconstruction, the Hiltons' identification seems possible but not the only possibility. A person can travel through the mountains from both al-Muwaylih and al-Wajh. In an era later than Lehi and Sariah's time, a spur of the incense trail connected al-Badʿ eastward and southward to the main road near Dedan (modern al-ʿUla). See Groom, *Frankincense and Myrrh,* 192 (map) and 206.

51. The Arabic term *al-Hijaz,* which generally refers to northwest Arabia, means something like "barrier." This sense is due not only to the mountain chain of al-Sarāt, which divides the lowlands of the Red Sea coast from the interior uplands, but also to the huge lava tracts that make it "a black barrier" (see George Rentz, "Al-Hidjāz," *Encyclopaedia of Islam*, 3:362).

52. In a few later scenes in the Book of Mormon, even allowing for language developments in later generations, the term *borders* may point to hilly or mountainous areas (see Alma 8:3 and 21:1). But also see Alma 50:15 and 51:22 for references to "borders" near a seashore and thus probably not meaning mountainous areas. The suggestion that "borders" may refer to mountainous areas

has come to me from Professor Paul Y. Hoskisson in a private conversation and from George D. Potter and Richard Wellington in their *Discovering the Lehi-Nephi Trail* (unpublished manuscript, July 2000), 21–28 (includes map).

53. The only classical source to describe this area in any detail notes the presence of "eaters of fish" and "nomadic encampments." The same source pointedly omits any mention of markets along the west coast of Arabia until one reaches Mouza, almost at the southern end of the Red Sea. See G. W. B. Huntingford, *The Periplus of the Erythraean Sea* (London: Hakluyt Society, 1980), 31–34, §§20–24.

54. The mountains of the west generally receive rain twice a year, in March and April and again from June through September (Grohmann and van Donzel, "Al-Sarāt," *Encyclopaedia of Islam*, 9:39). Those in the southeast see rain usually only during the summer monsoons (see, for example, Brian Doe, *Southern Arabia* [London: Thames and Hudson, 1971], 18–21).

55. Strabo, quoting Eratosthenes of Cyrene, who lived about 275–194 B.C., wrote that "farmers" inhabited the northern parts of Arabia. In the central region were "tent-dwellers and camel-herds," and water was obtained "by digging." In the "extreme parts toward the south" one finds "fertile" lands (*Geography*, 16.4.2). The suggestion that the "fertile parts" described by Nephi lay east of the mountains is that of Potter and Wellington (*Discovering the Lehi-Nephi Trail*, 105–25). Presumably, the expression "fertile parts" meant on one level that there was adequate fodder for the pack animals. What it may have meant for the individuals in the party—perhaps good sources of water—is more difficult to determine.

56. There is a problem here. It has to do with how far the extended family continued southward along the coastline. If they did not continue far, how did Nephi know that the mountains—the "borders"?—continued to run near the Red Sea farther south? For Nephi wrote that, after leaving Shazer, his party followed "the same direction" and traveled "in the borders [moun-

tains?] near the Red Sea" (1 Nephi 16:14). In our reconstruction, family members apparently turned into the mountains rather soon, near Shazer, leaving the Red Sea behind. My hypothesis is that the party met others along their trail, and these people evidently knew something about the geography of the coast of the Red Sea. The party members could not have avoided such contact. Even though the desert seems empty, it is not.

57. See Joseph Fielding Smith, comp., *Teachings of the Prophet Joseph Smith* (Salt Lake City: Deseret News Press, 1938), 267.

58. Nigel Groom estimates that the entire trip by land from the Dhofar region of modern Oman to Gaza on the Mediterranean Sea covered about 2,110 miles (*Frankincense and Myrrh*, 213, chart). Proposing a slightly different route, the Hiltons estimate the distance to be 2,156 miles (*Discovering Lehi*, 30).

59. Leucē Comē became a major port for the Nabateans in the second century B.C. A survey led by Michael Ingraham turned up significant numbers of Nabatean artifacts at ͨAynūnah. See Michael Lloyd Ingraham et al., "Saudi Arabian Comprehensive Survey Program: C. Preliminary Report on a Reconnaissance Survey of the Northwestern Province (with a Note on a Brief Survey of the Northern Province)," *Atlal: The Journal of Saudi Arabian Archaeology* 5 (1401 A.H.– A.D. 1981): 59–84, especially 76–78.

60. Strabo, *Geography*, 16.4.23–24; summarized briefly in Pliny, *Natural History* 6.32 (§160). Some scholars accept the identity of Marib with Strabo's Marsiaba (see Groom's review in *Frankincense and Myrrh*, 75–76). But Strabo writes that the Roman army broke off its siege at Marsiaba because of lack of water. This withdrawal from a city like Marib would seem odd because the Marib dam, which stored water in its reservoir, was only a few kilometers away. But the water was not fresh. On the question of time of travel over this distance, according to Groom the entire trip from Dhofar in southern Oman to Gaza took no more than four months (*Frankincense and Myrrh*, 213, chart). Walter M. Müller estimates that caravans starting from southwest Arabia (a different starting place) required at

least two months to reach the Mediterranean area (see Werner Daum, ed., *Yemen: 3000 Years of Art and Civilisation in Arabia Felix* [Innsbruck: Pinguin-Verlag, 1987], 49–50).

61. ʿAynūnah lies only thirty or so miles south of the al-Badʿ oasis and forty or so miles from Wadi Tayyib al-Ism. Like Lehi's party, the Romans would have crossed the mountains and traveled south-southeast along the incense trail because there were wells and fodder.

62. See note 6 above for hints that party members met other people.

63. Ahmed Fakhry offers a description based on his trip through the area in 1947 (*An Archaeological Journey to Yemen*, 1:139–40).

64. S. Kent Brown, "'The Place Which Was Called Nahom,'" *Journal of Book of Mormon Studies* 8/1 (1999): 66–68; and Warren P. Aston, "Newly Found Altars from Nahom," 56–61.

65. Following up a note by Ross T. Christensen ("The Place Called Nahom," 73), Warren and Michaela Aston made the first case that Nahom lay in the area of Wadi Jawf, to the south where the modern Nihm tribe dwells (*In the Footsteps of Lehi*, 3–25). Much of their work rests on ancient accounts by later Arab authors from the ninth and tenth centuries A.D. Paul Dresch holds that one can know the location of tribes only back to the beginning of the Islamic era, the seventh century A.D. (*Tribes, Government, and History in Yemen* [Oxford: Clarendon Press, 1989], 1). The altar inscriptions, however, show that the Nihm tribe has lived in that region for more than 2,600 years.

66. Perhaps significantly, Charles Doughty observed that tribal names in Arabia regularly go back to a mountain of the same name (*Travels in Arabia Deserta*, 1:464).

67. The Nihm tribe is one of several tribes in the so-called Bakīl confederation, which has inhabited the area in and around Wadi Jawf for centuries. See Andrey Korotayev, *Ancient Yemen: Some General Trends of Evolution of the Sabaic Language and Sabaean Culture*, Journal of Semitic Studies Supplement 5

(Oxford: Oxford University Press, 1995), 81–83; and Dresch, *Tribes, Government, and History in Yemen*, 24, table 1.2. Fakhry reports that he met some of "the bedouins of Nahm, who live in tents," while in the area of the Wadi Jawf (Fakhry, *Archaeological Journey to Yemen*, 1:13).

68. Consult Christian Robin's work on the tribal name *NHM* (and others), which has remained basically in the same place since it first appeared in inscriptions in the first millennium B.C. (*Les Hautes-Terres du Nord-Yemen avant l'Islam I: Recherches sur la geographie tribale et religieuse de Hawlān Quḍāʿa et du pays de Hamdān* [Istanbul: Nederlands historisch-archaeologisch Instituut, 1982], 27, 72–74).

69. In Arabic and in Old South Arabian, the letter *h* in *Nihm* represents a soft aspiration, whereas the *h* in the Hebrew word *Nahom* is the letter ḥet and carries a stronger, rasping sound.

70. *Nahōm/Nahūm* is translated as "mourners" in Isaiah 57:18 and as "repentings" in Hosea 11:8.

71. Nibley points out that the "Hebrew *Nahum*" means "comfort" (*Lehi in the Desert*, 79). See Ernst Jenni and Claus Westermann, eds., *Theological Lexicon of the Old Testament* (Peabody, Mass.: Hendrickson, 1997), 2:734–39.

72. For *NHM* in ancient Arabian dialects, see G. Lankester Harding, *An Index and Concordance of Pre-Islamic Arabian Names and Inscriptions* (Toronto: University of Toronto Press, 1971), 81, 602; and Joan Copeland Biella, *Dictionary of Old South Arabic: Sabaean Dialect*, Harvard Semitic Studies No. 25 (Chico, Calif.: Scholars Press, 1982), 296.

73. For reviews of what Joseph Smith could not have known about ancient Arabia, see England, "Through the Arabian Desert to a Bountiful Land," 143–56 (see n. 46 above); and Hilton and Hilton, *Discovering Lehi*, 183–89. Consult also the discussion in the section of this study titled "Ancient and Modern Writings on Arabia."

74. Certain Latter-day Saint investigators have mistakenly written that a branch of the incense trail ran along the west coast

of Arabia. For instance, George Reynolds and Janne M. Sjodahl hold that Lehi's party went along the shoreline of the Red Sea (*Commentary on the Book of Mormon* [Salt Lake City: Deseret News Press, 1955], 1:166). Nibley agrees (*Lehi in the Desert*, 45, 109–10; *An Approach to the Book of Mormon*, 3rd ed. [Salt Lake City: Deseret Book and FARMS, 1988], 63). The Hiltons also agree (*In Search of Lehi's Trail*, 29, 32–33, 39, 63, 77), as does Reed Durham (*The Gifts of the Magi: Gold, Frankincense and Myrrh* [published by author; rev. ed. 1993], 92–93). But research has not borne out this view, as the careful study by Groom shows (*Frankincense and Myrrh*, 189–213). To be sure, beginning in the second century B.C. the Nabataeans may have maintained a route along the west coast. But there is no evidence of a route before this era. Besides, the Nabataean road ran northward only from Leucē Comē (probably the modern town ʿAynūnah) and carried goods that came by ship through the Red Sea rather than by camel train from south Arabia. On this later route, see Groom, *Frankincense and Myrrh*, 207–8. A recent study plots an inland route only on the east side of the al-Sarāt mountain chain, not on the coastal side (Abdullah Saud al-Saud, "The Domestication of Camels and Inland Trading Routes in Arabia," *Atlal: The Journal of Saudi Arabian Archaeology* 14 [1416 A.H.– A.D. 1996]: 131–32). There is more. Although the author of the *Periplus* indicates that from the coastal town of Leucē Comē there was a route northward "to Petra, to Malikhas king of the Nabataioi," he does not indicate whether the route ran inland eastward from Leucē Comē, then north, or ran northward along the coast (Huntingford, *Periplus of the Erythraean Sea*, 31, §19). But if, as Lionel Casson argues from substantial evidence, Leucē Comē lay at ʿAynūnah, considerably north of al-Wajh and only a few miles south and east of al-Badʿ, there would have been no trail along the coast except as northbound travelers approached the area of modern Aqaba (Lionel Casson, *The Periplus Maris Erythraei* [Princeton, N.J.: Princeton University Press, 1989], 143–44). On this matter see also John

Healey, "The Nabataeans and Madā'in Sālih," *Atlal: The Journal of Saudi Arabian Archaeology* 10 (1406 A.H.– A.D. 1986): 110.

75. Richard Bowen points out that "the Greek mariner Eudoxus had undoubtedly reached India from the Red Sea c. 120 B.C.," thus initiating steps that would eventually cut Arabians out of the business of importing goods from India and farther east and then shipping them overland to the north through Arabia (in Richard LeBaron Bowen and Frank P. Albright, eds., *Archaeological Discoveries in South Arabia* [Baltimore: Johns Hopkins Press, 1958], 35). See also Groom, *Frankincense and Myrrh*, 61–62, 152–53.

76. Groom writes probably the most comprehensive description of the route of the trail (*Frankincense and Myrrh*, 165–213). For what could be known to Joseph Smith, consult England, "Through the Arabian Desert to a Bountiful Land," 143–56; Paul, "Joseph Smith and the Manchester (New York) Library," 333–56; and Hilton and Hilton, *Discovering Lehi*, 183–89.

77. There is no evidence that any books available in the Manchester, New York, library—the nearest to Joseph Smith's home—would have included any such information. See Paul, "Manchester (New York) Library," 333–56. Even though Carsten Niebuhr recorded that he and one of his companions came down with fever (malaria) in April 1763, Joseph Smith had no access to his writings, as we have already noted. See the summary in Thorkild Hansen, *Arabia Felix: The Danish Expedition of 1761–1767,* 240; and Niebuhr, *Reisebeschreibung nach Arabien und andern umliegenden Ländern*, 1:353, where Neibuhr writes that he and a colleague had come down with "ein starkes Fieber"—a high fever—on 6 April 1763.

78. Doughty, *Travels in Arabia Deserta*, 1:172, 182; also 259.

79. See Groom, *Frankincense and Myrrh*, 9–10, 55–95.

80. Along the coast, between Kanë [= Qana] and Dhofar, "the place is fearfully unhealthy, and pestilential even to those who sail past it; to those who work there it is always fatal; and in

addition they are killed off by sheer lack of food" (Huntingford, *Periplus of the Erythraean Sea*, 36, §29).

81. See Fakhry, *Archaeological Journey to Yemen*, 14; and Doughty, *Travels in Arabia Deserta*, 1:180, 259; 2:239; see also 1:298, 331, 568. Thomas generously characterized the water at Bin Hamuda as "brackish" (*Arabia Felix*, 175). Wilfred Thesiger noted that even camels would not drink from the Khaur bin Atarit well and that Bedouins had developed sores from washing in well water (*Arabian Sands* [New York: E. P. Dutton and Co., 1959], 111, 114). To be sure, the author of the *Periplus* wrote of debilitating disease in south Arabia (see Huntingford, *Periplus of the Erythraean Sea*, 36, §29), but this source was not available to Joseph Smith. Modern commentator Lionel Casson mistakenly considers such a report to be "propaganda" (*Periplus Maris Erythraei*, 166).

82. The survey undertaken by M. Ingraham and others found evidence of now-dry springs in northwest Arabia. But, except for a relatively rainy period about 500 B.C., the evidence supports the view that the last "wet" period of any significance ended 4,500 years ago, almost 2,000 years before Lehi's time. See M. L. Ingraham et al., "Saudi Arabian Comprehensive Survey Program: C," *Atlal: The Journal of Saudi Arabian Archaeology* 5:62, 72–73. See also P. R. Baduel, ed., *L'Arabie antique de Karib'îl à Mahomet*, 39; Jon Mandaville, "From the Lakes of Arabia," *Aramco World* 31/2 (1980): 8–13; and Karl W. Butzer, "Environmental Change in the Near East and Human Impact on the Land," *Civilizations of the Ancient Near East*, 1:123–51.

83. See Carsten Niebuhr, *Beschreibung von Arabien*. See also his *Reisebeschreibung nach Arabien und den umliegenden Ländern*, volume 1, which carries his description of his visit to Arabia. Niebuhr's work is summarized in handy fashion by Hansen in *Arabia Felix: The Danish Expedition of 1761–1767*, 202–301.

84. Consult the summaries of Nigel Groom ("Trade, Incense and Perfume") and J.-F. Breton ("Architecture") in Simpson, ed., *Queen of Sheba*, 88–94 and 142–48, respectively. The female

figures featured on pp. 148–49 are especially evocative of wealth in south Arabian societies.

85. See the bibliography of modern studies on inscriptions from Arabia, including publication series devoted to this emerging field, in Baduel, ed., *L'Arabie antique de Karib'îl à Mahomet*, 162–66.

86. "The early South Arabian language has been well recorded by metal plaques and carved stone inscriptions used as official and religious documents" (Doe, *Southern Arabia*, 21). Most inscriptions, of course, are preserved on stone. For a notice of recently discovered bronze inscriptions, see François Bron, "Quatre Inscriptions sabéennes provenant d'un temple de Dhū-Samawī," *Syria* 74 (1997): 73–80 (brought to my attention by Prof. David J. Johnson). Wendell Phillips also notes an inscribed bronze weight that his excavation team found at Sumhuram (Khor Rori) on the south coast of Oman (*Unknown Oman*, 198). For an exquisite example of an inscribed hand in bronze, dating from the early Christian era, see Baduel, ed., *L'Arabie antique de Karib'îl à Mahomet*, 143–44; and Simpson, ed., *Queen of Sheba*, 173. Frank P. Albright notes several bronze inscriptions of various dates found in southern Oman at Sumhuram, also known as Khor Rori, in *The American Archaeological Expedition in Dhofar, Oman, 1952–1953*, Publications of the American Foundation for the Study of Man Volume VI (Washington, D.C.: AFSM, 1982), 87–89, fig. 61, 71–74, 77 and 78 (also brought to my attention by Prof. Johnson).

Metal artifacts do not survive in large numbers because they were often melted down and used again for other purposes, as is the case with ancient, inscribed metallic weights. For such weights, see Marvin A. Powell Jr., "Ancient Mesopotamian Weight Metrology: Methods, Problems and Perspectives," in *Studies in Honor of Tom B. Jones*, ed. Marvin A. Powell Jr. and Ronald H. Sack (Neukirchen-Vluyn: Verlag Butzon & Bercker Kevelaer, 1979), 72.

87. See Brown, *From Jerusalem to Zarahemla*, 30–32.

88. For a review and photograph of the Anthon Transcript, see Danel W. Bachman, "Anthon Transcript," *Encyclopedia of Mormonism*, 1:43–44.

89. See the brief summary article "Similarities between the Anthon Transcript and Old South Arabian (Arabic)," *Journal of Book of Mormon Studies* 8/2 (1999): 83.

90. None of the ancient classical authors who have written about Arabia or about the incense trade there say anything about the directions that the incense trail followed in the region of the Ramlat Sabʿatayn desert. Pliny, who mentions "Sabota, a walled town containing sixty temples," which may be identified with Shabwah, does not indicate Sabota's locale vis-à-vis Marib, which he spells Mariba. Nor does Pliny say that there was a major road that connected his Sabota with important towns in the west (*Natural History*, 6.32 [§§155, 159]). Strabo does not mention the trail per se (*Geography*, 16.4.22–24), although he reports that Sabata (Shabwah) lies "farthest toward the east" among the four important interior cities of south Arabia (*Geography*, 16.4.2), implying a connecting road. But his work was not available in English translation during Joseph Smith's lifetime. No Western authors who wrote before Joseph Smith's time mention the eastward turn of the trail from the area of Wadi Jawf to Shabwah. Only the map of Arabia Felix that accompanies the Codex Ebnerianus of Ptolemy's *Geography*, which was copied about A.D. 1460 and is now owned by the New York Public Library, shows a trail that turns east in south Arabia. This trail probably comes from the influence of Arab cartographers on the maker of the map because Ptolemy does not describe the trail in the written part of his work where he lists towns and their locations. This codex, which is not one of the more important copies of Ptolemy's work because it does not make Lister's list, came into possession of the New York Public Library only in 1892 from a London book dealer named Bernard Quaritch and was not published until 1932. See Edward Luther Stevenson, ed. and trans., *Claudius Ptolemy, the Geography* (New York: Dover Publications, 1932), 137–40 and

the map of Arabia Felix; John Brian Harley and David Woodward, eds., *The History of Cartography: Cartography in the Traditional Islamic and South Asian Societies* (Chicago: University of Chicago Press, 1992), 3–4, 10, 94–95, 97–100, 168–69; and Raymond Lister, *Antique Maps and Their Cartographers*, 21–24. The acquisition information came from Dr. John M. Lundquist, head of the Oriental Division of the New York Public Library (28 March 2001).

91. For maps that show the eastward spurs of the trail that led to Shabwah, see Baduel, ed., *L'Arabie antique de Karib'îl à Mahomet*, map 1; and Groom, *Frankincense and Myrrh*, 167, 192.

92. Consult the discussion in Groom, *Frankincense and Myrrh*, 169–70, 181, 183–84.

93. See S. Kent Brown, "A Case for Lehi's Bondage in Arabia," *Journal of Book of Mormon Studies* 6/2 (1997): 205–17; Brown, *From Jerusalem to Zarahemla*, 55–59; and Warren P. Aston and Michaela J. Aston, "And We Called the Place Bountiful" (Provo, Utah: FARMS Preliminary Report, 1991), 3.

94. Earlier studies of south Arabia postulated that a leg of the incense trail ran east from the area of Shabwah. And most LDS authors have followed this view, assuming a reasonably well-traveled caravan route along the southern edge of the "empty quarter." (Nibley intimates such in *Lehi in the Desert*, 109–10; the Hiltons agree in *In Search of Lehi's Trail*, 101–2; the Astons speak of "the major [trade] route . . . to the east" in *In the Footsteps of Lehi*, 22). But the observations of Groom and Zarins are almost decisive against this view. For Groom, it was a matter of the huge distances between sources of water for humans and for large numbers of animals (see *Frankincense and Myrrh*, 165–68; and Phillips, *Unknown Oman*, 220). Phillips does, however, note the discovery of two inscriptions that both mention Shabwah, the incense-collecting city more than five hundred miles to the east of Dhofar. One is from Sumhuram on the seacoast, and the other is from Hanun on the northern slope of the Qara mountains (*Unknown Oman*, 195–97, 231). Hence, in antiquity

there was both a sea tie and apparently a land tie between Dhofar and Shabwah. The inscriptions thus open the possibility that caravans traveled overland from Dhofar to Shabwah, the reverse of the trip of Lehi and Sariah. But Phillips dates the ruins visible at Hanun only to the first century B.C., not to the earlier era when Lehi and Sariah were in Arabia, and he ties the inscription to the activity of collecting frankincense rather than to caravan travel (*Unknown Oman*, 200). Juris Zarins has written that in the northern Dhofar region, the Nejd area between the north slope of the mountains and the natural well at Shisur, there seems to be little evidence of settlement activity in the Iron Age A period (1000–300 B.C.), which points to the unlikelihood of caravans crossing westward from there to Shabwah. Most evidence for the Iron Age A era is to be found along the coast. See Juris Zarins, *Dhofar—Land of Incense: Archaeological Work in the Sultanate of Oman 1990–1995* (Muscat, Sultanate of Oman, unpublished manuscript), 48–49. Strabo adds that there were no major towns east of Sabata (Shabwah), an indicator of a lack of traffic in that part of Arabia (*Geography*, 16.4.2).

95. The dunes of the "Empty Quarter" rise to heights of seven hundred feet, which are almost impossible to cross. Even the lower dunes take several hours to negotiate on camelback. See Wilfred Thesiger, *Arabian Sands*, 129, 216–217, and plate 26; also Groom, *Frankincense and Myrrh*, 174. Of the fractured tableland terrain between the dunes and the ocean, J. G. T. Shipman said that it "is a maze of narrow gorges, some 1000 feet or more deep, winding and twisting around butresses of rock" ("The Hadhramaut," *Asian Affairs* 71/2 [1984]: 157).

96. According to Phillips, a traveler had to obtain the services of an escort known to and authorized by the tribe through whose territory the traveler was moving. If the controlling tribe discovered a person without escort, all property of the intruder was forfeit, and perhaps the person's life. In the case of a raid, however, a slave captured by the raiders was allowed to live because he or she had monetary value and, most important,

was not involved in any blood feud (*Unknown Oman*, 230–31, 292 n. 32). Bertram Thomas reports the same (*Arabia Felix*, 171–74; compare 9–10, 15, 36, 165, and 175 on constant tribal skirmishes).

Concerning slave trade in ancient Arabia, see Huntingford, *Periplus of the Erythraean Sea*, 31–32, §20, and 38, §31. See also Thomas, *Arabia Felix*, 32–33, 47. Most significantly, ancient inscriptions point to a similar situation (see Christian Robin in Baduel, ed., *L'Arabie antique de Karib'îl à Mahomet*, 55, 57; and Daum, ed., *Yemen: 3000 Years of Art and Civilisation in Arabia Felix*, 76). People in certain parts of Yemen are still today referred to in local parlance as "being ʿabīd (slaves, or at least sons of slaves)" (Dresch, *Tribes, Government, and History in Yemen*, 15).

97. Phillips speaks of "brief pastures" that come and go with the periods of rain (*Unknown Oman*, 211). Zarins points to evidence of Iron Age agriculture in the Dhofar region near the coast but not very far inland where the mountains recede into the desert (Zarins, *Dhofar—Land of Incense*, 44–48).

98. See Brown, *From Jerusalem to Zarahemla*, 55–59.

99. Doughty wrote of the "hostile and necessitous life of the Beduw" who "devour one another" and go for days without water and food. He wrote of others who were known as "desert fiends" and who endure "intolerable hardships" and attack others, leaving none alive (see his *Travels in Arabia Deserta*, 1:164; 322; see also 166, 174, 179, 308, and 387–93 for accounts of raiding, robbing, killing, and destroying property). Thomas paints a similar picture of life in south Arabia (*Arabia Felix*, xxiv, 9, 13, 36, 149–50, 165, 173–74). Nibley suggested that the Lord commanded members of Lehi's party not to "make much fire" (1 Nephi 17:12) in order to conceal them from marauders (*Lehi in the Desert*, 63–67).

100. As an indicator of the number of independent tribes and clans in southern Yemen, the peace brokered by the British representative Harold Ingrams in 1937 included the signatures of "1400 tribal leaders" (J. G. T. Shipman, "The Hadhramaut," *Asian*

Affairs 71/2 [1984]: 159). The unknown author of the *Periplus* writes that the southern coastal region of Arabia was evidently a penal area, the place of "men who have been sent there as punishment" (Huntingford, *Periplus of the Erythraean Sea*, 36, §29).

101. Phillips summarized: "This southern desert bordering *ar-rubᶜ al-khali* [the Empty Quarter] has remained a forbidding wilderness, intolerably hot and waterless, peopled only by a few illiterate and more or less barbarous nomads . . . who have lowered their needs to the irreducible minimum. . . . Lawrence wrote in the *Seven Pillars*, 'Bedouin ways are hard even for those brought up in them and for strangers terrible; a death in life'" (*Unknown Oman*, 216–17; compare 211).

102. That domesticated honey—different from wild honey—was available along the south coast of Arabia is recorded by Strabo, quoting Eratosthenes (ca. 275–194 B.C.) (cited in Groom, *Frankincense and Myrrh*, 64). But it is impossible that Joseph Smith could have known this.

103. Hugh Nibley was the first to point to Dhofar, "a paradise in the Qara Mountains on the southern coast of Arabia" (*Lehi in the Desert*, 109–12; the quotation is from p. 109). The Hiltons sought to narrow the locale of Bountiful to the area of the city of Salalah (*In Search of Lehi's Trail*, 40–41, 105–16), while the Astons argue for Wadi Sayq, almost fifty miles west of Salalah (*In the Footsteps of Lehi*, 43ff.). Paul Hedengren points to southeastern Oman, without being more specific (*The Land of Lehi* [Provo, Utah: Bradford and Wilson, 1995], 10–15). Potter and Wellington argue for Khor Rori (*Discovering the Lehi-Nephi Trail*, 209–12, 225–54).

As a caution, any attempt to identify a specific place in the Dhofar region as Bountiful faces impossible difficulties. First, no one can prove that a foreign family moved into a certain spot in Dhofar in the early sixth century B.C. because (1) there is no inscriptional evidence of the presence of such a party, and (2) archaeology cannot prove that a certain person or persons ever inhabited an area without such written proof. Under the right circumstances, an archaeologist could show, say, that the architecture of an area changed significantly in a certain era or that there is evidence of a sudden change in customs, such as food production or burial practices, which may indicate the arrival of a new people. But even if there were indicators that people had moved into a certain locale in Dhofar in the right time frame, these indicators would not prove that the newcomers were Israelites from Jerusalem. That sort of dimension is impossible to demonstrate without written materials that were left behind. If one wants a demonstration that this sort of attempt is fraught with serious difficulties, all one has to do is read about archaeology in the Holy Land. Every archaeological "fact" that decades ago seemed to point to the arrival of the Hebrews under Joshua in the thirteenth century B.C. has been disputed, including the reason for the site-wide burn layer at the Canaanite city of Hazor (north of the Sea of Galilee) that the Bible says was burned by Joshua and the Israelites (see Joshua 11).

104. Bertram Thomas similarly relates his deep relief and joy at seeing the greenery and the sea at Dhofar after a trip through the desert of only a few weeks (*Arabia Felix*, 48–49).

105. Phillips, *Unknown Oman*, 169.

106. Janzen, *Nomads in the Sultanate of Oman*, 38.

107. Quoted by Strabo and cited in Groom, *Frankincense and Myrrh*, 64.

108. F. W. Edwards and D. Aubertin listed the sites where their expedition found bees and wasps, including in the Dhofar area (see Thomas, *Arabia Felix*, 361–62). More recently on domesticated bees, see Eric Hansen, "The Beekeepers of Wadi Duʿan," *Aramco World* 46/1 (1995): 2–7.

109. Oral report at Brigham Young University by Professors Terry B. Ball, Loreen Wolstenhulme, and Gary Baird (Friday, 3 December 1999).

110. George F. Hourani, in *Arab Seafaring* (Princeton: Princeton University Press, 1951), also notes that Sumerian and Akkadian inscriptions of the third millennium B.C. mention "the

shipwrights of Magan," which lay on the Persian Gulf (5–6). The exact location of Magan/Makkan has been a subject of some discussion over the years. See, for example, Thierry Berthoud and Serge Cleuziou, "Farming Communities of the Oman Peninsula and the Copper of Makkan"; and Gerd Weisgerber, "Copper Production during the Third Millennium BC in Oman and the Question of Makkan," both published in *The Journal of Oman Studies* 6/2 (1983): 239–46 and 269–76, respectively.

111. Janzen, *Nomads in the Sultanate of Oman*, 35.

112. Thomas, *Arabia Felix*, 48–49.

113. See Janzen, *Nomads in the Sultanate of Oman*, 25, 29.

114. See Anthony G. Miller and Miranda Morris, *Plants of Dhofar: The Southern Region of Oman—Traditional, Economic, and Medicinal Uses* (Muscat, Oman: The Office of the Adviser for Conservation of the Environment, 1988). Bertram Thomas mentions wild animals such as ibex, panthers, wolves, hyenas, and fish in streams (*Arabia Felix*, 20, 40, 54–55, 146–48). Thesiger notes foxes, oryx, gazelles, hares, and a lot of snakes on the north slope of the Dhofar mountains (*Arabian Sands*, 92, 104, 108, etc.). Carsten Niebuhr offers a list of domesticated and wild animals living in Arabia in the eighteenth century, all in the southwestern sector (*Beschreibung von Arabien*, 161–80).

115. Nibley suggested this phenomenon (*Lehi in the Desert*, 43–44).

116. See Janzen, *Nomads in the Sultanate of Oman*, 19, 23–24, 30.

117. See James D. Muhly, "Metals," in *The Oxford Encyclopedia of Archaeology in the Near East*, ed. Eric M. Meyers et al. (New York: Oxford University Press, 1997), 4:3, 10; and "Mining and Metalwork in Ancient Western Asia," in *Civilizations of the Ancient Near East*, ed. Jack M. Sasson et al. (New York: Charles Scribner's Sons, 1995), 3:1505–6. See also Daniel T. Potts, "Distant Shores: Ancient Near Eastern Trade with South Asia and Northeast Africa," in *Civilizations of the Ancient Near East*, 3:1454–56; and Geoffrey Bibby, *Looking for Dilmun* (New York: Alfred A. Knopf, 1969), 191–92, 219–20.

118. Hourani, *Arab Seafaring*, 5.

119. Consult W. Revell Phillips, "Metals of the Book of Mormon," *Journal of Book of Mormon Studies* 9/1 (2000): 36–43. Eugene E. Clark earlier identified small deposits of iron ore in the area of Dhofar, specifically on the Mirbat plain east of Salalah. See "A Preliminary Study of the Geology and Mineral Resources of Dhofar, the Sultanate of Oman" (Provo, Utah: FARMS Preliminary Report, 1995). So did Revell Phillips in 1998; see "Planning Research in Oman," *Journal of Book of Mormon Studies* 7/1 (1998): 12–21.

120. My thanks go to Patricia J. Ward for typing and editorial assistance and to student assistants Levi R. Smylie, Heather Pabst Ward, and Robert D. Hunt for aid in gathering and checking sources for this study.

By Objective Measures: Old Wine into Old Bottles

Noel B. Reynolds

Over the last two decades, scholars have found new ways of bringing analytical tools and models from multiple disciplines to bear on studies of the Book of Mormon. This range of studies makes it possible to assess the validity of intuitively plausible arguments that were leveled against Joseph Smith's account of the divine origin of the Book of Mormon. Whereas the critics explain the Book of Mormon in terms of nineteenth-century origins, I assemble below eleven examples in which the application of careful and scientifically current scholarly research reverses those intuitions and argues strongly for ancient origins. These examples have come from such diverse fields of study and lines of investigation as the history of shipbuilding in ancient Arabia, demographic reconstructions of ancient populations, literary authorship, new discoveries in ancient Near Eastern literature, biblical literary devices, the history of warfare in the ancient world, and American political thought.

Shipbuilding in Ancient Arabia

SHIPBUILDING

In Joseph Smith's day the Arabian Peninsula was not well known to Americans and was generally understood to be a desert wasteland, devoid of timber that could have been used for shipbuilding.[1] There now exists convincing evidence that an obscure location at the extreme western end of Oman's Dhofar coast, Khor Kharfot, is the probable location of Nephi's Bountiful, where he and his family constructed the ship that carried them to the Americas.[2] Nephi recorded that the Lord instructed him in the manner of shipbuilding: "Now I, Nephi, did not work the timbers after the manner which was learned by men, neither did I build the ship after the manner of men; but I did build it after the manner which the Lord had shown unto me" (1 Nephi 18:2). He clearly was sufficiently familiar with the construction of vessels "after the manner of men" to know that the construction the Lord had shown him was not the same. Interestingly, ancient Oman, the likely location of Bountiful, has in the twentieth century been finally recognized for its ancient shipbuilding, a fact that allowed the ancient Omani to earn recognition as the Phoenicians of the Indian Ocean.

Oman, with its borders on the Arabian Gulf and the Indian Ocean, is relatively geographically isolated, and its history, according to archaeologist Michael Rice, is "most notably a record of Oman's marriage with the sea." He continues: "Her people have always been energetic and courageous seamen, probably from the earliest times. Oman's ships are distinctive and her sailors were foremost among the seamen of Islam."³ As early as 3000 B.C., evidence exists of Omani contact with other cultures in the Gulf region, and early records speak of the ships of Magan, an ancient place-name usually associated with Oman. Ancient Oman played an important role in early trade routes and, along with the city of Dilmun (probably situated on Bahrain Island to the north of Oman), served as an international center for trade by sea. Long before 600 B.C., their trade linked India, Persia, Mesopotamia, Africa, Egypt, and eventually China. In ancient times it was the natural location to build and launch a ship for a journey eastward into the Indian Ocean.

The Omani used a distinctive ship, the "sewn boat," which, though of very ancient origin, is still used by modern Omani. These sewn boats, also called "booms," are completely stitched together, without using nails; approximately 56,000 meters of coconut hair rope are required to sew together one complete ship. Using these vessels, the Omani have maintained trade between Mesopotamia, Africa, India, and even China over most of a five-thousand-year period. It is highly improbable that Joseph Smith or his contemporaries knew that southern Arabia was home to world-class mariners and shipbuilders for millennia. We do not know whether Nephi built his ship in the Omani style (which would have been different from "the manner of men" he would have known from the Mediterranean) or whether the construction style the Lord showed him was different from both of these. But the reputation of ancient Oman as a center of shipbuilding demonstrates clearly that the necessary materials for the successful constructions were available in that land in Lehi's day.

Nephi's Temple

NEPHI'S TEMPLE

Nephi records that after their separation from the Lamanites, his people built a temple "after the manner of the temple of Solomon save it were not built of so many precious things" (2 Nephi 5:16). Smaller temples patterned after the temple of Solomon existed in ancient Israel at the time of Lehi in areas distant from Jerusalem. Israeli archaeologist Avraham Negev commented on one of these temples: "The most remarkable discovery at Arad is the temple which occupied the north-western corner of the citadel. . . . Its orientation, general plan and contents, especially the tabernacle, are *similar to the Temple of Solomon*."[4] In other words, Nephi's construction of a simpler version of Solomon's temple in a remote location once he had established his people in a permanent city was not a unique event in Jewish history, but rather an expected occurrence, a fact of which Joseph Smith and his contemporaries (including especially his critic Alexander Campbell), lacking the aid of modern archaeology, would certainly have been unaware.

Nephite Population Numbers

CREDIBLE DEMOGRAPHICS

Thoughtful students of the Book of Mormon have sometimes questioned the seemingly large number of Nephites who descended from Lehi's original group. Critics have suggested on this basis that the Book of Mormon is demographically implausible.[5] But it has now been shown that the size and fluctuations in Nephite numbers resemble the patterns of known historical populations. James E. Smith, one of the chief architects of the widely used Cambridge model for estimating historical populations, refutes the critics' claim by comparing the Book of

Mormon account with other ancient civilizations and by utilizing the Cambridge demographic model to demonstrate possible numbers of Nephites.[6] He notes in passing that "if there is any hallmark of ancient historical records, it is their strong tendency to present [what might intuitively seem to be] puzzling, unrealistic, and inconsistent population figures."[7] Also, historical populations have generally experienced significant fluctuation and change similar to that depicted in the Book of Mormon.

Applying the Cambridge model with conservative assumptions about the growth of Nephite population, Smith calculated that the numbers in the text are on the high end of what would be predicted scientifically, but they remain plausible. For example, we know that "most of today's six million French Canadians descend from about five thousand immigrant pioneers of the seventeenth century," reflecting a much higher actual fertility rate than Smith assumes for his reconstruction of Nephite demographics. Relaxing any of Smith's perhaps unduly conservative assumptions would move the numbers closer to the middle of the expected range. Additionally, if the Nephites or Lamanites absorbed any unmentioned populations, the numbers cease to be at all problematic.[8] Because the demographic data in the Book of Mormon is incomplete, a precise picture of population sizes is impossible; however, as Smith concludes, "some plausible demographic inferences can be made, and the picture of Nephite population history that emerges is a realistic one."[9]

Joseph Smith went out on a limb when he included specific dates and population data in his translation of the Book of Mormon. Only in light of sophisticated analysis using tools far beyond the primitive Malthusian population projections of the early nineteenth century can modern readers appreciate how true to actual human experience such details in the Book of Mormon are.

Wordprinting

Wordprinting Evidence of Multiple Authors

In recent years scientists have utilized statistical models and new computer technology to demonstrate the existence of multiple writing patterns, or wordprints, in the Book of Mormon and to show that the Book of Mormon does not match Joseph Smith's writing pattern. This concept, termed wordprinting or stylometry, is based on the empirical discovery that authors unconsciously produce distinct writing patterns that are somewhat analogous to individual fingerprints. These writing patterns can be detected by analysis of authors' noncontextual word patterns. Because these patterns are not dependent on the context or genre of the writing, they remain remarkably consistent throughout an individual's adult lifetime. Many studies have shown that even the most skillful writers cannot change these patterns at will. Wordprinting models are thus based on analysis of the noncontextual words of an author that are statistically different from those of other authors. Wordprinting was first introduced in the middle of the twentieth century to determine the authorship of the disputed portions of texts such as *The Federalist* and the Pauline Epistles.[10] Wordprint analysis has come to occupy a unique niche in Book of Mormon studies because of its reliance on quantitative analysis of the text.

The concept of wordprinting in Book of Mormon analysis was first introduced in a 1980 study by Wayne A. Larsen and Alvin C. Rencher.[11] In their study Larsen and Rencher first carefully identified sections of the Book of

Wordprints and the Book of Mormon

By Objective Measures: Old Wine into Old Bottles • 133

	TESTS	\multicolumn{16}{c}{NUMBER OF REJECTIONS}
		0	1	2	3	4	5	6	7	8	9	10	11	12	13	14	15
Nephi vs. Nephi	3					x	x										
Alma vs. Alma	3			x	x												
Smith vs. Smith	3	x		xx													
Cowdery vs. Cowdery	1		x														
Spaulding vs. Spaulding	1			x													
Nephi vs. Alma	9			x			xx		x	x	x	x	x	x			
Smith vs. Nephi	6				x		xx		xx	x	x						
Smith vs. Alma	6				xx	x	x	xx	xx								
Cowdery vs. Nephi	6							x	x				xx				
Cowdery vs. Alma	6								xxxx	x	x	x	x		x	x	
Spaulding vs. Nephi	5											x	x	x		x	x
Spaulding vs. Alma	6							xxx		xx				x		x	x

Clearly different author →

The higher the number of "rejections," or differences in measurable stylometric elements, the less likely it is that two blocks of text were written by the same author. This chart shows results comparing blocks by the same authors and then by different authors.

Mormon that the text indicates are the products of different authors. They based their analysis on the twenty-four writers who contributed the most to the text, all with at least nearly one thousand words to their credit. They then utilized three separate statistical models to compare the writings of each author with those of the others and of Joseph Smith, Sidney Rigdon, Solomon Spaulding, Oliver Cowdery, and other nineteenth-century Mormon authors. All three models measured the frequency of letters and of both common (e.g., *the, and, of*) and less common (e.g., *out, after, among*) noncontextual words. They concluded that all three statistical models "strongly support multiple authorship of the Book of Mormon" and that the wordprint patterns in the text significantly differ from the writing patterns of Joseph Smith and the other nineteenth-century authors tested.[12]

During the 1980s John L. Hilton and several associates, some of whom were not Latter-day Saints, formed a group of scientists in Berkeley, California, to develop a more rigorous wordprinting model with which to test the Book of Mormon.[13] Rather than test the frequency of letters or noncontextual words, Hilton's model measures noncontextual word-pattern ratios (such as the percentage of sentences beginning with *a* and *and*) using a list of sixty-five ratios first suggested by Scottish forensics specialist A. Q. Morton. Hilton's model also has the distinct advantage of being based on a large body of control author studies, which helped to establish statistical significance; additionally, its more conservative assumptions require the use of authors with at least five thousand words in a text. Hilton's techniques were critically reviewed and accepted by the University of Chicago Press prior to its publication of a recent book that used his model to identify previously unrecognized writings of the seventeenth-century English philosopher Thomas Hobbes.[14]

There is much yet to be learned about wordprinting and its limits. One important discovery is that translators who attempt literal renderings of a text usually preserve a distinctive wordprint that maintains the statistical differences between that text and texts by other authors translated by the same or other persons. Looser approaches to translation, however, will stamp the translator's own wordprint on the resulting text. Thus we should not be too surprised to see the English-language edition of the Book of Mormon preserving differences between different Book of Mormon authors, even when many of the actual terms being counted in the English translation do not have specific parallels in the hypothesized original languages.

Hilton compared three independent texts of the didactic writings of Nephi and Alma with one another and with writings of Joseph Smith, Oliver Cowdery, and Solomon Spaulding. The results unambiguously showed that the wordprints of Nephi and Alma are distinct and significantly different from each other and from the wordprints of Smith, Cowdery, and Spaulding. The original findings were therefore confirmed, rendering it, in Hilton's words, "statistically indefensible" to claim that Joseph Smith or one of his contemporaries was the author of the Book of Mormon.[15]

Narrative of Zosimus

Another text that contains instructive parallels to the Book of Mormon is the Narrative of Zosimus, an early Christian document widely circulated in the first centuries A.D. that was listed in the ninth-century canon of Nicephorous

Zosimus

with apocryphal works that were to be discarded.[16] The traditions upon which this narrative is based most likely predate the birth of Christianity and are reflective of more ancient Jewish thought.[17] John W. Welch has demonstrated that the Zosimus narrative parallels the story of Lehi and Nephi in 1 Nephi in several key aspects.[18] On a general level, the text describes a righteous group that left Jerusalem at the time of Jeremiah, crossed the ocean, and arrived in a promised land. This striking initial connection to the Book of Mormon is further continued in many details of the Zosimus narrative, which suggests that both texts grew out of a common historical and cultural heritage.

History tells us nothing about Zosimus. In the narrative he is a righteous man who receives an angelic visitation in response to prayer. The angel informs him that he will be taken to a land of blessedness. Zosimus wanders without guidance through a wilderness and, though exhausted, arrives at the land of blessedness through prayer and divine intervention. He then encounters an "unfathomable river of water covered by an impenetrable cloud of darkness," which he crosses by grabbing the branches of a tree.[19] Reminiscent of the tree of life, the beautiful and fruit-laden tree next to a fountain of water gives nourishment to Zosimus, who then converses with an angelic escort who, after inquiring what he wants, allows him to see a vision of the Son of God.

After the vision, Zosimus is introduced to a gathering of the righteous sons of God, who share with him their history written upon stone plates. According to this history, these righteous sons of God were led from Jerusalem at the time of Jeremiah to this paradise on account of their righteousness. To Zosimus they stress the ideals of prayer and chastity and show him a book through which Zosimus learns that the inhabitants of Jerusalem, though wicked, will be shown mercy by God. Zosimus then returns from the land of blessedness to the world.

The parallels between Zosimus's journey and Lehi's and Nephi's vision of the tree of life—including the emphasis on prayer and faith, wandering through a dark and dreary wilderness, a river, a great mist, the tree of life next to the fountain of living waters, the angelic escort, the interrogation of desires, and the vision of the Son of God—are numerous and significant. Likewise, the intriguing similarities between the exodus of Lehi's family from Jerusalem at the time of Jeremiah and Zosimus's account of the history of the sons of God in the land of blessedness also strongly suggest that the two texts are connected in some significant manner. But the connection would seem to be an ancient one, as there is no evidence that the Zosimus narrative was available in English until decades after the publication of the Book of Mormon.[20]

Although the exact connection between the Narrative of Zosimus and the Book of Mormon will likely remain obscured by the passage of time, the similarities appear too extensive to explain by an appeal to mere coincidence. At the very least, Joseph Smith made a bold, bald assertion by claiming that Jesus had alluded to the Nephites—Israelites separated from the main body of Jews in Jerusalem at the time it was destroyed by the Babylonians and still living across the ocean—when he told his disciples in the Old World about the existence of "other sheep" whom he must also visit and bring (see John 10:16; 3 Nephi 15:16–17). Little could the young translator have dreamed that a text such as the Narrative of Zosimus would later surface, preserving just such a belief among early Palestinian Christians.

Orphic Gold Plates

Ancient Gold Plates

Verifying the authenticity of disputed ancient documents generally entails rigorous comparison of a document with the intellectual, cultural, and social heritage of the civilization it purports to describe. It is generally accepted that no forger of a text claiming to describe an area or time period with which he is not personally acquainted can possibly create a text that accurately describes another society in any detail. Indeed, historians usually have little trouble identifying forgeries of ancient documents, especially when those texts present a large amount of historical information, as does the Book of Mormon. If the Book of Mormon were a nineteenth-century concoction, this would have been easily and convincingly demonstrated a thousand times over. But this has not happened, and the attempts to pin such characterizations on the book have been largely refuted and replaced with a growing realization that the more carefully one examines the text, the more plausible its claimed ancient origins become.

Wilfred Griggs, a professor of classics, history, and ancient scripture at Brigham Young University, has compared Book of Mormon imagery with known Greek and Egyptian texts from around the time of Lehi.[21] In particular he has found powerful evidence that visions of the tree of life experienced by Lehi and Nephi share certain symbols and motifs with recently excavated Greek and Egyptian religious texts contemporary with Lehi's lifetime.

Symbols reminiscent of the tree of life visions described in the Book of Mormon are found in the ritual writings (recorded on gold plates) of the Orphic religious movement of Greek society, which became prominent throughout the eastern Mediterranean as early as the seventh century B.C. The Orphic plates, buried with the dead, were intended to guide the deceased in the afterworld, where he would encounter, among other items, two paths, one of which led to "a spring, near which is standing a white cypress."[22] Griggs explains that scholars have consistently associated the white cypress with the tree of life, and the plates themselves identify the spring as the "Lake of Memory," also symbolic of life. While scholars dispute the exact nature of the plates and the interpretation of the symbolism, there is broad consensus that they were the products of, or heavily influenced by, the ancient Near East.

Egyptian ritualistic funerary texts also contain similar references to a "tree growing by the fountain or spring of living water." Griggs explains that the rituals described in both the Orphic and Egyptian texts also would have been significant to the living, as a method of preparing "the living initiate for his journey into the world of departed spirits."[23] Given the ties between Greece and Egypt in this epoch, many scholars assert that the motifs on the Orphic plates have in reality an Egyptian origin. Griggs likewise suggests that the symbols used in the Book of Mormon were also influenced by the Egyptian ties, probably commercial, of Lehi and his family. Thus he suggests that the "most feasible and plausible explanation" for the similarities between the Orphic gold plates and the visions of the tree of life in the Book of Mormon is that "Egypt is the common meeting ground for the two traditions."[24] Growing evidence that symbols used in the Book of Mormon were part of the cultural milieu of Lehi's world—and not Joseph Smith's New York—strongly supports the divine and ancient origin of the Book of Mormon.

Forty-Day Literature

SIMILAR EARLY CHRISTIAN DOCUMENTS

The Book of Mormon text is supported by striking similarities to other ancient religious manuscripts that were unknown in 1830, when the Book of Mormon was published. Hugh Nibley has suggested that the texts of the "forty-day" literature, which are among the oldest Christian documents and purport to contain the postresurrectional teachings of Christ to his Old World apostles, have intriguing parallels in content to 3 Nephi, which records the visit and instruction of the resurrected Lord to his New World disciples.[25] A comparison between these relatively recently discovered texts, according to Nibley, allows 3 Nephi to take "its place in the bona fide apocalyptic library so easily and naturally that with the title removed, any scholar would be hard put to it to detect its irregular origin."[26] Elements in common include Christ's prophecy about the eventual apostasy of the church, after two generations in the Old World and four among the Nephites; references to the secrecy of certain teachings; statements about the visits of Christ to other peoples; a discussion of the history of the world in terms of dispensations; and the fact that Jesus physically ate food to show his status as a resurrected being. Additionally, Nibley notes that both accounts emphasize that the purpose of Christ's visit was to prepare his disciples for their missions to establish the church and that both stress the splendor and the intimacy of Christ's visits.

Nibley also engages in an extended comparison of 3 Nephi and the Coptic manuscript of the Gospel of the Twelve Apostles, discovered in 1904, seventy-four years after the Book of Mormon was published. Again, the parallels between the two texts in regard to general motifs and specific actions are consistent enough to suggest that they share a common origin in the teachings of the resurrected Christ. Among these similarities are the descriptions of Christ's condescension, his partaking of food with his disciples, a doctrinal emphasis on unity, the administering and withholding of the sacrament, the sacramental prayers, and three prayers by Christ. Additionally, both texts describe a private conversation between the Lord and either the Twelve Apostles or the twelve Nephite disciples. In both cases Christ encourages his disciples, who are at first abashed, to ask him what they are thinking; they eventually respond and inquire about the "type of the human who is dead but not dead, raised from the dead but still not resurrected,"[27] with Lazarus in the Old World and the Three Nephites in the New World representing this unique case. In both instances Jesus reassures them of the universality of the resurrection. The strong connections between the texts of the forty-day literature and 3 Nephi demonstrate the strong consistency of the latter with a genre of early Christian literature that was not known to early-nineteenth-century Americans and something that Joseph Smith could scarcely have imagined.

Merismus

In the Book of Mormon the Lord clearly outlines his gospel, particularly in 2 Nephi 31, 3 Nephi 11, and 3 Nephi 27, using a pattern with six major points of doctrine: faith in Jesus Christ, repentance, baptism of water, baptism of fire and of the Holy Ghost, endurance to the end, and eternal life. This same doctrinal pattern appears in the teachings of all the Book of Mormon prophets in the form of injunctions to the people. Throughout the Book of Mormon, the many statements regarding the gospel contain instructive variations on terminology and are often elliptical, leaving out one or more of the six points in any one articulation. However, for an audience familiar with the basic pattern, the allusion to that pattern is perfectly clear.

Merismus

The elliptical references often take the form of merismus, a classical rhetorical device in which the division of an important topic or statement into component parts allows for its full invocation by explicit listing of selected parts only. In the Hebrew Bible merismus occurs as concise or condensed expressions that, by mentioning the first and last or more prominent elements of a series, invoke the entire list.[28] In other words, once a pattern is established in the form of A, B, C, D, E, F (such as the list of elements of the gospel), the mere mention of two or more of these items, such as A and F, is used to represent the entire series. Understood as a formula composed of a list of ordered items, the gospel lends itself well to this rhetorical device. For example, a typical Book of Mormon merism states that believing in Jesus and enduring to the end is life eternal (see 2 Nephi 33:4). While repentance, baptism, and the gift of the Holy Ghost are not explicitly mentioned, they are implied by the use of merismus. Thus, using the pattern described above, the scripture uses the items A, E, and F to evoke the entire list in the minds of readers.

A conservative count of gospel-related merisms in the Book of Mormon gives at least 130 meristic statements of the gospel or doctrine of Christ.[29] The use of this ancient rhetorical device in the Book of Mormon, combined with the use of other ancient literary devices, most famously chiasmus, is strong evidence that the Book of Mormon was not the product of nineteenth-century America. Though not the way American writers would ordinarily have invoked formulas or lists, it is an appropriate rhetorical device for a book with ancient biblical connections.

Warfare

Readers of the Book of Mormon invariably wonder why so much attention is given to the preparation for, execution of, and recovery from war by the Jaredites, Nephites, and Lamanites. An estimated one-third of the text is somehow related to military matters, and the description of war-related items is further enhanced by the many prophets who were also military leaders. William J. Hamblin, a professor of history at Brigham Young University, has studied the Book of Mormon in the context of his knowledge regarding ancient warfare and has discovered that on general principles and specific details the Book of Mormon accurately describes an ancient system of warfare.[30] He states, "Despite the fact that Joseph Smith lived in the age of Modern, or technical, warfare, following the great military transformations of both the sixteenth century and the Napoleonic wars, the Book of Mormon consistently reflects the basic patterns of Pre-Modern warfare."[31]

COMPLEXITIES OF ACTUAL WARFARE

Ancient societies usually viewed warfare as inevitable, and thus they devoted most government resources to the military and maintained a martial mentality among the citizenry, who themselves constituted the bulk of the army. Such attitudes are readily recognizable in the Book of Mormon accounts. Historians of war divide the human experience into two broad categories, Modern and Pre-Modern warfare, with the rise of Modern warfare beginning in Europe in the sixteenth century. Pre-Modern warfare was always bound by certain environmental constraints, including the limitations of the human body, the terrain, the climate, and animal resources. Consistent with that fact, Book of Mormon accounts of war often explicitly speak of the constraints placed on the various armies by human, geographical, and seasonal circumstances. Significantly, Book of Mormon armies did not use animals during war, a situation that differed from much of the ancient world but that reflects exactly what archaeologists have discovered about ancient Mesoamerican warfare.[32] Weaponry mentioned in the Book of Mormon is likewise consistent with weapons used elsewhere in antiquity. In this regard the Book of Mormon most closely parallels Mesoamerican use of war technology, which lacked many of the elements, such as coats of mail and cavalry, that distinguished warfare in the ancient Near East. Additionally, the Book of Mormon does not present a static account of war technology but accurately portrays the constantly changing nature of warfare over the centuries.

Ancient warfare, which generally involved the entire society in its economic and social implications, was usually organized communally under the command of an elite hereditary military aristocracy. This also appears to be the case in the Book of Mormon. Military operations in the Book of Mormon also accurately reflect what is currently known about warfare throughout antiquity. War usually included complex preparations, an emphasis on marching to ensure that both supplies and men arrived in timely fashion at the correct locations, some guerrilla warfare, spies, a council of war, and a necessity of group cohesion on the battlefield—all elements of Book of Mormon warfare. Additionally, the pattern of organizing Book of Mormon armies in a decimal system (hundreds, thousands, ten thousands) is also found in ancient Israel and elsewhere in the ancient world.

Emphasis in the Book of Mormon on personal oaths of loyalty and of surrender is also typical of the ancient world, a fact that represents "perhaps the greatest distinction between modern and ancient international affairs."[33] Another major difference between Modern and Pre-Modern warfare is that war in antiquity was characterized by its religious connections, while war in modernity has become a secularized affair. In the Book of Mormon actions and beliefs associated with military culture (God's frequent intervention in battles on behalf of the righteous, consultation with prophets over military matters, the code of purity typified by Helaman's stripling warriors, to name a few examples), are representative of a ritualistic and sacral approach to warfare, paralleling patterns in the ancient Near East and Mesoamerica. Hamblin notes that of the three major themes of ancient literature and art—God, war, and love—the Book of Mormon accurately reflects the ancient world in its thematic emphases on two—God and war. Thus Hamblin concludes that the Book of Mormon describes a system of ancient warfare that in both general principles and specific practices would have been foreign to the world of Joseph Smith and yet is entirely consistent with what scholars now know about that feature of ancient societies.

Politics and the American Revolution

DISTINCTIVE POLITICS

Numerous critics of the Book of Mormon have asserted that the book contains political ideas that are a simple reflection of American thought in Joseph Smith's time. As Thomas O'Dea has claimed, "In it are found the democratic, the republican, the antimonarchical, and the egalitarian doctrines that pervaded the climate of opinion in which it was conceived."[34] However, in a careful study of the political philosophy and context of the Book of Mormon, Richard Bushman, a noted American historian, has demonstrated that it is "an anomaly on the political scene of 1830" and is much closer in government structure and philosophy to ancient Israelite monarchy than American republicanism.[35]

During his youth, Joseph Smith was undoubtedly imbued with the prevailing notion of the preeminent place of the American Revolution in world history. The victory of the American colonists was predominantly portrayed as a case of "heroic resistance" in which the colonists threw off the shackles of tyranny. However, the Book of Mormon account of the American Revolution emphasizes not courageous defiance but divine deliverance, a major theme and pattern in the entire book. Likewise, Bushman examined three separate cases in the Book of Mormon when the people of God faced situations similar to that of the American colonists; in each case, the people were delivered by fleeing, not by fighting. In fact, Book of Mormon peoples never overthrew an established government, no matter how tyrannical.

Joseph Smith was also exposed to a political context that celebrated the "true principles of government," meaning republicanism as opposed in principle to monarchy.

However, Bushman notes that "principled opposition to monarchy is scarcely in evidence" in the Book of Mormon.[36] In sharp contrast to this paradigm of early-nineteenth-century America—popular opposition to monarchy—the Nephite people often desired a king, while their leaders, the actual monarchs themselves, warned of the dangers of an evil king. In a reversal of roles from American images of enlightened patriots and despotic monarchs, "the people delighted in their subjection to the king, and the rulers were enlightened." Also, as Bushman argues, the Book of Mormon does not present monarchy as fundamentally evil; rather, "it was simply inexpedient because it was subject to abuse."[37]

Critics often cite the Nephite judges as an example of a democratic institution in the Book of Mormon. However, even though the judges were approved by the voice of the people, little else about them reflects American thought. The judges served for life, often inherited their positions, and wielded a concentration of powers without any functional checks and balances reminiscent of the American system. Nor is it obvious that they functioned like the biblical judges.

The Book of Mormon, in Bushman's analysis, is "strangely distant from the time and place of its publication."[38] On several key issues it stands in fundamental opposition to nineteenth-century-American political thought, not as a simple reflection of it as the book's critics have claimed. Parallels in ancient Israel more accurately stand as precedents to the political institutions and culture in the Book of Mormon narrative, though in subtle ways that Joseph Smith himself was not likely to have noticed: the motif of divine deliverance in Israelite history, popular desire for monarchy, and an emphasis on traditional law as opposed to constitutional rule of law with separation of powers and checks and balances. In terms of its political philosophy, the Book of Mormon fits much more comfortably into the tradition of Israelite thought than it does into the American context of Joseph Smith.

Consistency in Complexity

One of the strongest arguments for the antiquity of the Book of Mormon is the amazing depth of complexity addressed in a consistent manner throughout the book. This argument, first developed and perfected by Hugh Nibley, points to Joseph Smith's lack of education and his dictation of the Book of Mormon line by line without notes and without reviewing what was said minutes, hours, days, or even months earlier. Yet despite these circumstances, a large number of complex relationships are developed in the book and consistently maintained from beginning to end. Many of these relationships have taken scholars longer to sort out than it took Joseph Smith to translate the entire book.[39]

For example, the Book of Mormon employs at least three independent dating systems with remarkable accuracy. It also contains a complex system of religious teachings that is enriched as new sermons are added but is never confused or contradicted. The book's authors refer to a huge and complex set of sources—including official records, sermons, letters, monument inscriptions, and church records—that always maintain a consistent relationship in the final text. A large number of ancient literary forms, typical of ancient texts but virtually unknown in English in most cases, are woven into the narrative.

Subtle and complex political traditions evolve early in the text and surface in a variety of forms in later sections, always plausibly and consistently. The book describes various ebbs and flows of ethnic interaction without once losing track of even the most minor groups. Hundreds of individual characters are successfully introduced and coherently tracked. The geographical data in the text is diverse and complex, yet when carefully analyzed, it is perfectly consistent and matches an identifiable portion of Mesoamerica as well. This list of examples could go on at great length.

Melvin J. Thorne has argued that the improbability of alternative theories of the origin of the Book of Mormon increases rapidly as the number of elements establishing Book of Mormon complexity and parallels with the ancient world increases.[40] He utilizes the statistical rule that the probability of two events occurring by chance at the same time is equal to the product of their separate probabilities of occurring at all; in other words, two events that are likely to occur half the time independently are likely to occur jointly only one quarter of the time (.5 x .5 = .25). From a probabilistic point of view, the large number of ancient elements in the Book of Mormon, which would be natural in an ancient book but not in a nineteenth-century production, yields a joint probability that is astronomical against its being a nineteenth-century composition that just by chance is historically and culturally accurate.

Conclusion

These studies selected from such diverse fields as archaeology, historical demography, statistical authorship analysis, ancient history and literature, and American political culture all lead to a common conclusion: the Book of Mormon text displays a complexity of details and a richness of ancient patterns of life and literature that would have been impossible for anyone to compose on the basis of what was known in 1829. And scholarly discoveries and advances since that time have shown us that the facts and patterns embedded in that 1829 translation fit comfortably with the ancient world it purports to describe.

Notes

1. See Eugene England, "Through the Arabian Desert to a Bountiful Land: Could Joseph Smith Have Known the Way?" in *Book of Mormon Authorship Revisited: The Evidence for Ancient Origins,* ed. Noel B. Reynolds (Provo, Utah: FARMS, 1997), 144–56.

2. See Noel B. Reynolds, "Lehi's Arabian Journey Updated," in *Book of Mormon Authorship Revisited,* ed. Reynolds, 379–89.

3. Michael Rice, *The Archaeology of the Arabian Gulf, c. 5000–323 BC* (London and New York: Routledge, 1994), 246–48.

4. Quoted in Daniel C. Peterson, "Is the Book of Mormon True? Notes on the Debate," in *Book of Mormon Authorship Revisited,* ed. Reynolds, 154, emphasis added. See the original reports in Yohanan Aharoni and Ruth Amiran, "Arad: A Biblical City in Southern Palestine," *Archaeology* 17 (1964): 43–53; "Excavations at Tel Arad: Preliminary Report on the First Season," *Israel Exploration Journal* 14 (1964): 131–47; and "Excavations at Tel Arad: Preliminary Report of the Second Season," *Israel Exploration Journal* 17 (1967): 233–49. See also Yohanan Aharoni, "Arad: Its Inscriptions and Temple," *Biblical Archaeologist* 31 (1968): 232; and "The Israelite Sanctuary in Arad," in *New Directions in Biblical Archaeology,* ed. David Noel Freedman and Jonas Greenfield (Garden City: Doubleday, 1969), 28–44.

5. See John Tvedtnes's review of critic John C. Kunich, "Multiply Exceedingly: Book of Mormon Population Sizes," *Review of Books on the Book of Mormon* 6/1 (1994): 24–29.

6. See James E. Smith, "How Many Nephites? The Book of Mormon at the Bar of Demography," in *Book of Mormon Authorship Revisited,* ed. Reynolds, 255–93.

7. Smith, "How Many Nephites?" 258.

8. See the textual and other evidence for the presence of other peoples among Lehi's descendents in the New World assembled in John L. Sorenson, "When Lehi's Party Arrived in the Land, Did They Find Others There?" *Journal of Book of Mormon Studies* 1/1 (1992): 1–34.

9. Smith, "How Many Nephites?" 287.

10. See, for example, Frederick Mosteller and David L. Wallace, *Inference and Disputed Authorship: The Federalist* (Reading, Mass.: Addison-Wesley, 1964); and S. Michaelson and A. Q. Morton, "Last Words," *New Testament Studies* 8 (1972): 192–208.

11. See Wayne A. Larsen and Alvin C. Rencher, "Who Wrote the Book of Mormon? An Analysis of Wordprints," in *Book of Mormon Authorship: New Light on Ancient Origins*, ed. Noel B. Reynolds (Provo, Utah: FARMS, 1982), 157–88; or the earlier version in Wayne A. Larsen, Alvin C. Rencher, and Tim Layton, "Who Wrote the Book of Mormon? An Analysis of Wordprints," *BYU Studies* 20/3 (1980): 225–51.

12. Larsen and Rencher, "Analysis of Wordprints," 178.

13. See John L. Hilton, "On Verifying Wordprint Studies: Book of Mormon Authorship," in *Book of Mormon Authorship Revisited,* ed. Reynolds, 225–54; reprinted with changes from *BYU Studies* 30/3 (1990): 89–108.

14. See Thomas Hobbes, *Three Discourses: A Critical Modern Edition of Newly Identified Work of the Young Hobbes*, ed. (with explanatory essays) Noel B. Reynolds and Arlene W. Saxonhouse (Chicago: University of Chicago Press, 1995).

15. Hilton, "Verifying Wordprint Studies," 241.

16. See John W. Welch, "The Narrative of Zosimus (History of the Rechabites) and the Book of Mormon," in *Book of Mormon Authorship Revisited,* ed. Reynolds, 325.

17. James H. Charlesworth, in *The Pseudepigrapha and Modern Research* (Missoula, Mont.: Scholars Press, 1976), 225, speculates that it may be a Jewish text predating A.D. 70.

18. Welch, "Narrative of Zosimus," 323–74.

19. Ibid., 326.

20. The Zosimus narrative became generally available in English after 1867, when a translation appeared in the Edinburgh edition of *The Ante-Nicene Fathers,* published from 1867 to 1872.

21. See C. Wilfred Griggs, "The Book of Mormon as an Ancient Book," in *Book of Mormon Authorship,* ed. Reynolds, 75–101.

22. Ibid., 82.

23. Ibid., 91.

24. Ibid.

25. See Hugh W. Nibley, "Two Shots in the Dark: Christ among the Ruins," in *Book of Mormon Authorship,* ed. Reynolds, 121–41. Nibley draws here on his 1966 article in *Vigiliae christianae,* now reprinted and easily accessible as " Evangelium quadraginta dierum: The Forty-Day Mission of Christ—the Forgotten Heritage," in Hugh W. Nibley, *When the Lights Went Out: Three Studies on the Ancient Apostasy* (Provo, Utah: FARMS, 2001), 49–89.

26. Nibley, "Two Shots in the Dark," 122–23.

27. Ibid., 136.

28. See A. M. Honeyman, "*Merismus* in Biblical Hebrew," *Journal of Biblical Hebrew* 71 (1952): 14.

29. See Noel B. Reynolds, "The Gospel of Jesus Christ as Taught by the Nephite Prophets," *BYU Studies* 31/3 (1991): 31–50.

30. See William J. Hamblin, "The Importance of Warfare in Book of Mormon Studies," in *Book of Mormon Authorship Revisited,* ed. Reynolds, 523–43. See also, more generally, Stephen

D. Ricks and William J. Hamblin, eds., *Warfare in the Book of Mormon* (Salt Lake City: Deseret Book and FARMS, 1990).

31. Hamblin, "Importance of Warfare," 526.

32. See ibid., 529.

33. Ibid., 535. See Terrence L. Szink, "An Oath of Allegiance in the Book of Mormon," in *Warfare in the Book of Mormon*, ed. Ricks and Hamblin, 35–45.

34. Thomas F. O'Dea, *The Mormons* (Chicago: University of Chicago Press, 1957), 32.

35. See Richard L. Bushman, "The Book of Mormon and the American Revolution," in *Book of Mormon Authorship*, ed. Reynolds, 189–211. See also an earlier version in *BYU Studies* 17/1 (1976): 3–20.

36. Ibid., 198. An exception might be the brother of Jared, in an event recorded more than a thousand years before the Nephites existed (see Ether 6:23).

37. Ibid., 200.

38. Ibid., 203.

39. Many of the complexities that scholars have observed in the Book of Mormon are reported in John W. Welch, ed., *Rediscovering the Book of Mormon* (Salt Lake City: Deseret Book and FARMS, 1991).

40. See Melvin J. Thorne, "Complexity, Consistency, Ignorance, and Probabilities," in *Book of Mormon Authorship Revisited*, ed. Reynolds, 179–93.

Hebraisms and Other Ancient Peculiarities in the Book of Mormon

Donald W. Parry

At the end of the seventh century B.C., Lehi and his family lived in Jerusalem or its environs (see 1 Nephi 1:4), where Hebrew was spoken, written, and read. They took their knowledge of Hebrew with them to the New World, as Moroni 9:32–33 indicates: "We have written this record according to our knowledge, in the characters which are called among us the reformed Egyptian, being handed down and altered by us, according to our manner of speech. And if our plates had been sufficiently large *we should have written in Hebrew;* but the Hebrew hath been altered by us also." Because some form of Hebrew was used among the Nephites, the Book of Mormon reads like an ancient Hebrew book[1]—even in its English translation.

Indeed, many words, phrases, and expressions in the religious speeches and writings of Lehi, Nephi, and subsequent Book of Mormon prophets reflect biblical and idiomatic Hebrew rather than nineteenth-century American English. In the following pages I examine several such peculiarities in the Book of Mormon—literary forms and aspects of syntax, grammar, and usage that are unnatural in English yet characteristic of the language of Old World prophets as recorded in the Hebrew Bible (the basis of the Christian Old Testament). Of the numerous possible vestiges of ancient Hebrew in the Book of Mormon, I will discuss those that are conspicuously Hebraic and—particularly in their collective force—strongly indicative of the authenticity of the Book of Mormon.

Simile Curses

SIMILE
CURSES

Simile curses are well-attested literary forms in the Old Testament and ancient Near East.[2] They also appear in the Book of Mormon.[3] A simile curse combines the elements of a simile (a comparison of two things or a resemblance, customarily marked with *like* or *as*) with a curse (a statement that misfortune, injury, or death will befall the recipient of the curse). They are found in prophecies, treaties between suzerains and vassals, and in texts pertaining to religious covenants.

A treaty between Ashurnirari V, king of Assyria, and his vassal Matiʾilu contains an example of an ancient Near Eastern simile curse, wherein Matiʾilu is cautioned against breaking the treaty:

> If Matiʾilu sins against [this] treaty made under oath by the gods, then, just as this spring lamb, brought from its fold, will not return to its fold, will not behold its fold again, alas, Matiʾilu, together with his sons, daughters, officials, and the people of his land [will be ousted] from his country, will not return to his country, and not behold his country again.

This head is not the head of a lamb, it is the head of Matiʾilu, it is the head of his sons, his officials, and the people of his land. If Matiʾilu sins against this treaty, so may, just as the head of this spring lamb is torn off, . . . the head of Matiʾilu be torn off.[4]

An example of an Old Testament simile curse appears in 1 Kings 14, which registers Jeroboam's evil deeds and idolatries in verses 7–8 and then records the curse in verse 10: "Therefore, behold, I [the Lord] will bring evil upon the house of Jeroboam . . . and will take away the remnant of the house of Jeroboam, as a man taketh away dung, till it be all gone." Note the simile marker *as*, which connects the two points of comparison (house of Jeroboam and dung) to graphically portray the manner whereby the remnant of Jeroboam's family will be exiled. In another example, in 2 Kings 21:12–13, the Lord curses Judah's king Manasseh, members of the tribe of Judah, and Jerusalem for their considerable iniquities. The curse compares the destruction of Jerusalem and Judah to the cleaning of a dirty dish: "Thus saith the Lord God of Israel, Behold, I am bringing such evil upon Jerusalem and Judah, that whosoever heareth of it, both his ears shall tingle. . . . I will wipe Jerusalem as a man wipeth a dish, wiping it, and turning it upside down."

> **SIMILE CURSES**
>
> "I . . . will take away the remnant of the house of Jeroboam, as a man taketh away dung." (1 Kings 14:10)
>
> "I will wipe Jerusalem as a man wipeth a dish." (2 Kings 21:13)
>
> "The life of king Noah shall be valued even as a garment in a hot furnace." (Mosiah 12:3)
>
> Noah "shalt be as a stalk, even as a dry stalk of the field." (Mosiah 12:11)
>
> "God may cast us at the feet of our enemies, even as we have cast our garments at thy feet to be trodden under foot, if we shall fall into transgression." (Alma 46:22)

Given the ancient Near Eastern background of the Book of Mormon, the presence of simile curses therein is not surprising to those who embrace it as an authentic ancient record translated through divine inspiration. For those who believe otherwise, the presence of simile curses in that record is hard to explain, since not many examples of simile curses appear in the Old Testament and it is doubtful that Joseph Smith was aware of their form or setting in scripture.

In the Book of Mormon, the Lord, speaking through his prophet Abinadi, curses king Noah because of his great wickedness. Following the Lord's command, Abinadi stretches forth his hand, introduces his words with the phrase "Thus saith the Lord," and pronounces three curses upon Noah's head, each in the form of a simile. In the first, Abinadi says, "And it shall come to pass that the life of king Noah shall be valued even as a garment in a hot furnace; for he shall know that I am the Lord" (Mosiah 12:3; see v. 10). In the second, Abinadi promises that Noah shall be "as a stalk, even as a dry stalk of the field, which is run over by the beasts and trodden under foot" (v. 11); and in the third, the prophet promises the king, "Thou shalt be as the blossoms of a thistle, which, when it is fully ripe, if the wind bloweth, it is driven forth upon the face of the land" (v. 12). King Noah, the point of comparison in each similes, is likened to a garment, a dry stalk, and the blossoms of a thistle. Noah's subsequent death by fire is recorded in Mosiah 19:20.

The narrative of commander Moroni's raising the title of liberty contains three simile curses. The first is recorded in Alma 46:21: "And it came to pass that when Moroni had proclaimed these words, behold, the people came running together with their armor girded about their loins, rending their garments in token, or as a covenant, that they would not forsake the Lord their God; or, in other words, if they should transgress the commandments of God, or fall into transgression, and be ashamed to take upon them the name of Christ, *the Lord should rend them even as they had rent their garments.*" In the very next verse the people throw their garments at Moroni's feet and declare: "We covenant with our God, that *we shall be destroyed, even as our brethren in the land northward,* if we shall fall into transgression; yea, *he may cast us at the feet of our enemies, even as we have cast our garments at thy feet to be trodden under foot,* if we shall fall into transgression" (v. 22).

The simile curses in the Book of Mormon have the same form as those of the Bible and ancient Near East, and they appear in similar religious contexts, thus providing additional indications that this volume of scripture was framed in antiquity.

Peculiarities regarding Names

Of all the names of persons mentioned in the Old Testament, none are surnames. Biblical characters, whether notable or not, were known by one name only. And those names, as translated into the English language, neither use the letters *q, x,* or *w* nor begin with *F*.[5]

NAME PECULIARITIES

The Book of Mormon shares those same peculiarities: not one surname is mentioned among its 337 proper names, which, as transcribed into English, do not use the letters *q, x,* or *w* and do not begin with *F*. Had Joseph Smith authored the Book of Mormon in an attempt to pass it off as an ancient record, he might easily have slipped up by giving at least a few of his characters surnames, as was the custom for centuries before the coming forth of the Book of Mormon. And even if he were careful to model his expression after the Bible and thereby avoid obvious pitfalls, chances are slim that he would have noticed that in the Bible the letters *q, x,* and *w* are not used in proper names.

Poetic Parallelisms

POETIC
PARALLELISMS

In 1898 E. W. Bullinger, an Anglican clergyman and biblical scholar, authored *Figures of Speech Used in the Bible*,[6] which describes and illustrates in great detail seven types of parallelisms found in the Old Testament. Although Bullinger had expanded upon the work of other biblical scholars, especially the pioneering efforts of Robert Lowth,[7] no one before him had articulated the variety of poetic parallelisms in the Bible. These parallelisms are classified as synonymous, synthetic, antithetic, alternate, repeated alternate, extended alternate, and chiasmus.[8] Bullinger provided multiple examples of these parallelisms as well as brief reports regarding their significance.

The Book of Mormon contains numerous examples of each of the seven types of parallelism presented in Bullinger's work. Due to space considerations, I will discuss and illustrate only three kinds of parallelism in the Book of Mormon. Interested readers may wish to consult my book *The Book of Mormon Text Reformatted according to Parallelistic Patterns* for additional discussion and examples.[9]

Synonymous Parallelism

This form consists of two lines of text: the idea or subject of the first line is either repeated directly or echoed (in what is termed a "synonymous repetition") in the second line. An example appears in 2 Nephi 9:52:

> pray unto him continually by day,
> and give thanks unto his holy name by night

In this example the verb *pray* in line 1 is a synonymous counterpart to *give thanks* in line 2, and the phrase *by day* corresponds to *by night*. A third parallel is the correspondence between the pronoun *him* and *his holy name,* both referring to God.

A second example of synonymous parallelism is found in 2 Nephi 25:2:

> their works were works of darkness,
> and their doings were doings of abominations

Note the parallels between these two lines: the possessive pronoun *their* and the verb *were* are repeated, and the phrase *works of darkness* is a synonymous expression for *doings of abominations.*

Speaking of those who deny the works of God, the writer of 3 Nephi 29:5 crafted a synonymous parallelism by restating *wo unto him* and by pairing *that spurneth* with *that shall deny, Lord* with *Christ,* and *doings* with *works.*

> Wo unto him that spurneth at the doings of the Lord;
> yea, wo unto him that shall deny the Christ and his works!

Antithetic Parallelism

This form[10] is characterized by an opposition or contrast of thoughts, or an antithesis between two lines. A common feature that joins the two lines is the conjunction *and* or the disjunction *but* (both *and* and *but* are represented by a single character in the Hebrew, *waw*). Often the second line is introduced with one of these two words and immediately follows the contrasting element. 1 Nephi 17:45 is an example:

> Ye are swift to do iniquity
> but slow to remember the Lord your God.

The contrast is apparent, the word *swift* standing opposite of *slow* and the phrase *to do iniquity* counterpointing *to remember the Lord*.

The following antithetic parallelism from Alma 5:40 contrasts *good* with *evil* and *God* with the *devil*. The expressions *whatsoever is* and *cometh from* are featured in both lines:

> For I say unto you that whatsoever is good cometh
>   from God,
> and whatsoever is evil cometh from the devil.

Another example is found in Alma 22:6. When Aaron visits King Lamoni in the land of Nephi, the troubled king asks him what Ammon meant in saying

> If ye will repent ye shall be saved,
> and if ye will not repent, ye shall be cast off at the
>   last day.

The opposites in this simple summation of the gospel plan are evident: *repent ye* contrasts with *ye will not repent,* and *saved* stands opposite to *cast off.*

Repeated Alternate

In this form the parallel lines alternate, creating an AB, AB, AB pattern. The following verse, from 1 Nephi 19:10, features a number of prophecies concerning the crucifixion and burial of Jesus Christ.

> A the God of Jacob, yieldeth himself,
>   B according to the words of the angel,
> A as a man, into the hands of wicked men, to be lifted up,
>   B according to the words of Zenock,
> A and to be crucified,
>   B according to the words of Neum,
> A and to be buried in a sepulchre,
>   B according to the words of Zenos

Four messengers of the sufferings of Christ are mentioned: an unidentified angel, Zenock, Neum, and Zenos. Each prophetic message pertaining to the atoning sacrifice of the Lord alternates with the documentary citations of the prophet who delivered the message. In this manner the burden of the scriptures—the atonement of the Redeemer—is inseparably connected with those who carried the good tidings to humankind—the prophets.

The alternating AB, AB, AB pattern in Alma 30:10 sets forth violations of the law—murder, robbery, thievery, adultery (the lines marked with *A*)—followed by references to punishment (the lines marked with *B*).

A But if he murdered
    B he was punished unto death;
A and if he robbed
    B he was also punished;
A and if he stole
    B he was also punished;
A and if he committed adultery
    B he was also punished;
A yea, for all this wickedness
    B they were punished.

"And It Came to Pass"

The expression *and it came to pass*[11] is the translation of a Hebrew expression used frequently in scriptural histories and chronologies and far less frequently in poetry, prophecies, or direct speech. Although in its Hebrew form the expression is found in the Hebrew Bible some 1,200 times, it was translated in the King James Version as "and it came to pass" only about 727 times. The King James translators probably found the expression redundant and cumbersome,

"It Came to Pass"

which would explain why they often translated it as "and it became," "and it was," or "and." On a number of occasions they simply ignored the expression altogether.

Given the Semitic background of the Book of Mormon and the fact that it contains histories and chronologies comparable to those of the Old Testament, it is not surprising that *and it came to pass* is a characteristic feature of the book. Novelist and humorist Mark Twain once joked that if Joseph Smith had left out the many instances of *and it came to pass* from the Book of Mormon, the book would have been only a pamphlet.[12]

Similar to Old Testament usage, the phrase *and it came to pass* is rarely found in Book of Mormon psalms, lamentations, proverbs, blessings, curses, prayers, speeches, and dialogues where the first-person pronoun (*I* or *we*) is used. The expression is obviously missing from the Psalm of Nephi (2 Nephi 4:16–35); the speeches of such personalities as King Benjamin, Abinadi, Alma, and Jesus Christ; and the several epistles found in the Book of Mormon.

The Prophetic Perfect

Prophetic Perfect

The "prophetic perfect" is the use of the past tense or past participle verb forms (present and past perfect tenses) when referring to future events in prophecy. On occasion, Old Testament prophets prophesied using these forms "to express facts which are undoubtedly imminent, and therefore, in the imagination of the speaker, already accomplished."[13] Isaiah used the prophetic perfect in Isaiah 53 to prophesy of Jesus Christ's atoning sacrifice more than seven hundred years before Jesus' mortal ministry. Note the use of the past and perfect tenses (both in italics) in the following phrases, each of which expresses a future event:

he *has borne* our griefs and *carried* our sorrows (v. 4)
he *was wounded* for our transgressions (v. 5)
he *was bruised* for our iniquities (v. 5)
the chastisement of our peace *was* upon him (v. 5)
the Lord *hath laid* on him the iniquity of us all (v. 6)
he *was oppressed,* and he *was afflicted* (v. 7)
he *was cut off* out of the land of the living (v. 8)
for the transgression of my people *was he stricken* (v. 8)

Book of Mormon prophets also used the prophetic perfect in their prophecies. Lehi declared, "I have obtained a land of promise" (1 Nephi 5:5) long before he actually arrived in the promised land; and Nephi spoke of Jesus' baptism and reception of the Holy Ghost as though those events had already happened: "Wherefore, after he was baptized with water the Holy Ghost descended upon him in the form of a dove" (2 Nephi 31:8).

After quoting Isaiah 53, Abinadi taught a concept that seems to indicate he was aware of the prophetic perfect: "And now if Christ had not come into the world, *speaking of things to come as though they had already come,* there could have been no redemption" (Mosiah 16:6). Similarly, Jarom recorded, "Wherefore, the prophets, and the priests, and the teachers, did labor diligently, exhorting with all long-suffering the people to diligence; teaching the law of Moses, and the intent for which it was given; persuading them to look forward unto the Messiah, and believe in him to come *as though he already was*" (Jarom 1:11). Further, King Benjamin stated, "And the Lord God hath sent his holy prophets among all the children of men . . . that thereby whosoever should believe that Christ should come, the same might receive remission of their sins, and rejoice with exceedingly great joy, even as though he had already come among them" (Mosiah 3:13; compare Mormon 8:35).

The Book of Mormon, with its prophetic perfect forms, reads like an ancient scriptural work rather than a nineteenth-century text.

Climax: A Unique Poetic Form

Poetic Gradation

In 1898 the biblical scholar E. W. Bullinger identified a poetic form in the Bible that he called "climax" (Greek for "ladder").[14] He described this unique form in the Bible as "a beautiful figure, very expressive; and at once attracts our attention to the importance of a passage."[15] Climax occurs when the same word or words found at the end of one clause are repeated at or near the beginning of the next clause. Bullinger also refers to this form as "gradation," because the structure of a passage presents an ascension of thought, going up by steps from one level to the next.

Bullinger provides the following biblical example of climax, found in Joel 1:3–4. To make the form easily recognizable, the verse has been structured with the repeated words aligned on the left:

> Tell ye
> your children of it, and let
> your children tell
> their children, and
> their children another generation. That which the
> palmerworm hath left hath the
> locust eaten; and that which the
> locust hath left hath the
> cankerworm eaten; and that which the
> cankerworm hath left hath the
> > caterpiller eaten.

Note the four sets of repeated words: *your children, their children, locust,* and *cankerworm.* This duplication creates a continuation of thought from one segment to the next. In a dramatic way, four generations of one family are spoken of (*ye, your children, their children,* and *another generation*). This structure indicates an ascension of thought from the first generation to the last. The four generations parallel another gradation of thought—the four "generations" of the caterpillar family: the palmerworm, locust, cankerworm, and caterpillar.

The following climax, from Moroni 8:25–26, demonstrates the existence of this poetic form in the Book of Mormon:[16]

> And the first fruits of repentance is
> baptism; and
> baptism cometh by faith unto
> the fulfilling the commandments; and
> the fulfilling the commandments bringeth
> remission of sins; And the
> remission of sins bringeth
> meekness, and lowliness of heart; and because of
> meekness and lowliness of heart cometh the visitation
>   of the
> Holy Ghost, which
> Comforter filleth with hope and perfect
> love, which
> love endureth by diligence unto prayer,
>   until the end shall come, when all the saints shall
>   dwell with God.

There are six repeated words or phrases in this climax—*baptism, the fulfilling the commandments, remission of sins, meekness and lowliness of heart, Holy Ghost* (paralleling *Comforter*), and *love.* The beginning point of the climax (or ascension of expression) is repentance, an essential step onto the path of eternal life. Repentance is followed by baptism, obedience, and so on, finally culminating in salvation as the righteous receive an eternal station with God.

A climactic passage in Mormon 9:12–13 begins with the fall of Adam but concludes with humankind's being "brought back into the presence of the Lord" because of Jesus Christ.

> Behold, he created
> Adam, and by
> Adam came
> the fall of man. And because of
> the fall of man came
> Jesus Christ, even the Father and the Son; and because of
> Jesus Christ came the
> redemption of man. And because of the
> redemption of man, which came by
> Jesus Christ, they are brought back into the
> presence of the Lord.

The key words and concepts repeated in this passage—*Adam, fall of man, Jesus Christ,* and *redemption of man*—create a series of parallel statements. Through the alternating parallelism coupled with these climactic lines, Adam is seen as a character complementary to Jesus Christ, and the concept of the fall of man stands opposite to the redemption of man. Through Adam (the "first man Adam," the Apostle Paul says) came the fall of man, but through Jesus Christ (the "last Adam") came the redemption of man (see 1 Corinthians 15:45). A similar passage is found in 1 Corinthians 15:22, where the words *Adam* and *Jesus* and *die* and *alive* are found in the couplet—"For as in

Adam all die, even so in Christ shall all be made alive." Because of Jesus Christ's infinite atonement, repentant souls "are brought back into the presence of the Lord."

The fact that climactic forms appear in the Book of Mormon is good evidence that this volume of scripture belongs to the ancient world of its companion volume, the Bible. Bullinger discovered climax in the Bible more than six decades *after* the coming forth of the Book of Mormon. For that reason, and because of the scarcity of climax in the Old Testament, it is highly improbable that Joseph Smith was aware of this poetic device. Rather than attribute the approximately twenty examples[17] of climax in the Book of Mormon to happenstance or to Joseph Smith's uncommon literary knowledge and skill, it is more reasonable to accept that the Book of Mormon authors who used climax belonged to an ancient Near Eastern literary tradition corresponding to that of the Old Testament.

Prophetic Speech Formulas

In *Prophecy in Early Christianity and the Ancient Mediterranean World*, biblical scholar David E. Aune sets forth the various formulaic expressions that characterize prophetic speech in the Old Testament.[18] Often employed at the beginning of a prophetic speech, prophecy, or revelation, these expressions serve to formally introduce vital, sacred utterances and to announce that the Lord is the source behind them. The Book of Mormon prophets used the same formulas in their prophetic discourse. The formulas are as follows:

PROPHETIC SPEECH FORMULAS

The messenger formula—"Thus saith the Lord..." (e.g., Amos 1:3, 6). The purpose of the expression, found thirty-nine times in the Book of Mormon (e.g., 1 Nephi 20:17;

Mosiah 3:24; Alma 8:17), is to indicate the origin of the revelation. The revelation is directed to the messenger (i.e., a prophet) from the Lord himself.

The proclamation formula—"Hear the word of the Lord . . ." (e.g., 1 Kings 22:19; Amos 7:16; Isaiah 49:1). The declaration is an emphatic summons to hear God's word. Book of Mormon instances of this formula include "hearken to the word of the Lord" (Jacob 2:27), "hear the words of Jesus" (3 Nephi 30:1), and "hearken unto the words which the Lord saith" (Helaman 13:21).

The oath formula—"The Lord God hath sworn . . ." (e.g., Amos 4:2; 8:7) or "as the Lord liveth" (e.g., Judges 8:19; Ruth 3:13). This formula presents an oath. The phrase *As the Lord liveth* is found in 1 Nephi 3:15 and 4:32 and elsewhere in the Book of Mormon.

The revelation formula—"The word of the Lord came to . . ." (e.g., 1 Samuel 15:10; Zechariah 7:1). This expression indicates the origin of the message and the authority of the speaker. Of the Lamanite prophet Samuel, the Book of Mormon states, "Behold, the voice of the Lord came unto him" (Helaman 13:3; see also vv. 5, 7; Jacob 2:11; Alma 43:24).

The woe oracle—"Woe unto . . ." (e.g., Isaiah 5:8, 11, 20; Habakkuk 2:9, 12, 15). Approximately forty examples of this formula are found in the Book of Mormon (e.g., 1 Nephi 1:13; 2 Nephi 9:27; 15:21). Often part of a judgment speech, it is used to pronounce anguish and distress upon a person or group of people.

It is not by chance that the Book of Mormon contains these formulas, and a writer who wished to imitate the Bible would likely have overlooked them, employed them in improper contexts, or failed to integrate them into the text in a natural manner.

Names and Titles of Deity

Many of the ancient Babylonian gods, including Enlil, Adad, Nannar, Shamash, Nergal, Ishtar, and Marduk, had multiple names and titles. The chief weather god, Adad, for example, was known as God of Clouds, God of the Storm Cloud, God of Earthquake, God of Thunder, God of Lightning, God of Inundation, God of Rain, God of Storm, and God of the Deluge; and Shamash, the sun god, was called God of Brightness, God of Sunrise, God of Offerings, God of Peoples, and God of Hosts.[19] Deities from ancient Near Eastern religions also had multiple names: "Certain deities in the Ancient Near East are celebrated for the multiplicity of their names or titles, e.g. the 50 names of Marduk in Enuma Elish, the 74 names of Re in the tomb of Thutmosis III and the 100–142 names of Osiris in Spell 142 of the Book of the Dead."[20]

MULTIPLE NAMES OF GOD

Similarly, the Old Testament contains scores of names and titles of deity, including Shepherd, Savior, Redeemer, Lord, God, Rock, Almighty, Branch, Creator of Israel, Deliverer, Everlasting Father, God of Abraham, God of Isaac, God of Jacob, Shield, Jehovah, Lawgiver, Light, Ruler, Stone, Star, Prince of Peace, Servant. Such divine epithets are found in every Old Testament book except Esther. Isaiah and other books of the Old Testament attest scores of different names for God.

According to Book of Mormon scholar Susan Easton Black, the Book of Mormon contains 101 epithets for Christ.[21] Black's tally includes Redeemer of Israel, Son of the Living God, and Lord God Omnipotent (each of which appears once); True Messiah, Great Creator, and Stone (each found twice); Lamb of God, Lord Jesus Christ, Holy One of Israel, and Messiah (each found 10 or more times);

and God, Jesus, Lord, Lord God, and Christ (each found at least 100 times in the book). In all, the 101 names or titles of Christ appear 3,925 times in the Book of Mormon's 6,607 verses. Black's tabulation shows that, on average, a name or title of Christ appears once every 1.7 verses.

The frequent occurrence and variety of deific names and titles in the Book of Mormon distinguish the book from religious works created in the nineteenth century and place it squarely within the tradition of ancient religious texts.

Compound Prepositions

Compound Prepositions

Describing a characteristic feature of Hebrew grammar, Bruce K. Waltke and M. O'Connor write: "Compound prepositions are the result of the piling up of two or more simple prepositions. . . . Hebrew frequently piles up prepositions to represent more accurately the relation in question. . . . The combinations and their nuances are too numerous to catalog here."[22]

The expressions *from before, from behind,* and *to behind* are examples of compound prepositions from the Old Testament. For instance, "The Lord God of Israel hath dispossessed the Amorites *from before* his people Israel" (Judges 11:23, emphasis added). Sometimes the compound preposition is lost in the English translation, as in 2 Kings 9:18, which reads "turn thee behind me," though the Hebrew literally reads "turn *to behind* me."

The Book of Mormon, with its Hebrew background, similarly features compound prepositions. For example, the expression *from before* is found in 1 Nephi 4:28; 11:12; 2 Nephi 9:8; Mosiah 17:4; Alma 44:12; and 3 Nephi 4:12. The latter reads, "And notwithstanding the threatenings and the oaths which Giddianhi had made, behold, the

Nephites did beat them, insomuch that they did fall back *from before* them."

Plural Amplification

In order to amplify or emphasize an idea, biblical Hebrew sometimes uses a noun in the plural when a singular is expected.[23] The King James translators translated these Hebrew plural nouns into the English singular. In the following examples from the Old Testament the Hebrew readings appear in brackets.

PLURAL AMPLIFICATION

> thy brother's blood [bloods] crieth unto me from the ground (Genesis 4:10)
> and strength of salvation [salvations] (Isaiah 33:6)
> O Lord God, to whom vengeance [vengeances] belongeth (Psalm 94:1)
> Wisdom [wisdoms] crieth without; she uttereth her voice in the streets (Proverbs 1:20)
> the wicked . . . shall be brought forth to the day of wrath [wraths] (Job 21:30)

In many instances the Book of Mormon contains Hebrew-like plural nouns instead of the expected singular:

> there shall be bloodsheds (2 Nephi 1:12)
> the understandings of the children of men (Mosiah 8:20)
> great condescensions unto the children of men (Jacob 4:7)
> labor with their mights (Jacob 5:72)
> great slaughters with the sword (1 Nephi 12:2)
> there were . . . magics (Mormon 1:19)
> their cunning and their lyings (Alma 20:13)
> mine afflictions were great above all (1 Nephi 15:5)
> destructions[24] of my people (1 Nephi 15:5)
> foolish imaginations of his heart (1 Nephi 2:11)

Notes on Numbers

Number Usage

The Book of Mormon consistently agrees with the usage of numbers in the Old Testament, as illustrated in the following three items:

1. *Avoidance of complex numeric forms.* Biblical Hebrew uses cardinals *(one, two, three)*, ordinals *(first, second, third)*, multiplicatives *(double, sevenfold)*, and fractions *(half, third, tenth)* but avoids complex numeric forms using prefixes such as *mono-, bi-, di-, uni-, tri-, multi-,* and *poly-*.

2. *The number without the noun.* Often in biblical Hebrew, an expected noun does not follow a number. For instance, Genesis 45:22 states that Joseph "gave three hundred of silver" to Benjamin, without stating that the three hundred probably refers to pieces of silver. In order to fix what would have been an awkward omission in English, the King James translators supplied the word *pieces* but italicized it to show that it is not part of the original text. Other biblical examples of the number without the noun include "ten weight of gold" (Genesis 24:22; the KJV adds *shekels* to its translation: "ten *shekels* weight of gold"), "he measured six of barley" (Ruth 3:15; the KJV adds *measures:* "he measured six *measures* of barley"), and "a captain of fifty with his fifty" (2 Kings 1:9).

In the Book of Mormon, Laman and Lemuel ask, "How is it possible that the Lord will deliver Laban into our hands? Behold, he is a mighty man, and he can command fifty, yea, even he can slay fifty; then why not us?" (1 Nephi 3:31). The number fifty, used twice in this passage, is not followed by a noun. Does *fifty* refer to men, warriors, princes, commanders of armies? The context does not make this certain. Other Book of Mormon examples include "my little band of two thousand and sixty fought most desperately" (Alma 57:19); "Wherefore, by the words of three, God hath said, I will establish my word" (2 Nephi 11:3); "And it came to pass that there were two hundred, out of my two thousand and sixty" (Alma 57:25).

3. *Joining two or more numbers with the conjunction "and."* It is common in biblical Hebrew to join two or more numbers with the conjunction *and;* for instance, "thirty and two kings" (1 Kings 20:1) rather than "thirty-two kings." Examples in the Book of Mormon include "an army of forty and two thousand" (Mormon 2:9), "three hundred and twenty years" (Omni 1:5), and "being sixty and three years old" (Mosiah 17:6).

The Construct State

Biblical Hebrew juxtaposes two or more nouns to form a construct chain. When this Hebrew form is translated into English, the term *of* is often added to show the relationship between the nouns. In Hebrew one says "tables of stone" (Exodus 24:12) or "the word of the Lord" (Genesis 15:4), not "stone tables" or "the Lord's word."

CONSTRUCT STATE

There are numerous examples of the construct state in the Book of Mormon. These include "plates of brass" (1 Nephi 3:24), "rod of iron" (1 Nephi 8:19), "sword of Laban" (2 Nephi 5:14), "temple of Solomon" (2 Nephi 5:16), "the commandments of the Lord" (2 Nephi 5:19), "land of promise" (1 Nephi 17:33), "works of darkness" (2 Nephi 25:2), and "plans of awful wickedness" (Helaman 6:30). Also, the term *Lord's* is found "but twice in the entire Book of Mormon, while the equivalent of the construct state of nouns using his name occurs about three hundred times in a possessive sense in expressions such as 'commandments of the Lord,' 'name of the Lord,' 'people of the Lord,' 'presence of the Lord,' 'promises of the Lord.'"[25] Similarly, the term *God's* is found twice in the Book of Mormon, while the construct forms "church of God," "commandments of God," "kingdom of God," "Spirit of God," and so on are found more than 450 times.[26] The overwhelming practice of preferring the construct state over the possessive and related forms is a strong indication of Hebraic writing.

Repetition of the Definite Article

Repetition of "The"

Unlike English, in which a series of nouns can be introduced by a single definite article *(the)*, Hebrew repeats the definite article for each noun. This kind of repetition is seen throughout the Book of Mormon. A prime example is "We did observe to keep *the* judgments, and *the* statutes, and *the* commandments of the Lord" (2 Nephi 5:10). Of course, it would be much more usual in English to render this as "We did observe to keep the judgments, statutes, and commandments of the Lord." Similarly, Hebrew also repeats the conjunction *and* in some sequences (see the section titled "Many 'Ands.'")

Cognate Accusative

Cognate Accusative

The cognate accusative is a direct object noun that shares the same root as the preceding verb, as in Joseph "dreamed a dream" (Genesis 37:5) instead of the more customary English rendering "Joseph had a dream." The Hebrew Bible contains numerous examples of the cognate accusative (e.g., Genesis 1:11; 9:14; Numbers 11:4; Psalm

14:5; 144:6; Isaiah 35:2; Joel 3:1), although literal representations of this form is generally not used in translation.

The Book of Mormon contains many instances of the cognate accusative, including "I will curse them even with a sore curse" (1 Nephi 2:23; see 2 Nephi 1:22; Jacob 3:3), "Behold I have dreamed a dream" (1 Nephi 3:2; 8:2), "yoketh them with a yoke" (1 Nephi 13:5), "I will work a great and a marvelous work" (1 Nephi 14:7), "build buildings" (2 Nephi 5:15; Mosiah 23:5), "this was the desire which I desired of him" (Enos 1:13), "succor those that stand in need of your succor" (Mosiah 4:16), "taxed with a tax" (Mosiah 7:15), "work all manner of fine work" (Mosiah 11:10; Ether 10:23), "judge righteous judgments" (Mosiah 29:29, 43), "sing the song" (Alma 5:26), and "fear exceedingly, with fear" (Alma 18:5).

Cognate Accusatives

"I will curse them even with a sore curse." (1 Nephi 2:23)

"Behold, I have dreamed a dream." (1 Nephi 3:2; 8:2)

"yoketh them with a yoke" (1 Nephi 13:5)

"I will work a great and marvelous work." (1 Nephi 14:7)

"build buildings" (2 Nephi 5:15; Mosiah 23:5)

"This is the desire which I desired of him." (Enos 1:13)

"work all manner of fine work" (Mosiah 11:10)

"judge righteous judgments" (Mosiah 29:29, 43)

"sing the song" (Alma 5:26)

Many "Ands"

Biblical Hebrew uses the equivalent of the conjunction *and* much more than English uses *and*, especially in historical narrative and prose but also in poetry and direct speech. Its frequent appearance in English sounds irregular and repetitive. Consider the ten *and*s in the King James Version of 1 Samuel 17:34–35:

Many "Ands"

> *And* David said unto Saul, Thy servant kept his father's sheep, *and* there came a lion, *and* a bear, *and* took a lamb out of the flock:

And I went out after him, *and* smote him, *and* delivered it out of his mouth: *and* when he arose against me, I caught him by his beard, *and* smote him, *and* slew him. (emphasis added)

Compare also the thirteen *and*s in a single verse of Joshua:

And Joshua, *and* all Israel with him, took Achan the son of Zerah, *and* the silver, *and* the garment, *and* the wedge of gold, *and* his sons, *and* his daughters, *and* his oxen, *and* his asses, *and* his sheep, *and* his tent, *and* all that he had: *and* they brought them unto the valley of Achor. (Joshua 7:24, emphasis added)

The Book of Mormon corresponds to the Old Testament in its use of many *and*s throughout its historical and prose sections. There are twenty-two *and*s in 1 Nephi 11:30–32, which describes Nephi's vision of the Lamb of God ministering among his people; 1 Nephi 12:4 contains twelve *and*s in a single verse pertaining to Nephi's vision of the destruction of the land shortly before Christ's coming; Mosiah 10:8 contains eight *and*s in a list of weapons; and Alma 46:12–13 contains fifteen *and*s in a description of Moroni and his title of liberty. Helaman 3:14, with its eighteen *and*s in a single verse, is a good example of how an awkward construction in the English translation of the Book of Mormon makes perfectly good sense in Hebrew and reflects the ancient character of the book:

But behold, a hundredth part of the proceedings of this people, yea, the account of the Lamanites *and* of the Nephites, *and* their wars, *and* contentions, *and* dissensions, *and* their preaching, *and* their prophecies, *and* their shipping *and* their building of ships, *and* their building of temples, *and* of synagogues *and* their sanctuaries, *and* their righteousness, *and* their wickedness, *and* their murders, *and* their robbings, *and* their plundering, *and* all manner of abominations *and* whoredoms, cannot be contained in this work. (emphasis added)

Repetition of the Possessive Pronoun

In lists the Hebrew language repeats the possessive pronoun (e.g., *their, our, your, thy, his, her*) before each of the nouns to which it refers, a convention that is uncommon in English usage. The Old Testament (Hebrew Bible) preserves many examples of this Hebrew usage. For instance, the pronoun *our* is used six times in the King James Version of Exodus 10:9: "And Moses said, We will go with *our* young and with *our* old, with *our* sons and with *our* daughters, with *our* flocks and with *our* herds will we go" (emphasis added). Other biblical examples include the repetition of *our* five times in Deuteronomy 26:7, *their* four times in Genesis 10:20, *your* five times in Exodus 12:11, *your* four times in Leviticus 26:30, and *our* six times in Nehemiah 9:32.

Pronoun Repetition

Many examples of this usage appear in the Book of Mormon. For instance, the possessive pronoun *your* is used twelve times in 3 Nephi 30:2:

> Turn, all ye Gentiles, from *your* wicked ways; and repent of *your* evil doings, of *your* lyings and deceivings, and of *your* whoredoms, and of *your* secret abominations, and *your* idolatries, and of *your* murders, and *your* priestcrafts, and *your* envyings, and *your* strifes, and from all *your* wickedness and abominations, and come unto me, and be baptized in my name, that ye may receive a remission of *your* sins, and be filled with the Holy Ghost. (emphasis added)

Other examples of the repeated possessive pronoun in the Book of Mormon include *your* four times in Mosiah 4:30, *their* eight times in Mosiah 11:3, *your* three times in Alma 32:42, *our* nine times in Alma 44:5, *thy* four times in Alma 38:3, and *their* twelve times in Helaman 3:14.

Emphatic Pronoun

Pronoun Emphasis

For purposes of emphasis, biblical Hebrew sometimes repeats the personal pronoun. This usage, termed the "emphatic pronoun," occurs when the pronoun is the subject, as in Genesis 6:17, where the Lord states, "Behold, *I, even I*, do bring a flood of waters upon the earth" (emphasis added); or when the pronoun is the object, as in Genesis 27:38, where Esau implores his father to "bless *me, even me* also, O my father" (emphasis added). Some translators do not translate the emphatic pronoun, perhaps considering it unnatural or simply redundant in English.

The Book of Mormon also has examples of the emphatic pronoun. King Benjamin, speaking to a Nephite multitude, says, "*And I, even I*, whom ye call your king, am no better than ye yourselves are" (Mosiah 2:26; see v. 4).

Conclusion

The seventeen topics covered in this paper are but a sampling of the linguistic evidence that supports the Book of Mormon's claim of ancient authorship. The scriptural examples for each topic could be multiplied, and many related topics could be added. The present coverage, however, seems more than adequate to support these concluding observations:

1. The Hebraisms in the Book of Mormon attest to the book's Near Eastern background and antiquity. Their presence cannot be explained as a matter of coincidence, nor could a modern writer have integrated them so effectively (naturally and correctly) throughout the narrative. It is very unlikely that Joseph Smith had technical knowledge of these various archaic modes of expression, for many of them are subtle in their Book of Mormon contexts and are similarly inconspicuous in the Old Testament. Joseph's level of education and familiarity with the Bible could not have equipped him with the requisite literary knowledge and skill to craft so many Hebraisms so seamlessly and correctly into the Book of Mormon text. This is especially obvious in light of statements by his mother, Lucy Mack Smith, and his wife.[27]

2. The literary forms covered in this paper were generally uncommon in, if not altogether foreign to, the English of Joseph Smith's day. One must search beyond the nineteenth century for the origin of the Book of Mormon text.

3. It is significant that many changes in the Book of Mormon from the first edition in 1830 to subsequent editions pertain to Hebrew literary style. Joseph Smith and others apparently changed many awkward-sounding Hebraisms to idiomatic English. This does not mean, however, that the meaning of the text has changed. For instance, English and linguistics professor Royal Skousen has found in the original manuscript of the Book of Mormon fourteen examples of a common Hebrew-like construction whose literal translation ("if . . . and") is not significantly different in meaning from its present adjusted version. One passage is Moroni 10:4, which originally read, "If ye shall ask with a sincere heart with real intent

having faith in Christ and he will manifest the truth of it unto you." The passage now reads, "If ye shall ask with a sincere heart, with real intent, having faith in Christ, he will manifest the truth of it unto you."

4. When properly understood, the topics discussed in this paper enhance the readability of the Book of Mormon. For example, readers who come upon a simile curse will recognize its form and function and will thus better appreciate the cultural and religious world of the prophets of both the Old and New Worlds. Similarly, readers who encounter the cognate accusative (e.g., "dreamed a dream") will recognize it is an ancient Hebrew form instead of being distracted by it.

5. The peculiar expressions in the Book of Mormon that reflect ancient literary forms in the underlying text reveal Joseph Smith to be a careful, faithful translator of the text inscribed on the gold plates.

6. The seventeen topics covered in this paper, as significant and interesting as they are, are far less important than the primary objective of the Book of Mormon: to bring people to Christ and his atonement. Although some people may attempt to argue against the validity, significance, or even existence of the ancient literary forms I have identified in the Book of Mormon, they cannot argue against the fact that the book has the power to transform lives, a power that has converted millions of people into followers of Christ. The Book of Mormon accomplishes that by encouraging people to believe in Jesus Christ and his gospel, to repent of and forsake their sins, to become Christlike in their dealings with others, and to make the atonement meaningful in their lives (see Jacob 1:7; Omni 1:26; Moroni 10:30, 32).

In connection with the power of the Book of Mormon to change lives, I refer to an article by Robert Detweiler titled "What Is a Sacred Text?" in which he establishes seven traits of a sacred text:

1. Sacred texts claim to be divinely inspired.
2. They reveal sacred messages from deity or deities.
3. They have veiled or hidden messages in the form of mysteries, parables, and so on.
4. They require an authoritative interpreter.
5. They effect the "transformation of lives."
6. They serve as the foundation of religious ritual.
7. They are "evocative of divine presence."[28]

The Book of Mormon bears all seven traits. Concerning the fifth trait (the one I consider most important), Detweiler states that sacred texts "purport to change lives. They effect such transformations indirectly or directly. Indirectly they do so by describing some extra-textual path to salvation. . . . Generally it involves a formula to follow, a discipline to exercise, a trip to undertake, a savior figure to recognize, emulate, and obey. In these instances the text is not the instrument of transformation but the document of instruction toward change. But sometimes the sacred text is actually the instrument itself. Its very language claims a redemptive or transformational power, as if divinity indwelt the words and caused them, through articulation of them, to bring about altered states of being."[29]

The fact that the Book of Mormon changes lives is evident worldwide in the Church of Jesus Christ of Latter-day Saints—one simply needs to witness the testimonies of young and old church members at a monthly testimony meeting in a local chapel to understand the effect of this ancient record on its believers. Note its life-changing influence on Willard Richards, who read the Book of Mormon in the summer of 1835:

> [He] opened the book, without regard to place, and totally ignorant of its design or contents, and before reading half a page, declared that, "God or the devil has had a hand in that book, for man never wrote it." He read it twice through in about ten days; and so firm was his conviction of the truth, that he immediately commenced settling his accounts, selling his medicine, and freeing himself from every incumbrance, that he might go to Kirtland, Ohio, seven hundred miles west, the nearest point he could hear of a Saint, and give the work a thorough investigation; firmly believing that if the doctrine was true, God had some greater work for him to do than peddle pills.[30]

Parley P. Pratt, another early convert, had a similar experience when reading the Book of Mormon for the first time. Note how the book filled his soul with "joy and gladness":

> I opened [the Book of Mormon] with eagerness, and read its title page. I then read the testimony of several witnesses in relation to the manner of its being found and translated. After this I commenced its contents by course. I read all day; eating was a burden, I had no desire for food; sleep was a burden when the night came, for I preferred reading to sleep.
>
> As I read, the spirit of the Lord was upon me, and I knew and comprehended that the book was true....
>
> This discovery greatly enlarged my heart, and filled my soul with joy and gladness. I esteemed the Book, or the information contained in it, more than all the riches of the world.[31]

Just as the Book of Mormon changed the lives of Willard Richards and Parley P. Pratt, it continues to speak from the dust across the ages to change the lives of hundreds of thousands of people as it brings them to Jesus Christ and his atonement.

NOTES

1. Thomas W. Brookbank pioneered the study of Hebraisms in the Book of Mormon. See his multipart article "Hebrew Idioms and Analogies in the Book of Mormon," *Improvement Era,* December 1909–April 1910, January 1914–October 1914, December 1915. Others have also discussed this phenomenon. See Sidney B. Sperry, "Hebrew Idioms in the Book of Mormon," *Improvement Era,* October 1954, 703, 728–29; E. Craig Bramwell, "Hebrew Idioms in the Small Plates of Nephi," *Improvement Era,* July 1961, 496, 517; Angela Crowell, "Hebraisms in the Book of Mormon," *Zarahemla Record,* nos. 17–18 (summer/fall 1982): 1–7, 16; and, more recently, three studies by John A. Tvedtnes, "Hebraisms in the Book of Mormon: A Preliminary Survey," *BYU Studies* 11 (autumn 1970): 50–60; "Since the Book of Mormon is largely the record of a Hebrew people, is the writing characteristic of the Hebrew language?" I Have a Question, *Ensign,* October 1986, 64–66; and "The Hebrew Background of the Book of Mormon," in *Rediscovering the Book of Mormon,* ed. John L. Sorenson and Melvin J. Thorne (Salt Lake City: Deseret Book and FARMS, 1991), 77–91.

2. For a discussion of curses found in the Old Testament and ancient Near East, see Delbert R. Hillers, *Treaty-Curses and the Old Testament Prophets* 16 (Rome: Pontifical Biblical Institute, 1964), Ph.D. diss.; Herbert Chanan Brichto, *The Problem of the "Curse" in the Hebrew Bible* (Philadelphia: Society of Biblical Literature, 1963); Stanley Gevirtz, "West-Semitic Curses and the Problem of the Origins of Hebrew Law," *Vetus Testamentum* 11 (1961): 157–58;

and Sheldon H. Blank, "The Curse, Blasphemy, the Spell, and the Oath," *Hebrew Union College Annual* 23 (1950–51): 73–95.

3. For a brief but systematic study of Book of Mormon simile curses, see Mark J. Morrise, "Simile Curses in the Ancient Near East, Old Testament, and Book of Mormon," *Journal of Book of Mormon Studies* 2/1 (1993): 124–38.

4. In James B. Pritchard, ed., *Ancient Near Eastern Texts Relating to the Old Testament* (Princeton, N.J.: Princeton University Press, 1969), 532.

5. See Arthur G. Pledger, "The *W* and *I*," *Ensign,* September 1976, 24–25. See also Donald W. Parry, "The Book of Mormon: Integrity and Internal Consistency," in *Expressions of Faith: Testimonies of Latter-day Saint Scholars,* ed. Susan Easton Black (Salt Lake City: Deseret Book, 1996), 211.

6. E. W. Bullinger, *Figures of Speech Used in the Bible* (Grand Rapids, Mich.: Baker Book House, 1968).

7. Robert Lowth, *Lectures on the Sacred Poetry of the Hebrews,* 2 vols. (1787; reprint, New York: Garland, 1971).

8. See Bullinger, *Figures of Speech,* 349–62.

9. Donald W. Parry, *The Book of Mormon Text Reformatted according to Parallelistic Patterns* (Provo, Utah: FARMS, 1992). See also Hugh W. Pinnock, *Finding Biblical Hebrew and Other Ancient Literary Forms in the Book of Mormon* (Provo, Utah: FARMS, 1999).

10. See my discussion of antithetic parallelism in "Teaching in Black and White: Antithetic Parallel Structure in the Book of Alma, Its Form and Function," in *The Book of Mormon: Alma, the Testimony of the Word,* ed. Monte S. Nyman and Charles D. Tate Jr. (Provo, Utah: BYU Religious Studies Center, 1992), 281–90.

11. This expression is commonly mentioned in Hebrew grammars. See, for example, Joshua Blau, *A Grammar of Biblical Hebrew* (Wiesbaden: Otto Harrassowitz, 1976), 107. For a brief, popular discussion on this phrase, see Donald W. Parry, "Why is the phrase 'and it came to pass' so prevalent in the Book of Mormon?" I Have a Question, *Ensign,* December 1992, 29.

12. Mark Twain, *Roughing It* (Hartford, Conn.: American Publishing, 1901), 133.

13. Friedrich Heinrich Wilhelm Gesenius, *Gesenius' Hebrew Grammar* (Oxford: Clarendon, 1970), 312–13; cited by Stephen D. Ricks, "Many times in prophecy, the present and past tenses are used, even though the prophecy refers to a future event. Can you explain the use of verb tenses in prophecy?" I Have a Question, *Ensign*, August 1988, 27–28.

14. See Bullinger, *Figures of Speech Used in the Bible*, 256–59.

15. Ibid., 256.

16. See Donald W. Parry, "Climactic Forms in the Book of Mormon," in *Reexploring the Book of Mormon*, ed. John W. Welch (Salt Lake City: Deseret Book, 1992), 290–92.

17. See, for example, 1 Nephi 15:13–20, 33–35; 2 Nephi 1:13; Mosiah 2:17–19; Alma 42:17–20; Helaman 5:6–8; Ether 3:15–16; Mormon 9:12–13.

18. David E. Aune, *Prophecy in Early Christianity and the Ancient Mediterranean World* (Grand Rapids, Mich.: Eerdmans, 1991), 88–97. See Donald W. Parry, "'Thus Saith the Lord': Prophetic Language in Samuel's Speech," *Journal of Book of Mormon Studies* 1/1 (1992): 181–83.

19. For the multiple names and titles of these Babylonian deities, see *Cuneiform Texts from Babylonian Tablets in the British Museum, Part XXIV* (London: Trustees of the British Museum, 1967), 10–13.

20. H. B. Huffmon, "Name," in *Dictionary of Deities and Demons in the Bible*, ed. Karel van der Toorn, Bob Becking, and Pieter W. van der Horst (Leiden: Brill, 1995), 1148.

21. See Susan Easton Black, "Names of Christ in the Book of Mormon," *Ensign*, July 1978, 60–61. See also Susan Easton Black, *Finding Christ through the Book of Mormon* (Salt Lake City: Deseret Book, 1987), passim.

22. *An Introduction to Biblical Hebrew Syntax*, 220–21.

23. For a brief discussion of this phenomenon, see E.

Kautzsch, ed., *Gesenius' Hebrew Grammar* (Oxford: Clarendon, 1949), 396–98.

24. The printer's manuscript and the 1830 edition of the Book of Mormon read the plural *destructions*. See Royal Skousen, ed., *The Printer's Manuscript of the Book of Mormon: Typographical Facsimiles of the Entire Text in Two Parts* (Provo, Utah: FARMS, 2001), 1:101.

25. T. W. Brookbank, "Hebrew Idioms and Analogies in the Book of Mormon," *Improvement Era*, September 1914, 1062.

26. Ibid.

27. Both Lucy Mack Smith and Emma Smith made statements that indicated that the Prophet had only a partial knowledge of the Bible. Emma recalled assisting her husband as he translated the Book of Mormon: "When my husband was translating the Book of Mormon, I wrote a part of it, as he dictated each sentence, word for word, and when he came to proper names he could not pronounce, or long words, he spelled them out, and while I was writing them. . . . When he stopped for any purpose at any time he would, when he commenced again, begin where he left off without any hesitation, and one time while he was translating he stopped suddenly, pale as a sheet, and said, 'Emma, did Jerusalem have walls around it?' When I answered, 'Yes,' he replied, 'Oh! I was afraid I had been deceived.' He had such a limited knowledge of history at that time that he did not even know that Jerusalem was surrounded by walls" (as quoted in Russell M. Nelson, "A Treasured Testament," *Ensign*, July 1993, 61).

On one occasion the Prophet's mother revealed: "From this time forth, Joseph continued to receive instructions from the Lord, and we continued to get the children together every evening for the purpose of listening while he gave us a relation of the same. I presume our family presented an aspect as singular as any that ever lived upon the face of the earth—all seated in a circle, father, mother, sons and daughters, and giving the most profound attention to a boy, eighteen years of age, who had never read the Bible through in his life: he seemed much less inclined to the perusal of books than any of the rest of our children, but far more given to meditation and deep study" (Lucy Mack Smith, *History of Joseph Smith by His Mother, Lucy Mack Smith*, ed. Preston Nibley [Salt Lake City: Bookcraft, 1958], 82).

28. Robert Detweiler, "What Is a Sacred Text?" *Semeia* 31 (1985): 213–30. See page 223 for an explanation of the characteristics of the seven traits on pages 218–23.

29. Ibid., 220–21.

30. Susan Easton Black, ed., *Stories from the Early Saints Converted by the Book of Mormon* (Salt Lake City: Bookcraft, 1992), 66.

31. Ibid., 64.

Not Joseph's, and Not Modern

Daniel C. Peterson

At the dawn of the twentieth century, essentially no scholarship existed in support of the historical authenticity and divine inspiration of the Book of Mormon. Even at the midpoint of the past century, little of any merit was to be found. Since then, however, Book of Mormon scholarship has grown exponentially, and, as the twenty-first century gets fully under way, the book can claim far more support than at any previous time in its modern history. The trajectory of the discussion itself seems to support the book's claims. A simple fraud, a naive hoax, should have collapsed many decades ago. The collapse should, one would think, be obvious and unmistakable. Yet the Book of Mormon not only survives, it flourishes.

I shall attempt, within the confines of this brief essay, to sketch a few interesting pieces of evidence and to demonstrate how, together, they point to the reliability of the explanation for the Book of Mormon that has been taught by the Church of Jesus Christ of Latter-day Saints since its beginning.

The Exodus Motif

Depth of Exodus Motif

As careful scholarship continues to demonstrate, and contrary to the expectations of many, the Book of Mormon is a work of impressive literary depth, subtlety, and complexity.[1]

Terrence L. Szink, for example, has demonstrated that Nephi's account of the journey of his father's family from Jerusalem to the land of promise is modeled, unmistakably and in some detail, on the biblical story of the exodus of Moses and Israel out of the land of Egypt.[2] Obviously, both groups were led by visionary prophetic figures to leave lands that were under divine condemnation and to journey to lands of "promise," miraculously crossing major water barriers in order to reach safety from those who pursued or threatened them. In both accounts, rebellious members of the group "murmured" because of their hunger, lamented being taken from their previous home to perish in the wilderness, declared that they would rather have died than to have embarked on their present journey, and expressed a desire to return, instead, to the oppressive or dangerous lands from which God had delivered them. In both, a metallic object (the Liahona for the Lehites, the brazen serpent for the Israelites) played a major role, and we are told that to "look" upon it in a proper attitude was to "live." Both peoples were led by the Lord, who is represented by a figurative or literal "light." Both Nephi and Moses were summoned by the Lord to ascend a mountain, where Moses was given instructions on how to build a tabernacle and Nephi was given instructions on how to build a ship. In both accounts, the group's rebellious members drew divine wrath down upon themselves and their fellows when they engaged in wild and inappropriate partying, forgetting the Lord who had delivered them. The similarities appear in nuances of language as well as in broader themes.

"It seems to me," Szink concludes,

> that such a large body of parallels cannot be accounted for by coincidence. It appears that Nephi purposefully wrote his account in a way that would reflect the Exodus. His intention was to prove that God loved and cared for the Nephites just as he did the children of Israel during the Exodus from Egypt.[3]

That the parallels are likely to have been intentional appears, too, in the fact that, at 1 Nephi 4:1–3, and 17:23–44, Nephi expressly compares himself and the experiences of his people to portions of the biblical exodus story, in the latter passage using language that seems to recall the crossing of the Red Sea.[4]

"Certainly," Szink further suggests,

> this connection could not have been a product of Joseph Smith's writing. The parallels to Exodus occur at dozens of places throughout the Book of Mormon record. No hasty copying of the Bible could have produced such complex similarities, not to mention the differences that remain. In fact, because they are so quiet and underlying, no Latter-day Saint until our day has even noticed these comparisons. Nephi clearly composed a masterpiece full of subtle literary touches that we are only now beginning to appreciate.[5]

Significantly, as Szink observes, comparisons between the Israelite exodus and the Lehite journey are made by later Book of Mormon figures as well.⁶ This is what we would expect from a genuinely historical narrative, since Lehi's exodus from Jerusalem inevitably had a powerful impact on his family and their descendants, marking them forever. Jacob, Lehi's "firstborn in the wilderness," for instance, spent his earliest years traveling in the Arabian desert as an exile. Many decades later, near the end of his life, he reflected that "the time passed away with us, and also our lives passed away like as it were unto us a dream, we being a lonesome and a solemn people, wanderers."⁷ Jacob, like his brother Nephi and his father, Lehi, had been born and raised in a culture where the mighty acts of God in the exodus were commemorated not only in frequent retellings of the story but in ritual form at Passover. It was natural that they should think of their deliverance from doomed Jerusalem as a second exodus, though

> it is sadly ironic that Jerusalem, the promised land the Israelites had struggled so hard to obtain, had become at the time of Lehi analogous to the land of Egypt at the time of the Exodus. Lehi, a man of God, and his family were no longer safe there, and were forced to seek a *new* promised land.⁸

However, Lehi's is not the only "exodus" recorded in the Book of Mormon. Shortly after the group's arrival in the Americas, Nephi, feeling menaced by the people of Laman and Lemuel, led his faithful followers—including Jacob—away from the land of their "first inheritance." Still later, groups led by Mosiah, Alma₁, and Limhi, as well as the entire people of Anti-Nephi-Lehi, similarly abandoned their homes for new lands, impelled by deep religious visions and led by prophets. In fact, the Nephites appear to have seen their repeated exodus experiences as archetypal expressions of their individual and collective spiritual journeys.[9] They were, as Alma$_2$ said more than five centuries after their arrival in the Americas, "wanderers in a strange land."[10]

These later deliverances were likewise recounted in terms of the original biblical exodus, so that what David Daube says about the biblical narrative is no less true with regard to subsequent events recorded in the Book of Mormon: "By being fashioned on the exodus, later deliverances became manifestations of this eternal, certainty-giving relationship between God and his people."[11] In very Hebraic fashion, the Nephites knew that one of their primary responsibilities before God was to "remember," to never forget his glorious and mighty acts on their behalf.[12]

George S. Tate has likewise argued that Nephi's account of the Lehite journey to the New World deliberately echoes the Israelite exodus.[13] He notes such motifs, beyond those already mentioned above, as references in both the Nephite and Israelite accounts to a (paschal?) lamb, miraculous provision of food in the wilderness when murmuring erupts among the hungry travelers, and even references in both accounts to the passage of forty years. To these, Mark J. Johnson has added such details as the burial of a deceased patriarch at a significant location, after (in the biblical instance certainly, and in the Book of Mormon account probably) the body has been transported for some length of time, as well as the transfiguration of Moses and Nephi before their people.[14] Tate goes still further, though, to contend that exodus typology runs through the entire Book of Mormon until it finds its ultimate and explicit fulfillment in the account of the visitation of Christ to the Americas, as recorded in 3 Nephi. S. Kent Brown agrees that Christ's appearance at Bountiful is depicted in terms at least partially borrowed from the exodus story, and argues that the presentation of the Savior's atonement in the Book of Mormon is itself rendered in a manner that has been colored by reflection upon the deliverance of Israel from Egyptian bondage.[15] This is, of course, precisely what we would expect, given the Book of Mormon's claim to roots in the culture of ancient Israel. As biblical scholar James Plastaras has observed,

> It was the . . . exodus which shaped all of Israel's understanding of history. It was only in light of the exodus that Israel was able to look back into the past and piece together her earlier history. It was also the exodus which provided the prophets with a key to the understanding of Israel's future. In this sense, the exodus stands at the center of Israel's history.[16]

"In summary," Brown writes regarding the implications of what he and others have discovered in researching this topic,

> the Book of Mormon can be seen as the repository of an extraordinarily rich tradition with deep, ancient roots. Taken as a whole, the work proves to be one of stunning complexity and nuanced subtlety—no small conclusion.[17]

Such sophisticated and authentic usage of the Israelite exodus narrative strongly suggests that the author of 1 Nephi in particular, like the authors of the Book of Mormon in general, was someone thoroughly steeped in the Hebrew Bible. Of course, that description seems appropriate to Nephi, the privileged and well-educated son of a wealthy Hebrew father. But it doesn't fit young Joseph Smith, who appears to have been anything but a systematic, regular student of the Bible. Even by the age of eighteen, according to his mother—that is, in roughly 1823, when he received the first visitation from Moroni—he "had never read the Bible through in his life."[18] Later in the 1820s, when the Book of Mormon was translated, his knowledge of the Bible does not appear to have been dramatically greater.[19]

Joseph Smith an Unlikely Author

In fact, the youthful Joseph does not appear to have been an avid reader at all. His mother recalls that "he seemed much less inclined to the perusal of books than any of the rest of our children," and there seems no reason to doubt her word.[20] Very few volumes sat on the shelves of the local library, and the Smiths do not appear to have had access to that library in any case.[21] Yet the Book of Mormon that Joseph Smith somehow produced contains a great deal of information that is unlikely to have emerged out of his own experience.

For example, Joseph Smith never fought in a war. His military experience, such as it was, was limited almost entirely to the parades and drills of the Nauvoo Legion, with all the patriotic panoply of fife and drum that an early-nineteenth-century-American frontier militia could muster. However, in the Book of Mormon's portrayal of the Gadianton robbers we find a detailed, realistic depiction of a prolonged guerrilla struggle—lacking any trace of romanticism, uniforms, glamour, or parades, but matching up remarkably well with the actual conduct of such unconventional conflict. Yet this portrayal was published well over a century before the great guerrilla warfare theorists of the twentieth century (such as Mao Tse Tung,

GUERRILLA WARFARE

Ernesto "Che" Guevara, and Vo Nguyen Giap) put their pens to paper.²²

GEOLOGY

The modern scientific disciplines of seismology and vulcanology also have something to contribute to this matter: Joseph Smith lived in an area that was, geologically speaking, very quiet. He never saw a volcano, never experienced an earthquake of any notable magnitude (if, indeed, he ever felt one at all). Yet the Book of Mormon's portrayal of the great New World catastrophes that marked the crucifixion of Christ is remarkably realistic, down to the aftershocks, the choking vapors, and the lightning storms that arise when volcanic particles churn at high velocities in the cloud above an eruption. It seems very likely that 3 Nephi was written either by someone who was an eyewitness to a major volcanic and seismic event (which Joseph never was) or, alternatively, by someone who had read accounts of the Nephite destruction. A third possibility is that someone employed similar accounts from other sources in order to formulate a fictional though deceptively realistic tale. However, it seems extremely unlikely that Joseph Smith had done any vulcanological or seismological research.²³

OLIVE CULTURE

Similarly, the lengthy allegory of the olive tree given in Jacob 5 betrays a knowledge of olive cultivation considerably beyond what Joseph Smith, growing up in the cool, wet deciduous forests of the American Northeast, likely possessed. In fact, the allegory is remarkably consistent in detail with what we learn from ancient manuals on Mediterranean olive culture.²⁴

Christopher Columbus and the *Libro de las profecías*

One of the best-known prophecies in the Book of Mormon has generally been understood to predict the career of Christopher Columbus, who is usually reckoned the effective European "discoverer" of the New World. Accordingly, Columbus emerges from the very pages of scripture itself as an important and foreordained actor in the divine plan:

INSPIRATION OF
CHRISTOPHER
COLUMBUS

> And I looked and beheld a man among the Gentiles, who was separated from the seed of my brethren by the many waters; and I beheld the Spirit of God, that it came down and wrought upon the man; and he went forth upon the many waters, even unto the seed of my brethren, who were in the promised land.[25]

Skeptical readers of the Book of Mormon, however, have tended to dismiss this passage as a cheap and easy instance of prophecy after the fact, composed centuries after Columbus's death—but postdated, as it were, in order to create a seemingly impressive and self-validating prediction by an ancient prophetic writer. At the very most, some have observed, a "prophecy" of Columbus hardly constitutes evidence for the antiquity or inspiration of the Book of Mormon.

On a surface level, such critics seem to be right. It would have taken little talent in the late 1820s for someone to prophesy the discovery of America nearly three and a half centuries earlier. But the description of Columbus provided by 1 Nephi 13:12 nonetheless remains a remarkable demonstration of the revelatory accuracy of the Book of Mormon. It is only with the growth of Columbus scholarship in recent years, and particularly with the translation and publication of Columbus's *Libro de las profecías* in 1991, that English-speaking readers have been fully able to see how remarkably the admiral's own self-understanding parallels the portrait of him given in the Book of Mormon.

The Columbus revealed in very recent scholarship is quite different from the gold-driven secular adventurer celebrated in the textbooks and holidays most of us grew up with.[26]

We now understand, for example, that the primary motivation for Columbus's explorations was not financial gain but the spread of Christianity. He was zealously committed to the cause of taking the gospel, as he understood it, to all the world. He felt himself guided by the Holy Spirit, and a good case can indeed be made that his first transoceanic voyage, in particular, was miraculously well executed.

Columbus was a serious and close student of the Bible. Among his very favorite passages of scripture was John 10:16: "And other sheep I have that are not of this fold: them also I must bring, and they shall hear my voice; and there shall be one fold and one shepherd." This verse provided significant support for his image of himself as a bearer of the gospel to the New World. And, though he was unfamiliar with the writings of Nephi, Columbus was convinced that his role had been predicted by ancient prophets. "The Lord purposed," he wrote to Ferdinand and Isabella,

> that there should be something clearly miraculous in this matter of the voyage to the Indies. . . . I spent seven years here in your royal court discussing this subject with the leading persons in all the learned arts, and their conclusion was that it was vain. That was the end, and they gave it up. But afterwards it all turned out just as our redeemer Jesus Christ had said, and as he had spoken earlier by the mouth of his holy prophets.[27]

"For the execution of the journey to the Indies," he said, "I was not aided by intelligence, by mathematics or by maps. It was simply the fulfillment of what Isaiah had prophesied."²⁸ Referring to his first crossing of the Atlantic, Columbus declared,

> With a hand that could be felt, the Lord opened my mind to the fact that it would be possible to sail from here to the Indies, and he opened my will to desire to accomplish the project. This was the fire that burned within me. . . . Who can doubt that this fire was not merely mine, but also of the Holy Spirit who encouraged me with a radiance of marvelous illumination from his sacred Holy Scriptures, by a most clear and powerful testimony . . . urging me to press forward? Continually, without a moment's hesitation, the Scriptures urge me to press forward with great haste.²⁹

As noted, the quite recent publication of Columbus's *Book of Prophecies* in English translation—much too late for Joseph Smith to have used it—now permits us a window into the great admiral's soul. And what we find there is strikingly reminiscent of prominent themes in the Book of Mormon. Columbus was fascinated, for instance, by such subjects as the recovery of the Holy Land and the rebuilding of the ancient Jewish temple in Jerusalem. One of his favorite scriptures, in this regard, was Isaiah 2:2 (= 2 Nephi 12:2): "And it shall come to pass in the last days, that the mountain of the Lord's house shall be established in the top of the mountains, and shall be exalted above the hills; and all nations shall flow unto it." He was also, as mentioned, deeply committed to the notion that the gospel had to be preached to the ends of the earth and the inhabitants thereof brought to Christ before the end of the world. For much of this, as careful readers of the Book of Mormon might have guessed, Columbus's favorite author was the prophet Isaiah. Indeed, it was in that prophet's book that Columbus thought he could see himself and his voyages divinely foretold. Among the passages that caught his attention was Isaiah 55:5:

> Behold, thou shalt call a nation that thou knowest not, and nations that knew not thee shall run unto thee because of the Lord thy God, and for the Holy One of Israel; for he hath glorified thee.

Columbus seems to have regarded this as a prophecy of his own mission, along with Isaiah 42:1–4 ("Behold my servant, whom I uphold; mine elect, in whom my soul delighteth; I have put my spirit upon him. . . . and the isles shall wait for his law"), which students of the Book of Mormon will have no difficulty connecting with the prophet Jacob's remarks at 2 Nephi 10:20–22:

> And now, my beloved brethren, seeing that our merciful God has given us so great knowledge concerning these things, let us remember him, and lay aside our sins, and not hang down our heads, for we are not cast off; nevertheless, we have been driven out of the land of our inheritance; but we have been led to a better land, for the Lord has made the sea our path, and we are upon an isle of the sea.
>
> But great are the promises of the Lord unto them who are upon the isles of the sea; wherefore as it says isles, there must needs be more than this, and they are inhabited also by our brethren.
>
> For behold, the Lord God has led away from time to time from the house of Israel, according to his will and pleasure. And now behold, the Lord remembereth all them who have been broken off, wherefore he remembereth us also.
>
> Therefore, cheer up your hearts.

"Our Lord," Columbus said in 1500, "made me the messenger of the new heaven and the new earth, of which he spoke in the Book of Revelation by St. John, after having spoken of it by the mouth of Isaiah; and he showed me the place where to find it."³⁰ Christopher Columbus would have heartily agreed with the Book of Mormon's description of him as a man "wrought upon" by "the Spirit of God."

Witnesses to the Book of Mormon

On the basis of the kinds of considerations that we have already discussed, as well as many others (some of them treated elsewhere in this volume), it appears highly unlikely that Joseph Smith could simply have created the Book of Mormon out of the learning and experience naturally available to him. And the testimony of contemporary witnesses to the Book of Mormon makes it virtually impossible to maintain that the angel Moroni and the book he delivered were figments merely of Joseph's imagination, whether skeptics prefer to think of him as sincerely deceived or intentionally deceptive. The claim by a sympathetic, insightful, but often severely misinformed European scholar, that the plates of the Book of Mormon were visible, if at all, only to Joseph Smith, "never seen by anyone else," is simply false.³¹ It cannot be sustained in the face of the evidence. And the importance of that fact can hardly be overstated.

THE WITNESSES

First of all, there are the "official" accounts of the Three and the Eight Witnesses to the Book of Mormon, whose honesty and consistency are manifest in the many surviving documents by and about them. Space permits only a brief treatment of the voluminous evidence on this subject.[32]

On the day following the death of David Whitmer, in 1888, the *Chicago Times* reported an interview with an unnamed "Chicago Man." This man related a conversation that he had engaged in with another individual some years before, a prominent resident of the county in which David Whitmer had lived who had been a lawyer and a sheriff there and who had, the Chicago Man said, known the witness very well. The prominent Clay County resident had given him a remarkable portrait of David Whitmer's character and later life.

> In the opinion of this gentleman, no man in Missouri possessed greater courage or honesty than this heroic old man [David Whitmer]. "His oath," he said, "would send a man to the gallows quicker than that of any man I ever knew." He then went on to say that no person had ever questioned [David Whitmer's] word to his knowledge about any other matter than finding the Book of Mormon. [Whitmer] was always a loser and never a gainer by adhering to the faith of Joseph Smith. Why persons should question his word about the golden plates, when they took it in relation to all other matters, was to him a mystery.[33]

Yet this very David Whitmer persisted, literally to his dying day, despite ridicule and skepticism from those around him and despite his own deep disaffection from the institutional church led by Joseph Smith and then by Brigham Young and the apostles, in stating that he had been in the presence of an angel, had seen the gold plates and other objects related to the Book of Mormon, and had heard the voice of God declare the book true. In an 1878 interview with Orson Pratt and Joseph F. Smith, for example, he gave dramatic and emphatic testimony of his experience as a witness:

> I saw [the plates and other Lehite artifacts] just as plain as I see this bed (striking his hand upon the bed beside him), and I heard the voice of the Lord, as distinctly as I ever heard anything in my life, declaring that the records of the plates of the Book of Mormon were translated by the gift and power of God.[34]

Six years later, Whitmer was interviewed by Joseph Smith III, in the presence of others, not all of whom were disposed to believe his account. Significantly, he listed several items that he had seen, besides the golden plates:

> Rather suggestively [Colonel Giles] asked if it might not have been possible that he, Mr. Whitmer, had been mistaken and had simply been moved upon by some mental disturbance, or hallucination, which had deceived them into *thinking* he saw the Personage, the Angel, the plates, the Urim and Thummim, and the sword of Laban. How well and distinctly I remember the manner in which Elder Whitmer arose and drew himself up to his full height—a little over six feet—and said, in solemn and impressive tones: "No, sir! I was not under any hallucination, nor was I deceived! I saw with these eyes and I heard with these ears! *I know whereof I speak!*"[35]

Unlike the Three Witnesses, who saw an angel and heard a divine voice testify to the truth of the translation of the metallic record—and whose testimony, for that reason, has been discounted by some determined skeptics as simple hallucination—the Eight Witnesses saw and handled the plates under quite matter-of-fact circumstances. Yet their testimony is no less impressive.

Hyrum Smith, for example, who besides being the Prophet's loyal elder brother was also one of the Eight Witnesses, wrote in December 1839 of his recent sufferings in Missouri:

> I had been abused and thrust into a dungeon, and confined for months on account of my faith, and the testimony of Jesus Christ. However I thank God that I felt a determination to die, rather than deny the things which my eyes had seen, which my hands had handled, and which I had borne testimony to . . . ; and I can assure my beloved brethren that I was enabled to bear as strong a testimony, when nothing but death presented itself, as ever I did in my life.[36]

These were not empty words. Four and a half years later, Hyrum Smith sealed his testimony with his blood at Carthage, Illinois, when an armed anti-Mormon mob with painted faces assassinated him and his brother. The historical evidence indicates that Hyrum understood his likely fate, and that he went to it willingly.[37]

Another of the Eight Witnesses, John Whitmer, was excommunicated on 10 March 1838, one month before his brother David. Like David, he never returned to the Church. In fact, for a brief period it even appears that John's spiritual confidence in the Book of Mormon had been shaken by his separation from his former associates and by his bitterness over the economic and other issues that had arisen during the Latter-day Saints' brief sojourn in Missouri. (He was sorrowful and dejected about his excommunication, but also, for at least a time, quite angry at the church in general and Joseph Smith in particular.)[38] During an 1839 exchange with Theodore Turley, the Mormon business agent who had stayed behind in Far West to settle financial affairs there after the expulsion of the Saints, Whitmer confessed to doubts about whether the Book of Mormon was true. After all, he had heard no divine voice confirming the accuracy of the translation. Speaking of the original text on the plates, he said, "I cannot read it, and I do not know whether it is true or not." Nonetheless, he insisted, "I handled those plates; there were fine engravings on both sides. I handled them."[39]

Thus, even in the depths of his alienation and bitterness, even when he was most inclined to doubt what he could not see for himself—even living, as he did, in the area of the worst anti-Mormon persecutions, when continuing to affirm faith in anything connected with the Latter-day Saint movement could have been personally dangerous—John Whitmer did not deny that he had "lifted and handled a metal object of substantial weight."[40] There was nothing mystical, visionary, or immaterial about his experience. It was a simple matter of hefting and examining something entirely tangible, something quite literally physical.

It appears, however, that John Whitmer's bitterness, or at least his skepticism, was short-lived. By 1856, he was the last survivor from among the Eight Witnesses. In 1861, Jacob Gates spoke with him for more than four hours, thereafter entering the following summary comment in his journal: "[H]e still testified that the Book of Mormon is true and that Joseph Smith was a Prophet of the Lord."[41]

Fifteen years after that interview, in 1876, Whitmer wrote a lengthy letter to Mark Forscutt, which included the following:

> Oliver Cowdery lived in Richmond, Mo., some 40 miles from here, at the time of his death. I went to see

him and was with him for some days previous to his demise. I have never heard him deny the truth of his testimony of the Book of Mormon under any circumstances whatever.... Neither do I believe that he would have denied, at the peril of his life; so firm was he that he could not be made to deny what he has affirmed to be a divine revelation from God....

... I have never heard that any one of the three or eight witnesses ever denied the testimony that they have borne to the Book as published in the first edition of the Book of Mormon. There are only two of the witnesses to that book now living, to wit., David Whitmer, one of the three, and John Wh[itmer], one of the eight. Our names have gone forth to all nations, tongues and people as a divine revelation from God. And it will bring to pass the designs of God according to the declaration therein contained.[42]

Several other people handled the plates and described them as quite heavy. Thus, for example, William Smith, in an interview with J. W. Peterson, later recalled an experience with the plates that occurred under wholly nonvisionary circumstances: "I handled them and hefted them while [they were] wrapped in a tow frock and judged them to have weighed about sixty pounds. I could tell they were plates of some kind and that they were fastened together by rings running through the back."[43] Martin Harris, not yet invited to be one of the Three Witnesses, once lifted the box in which he had been told that the plates were concealed, to see what he could determine. He knew from the weight of the box that it had to contain something as dense and heavy as either gold or lead, he later recalled, "and I knew that Joseph had not credit enough to buy so much lead."[44]

Furthermore, as already noted, the plates were not the only tangible objects involved in these accounts, nor were the official witnesses the only people who saw such things. Lucy Mack Smith, for instance, "examined" the Urim and Thummim and "found that it consisted of two smooth three-cornered diamonds set in glass, and the glasses were set in silver bows, which were connected with each other in much the same way as old fashioned spectacles."[45] Regarding the breastplate that Joseph found with the plates, she wrote:

> It was wrapped in a thin muslin handkerchief, so thin that I could see the glistening metal, and ascertain its proportions without any difficulty.
>
> It was concave on one side and convex on the other, and extended from the neck downwards, as far as the centre of the stomach of a man of extraordinary size. It had four straps of the same material, for the purpose of fastening it to the breast, two of which ran back to go over the shoulders, and the other two were designed to fasten to the hips. They were just the width of two of my fingers, (for I measured them,) and they had holes in the ends of them, to be convenient in fastening.[46]

Joseph Smith's wife Emma frequently encountered the plates while engaged in the utterly unmystical labor of early-nineteenth-century housework. She later recalled that

> the plates often lay on the table without any attempt at concealment, wrapped in a small linen table cloth, which I had given him to fold them in. I once felt of the plates as they thus lay on the table, tracing their outline and shape. They seemed to be pliable like thick paper, and would rustle with a metallic sound when the edges were moved by the thumb, as one sometimes thumbs the edges of a book.[47]

Even now, despite the passage of nearly two centuries and countless attempts, no credible counterexplanation has been offered by any critic for the experiences claimed by the Witnesses to the Book of Mormon. Their still-unimpeached testimony clearly demonstrates that the Book of Mormon plates and the other artifacts mentioned in the historical accounts were physical, that they were neither a figment of Joseph Smith's imagination nor generated by the credulous fantasies of a band of rustic religious zealots.

Ancient Near Eastern Origins

So the Book of Mormon does not appear to have emerged out of Joseph Smith's subjective experience. He had objectively real plates and related objects in his possession. Others saw them. Where, then, did the Book of Mormon come from? Considerable evidence suggests that it came from precisely the kind of ancient Near Eastern cultural background that it claims for itself. A few examples will have to suffice.

THE NAME "ALMA"

Thus, for instance, two male characters named Alma appear in the Book of Mormon. And, of course, this seems to run counter to what we might have expected: If Joseph Smith knew the name *Alma* at all from his environment, it is highly likely that he would have known it as a Latinate *woman's* name rather than as a masculine one. (Many will recognize the Latin phrase *alma mater,* which means "beneficent mother.") Recent documentary finds demonstrate, however, that *Alma* also occurs as a Semitic masculine personal name in the ancient Near East—just as it does in the Book of Mormon.⁴⁸ How did Joseph know this? How could he have learned it? Quite simply, so far as modern scholarship has been able to determine, he could not have known it from any source existing in his frontier American environment.

The Book of Mormon's use of *Alma* as a man's name has occasioned considerable amusement among uninformed critics of the book. So has the prophecy in Alma 7:10, predicting that Jesus "shall be born of Mary, at Jerusalem, which is the land of our forefathers." As everybody who knows anything at all about Christianity also knows, Jesus was born in the little town of Bethlehem. However, although identifying a "land of Jerusalem" as the birthplace of Jesus would have seemed an obvious mistake for at least a century after the publication of the Book of Mormon, it is now plain that Bethlehem could be, and indeed anciently was, regarded as a town in the "land of Jerusalem." A recently released text from the Dead Sea Scrolls, for example—a text claiming to have originated in the days of Jeremiah (and, therefore, in Lehi's time)—says that the Jews of that period were "taken captive from the land of Jerusalem."[49] Texts discovered earlier in the twentieth century seem to include Bethlehem within that "land." Joseph Smith could not have learned this from the Bible, though, for no such language appears in it.[50]

LAND OF JERUSALEM

He is also very unlikely, even had he been a diligent and deep student of it, to have deduced from his Bible the complex patterns associated with the calling of prophets that contemporary scholarship has begun to notice and discuss. Yet those patterns appear with striking clarity in the Book of Mormon—arguably, indeed, more clearly in the Book of Mormon than in the Bible or in any other single text coming to us from the ancient Near East. Diligent researchers have been obliged to piece the general pattern together from widely scattered documents. Yet Lehi's vision of God and

PROPHETIC CALL

his accompanying prophetic call, we now know, could serve as a textbook illustration of such visions and calls as they are recounted in ancient literature, complete with motifs of the heavenly book and the divine council that have only garnered scholarly attention in recent decades.[51]

The Book of Mormon relates that Lehi was

> overcome with the Spirit, [and] he was carried away in a vision, even that he saw the heavens open, and he thought he saw God sitting upon his throne, surrounded with numberless concourses of angels in the attitude of singing and praising their God.[52]

This is clearly a vision of the divine council, known today from many ancient Near Eastern texts, that surrounds God and over which he presides. The Hebrew word *sôd*, which denotes that council, also refers to the counsel issued from it. It can often be interchanged, in this sense, with the Greek word *mysterion*. In ancient conceptions, it is frequently the prophet's admission to this council as a mortal human being, and his knowledge of its decrees and secrets, that lends him authority as an earthly spokesman for God. "Surely the Lord God will do nothing," said the ancient Israelite prophet Amos of Tekoa, "but he revealeth his secret *[sôd]* unto his servants the prophets."[53]

Hebrew Conditional Sentences

Another helpful indicator of the true origin of the Book of Mormon is the presence of the *if-and* conditional construction in the 1830 first English printing of the book.[54] A little background will help to make the significance of this indicator clear. In English conditional sentences, we typically say things like "If you study hard, you will succeed," and "If you don't exercise and eat well, you will damage your health." The first part of such sentences is the "condition." If that condition is fulfilled, the second part of the sentence will occur.[55] In the earliest manuscript of the Book of Mormon, however, a strikingly different kind of conditional sentence occurs several times. Thus, in the 1830 edition, Helaman 12:13–21 read as follows:

> [Y]ea, and *if* he saith unto the earth, Move, *and* it is moved; yea, *if* he say unto the earth, Thou shalt go back, that it lengthen out the day for many hours, *and* it is done.... And behold, also, *if* he saith unto the waters of the great deep, Be thou dried up, *and* it is done. Behold, *if* he saith unto this mountain, Be thou raised up, and come over and fall upon that city, that it be buried up, *and* behold it is done.... and *if* the Lord shall say, Be thou accursed, that no man shall find thee from this time henceforth and forever, *and* behold, no man getteth it henceforth and forever. And behold, *if* the Lord shall say unto a man, Because of thine iniquities thou shalt be accursed forever, *and* it shall be done. And *if* the Lord shall say, Because of thine iniquities, thou shalt be cut off from my presence, *and* he will cause that it shall be so.[56]

Another, much more familiar passage also read rather differently in the 1830 edition of the Book of Mormon:

> And when ye shall receive these things, I would exhort you that ye would ask God, the Eternal Father, in the name of Christ, if these things are not true; and *if* ye shall ask with a sincere heart, with real intent, having faith in Christ, *and* he will manifest the truth of it unto you, by the power of the Holy Ghost.[57]

Of course, Joseph Smith was poorly educated. He spoke and wrote nonstandard English. But it is extraordinarily doubtful that he or any other native speaker of English has ever spoken or written this way. An *if-and* conditional sentence grates on our ears. If someone were to use it in our presence, and we would find it very odd. Yet it is perfectly appropriate Hebrew. It is common in the Hebrew Bible, yet, to the best of my knowledge, it never appears in any biblical translation into English or any other Western language.[58]

Nephi and His Asherah

Nephi's vision of the tree of life, one of the most loved passages in the Book of Mormon, is an expanded repetition of the vision received earlier by his father, Lehi.

NEPHI AND
HIS ASHERAH

> And it came to pass that the Spirit said unto me: Look! And I looked and beheld a tree; and it was like unto the tree which my father had seen; and the beauty thereof was far beyond, yea, exceeding of all beauty; and the whiteness thereof did exceed the whiteness of the driven snow.
>
> And it came to pass after I had seen the tree, I said unto the Spirit: I behold thou hast shown unto me the tree which is precious above all.
>
> And he said unto me: What desirest thou?
>
> And I said unto him: To know the interpretation thereof. . . .[59]

Nephi wanted to know the meaning of the tree that his father had seen and that he himself now saw. Accordingly, we would expect "the Spirit" to answer Nephi's question. But the response to Nephi's question, when it comes, is rather surprising:

> And it came to pass that he said unto me: Look! And I looked as if to look upon him, and I saw him not; for he had gone from before my presence.

> And it came to pass that I looked and beheld the great city of Jerusalem, and also other cities. And I beheld the city of Nazareth; and in the city of Nazareth I beheld a virgin, and she was exceedingly fair and white.
>
> And it came to pass that I saw the heavens open; and an angel came down and stood before me; and he said unto me: Nephi, what beholdest thou?
>
> And I said unto him: A virgin, most beautiful and fair above all other virgins.
>
> And he said unto me: Knowest thou the condescension of God?
>
> And I said unto him: I know that he loveth his children; nevertheless, I do not know the meaning of all things.
>
> And he said unto me: Behold, the virgin whom thou seest is the mother of the Son of God, after the manner of the flesh.
>
> And it came to pass that I beheld that she was carried away in the Spirit; and after she had been carried away in the Spirit for the space of a time the angel spake unto me, saying, Look!
>
> And I looked and beheld the virgin again, bearing a child in her arms.
>
> And the angel said unto me: Behold the Lamb of God, yea, even the Son of the Eternal Father![60]

Next, "the Spirit" asks Nephi the question that Nephi himself had posed only a few verses before: "Knowest thou the meaning of the tree which thy father saw?"[61]

Strikingly, though the vision of Mary seems irrelevant to Nephi's original inquiry about the significance of the tree—for the angelic guide's response doesn't mention the tree at all—Nephi himself now replies that, yes, he knows the answer to his question.

And I answered him, saying: Yea, it is the love of God, which sheddeth itself abroad in the hearts of the children of men; wherefore it is the most desirable above all things.

And he spake unto me, saying: Yea, and the most joyous to the soul.[62]

How has Nephi come to this understanding? Clearly, the answer to his question about the meaning of the tree somehow lies in the image of the virgin mother with her child. In some sense, it seems that the virgin *is* the tree.[63] Even the language used to describe her echoes the vocabulary previously used for the tree. Just as she was "exceedingly fair and white," "most beautiful and fair above all other virgins," so was the tree's beauty "far beyond, yea, exceeding of all beauty; and the whiteness thereof did exceed the whiteness of the driven snow." Significantly, though, it is only when she appears with a baby and is identified as "the mother of the Son of God" that Nephi grasps the tree's meaning.

Why would Nephi, whether consciously or unconsciously, see a connection between a tree and the virginal mother of a divine child? The ancient Near Eastern religious world is very foreign to us, as it was to Joseph Smith. Nephi's vision appears to reflect a meaning of the "sacred tree" that is unique to the ancient Near East, and that, indeed, can only be fully appreciated when the ancient Canaanite and Israelite associations of that tree are borne in mind.[64]

A feminine divine being, generally called by some form of the name *Asherah,* seems to have been known and worshipped not only among the Canaanites but among the Israelites. Her veneration can be documented over a period extending from the conquest of Canaan in the second millennium before Christ to the fall of Jerusalem in 586 B.C.—the time of Lehi's departure with his family from the Old World. Belief in Asherah seems, in fact, to have been a conservative position in ancient Israel; it was *criticism* of her that appears to have been a religious innovation. In fact, an image or symbol of Asherah stood in Solomon's temple at Jerusalem for nearly two-thirds of its existence, until the reforms of King Josiah (who reigned from roughly 639 to 609 B.C.). This means that her presence in the temple extended into the lifetime of Lehi and perhaps even into the lifetime of Lehi's son Nephi. Since that time, though, she has been fiercely suppressed. In the text of the Bible as we now read it, although hints of the goddess remain, little survives that would enable us to form an accurate or detailed understanding of her character or nature. Greater understanding has only begun to come through relatively recent archaeological discoveries, including but not limited to the immensely important Canaanite texts from ancient Ugarit, in Syria.

What was the symbol of Asherah that stood in the temple at Jerusalem? Asherah was associated with trees. The tenth-century cultic stand from Ta'anach, near Megiddo, for instance, features two representations of Asherah, first in human form and then as a sacred tree. She *is* the tree.[65] Israelite goddess figurines that represent her typically feature upper bodies that are unmistakably anthropomorphic and female while their lower bodies are simple columns, very possibly representing tree trunks. Asherah "is a tree goddess, and as such is associated with the oak, the tamarisk, the date palm, the sycamore, and many other species. This association led to her identification with sacred trees or the tree of life."[66] The rabbinic authors of the Jewish Mishna (second–third century A.D.) explain the *asherah* as a tree that was worshipped.⁶⁷

She seems to have been represented by a carved, wooden image, perhaps some kind of pole. Very probably it symbolized a tree, and it may itself have been a stylized tree. It was not uncommon in the ancient Near East for a god or goddess to be essentially equated with his or her symbol, and Asherah seems to have been no exception: Asherah was both goddess *and* cult symbol. She *was* the "tree."

The menorah, the seven-branched candelabra that stood for centuries in the temple of Jerusalem, supplies an interesting parallel to all of this: Leon Yarden maintains that the menorah represents a stylized almond tree. He points to the notably radiant whiteness of the almond tree at certain points in its life cycle. Yarden also argues that the archaic Greek name of the almond (*amygdale,* reflected in its contemporary botanical designation as *Amygdalis communis*), almost certainly not a natively Greek word, is most likely derived from the Hebrew *em gədullāh,* meaning "Great Mother."⁶⁸

Among the Hebrews, Asherah seems to have been known as a maternal *dea nutrix,* a nourishing or nurturing goddess. Paradoxically, though, it appears that she may also have been considered a virgin. The Punic western goddess Tannit, whom Saul Olyan has identified with Israelite-Canaanite Asherah, the consort of the chief god El, the mother and wet nurse to the gods, was depicted as a virgin and symbolized by a tree.⁶⁹

Although Asherah remains imperfectly understood, and although we cannot be certain of all the details, it should be apparent by now why Nephi, an Israelite living at the end of the seventh and the beginning of the sixth century before Christ, might have recognized an answer to his question about a marvelous tree in the otherwise unexplained image of a virginal mother and her divine child. His perception seems to derive from precisely the preexilic Palestinian culture into which, the Book of Mormon tells us, Nephi had been born. This is a culture very foreign to ours, and to that of Joseph Smith.

The evidence (barely) sampled here strongly suggests that Joseph Smith was not, and could not have been, the author of the Book of Mormon. Furthermore, it simply does not permit the notion, popular among some skeptics who seek a less confrontational mode of dismissing the claims of the restoration, that the whole thing can be explained purely on the basis of subjective events in Joseph Smith's mind. It forces the question, Truth or fraud? There is no middle ground. But it also whispers the correct answer to that question. It points to a culture with roots in the ancient Semitic Near East as a source for many of the peculiar characteristics of the Book of Mormon. It thereby supports the spiritual conviction of millions of Latter-day Saints, living and dead, that the Book of Mormon is a divinely provided testimony to the deity of Jesus Christ, the atoning Redeemer of humankind, and to the prophetic calling of Joseph Smith, the founding prophet of the restoration.

Notes

1. Recent literary appreciations of the Book of Mormon include Bruce W. Jorgensen, "The Dark Way to the Tree: Typological Unity in the Book of Mormon," in *Literature of Belief: Sacred Scripture and Religious Experience,* ed. Neal E. Lambert (Provo, Utah: BYU Religious Studies Center, 1981), 217–31; Grant R. Hardy, "Mormon as Editor," in *Rediscovering the Book of Mormon,* ed. John L. Sorenson and Melvin J. Thorne (Salt Lake City: Deseret Book and FARMS, 1991), 15–28; John S. Tanner, "Jacob and His Descendants as Authors," in *Rediscovering the Book of Mormon,* ed. Sorenson and Thorne, 52–66; Alan Goff, "The Stealing of the Daughters of the Lamanites," in *Rediscovering the Book of Mormon,* ed. Sorenson and Thorne, 67–74; Marilyn Arnold, *Sweet Is the Word—Reflections on the Book of Mormon—Its Narrative, Teachings, and People* (American Fork, Utah: Covenant, 1996); Eugene England, "A Second Witness for the *Logos,*" in *By Study and Also by Faith,* ed. John M. Lundquist and Stephen D. Ricks, (Salt Lake City: Deseret Book and FARMS, 1990), 2:91–125; Richard Dilworth Rust, *Feasting on the Word: The Literary Testimony of the Book of Mormon* (Salt Lake City: Deseret Book and FARMS, 1997); Hugh W. Pinnock, *Finding Biblical Hebrew and Other Ancient Literary Forms in the Book of Mormon* (Provo, Utah: FARMS, 1999); and John S. Tanner, "The World and the Word: History, Literature and Scripture," in *Historicity and the Latter-day Saint Scriptures,* ed. Paul Y. Hoskisson (Provo, Utah: BYU Religious Studies Center, 2001), 217–35. Mark D. Thomas, in *Digging in Cumorah: Reclaiming Book of Mormon Narratives* (Salt Lake City: Signature Books, 1999), while apparently not accepting the historical authenticity of the Book of Mormon, nonetheless celebrates the book's multilayered and complex literary quality. Two forthcoming studies by literature scholar Robert A. Rees, on "Joseph Smith, the Book of Mormon, and the American Renaissance"

and "Irony in the Book of Mormon," argue that "Joseph Smith lacked the literary imagination and talent, authorial maturity, time, education, knowledge, or sophistication that would have been required to write the Book of Mormon."

2. See Terrence L. Szink, "Nephi and the Exodus," in *Rediscovering the Book of Mormon,* ed. Sorenson and Thorne, 38–51; and Terrence L. Szink, "To a Land of Promise (1 Nephi 16–18)," in *First Nephi to Alma 29,* Studies in Scripture, vol. 7, ed. Kent P. Jackson (Salt Lake City: Deseret Book, 1987), 60–72. Compare Alan Goff, "Mourning, Consolation, and Repentance at Nahom," in *Rediscovering the Book of Mormon,* ed. Sorenson and Thorne, 92–99.

3. Szink, "Nephi and the Exodus," 50.

4. For Nephi's self-comparison to Moses, see Noel B. Reynolds, "The Political Dimension in Nephi's Small Plates," *BYU Studies* 27/4 (fall 1987): 15–37.

5. Szink, "Nephi and the Exodus," 50–51.

6. For instance, at Mosiah 7:19–20 and Alma 36:28–29.

7. Jacob 7:26.

8. Szink, "To a Land of Promise," 71, emphasis in original.

9. This is the argument of Bruce J. Boehm, "Wanderers in the Promised Land: A Study of the Exodus Motif in the Book of Mormon and Holy Bible," *Journal of Book of Mormon Studies* 3/1 (spring 1994): 187–203.

10. Alma 13:23.

11. David Daube, *The Exodus Pattern in the Bible* (London: Faber and Faber, 1963), 14.

12. For a helpful exploration of this theme in the Book of Mormon, see Louis Midgley, "The Ways of Remembrance," in *Rediscovering the Book of Mormon,* ed. Sorenson and Thorne, 168–76; and Louis Midgley, "'To Remember and Keep': On the Book of Mormon as an Ancient Book," in *The Disciple as Scholar: Essays on Scripture and the Ancient World in Honor of Richard Lloyd Anderson,* ed. Stephen D. Ricks, Donald W.

Parry, and Andrew H. Hedges (Provo, Utah: FARMS, 2000), 95–137.

13. See George S. Tate, "The Typology of the Exodus Pattern in the Book of Mormon," in *Literature of Belief,* ed. Lambert, 245–62. On pages 258–59, Tate offers a helpful chart of exodus motifs recurring in the Old and New Testaments and the Book of Mormon. For another chart comparing Lehi's journey from Jerusalem to the land of promise with the exodus of the children of Israel out of Egypt, see John W. Welch and J. Gregory Welch, *Charting the Book of Mormon: Visual Aids for Personal Study and Teaching* (Provo, Utah: FARMS, 1999), chart 91.

14. See Mark J. Johnson, "The Exodus of Lehi Revisited," *Journal of Book of Mormon Studies* 3/2 (1994): 123–26, reprinted in *Pressing Forward with the Book of Mormon,* ed. John W. Welch and Melvin J. Thorne (Provo, Utah: FARMS, 1999), 54–58.

15. S. Kent Brown, "The Exodus Pattern in the Book of Mormon," in his *From Jerusalem to Zarahemla: Literary and Historical Studies of the Book of Mormon* (Provo, Utah: BYU Religious Studies Center, 1998), 75–98. This is a revised version of an article originally published under the same title in *BYU Studies* 30/3 (summer 1990): 111–26.

16. James Plastaras, *The God of Exodus: The Theology of the Exodus Narratives* (Milwaukee: Bruce Publishing, 1966), 7.

17. Brown, "Exodus Pattern," 89.

18. Lavina Fielding Anderson, ed., *Lucy's Book: A Critical Edition of Lucy Mack Smith's Family Memoir* (Salt Lake City: Signature Books, 2001), 344.

19. A notable example illustrating Joseph's lack of intimate familiarity with the Bible during the production of the English Book of Mormon is briefly given in Daniel C. Peterson, "What the Manuscripts and the Eyewitnesses Tell Us about the Translation of the Book of Mormon," in *Uncovering the Original Text of the Book of Mormon: History and Findings of the Critical Text*

Project, ed. M. Gerald Bradford and Alison V. P. Coutts (Provo, Utah: FARMS, 2002), 67–71. On the other hand, the Finnish Lutheran scholar Heikki Räisänen contends that Joseph's reading of the Bible in the years immediately following publication of the Book of Mormon was acutely perceptive (although, from Räisänen's perspective, ultimately mistaken). See Räisänen's "Joseph Smith und die Bibel: Die Leistung des mormonischen Propheten in neuer Beleuchtung," *Theologische Literaturzeitung* 109 (1984): 81–92.

20. Anderson, *Lucy's Book,* 344.

21. See Erich Robert Paul, "Joseph Smith and the Manchester (New York) Library," *BYU Studies* 22/3 (1982): 333–56; also Erich Robert Paul, *Science, Religion, and Mormon Cosmology* (Urbana: University of Illinois, 1992), 83.

22. See Daniel C. Peterson, "The Gadianton Robbers as Guerrilla Warriors," in *Warfare in the Book of Mormon,* ed. Stephen D. Ricks and William J. Hamblin (Salt Lake City: Deseret Book and FARMS, 1990), 146–73.

23. For discussions of this topic, see Hugh Nibley, *Since Cumorah,* 2nd ed. (Salt Lake City: Deseret Book and FARMS, 1988), 231–38; Bart J. Kowallis, "In the Thirty and Fourth Year: A Geologist's View of the Great Destruction in 3 Nephi," *BYU Studies* 37/3 (1997–98): 136–90; Benjamin R. Jordan, "'Many Great and Notable Cities Were Sunk': Liquefaction in the Book of Mormon," *BYU Studies* 38/3 (1999): 115–18; Russell H. Ball, "An Hypothesis concerning the Three Days of Darkness among the Nephites," *Journal of Book of Mormon Studies* 2/1 (spring 1993): 107–23; and John Gee, "Another Note on the Three Days of Darkness," in *Pressing Forward with the Book of Mormon,* ed., Welch and Thorne, 219–27 (originally published in *Journal of Book of Mormon* Studies 6/2 [1997]: 235–44).

24. See the essays in Stephen D. Ricks and John W. Welch, eds., *The Allegory of the Olive Tree: The Olive, the Bible, and Jacob 5* (Salt Lake City: Deseret Book and FARMS, 1994).

25. 1 Nephi 13:12.

26. A good treatment of this subject is Arnold K. Garr, *Christopher Columbus: A Latter-day Saint Perspective* (Provo, Utah: BYU Religious Studies Center, 1992). Prof. Garr's book is reviewed and summarized by Daniel C. Peterson, "Christ-Bearer," in *FARMS Review of Books* 8/1 (1996): 104–11. See also Pauline Watts, "Prophecy and Discovery: On the Spiritual Origins of Christopher Columbus's 'Enterprise of the Indies,'" *American Historical Review* (February 1985): 73–02, of which a brief summary appears in *Reexploring the Book of Mormon,* ed. John W. Welch (Salt Lake City: Deseret Book and FARMS, 1992), 32–35.

27. Delno C. West and August Kling, *The "Libro de las profecías" of Christopher Columbus* (Gainesville: University of Florida Press, 1991), 107.

28. Ibid., 111.

29. Ibid., 105.

30. Cited in Kay Brigham, *Christopher Columbus: His Life and Discovery in the Light of His Prophecies* (Barcelona: CLIE, 1990), 50 (or 57 n).

31. I quote Heikki Räisänen, *Marcion, Muhammad and the Mahatma: Exegetical Perspectives on the Encounter of Cultures and Faiths* (London: SCM Press, 1997), 153, but any number of other authors, of varying degrees of competence and sympathy, could have been cited to the same effect.

32. For more detailed treatment, see especially Richard Lloyd Anderson, *Investigating the Book of Mormon Witnesses* (Salt Lake City: Deseret Book, 1981); and Lyndon W. Cook, ed., *David Whitmer Interviews: A Restoration Witness* (Orem, Utah: Grandin Book, 1991). Eldin Ricks, *The Case of the Book of Mormon Witnesses* (Salt Lake City: Olympus, 1961); Milton V. Backman Jr., *Eyewitness Accounts of the Restoration* (Orem: Grandin Book, 1983), republished in 1986 by Deseret Book; and Rhett Stephens James, *The Man Who Knew: The Early Years* (Cache Valley, Utah: Martin Harris Pageant Committee, 1983), are also worthwhile.

Even those seeking to dismiss the testimony of the witnesses now often find themselves obliged to concede the witnesses' honesty and sincerity. A good example of this is Dan Vogel, "The Validity of the Witnesses' Testimonies," in *American Apocrypha: Essays on the Book of Mormon,* ed. Dan Vogel and Brent Lee Metcalfe (Salt Lake City: Signature Books, 2002), 79–121, which, although attempting to defeat the testimonies of the witnesses by claiming that they rest on nothing more than hallucinations (induced by some *ad hoc* combination or other of morbid psychological obsession, religious fanaticism, excitability, low blood sugar, hypnosis, and, if those notions somehow fail to convince, a stage-prop box and some bogus tin plates), concedes the character issue.

33. Cited in Cook, ed., *David Whitmer Interviews,* 224.

34. Interview with Orson Pratt and Joseph F. Smith (Richmond, Missouri, 7–8 September 1878), reported in a letter to President John Taylor and the Quorum of the Twelve dated 17 September 1878. Originally published in the *Deseret News* (16 November 1878) and reprinted in Cook, ed., *David Whitmer Interviews,* 40.

35. Interview with Joseph Smith III et al. (Richmond, Missouri, July 1884), originally published in *The Saints' Herald* (28 January 1936) and reprinted in Cook, ed., *David Whitmer Interviews,* 134–35, emphasis in the original.

36. Susan Easton Black, ed., *Stories from the Early Saints: Converted by the Book of Mormon* (Salt Lake City: Bookcraft, 1992), 96.

37. See, for example, Donna Hill, *Joseph Smith: The First Mormon* (Garden City, N.Y.: Doubleday, 1977), 402.

38. See F. Mark McKiernan and Roger D. Launius, eds., *An Early Latter Day Saint History: The Book of John Whitmer Kept by Commandment* (Independence, Mo.: Herald Publishing House, 1980), 20.

39. Cited by Anderson, *Investigating the Book of Mormon Witnesses,* 131, from memoranda written by Theodore Turley and dated 4 April 1839.

40. The quoted phrase comes from Anderson, *Investigating the Book of Mormon Witnesses*, 132.

41. Journal of Jacob Gates for 18 March 1861, as cited in Anderson, *Investigating the Book of Mormon Witnesses*, 131.

42. Letter of John Whitmer to Mark Forscutt, dated 5 March 1876, cited in Richard L. Anderson, "Personal Writings of the Book of Mormon Witnesses," in *Book of Mormon Authorship Revisited: The Evidence for Ancient Origins*, ed. Noel B. Reynolds (Provo, Utah: FARMS, 1997), 55–56.

43. Anderson, *Investigating the Book of Mormon Witnesses*, 24.

44. Cited in ibid., 107–8.

45. Anderson, *Lucy's Book*, 379.

46. Ibid., 390.

47. Cited by Black, *Stories from the Early Saints*, 91–92.

48. See Paul Y. Hoskisson, "Alma as a Hebrew Name," *Journal of Book of Mormon Studies* 7/1 (1998): 72–73; Terrence L. Szink, "Further Evidence of a Semitic Alma," *Journal of Book of Mormon Studies* 8/1 (1999): 70; and Terrence L. Szink, "The Personal Name 'Alma' at Ebla," *The Religious Educator* 1/1 (2000): 53–56.

49. For the original text and a translation of 4Qapocryphon of Jeremiah C (4Q385b [4QapocrJer C]), see Robert Eisenman and Michael Wise, *The Dead Sea Scrolls Uncovered* (Shaftesbury, England: Element, 1992), 57–58. Florentino García Martínez, in *The Dead Sea Scrolls Translated: The Qumran Texts in English*, trans. Wilfred G. E. Watson (Leiden: E. J. Brill, 1994), 285, inadequately renders the Hebrew.

50. See Daniel C. Peterson, William J. Hamblin, and Matthew Roper, "On Alma 7:10 and the Birthplace of Jesus Christ" (Provo, Utah: FARMS, 1995); John A. Tvedtnes, "Cities and Lands in the Book of Mormon," *Journal of Book of Mormon Studies* 4/2 (1995): 147–50 [= Welch and Thorne, eds., *Pressing Forward with the Book of Mormon*, 164–68]; Robert F. Smith, "The Land of Jerusalem: The Place of Jesus' Birth," in *Reexploring the Book of Mormon*, ed. Welch 170–72; and Welch and Thorne, eds., *Pressing Forward with the Book of Mormon*, 139–41.

51. The relevant passage in the Book of Mormon is 1 Nephi 1. See John W. Welch, "The Calling of a Prophet," in *The Book of Mormon: First Nephi, The Doctrinal Foundation,* ed. Monte S. Nyman and Charles D. Tate Jr. (Provo, Utah: BYU Religious Studies Center, 1988), 35–54; Blake Thomas Ostler, "The Throne-Theophany and Prophetic Commission in 1 Nephi: A Form-Critical Analysis," *BYU Studies* 26/4 (1986): 67–95; Welch, ed., *Reexploring the Book of Mormon,* 24–28; compare Daniel C. Peterson and Stephen D. Ricks, "The Throne-Theophany/Prophetic Call of Muhammad," in *The Disciple as Scholar: Essays on Scripture and the Ancient World in Honor of Richard Lloyd Anderson,* ed. Stephen D. Ricks, Donald W. Parry, and Andrew H. Hedges (Provo, Utah: FARMS, 2000), 323–37; and Daniel C. Peterson, "'Ye are Gods': Psalm 82 and John 10 as Witnesses to the Divine Nature of Humankind," in *The Disciple as Scholar,* ed. Ricks, Parry, and Hedges, 471–594.

52. 1 Nephi 1:8.

53. Amos 3:7. See Raymond E. Brown, "The Pre-Christian Semitic Concept of 'Mystery,'" *Catholic Biblical Quarterly* 20 (1958): 417–43; and Welch, ed., *Reexploring the Book of Mormon,* 24–25.

54. On this, see the short article by Royal Skousen entitled "Hebraic Conditionals in the Book of Mormon," in *Pressing Forward with the Book of Mormon,* ed. Welch and Thorne, 201–3.

55. This, of course, is yet another conditional sentence.

56. Royal Skousen, ed., *The Printer's Manuscript of the Book of Mormon: Typographical Facsimile of the Entire Text in Two Parts* (Provo, Utah: FARMS, 2001), 2:760, emphasis added, spelling and punctuation regularized.

57. Moroni 10:4, as given in Skousen, *The Printer's Manuscript of the Book of Mormon,* 2:973–74, emphasis added, spelling and punctuation regularized.

58. In the Hebrew of the book of Genesis alone, the *if-and* conditional construction occurs at 18:26; 24:8, 41; 28:20–21; 31:8 (twice); 34:17 (twice); 44:26; and 47:6.

59. 1 Nephi 11:8–11.

60. 1 Nephi 11:12–21.

61. 1 Nephi 11:21.

62. 1 Nephi 11:22–23.

63. Not necessarily in every sense. At 1 Nephi 11:25, Nephi himself declares that he "beheld that the tree of life was a representation of the love of God." (In Hosea 14:8, God compares *himself* to a tree.) Metaphor, as opposed to allegory, is open to multiple (and therefore multivalently rich) meaning. The tree may well represent the love of God while, at the same time, it might have represented the virgin mother of God to an ancient resident of Jerusalem. The two are not mutually exclusive.

64. For a much more complete presentation of analysis and evidence on this subject, see Daniel C. Peterson, "Nephi and His Asherah: A Note on 1 Nephi 11:8–23," in *Mormons, Scripture, and the Ancient World: Studies in Honor of John L. Sorenson*, ed. Davis Bitton (Provo, Utah: FARMS, 1998), 191–243. A greatly condensed version of the same article is Daniel C. Peterson, "Nephi and His Asherah," *Journal of Book of Mormon Studies* 9/2 (2000): 15–25, 80–81.

65. See J. Glen Taylor, "The Two Earliest Known Representations of Yahweh," in *Ascribe to the Lord: Biblical and Other Studies in Memory of Peter C. Craigie*, ed. Lyle Eslinger and Glen Taylor, Journal for the Study of the Old Testament Supplement Series 67 (Sheffield, England: JSOT Press, 1988), 558–60, 565 n. 19; and J. Glen Taylor, *Yahweh and the Sun: Biblical and Archaeological Evidence for Sun Worship in Ancient Israel* (Sheffield, England: JSOT Press, 1993), 29.

66. Steve A. Wiggins, "The Myth of Asherah: Lion Lady and Serpent Goddess," *Ugarit-Forschungen: Internationales Jahrbuch für die Altertumskunde Syrien-Palästinas* 23 (1991): 383, with references to the relevant literature.

67. See John Day, "Asherah in the Hebrew Bible and Northwest Semitic Literature," *Journal of Biblical Literature* 105/3 (1986), 397–98, 401–4 and references supplied there.

68. See Leon Yarden, *The Tree of Light: A Study of the Menorah, the Seven-Branched Lampstand* (Uppsala, Sweden: Skriv Service AB, 1972), 44–47, 103–6.

69. See Saul M. Olyan, *Asherah and the Cult of Yahweh in Israel* (Atlanta: Scholars Press, 1988), 56–61, 65–67.

Ancient Texts in Support of the Book of Mormon

John A. Tvedtnes

In recent years it has become more and more clear that elements of the Book of Mormon account have ancient precedents. Some of these elements are attested in ancient texts that were unknown in Joseph Smith's day and could therefore not have been known to him. Typically, these texts are traditional tales passed down from one generation to another until they were written down or are based on now-lost earlier writings. Critics might argue that these are not historical records and therefore cannot be used in support of the Book of Mormon. But this fails to answer how the Book of Mormon came to include so many of the elements known in these texts.

This essay examines some of these elements, describing their sources and how they can help us appreciate the antiquity and historicity of the Book of Mormon account.

Hidden Texts

OTHER
HIDDEN
RECORDS

Joseph Smith said he found the plates from which he translated the Book of Mormon hidden in a stone box buried in the ground and covered by another large stone (see Joseph Smith—History 1:51–52). Though the claim seemed incredible to critics of the day, such discoveries are now considered almost commonplace. In 1945 several leather-bound volumes of gnostic Christian writings from the fifth century A.D. were found at Chenoboskion, Egypt, also known as Nag Hammadi. Their contents included books purportedly composed by some of the early apostles. Like the Book of Mormon, these books had been hidden away in the ground (though they were buried in a large pottery jar instead of a stone box).

Two years later a larger set of documents was found concealed in caves near the Dead Sea. Some of them had been placed inside fired clay pots. In all, fragments of approximately eight hundred separate scrolls were found. These Dead Sea Scrolls included multiple copies of all of the books of the Old Testament except Esther, along with many other ancient religious texts. The scrolls had been written two thousand years ago. The text of one scroll, inscribed on a long copper plate that had been rolled up, described where other books and various treasuries had been hidden.

Over the last few years, I have found dozens of stories of ancient records hidden away for future discovery and have recently published a book on the subject.[1] H. Curtis Wright has noted that the burial of metallic records in stone boxes was common in ancient times, particularly in the ancient Near East, where Lehi lived.[2] In addition, hundreds of other metallic records have been found in other circumstances.³ Moreover, a number of ancient texts speak about records kept on metallic plates. These sources include 1 *Maccabees* 8:22, the *Cologne Mani Codex*,⁴ the *Apocalypse of Enosh* (cited in the *Cologne Mani Codex*),⁵ and the accounts of the eleventh-century Arab historian al-Thaʿlabī⁶ and the thirteenth-century Arab historian Idrīsī.⁷ With hundreds of examples of ancient texts hidden away for future discovery and hundreds more written on metallic plates, many of them buried in stone boxes, it seems clear that the story of the Book of Mormon has abundant precedent in documents of its time and earlier.

Semitic Texts Written in Egyptian Script

Moroni noted that, while his people still used the Hebrew language, Mormon's abridgment of their records had been written in "reformed Egyptian" (see Mormon 9:32–33). Nephi, whose writings became the pattern for the records constituting the Book of Mormon, wrote: "Yea, I make a record in the language of my father, which consists of the learning of the Jews and the language of the Egyptians. And I know that the record which I make is true; and I make it with mine own hand; and I make it according to my knowledge" (1 Nephi 1:2–3).

REFORMED EGYPTIAN

It was not until the twentieth century that ancient Hebrew texts written in Egyptian script became known to scholars. We now have a number of Northwest Semitic texts (Hebrew or related to Hebrew) in Egyptian magical papyri. These are mostly incantations that, instead of being translated, were merely transcribed in hieratic, a cursive or reformed version of the hieroglyphic characters most people think of as Egyptian writing. The underlying language, however, is an early form of Hebrew/Canaanite.⁸ The texts are found on the London Magical Papyrus (fourteenth century B.C.),[9] the Harris Magical Papyrus (thirteenth century B.C.),[10] Papyrus Anastasi I (thirteenth century B.C.),[11] and Ostracon 25759 recto (eleventh century B.C.).[12] The latter is interesting because the text on one side is purely Egyptian hieratic, while the text on the other is an early form of Hebrew written in hieratic characters. All of these documents were discovered and translated long after the Book of Mormon was published.

Of particular interest is Amherst Papyrus 63, a document of the fourth century B.C. written in a cursive (reformed) Egyptian script called demotic but whose underlying language is Aramaic, a sister language to Hebrew.[13] Among the writings included in the religious text is a version of Psalm 20:2–6.[14]

An ostracon uncovered at the ancient Judean site of Arad in 1967 and dating to the time of Lehi has a text that, although written in a combination of ten Egyptian hieratic and seven Hebrew characters, can be read entirely as Egyptian.[15] Other texts of the same time period that commingle Hebrew and Egyptian scripts were discovered during archaeological excavations at Tel Ein-Qudeirah (biblical Kadesh-Barnea), in the Sinai Peninsula near the border of ancient Judah, during the latter half of the 1970s.[16]

To most of Joseph Smith's contemporaries, the term *reformed Egyptian* seemed to be so much nonsense. Alexander Campbell, who wrote the first book critical of the Book of Mormon, scoffed at the fact that it had been translated "from the reformed Egyptian!!!"[17] Many critics still suggest, despite long-standing evidence to the contrary, that there is no such thing as "reformed Egyptian" and insist that no ancient Israelite would have written sacred scripture using Egyptian. We now know the opposite to be true.

The Oldest Bible Texts Fit the Book of Mormon Pattern

It is interesting that the earliest extant manuscripts containing biblical text fit the same pattern as the Book of Mormon. One of these manuscripts was written on small metal scrolls, another was written in a reformed Egyptian script, and a set of biblical manuscripts was concealed for future recovery.[18]

OLD BIBLE TEXTS

The earliest known manuscripts containing biblical text were found in 1980 in a tomb in Jerusalem. Dating from the end of the seventh century B.C. (the time of Lehi), they consisted of two rolled-up silver leaves inscribed with the priestly blessing found in Numbers 6:24–26.[19]

The second oldest known manuscript citing a Bible text is the fourth-century B.C. Amherst Papyrus 63, discussed earlier, which includes a quote of Psalm 20:2–6. Though the language of the text is Aramaic (a close relative of Hebrew that the Jews had adopted after the fall of Jerusalem in 587 B.C.), it is not written in the Aramaic alphabet but in Egyptian demotic script, a type of cursive or reformed Egyptian.

Third in age among known Bible manuscripts are the Dead Sea Scrolls, discovered between the years 1947 and 1956. The oldest of these, a copy of the book of Exodus (denominated 4Q17) discovered in 1948, was written in the middle of the third century B.C. Like the Book of Mormon, the Dead Sea Scrolls were concealed in the earth to come forth at a later time.

The fact that the three earliest known manuscripts with Bible text are, respectively, written on metallic plates, written in a reformed Egyptian script reflecting an underlying Semitic language, and hidden away for future discovery demonstrates that the Book of Mormon fits an ancient pattern.

Joseph's Garment

Joseph's Rent Garment

In Alma 46 we read that the Nephite chief captain Moroni tore out a piece of his garment, wrote a motto on it, and mounted it as a standard to rally his troops. Soldiers dressed in their armor ran to him, "rending their garments . . . as a covenant" that if they should forsake God, "the Lord should rend them even as they had rent their garments" (Alma 46:21). They then "cast their [rent] garments at the feet of Moroni" as a sign that if they should "fall into transgression," God might "cast us at the feet of our enemies, even as we have cast our garments at thy feet to be trodden under foot" (Alma 46:22).

Taking his cue from this act, Moroni then exhorted his people, referring to them as "a remnant of the seed of Joseph, *whose coat was rent by his brethren into many pieces*" and citing the words of Joseph's father, Jacob, who, "before his death . . . saw that a part of the remnant of the coat of Joseph was preserved and had not decayed. And he said—Even as this remnant of garment of my son hath been preserved, so shall a remnant of the seed of my son be preserved by the hand of God, and be taken unto himself" (Alma 46:23, 24).

The biblical account in Genesis 37 indicates that Joseph's brothers stripped him of his garment and later dipped it in goat's blood to make it appear that he had been slain by a wild beast (see Genesis 37:23, 31). It does not say that they tore the garment, though Jacob, upon seeing it, said that Joseph had been "rent in pieces" by some wild beast (Genesis 37:33).

Aside from Alma 46:23, the only document I know of that clearly indicates that the brothers tore Joseph's garment is the thirteenth-century collection of earlier Jewish stories known as the *Book of Jasher:* "And they hastened and took Joseph's coat and tore it, and they killed a kid of the goats and dipped the coat into the blood of the kid, and then trampled it in the dust, and they sent the coat to their father Jacob" (*Jasher* 43:13). One cannot fail to note the parallel with Moroni's soldiers, who cast their garments down "to be trodden under foot" (Alma 46:22). Since the *Book of Jasher* did not come to Joseph Smith's attention until it was published in English in 1840, it seems that this medieval Jewish document shares an ancient tradition also found in the Book of Mormon.

The preservation of Joseph's garment is noted in the *Zênâhu La-Yosêf,* an Ethiopic manuscript from the Dabra Bizon monastery, in which Benjamin, eating with the Egyptian official he did not yet know to be his brother Joseph, told him of his lost brother and of his father Jacob's mourning: "He looks at his [Joseph's] garment stained in his blood. He puts it in front of him, and soaks it every day with the tears of his eyes."[20] According to a Muslim tradition reported by al-Kisaʾi, Jacob, before sending his sons to Egypt for the second time, gave "Joseph's shirt to Benjamin to wear, the one that had been brought to him spattered with blood."[21]

According to Alma 46:24, it was the preservation of a remnant of Joseph's garment that led Jacob to exclaim, " . . . so shall a remnant of the seed of my son be preserved by the hand of God." A similar story is found in early

238 • Echoes and Evidences of the Book of Mormon

Jewish and Muslim traditions, which vary in that it was a second garment, brought to Joseph by the angel Gabriel, that gave Jacob to know that Joseph had been preserved.²² According to al-Kisaʾi, after revealing his identity to his brethren, Joseph "took off the shirt that God had given him in the well and gave it to Judah, saying, 'Depart ye with this my inner garment, and throw it on my father's face; and he shall recover his sight.'"²³ When Judah was yet ten days' distance from his father's camp, Jacob declared, "I perceive the smell of Joseph" and knew that his son was yet alive.²⁴ ʿAl-Ṭabarî's account also includes the tale of Joseph's sending his garment to heal his father's blindness and of Jacob's smelling "the scent of Joseph" before Judah arrived.²⁵

With so many details of the story told in Alma 46 reflected in early Jewish and Muslim texts, the suggestion that the Book of Mormon account reflects an ancient tradition seems inescapable.

Joseph's Prophecy

PROPHECY
BY JOSEPH
OF OLD

According to 2 Nephi 3:5–15, the Old Testament patriarch Joseph foresaw that the Lord would raise up a man named Moses to deliver the Israelites from Egyptian bondage. This great prophecy is also found in the Joseph Smith Translation of Genesis 50:24–38, which contains the words uttered by Joseph on his deathbed. This translation adds, in Genesis 50:35, that Joseph also prophesied of Aaron as Moses' companion, saying, "And I will make a spokesman for him, and his name shall be called Aaron."

The antiquity of the story is confirmed in Jewish tradition, notably in one of the second-century A.D. *targumim*, or translations of the Bible into Aramaic.²⁶ In a lengthy addition to Genesis 40:12, *Targum Neofiti* has Joseph interpreting the three branches of the butler's dream as follows: "The three branches are the three fathers of the world: namely; Abraham, Isaac, and Jacob, the sons of whose sons are to be enslaved in the slavery of the land of Egypt and are to be delivered by the hands of three faithful leaders: Moses, Aaron, and Miriam, who are to be likened to the clusters of grapes."[27] Similarly, the Talmud has Rabbi Eleazar explaining that "the 'vine' is the world, the 'three branches' are [the patriarchs] Abraham, Isaac and Jacob," with Rabbi Joshua correcting him by saying, "The 'vine' is the Torah, the 'three branches' are Moses, Aaron and Miriam" (TB *Hillun* 92a).

From the standard account in Genesis 50:24–25, it is clear that Joseph was aware that the Israelites would someday leave Egypt, though he says nothing about the bondage they would endure in the meanwhile. But *Pirqe de Rabbi Eliezer* 48 (attributed to Rabbi Eliezer ben Hyrqanos, who lived in the latter half of the first century A.D. through the first decades of the second century), citing the Genesis passage, has Joseph prophesying the bondage of the Israelites and their deliverance by God. The second-century A.D. *Targum Pseudo-Jonathan* on Genesis 50:24 has Joseph telling his family, "Behold you will be enslaved in Egypt, but do not make plans to go up out of Egypt until the time that two deliverers come and say to you, 'The Lord surely remembers you.'"[28] This suggests that he knew about the coming of Moses and Aaron to liberate Israel and confirms the accuracy of Joseph Smith's addition to that verse and the one that follows.

In this case, we have confirmation from early Jewish texts not only for the Book of Mormon account of Joseph's prophecy but also for the account of that prophecy found in Joseph Smith's revision of Genesis 50.

Abinadi's Interpretation of Isaiah 52–53

ABINADI ON ISAIAH 52–53

A century before Lehi left Jerusalem, the prophet Isaiah prophesied, "How beautiful upon the mountains are the feet of him that bringeth good tidings, that publisheth peace; that bringeth good tidings of good, that publisheth salvation; that saith unto Zion, Thy God reigneth!" (Isaiah 52:7). The Book of Mormon prophet Abinadi explained that the passage referred to "all the holy prophets . . . who have published peace, who have brought good tidings of good, who have published salvation; and said unto Zion: Thy God reigneth! And O how beautiful upon the mountains were their feet!" (Mosiah 15:13–15). He added, "O how beautiful upon the mountains are the feet of him that bringeth good tidings, that is the founder of peace, yea, even the Lord, who has redeemed his people; yea, him who has granted salvation unto his people" (v. 18).

Abinadi saw in Isaiah's prophecy reference to both the Lord, who redeems his people, and the prophets he sends to preach salvation and peace. This interpretation is strikingly similar to the one found in one of the Dead Sea Scrolls, 11QMelchizedek (also known as 11Q13), which cites the Isaiah passage, then explains that "the mountains are the pro[phets . . .] And the messenger is [the ano]inted of the spirit about whom Dan[iel] spoke [. . . and the messenger of] good who announces salv[ation is the one about whom it is written that] he will send him 'to comfo[rt the afflicted, to watch over the afflicted ones of Zion']."29 The Hebrew term rendered "anointed" here is *mašiaḥ,* Messiah. The interpretation of the Isaiah passage in the scroll agrees with Abinadi's teachings in mentioning both the Messiah and the prophets. But while both documents compare the messenger to the Messiah, the Jewish text differs by associating the prophets with the mountains. Similarly, a number of other early Jewish texts compare the patriarchs and their wives to mountains.[30] One text, *Midrash Tanhuma,* suggests that the mountain mentioned in Zechariah 4:7 is the Messiah.

Abinadi further explained that the "generation" and "seed" of the Messiah mentioned in Isaiah 53:8, 10 consisted of the prophets who had foreseen the advent of Christ to the earth (see Mosiah 15:10–13). This interpretation is also found in a thirteenth-century Ethiopian Christian document unavailable in English until 1935, more than a century after the Book of Mormon was first published. Commenting on the placing of vegetation on the earth as described in Genesis 1:11–12, the *Book of the Mysteries of the Heavens and the Earth* says that "the trees are symbols of the Apostles, and must be so interpreted. And the green herbs are the symbols of the children of the Apostles, and the children of the Apostles are those who have believed through their hands. And the seed are those servants who have sown seed on the face of the earth. The words 'each kind of seed' refer to their various companies, and to their various preachings." The apostles, like the prophets before them, taught of Christ, and those who accepted their testimony are here called their "seed."[31]

That the first-century B.C. Nephite prophet Abinadi should interpret these Isaiah passages in the same way as early Jewish and Christian texts that were unknown when the Book of Mormon was published suggests that the story is authentic and draws on early traditions.

Foreknowledge of Christ's Advent

Prophecies of Christ

Book of Mormon prophets often spoke of Jesus Christ long before his birth and referred to him as "that which is to come."³² Lehi and his sons Nephi and Jacob knew of Christ's name and title, his baptism by John, his teachings, his selection of twelve apostles, his miraculous healings and casting out of devils, and his death on the cross (see 1 Nephi 10:7–10; 11:27–33; 2 Nephi 10:3; 25:19). Alma knew the name of Christ's mother, Mary, and of Christ's sufferings and death (see Alma 7:10–12). King Benjamin also knew the name of Christ's mother, along with other details of the Savior's life, such as the kinds of miracles he would perform, his temptation and suffering, his crucifixion, and his resurrection after three days (see Mosiah 3:5–10). Samuel the Lamanite spoke of the heavenly signs that would accompany the birth and death of the Savior (see Helaman 14:3–6, 20–27).

Equally significant is that the Book of Mormon suggests that various Old World prophets also knew details of Christ's life long before he was born. Nephi noted that Zenock and Neum had written of the Messiah's crucifixion, while Zenos wrote of his burial and the three days of darkness that would be a sign of his death (see 1 Nephi 19:10). A later Nephi, son of Helaman, declared that "many prophets" of old had testified of Christ, including Moses, Abraham, Zenock, Ezias, Isaiah, Jeremiah, and "all the holy prophets" between the time of Abraham and the time of Moses (see Helaman 8:13–20).

Critics of the Book of Mormon claim that such details of Christ's life could not have been known before he was born. But early Christians readily accepted the idea. Ignatius, bishop of Antioch (died A.D. 107), wrote to the Magnesians: "The divinest prophets lived according to Christ Jesus. On this account also they were persecuted, being inspired by His grace to fully convince the unbelieving that there is one God, who has manifested Himself by Jesus Christ His Son."³³ The *Epistle of Barnabas,* which was widely read in Christian congregations of the second century A.D., indicates in its twelfth chapter that Moses knew that the Messiah would be called Jesus.

Chapter 32 of the *Book of the Bee,* a thirteenth-century text first published fifty-six years after the Book of Mormon, preserves a number of early Christian traditions about prophecies of Christ uttered by various Old Testament prophets. According to the account, the prophet Hosea "prophesied mystically about our Lord Jesus Christ who was to come; saying that when He should be born, the oak in Shiloh should be divided into twelve parts; and that He should take twelve disciples of Israel."³⁴ The prophet Nahum "prophesied that when the Messiah should be slain, the vail of the temple should be rent in twain, and that the Holy Spirit should depart from it."³⁵ The prophet Habakkuk "prophesied concerning the Messiah, that He should come, and abrogate the laws of the Jews."³⁶ The prophet Zephaniah "prophesied concerning the Messiah, that He should suffer, and that the sun should become dark, and the moon be hidden."³⁷ The prophecy in this document attributed to Nahum was attributed by the fourth-century Christian Father Epiphanius to Habakkuk. The fact that Epiphanius predated the writing of the *Book of the Bee* by nine centuries demonstrates the antiquity of the stories recounted in it.³⁸

Nephi, the son of Helaman, specifically noted that the Old Testament prophet Jeremiah had foretold the coming of Christ (see Helaman 8:20).³⁹ Two second-century church fathers, Justin Martyr and Irenaeus, writing of Christ's preaching to the dead while his body lay in the tomb, attributed to Jeremiah a prophecy (one not found in the biblical account) in which the prophet wrote that the Lord would descend to preach salvation to the dead. In *Dialogue with Trypho* 72, Justin Martyr wrote, "And again, from the sayings of the same Jeremiah these have been cut out [by the Jews]: 'The Lord God remembered His dead people of Israel who lay in the graves; and He descended to preach to them His own salvation.'"[40] Irenaeus cited the same passage in *Against Heresies* 4.22.[41]

The *Book of the Bee* also preserves an earlier tradition of another nonbiblical prophecy of Jeremiah, declaring that "this (prophet) during his life said to the Egyptians, 'a child shall be born—that is the Messiah—of a virgin, and He shall be laid in a crib, and He will shake and cast down the idols.' From that time and until Christ was born, the Egyptians used to set a virgin and a baby in a crib, and to worship him, because of what Jeremiah said to them, that He should be born in a crib."[42] The story is drawn from *The Lives of the Prophets* 2:8–10, a text that a number of scholars have suggested was originally written in Hebrew by Egyptian Jews during the lifetime of Jesus himself.[43] The text was not published in any Western languages until nearly eighty years after the Book of Mormon first appeared.

Another Christian document known from medieval manuscripts in various languages is *4 Baruch*, which is subtitled "The Things Omitted from Jeremiah the Prophet." The Ethiopic version attributes the book to Jeremiah's scribe Baruch, but the Greek says it was written by Jeremiah. Chapter 9 has Jeremiah prophesying of the coming of Jesus Christ, the Son of God; of his selection of twelve apostles; of his death and resurrection after three days; and of his return in glory to the Mount of Olives. According to the account, Jeremiah was stoned for this declaration.[44]

The New Testament suggests in passing that Abraham knew of Christ's coming (see John 8:56; Galatians 3:8), though the Old Testament story of Abraham itself does not demonstrate this. The Book of Mormon prophet Jacob noted that Abraham's offering of Isaac was "a similitude of God and his Only Begotten Son" (Jacob 4:5)—something that is confirmed in several early Christian sources, such as *Epistle of Barnabas* 7:3; Irenaeus, *Against Heresies* 4.4, 5; and Augustine, *City of God* 16.32.

But foreshadowing is not the same as outright prophecy or revelation. From the Book of Abraham that Joseph Smith restored, we learn that the ancient patriarch actually saw Christ in the premortal council (see Abraham 3:22–28). This kind of intimate knowledge of the Savior on the part of Abraham is suggested in a centuries-old Ethiopic text that derives from a Coptic text dated by the translator to the sixth century but not published until 1922. In *Kebra Nagast* 14, we read: "And God held converse with Abram, and He said unto him, 'Fear thou not. From this day thou art My servant, and I will establish My Covenant with thee and with thy seed after thee . . . and afterwards I will send My Word for the salvation of Adam and his sons for ever.'"[45] Chapter 104 of the same work says, "And thou dost not understand that they were justified by faith—Abraham, and David and all the Prophets, one after the other, who prophesied concerning the coming of the Son of God. And Abraham said, 'Wilt Thou in my days, O Lord, cast Thy word upon the ground?' And God said unto him, 'By no means. His time hath not yet come, but I will shew thee a similitude of His coming.'" God then has Abraham meet with Melchizedek, who "gave him the mystery of the bread and wine, that same which is celebrated in our Passover for our salvation through our Lord Jesus Christ."[46]

From these early accounts, we see that the idea that details of the life of Christ were known by a number of prophets prior to his birth was common in early Christianity, as it is in the Book of Mormon.

The Jaredite Barges

Ancient Vessels

Ether 6:7 says that the Jaredite barges "were tight like unto the ark of Noah." This comparison with the vessel constructed by Noah enables us to draw several parallels between the two vessels, each of which had been constructed according to the Lord's instructions. In order to provide light inside the vessels during the ocean crossing, the brother of Jared prepared sixteen crystalline stones that the Lord touched, making them glow (see Ether 3:1–6; 6:2–3).[47] Similar stories are told of the ark of Noah.[48]

A number of early Jewish sources say that God had Noah suspend precious stones or pearls inside the ark to lighten it. The gems would glow during the night and dim during the day so Noah could tell the time of day and how many days had passed.[49] This was the explanation the rabbis gave for the ṣôhar that the Lord told Noah to construct in the ark. Though called a "window" in the King James version of Genesis 6:16, the ṣôhar is rendered "light" in some Bible translations."[50] In a medieval Arabic text we read that it was the pegs that Noah used to construct the ark that shone.[51]

The Book of Mormon speaks of "the mountain waves" and the "furious wind" that the Jaredites encountered during their ocean voyage to the New World, stressing that "the wind did never cease to blow towards the promised land while they were upon the waters" (see Ether 6:5–8; see also 2:24–25), reminding us of the experience of Noah during the great flood.[52]

An Ethiopic Christian text, *Conflict of Adam and Eve* III, 9:6–7, describes the flood of Noah in terms similar to those used to describe the great storm that blew the Jaredite barges to the New World, including the description of "waves . . . high like mountains," as in Ether 2:24 and 6:6.[53] The Book of Mormon indicates that the high waves resulted from intense winds from the Lord. Early Jewish and Christian traditions indicate that God sent strong winds to destroy the Tower of Babel, from which the Jaredites fled (see Ether 1:33). The story is found in the *Chronography . . . of Bar Hebraeus* 1, *Jubilees* 10:26, and *Sibylline Oracles* 3:101–107. Other texts (*Conflict of Adam and Eve* III, 24:8; *Book of the Rolls,* folio 120a; *Book of the Cave of Treasures,* folios 23b.2–24a.1; and *Book of the Bee* 23) have the wind, sometimes called a "wind-flood," destroying the idols erected by Nimrod, to whom both Jewish and Christian traditions attribute the building of the tower.

The existence of details such as the glowing stones and furious winds in both the Book of Mormon story of the Jaredites and other ancient traditions about Noah's flood and the great "wind-storm" suggests more than coincidence.

The Translation of Moses and John

The Book of Mormon indicates that the prophet Moses and the apostle John were both translated. Again, there is ancient textual support for these declarations that are not mentioned in the Bible.

Moses' and John's Translation

Alma 45:18–19 says that after the disappearance of Alma, some Nephites came to believe that he might have been taken in the same way "the Lord took Moses unto himself." That Moses was translated may be suggested in Doctrine and Covenants 84:25, where we read that the Lord "took Moses out of their midst." Only one text known in Joseph Smith's day suggested that Moses had not died. The first-century A.D. Jewish historian Flavius Josephus wrote that when Moses went atop a high mountain with "Eleazar and Joshua, and was still discoursing with them, a cloud stood over him on the sudden, and he disappeared in a certain valley, although he wrote in the holy books that he died, which was done out of fear, lest they should venture to say that, because of his extraordinary virtue, he went to God" (*Antiquities of the Jews* 4.8.48).[54] The story is confirmed in a fourth-century A.D. Samaritan document, *Tibat Marqa* (also called *Memar Marqa*) 269a, which says that "when he got to the top of the mountain, a cloud came down and lifted him up from the sight of all the congregation of Israel."[55]

A number of early Jewish texts unavailable to Joseph Smith confirm that Moses never died but was alive and serving God in heaven. Among these are the Talmud (TB *Sotah* 13b); *Midrash ha-Gadol, Zot habberakhah* 4:5; *Sifre* to Deuteronomy 357;[56] and *Midrash Leqah Tob*.[57] The medieval *Zohar* reflects the same tradition (*Zohar* Genesis 37b; Exodus 88b–89a, 174a; Leviticus 59a).

Some of the early Christian fathers also held that Moses had not died but had been taken by God. Among these are St. Ambrose (died A.D. 397) in his *On Cain and Abel* 1.2.8 and Cassiodorus (ca. A.D. 468–560) in his Latin translation of Clement of Alexandria, commenting on Jude 1:9.

We learn of the apostle John's translation in 3 Nephi 28:6–9, where Christ promises three of the Nephite disciples that they will not die and compares their situation to that of John. That John may have been spared death is merely hinted at in John 21:20–23, which cautions that while "this saying [went] abroad among the brethren, that that disciple should not die: yet Jesus said not unto him, He shall not die; but, If I will that he tarry till I come, what is that to thee?" A revelation given to Joseph Smith in April 1829 confirmed that John had, indeed, been translated (Doctrine and Covenants 7).⁵⁸

A fourth-century Christian document, the *Discourse on Abbatôn*, first published in 1914, confirms that John had been translated. The preface speaks of "the Holy Apostle Saint John, theologian and virgin, who is not to taste death until the thrones are set in the Valley of Jehoasaphat."⁵⁹ The text itself has the resurrected Jesus saying, "And as for thee, O My beloved John, thou shalt not die until the thrones have been prepared on the Day of the Resurrection. . . . I will command Abbaton, the Angel of Death, to come unto thee on that day. . . . Thou shalt be dead for three and a half hours, lying upon thy throne, and all creation shall see thee. I will make thy soul to return to thy body, and thou shalt rise up and array thyself in apparel of glory."⁶⁰

The Executions of Laban and Zemnarihah

John W. Welch and some of his students have discussed the executions of Laban and Zemnarihah in terms of Jewish law. In the case of Laban, they have noted the concepts of justifiable homicide and the slaying of one for the good of the many.⁶¹ Welch has briefly compared Nephi's killing of Laban (see 1 Nephi 4:10–23) with Moses'

LABAN'S AND
ZEMNARIHAH'S
EXECUTIONS

slaying of the Egyptian who had stricken a Hebrew slave. The following adds to that discussion a few further points found in ancient Jewish texts.[62]

Nephi wrote, "I was constrained by the Spirit that I should kill Laban" and then noted his hesitation and the insistence of the Spirit that he perform the deed (see 1 Nephi 4:10–12). Interestingly, Moses is also said to have hesitated to kill the Egyptian overseer until he received a divine revelation on the matter. According to ʾAbot de Rabbi Nathan 20, thought to have been written in the second century A.D. but not available in English until the twentieth century, Moses summoned a court of ministering angels and asked them if he should kill the Egyptian, to which the angels responded, "Kill him." The same story is told in *Midrash Rabbah* Exodus 1:29, which adds that, before calling on the angels for counsel, Moses perceived that no righteous persons would descend from the Egyptian man.[63] A similar story is found in an early Jewish text, *Tosephta-Targum* (V. 1) 2 on 1 Samuel 17:43, which says that just before he slew Goliath, David "lifted up his eyes to heaven and saw angels deliberating on Goliath the Philistine."[64]

Regarding the execution of Zemnarihah, leader of the band of Gadianton (see 3 Nephi 4:28–29), Welch has discussed the concept of hanging in early Judaism and the symbolism of felling the tree as a warning to other potential wrongdoers.[65] My attention has been particularly drawn to the reasons Zemnarihah was hanged rather than, say, stoned—the more usual method of execution under the law of Moses.[66]

One of the Dead Sea Scrolls, the *Temple Scroll* (also called 11Q19), calls for execution of a spy—one who defects to another nation and curses his own people, or one who "betrays his people to a foreign nation or causes evil against his people"—by hanging.[67] The Israelites who joined themselves to their enemies, the Midianites, in the worship of the false god Baal-Peor and were hanged by Moses fit this description of a traitor (see Numbers 25:1–9).

The Gadianton band led by Zemnarihah consisted of dissenters who had turned against the Nephites (see Helaman 11:24–26; 3 Nephi 1:27–28). In Gadianton's day they had fled the land to avoid being apprehended for their treasonous acts in killing the chief judge Pahoran and attempting to slay his successor, Helaman (see Helaman 2:11). Because of this flight, they fit the description found in the *Temple Scroll* of the man who "escapes amongst the nations." Giddianhi, Zemnarihah's predecessor as leader of the band, admitted that his people had dissented from the Nephites (see 3 Nephi 3:9–11). It is also of interest that Giddianhi swore "with an oath" to destroy the Nephites (3 Nephi 3:8), clearly plotting evil against the people as also mentioned in the *Temple Scroll*. His successor's execution by hanging is entirely in line with early Jewish law.

From this information we can see that even the minutest details of the executions of Laban and Zemnarihah are in conformity with ancient Jewish traditions unavailable to Joseph Smith.

Conclusion

This is but a sampling of ancient texts that lend support to the Book of Mormon. I have discussed others elsewhere[68] and plan to publish many more in the near future. Such texts are, of course, only a small portion of the vast array of evidences for the antiquity and authenticity of the Book of Mormon.

Notes

1. See John A. Tvedtnes, *The Book of Mormon and Other Hidden Books: "Out of Darkness unto Light"* (Provo, Utah: FARMS, 2000); see also John A. Tvedtnes, "Hidden Records," in his *The Most Correct Book: Insights from a Book of Mormon Scholar* (Salt Lake City: Covenant, 1999), 25–28.

2. For an in-depth discussion, see H. Curtis Wright, "Ancient Burials of Metal Documents in Stone Boxes," in *By Study and Also by Faith,* ed. John M. Lundquist and Stephen D. Ricks (Salt Lake City: Deseret Book and FARMS, 1990), 273–334.

3. See H. Curtis Wright, "Metallic Documents of Antiquity," *BYU Studies* 10/4 (1970): 457–75.

4. P. Colon. inv. nr. 4780, 50–52, in Ron Cameron and Arthur J. Dewey, *The Cologne Mani Codex* (Missoula, Mont.: Scholars Press, 1979), 39–43.

5. John C. Reeves, *Heralds of That Good Realm: Syro-Mesopotamian Gnosis and Jewish Traditions* (Leiden: Brill, 1996), 142.

6. Al-Tha'labī, *Qisas al-Anbiya'* (Cairo: Mustafa al-Babi al-Halabi wa-Awladuhu, 1340 A.H.), 102, 202. Hugh Nibley was the first to bring this information to the attention of Latter-day Saints.

7. The story is reported in Sir Ernest A. Wallis Budge, *The Book of the Dead* (New Hyde Park, N.Y.: University Books, 1966), 15 n. 5.

8. Hebrew is part of the Canaanite language family, usually called Northwest Semitic. This includes later forms of the Canaanite language, called Phoenician and Punic. Closely related is Ugaritic, known from thirteenth- and fourteenth-century B.C. inscriptions at the northwest Syrian city of Ugarit, and less closely related is Eblaite, known from second-millennium B.C. inscriptions from nearby Ebla.

9. See Richard C. Steiner, "Northwest Semitic Incantations in an Egyptian Medical Papyrus of the Fourteenth Century B.C.E.," *Journal of Near Eastern Studies* 51/3 (1992): 196–97.

Steiner briefly mentions the other Northwest Semitic texts noted herein and also draws our attention to a later Arabic text written in Coptic characters; see J. Blau, "Some Observations on a Middle Arabic Egyptian Text in Coptic Characters," *Jerusalem Studies in Arabic and Islam* 1 (1979): 215–62.

10. See T. Schneider, "Mag.pHarris XII, 1–5; Eine kanaanäische Beschwörung für die Löwenjagd?" *Göttinger Miszellen* 112 (1989): 53–63.

11. See William Foxwell Albright, *The Vocalization of the Egyptian Syllabic Orthography* (New Haven: Yale University Press, 1934), 33, 37, 42; W. Helck, *Die Beziehungen Ägyptens zu Vorderasien im 3, Und 2, Jahrtausend v. Chr.*, Ägyptologische Abhandlungen, vol. 44 (Wiesbaden: Harrassowitz, 1971), 528–29; and H.-W. Fischer Elfert, *Die satirische Streitschrift des Papyrus Anastasi I*, Ägyptologische Abhandlungen, vol. 44 (Wiesbaden: Harrassowitz, 1986), 152.

12. This ostracon is from the Cairo Museum. See Ariel Shisha-Halevy, "An Early North-West Semitic Text in the Egyptian Hieratic Script," *Orientalia* n.s. 47 (1978): 145–62. An ostracon (plural ostraca) is a piece of pottery on which writing appears. In the ancient Near East, when a jar was broken, pieces suitable for writing were kept, much as we keep scratch paper.

13. For information on the text, see Raymond A. Bowman, "An Aramaic Religious Text in Demotic Script," *Journal of Near Eastern Studies* 3 (1944): 219–31; Charles F. Nims and Richard C. Steiner, "A Paganized Version of Psalm 20:2–6 from the Aramaic Text in Demotic Script," *Journal of the American Oriental Society* 103 (January–March 1983): 261–74; Richard C. Steiner and Charles F. Nims, "You Can't Offer Your Sacrifice and Eat It Too: A Polemical Poem from the Aramaic Text in Demotic Script," *Journal of Near Eastern Studies* 43/2 (1984): 89–114; Richard C. Steiner and Charles F. Nims, "Ashurbanipal and Shamash-shum-ukin: A Tale of Two Brothers from the Aramaic Text in Demotic Script," *Revue Biblique* 92/1 (1985): 60–81; Richard C. Steiner, "The Aramaic Text in Demotic Script: The

Liturgy of a New Year's Festival Imported from Bethel to Syene by Exiles from Rash," *Journal of the American Oriental Society* 111/2 (1991): 362–63; and Richard C. Steiner, "Northwest Semitic Incantations in an Egyptian Medical Papyrus of the Fourteenth Century B.C.E.," *Journal of Near Eastern Studies* 51/3 (1992): 191–200.

14. For discussions of the various Semitic texts written in Egyptian script, see John Gee, "La Trahison des Clercs: On the Language and Translation of the Book of Mormon," *Review of Books on the Book of Mormon* 6/1 (1994): 79–99, especially pp. 96–99 and n. 147; Stephen D. Ricks and John A. Tvedtnes, "Jewish and Other Semitic Texts Written in Egyptian Characters," *Journal of Book of Mormon Studies* 5/2 (1996): 156–63, reprinted as "Semitic Texts Written in Egyptian Characters," in *Pressing Forward with the Book of Mormon,* ed. John W. Welch and Melvin J. Thorne (Provo, Utah: FARMS, 1999), 237–43; and John A. Tvedtnes, "Reformed Egyptian," in his *Most Correct Book,* 22–24.

15. Shlomo Yeivin, "An Ostracon from Tel Arad Exhibiting a Combination of Two Scripts," *Journal of Egyptian Archaeology* 55/2 (1969): 98–102. The importance of this find for the Book of Mormon was discussed by John A. Tvedtnes in "The Language of My Father," *New Era,* May 1971, 19, and "Linguistic Implications of the Tel Arad Ostraca," *Newsletter and Proceedings of the Society for Early Historic Archaeology,* no. 127 (October 1971).

16. For photos of the ostraca and a brief discussion, see Rudolph Cohen, "Excavations at Kadesh-barnea, 1976–78," *Biblical Archaeologist* 44/2 (1981): 98–99; and Rudolph Cohen, "Did I Excavate Kadesh-Barnea?" *Biblical Archaeology Review* 7/3 (1981): 25–30.

17. Campbell published a series of articles critical of the Book of Mormon in his paper, the *Millennial Harbinger,* at Bethany, Virginia, beginning in February 1831. The articles were later collected into a book entitled *Delusions,* published by E. H. Green & Co. of Boston in 1832.

18. See the discussion by John Gee and John A. Tvedtnes in the FARMS Update published in the newsletter of the Foundation for Ancient Research and Mormon Studies, Brigham Young University, "Ancient Manuscripts Fit Book of Mormon Pattern," *Insights* (February 1999): 3–4.

19. The finds were reported by Gabriel Barkay in "The Divine Name Found in Jerusalem," *Biblical Archaeology Review* 9/2 (1983): 14–19, and in his "Priestly Blessings on Silver Plates" (in Hebrew), *Cathedra* 52 (1989): 46–59. See also the discussion in William J. Adams Jr., "Lehi's Jerusalem and Writing on Metal Plates," *Journal of Book of Mormon Studies* 3/1 (1994): 204–6, reprinted as "Lehi's Jerusalem and Writing on Silver Plates," in *Pressing Forward with the Book of Mormon,* ed. Welch and Thorne, 23–25; and in "More on the Silver Plates from Lehi's Jerusalem," *Journal of Book of Mormon Studies* 4/2 (1995): 136–37; reprinted in *Pressing Forward with the Book of Mormon,* ed. Welch and Thorne, 27–28.

20. E. Isaac, "The Ethiopic History of Joseph: Translation with Introduction and Notes," *Journal for the Study of the Pseudepigrapha* 6/1 (1990): 88.

21. W. M. Thackston Jr., trans., *The Tales of the Prophets of al-Kisaʾi* (Boston: Twayne, 1978), 2:182; see p. 183.

22. For the story of this second garment from paradise, see *Midrash Bereshit Rabbah* 89:9; *Zohar* Genesis 194b; and Thackston Jr., trans., *Tales of the Prophets of al-Kisaʾi,* 2:170.

23. Thackston Jr., trans., *Tales of the Prophets of al-Kisaʾi,* 2:188.

24. See ibid., 2:188–89.

25. See William M. Brinner, trans., *The History of al-Ṭabarī,* vol. 2 of *Prophets and Patriarchs* (Albany: SUNY, 1987), 180–81.

26. The Hebrew word *targum* (plural *targumim*) means "translation" and refers to the Aramaic translations of the Bible made after the Jews had adopted Aramaic instead of Hebrew as their native tongue during the Babylonian captivity.

27. Martin McNamara, trans., *Targum Neofiti 1: Genesis* (The Aramaic Bible, vol. 1A) (Collegeville, Minn.: Liturgical Press,

1992), 182. Compare *Pirqe de Rabbi Eliezer* 48 and *Targum Pseudo-Jonathan* on Genesis 50:25, which speak of Moses and Aaron as redeemers of Israel.

28. Michael Maher, *Targum Pseudo-Jonathan: Genesis* (The Aramaic Bible, vol. 1B) (Collegeville, Minn.: Liturgical Press, 1992), 166

29. Column II, lines 15–19, cited from Florentino García Martínez, *The Dead Sea Scrolls Translated*, 2nd ed. (Leiden: Brill, 1996), 140. The scroll cites the Messianic prophecy in Isaiah 61:2–3 and mistakenly attributes it to Daniel, who also prophesied of the Messiah (see Daniel 9:24–26). Jesus cited the Isaiah 61 passage in reference to his own calling in Luke 4:18–19. For a discussion of 11QMelchizedek in connection with Abinadi's interpretation, see Dana M. Pike, "The Imagery of Isaiah 52:7–10," in *Isaiah in the Book of Mormon,* ed. Donald W. Parry and John W. Welch (Provo, Utah: FARMS, 1998), 261–65. See also John A. Tvedtnes, "How Beautiful upon the Mountains," in his *Most Correct Book,* 172–75.

30. *Mekilta RI* Exodus 17:9, *Midrash Tanhuma* A Be-Shallah 26, *Targum Pseudo-Jonathan* on Exodus 17:9, *Targum Neofiti* and *Targum Pseudo-Jonathan* on Numbers 23:9 and Deuteronomy 33:15, *Pesikta Rabbati* 33:4, and *Zohar* Exodus 58b.

31. Sir Ernest A. Wallis Budge, *The Book of the Mysteries of the Heavens and the Earth and Other Works of Bakhayla Mîkâʾêl (Zôsîmâs)* (Oxford: n.p., 1935), 131. In 1 Corinthians 3:5–9 Paul also compares those converted to Christ to agricultural produce, though the connection is less clear than that of the former source.

32. See the discussion in John A. Tvedtnes, "That Which Is to Come," in his *Most Correct Book,* 235–41. In an Ethiopic text describing the tabernacle of Moses, Christ is called "Him that is to come." See Budge, *Book of the Mysteries,* 159.

33. Alexander Roberts and James Donaldson, eds., *Ante-Nicene Fathers* (1885; reprint, Peabody, Mass.: Hendrickson, 1994), 1:62.

34. Sir Ernest A. Wallis Budge, trans., *The Book of the Bee*, (Oxford: Clarendon, 1886), 69.

35. Ibid., 71.

36. Ibid.

37. Ibid., 71–72.

38. See ibid., 71 n. 2.

39. See the discussion in John A. Tvedtnes, "Jeremiah's Prophecies of Jesus Christ," in his *Most Correct Book,* 99–103.

40. Roberts and Donaldson, eds., *Ante-Nicene Fathers,* 1:235. Many early Christian texts refer to Christ's preaching in the spirit world, an event additionally recorded in 1 Peter 3:18–20; 4:6 and Doctrine and Covenants 138.

41. Ibid., 1:493–94. In ibid., 451, Irenaeus also cites the passage in *Against Heresies* 3.20.4, where he mistakenly attributes it to Isaiah.

42. Budge, trans., *Book of the Bee,* 72. Compare Isaiah 19:1.

43. For an English translation of the Jeremiah passage, see James H. Charlesworth, *The Old Testament Pseudepigrapha* (Garden City: Doubleday, 1985), 2:387–88. Both *The Lives of the Prophets* and *The Book of the Bee* include prophecies of Christ attributed to other Old Testament prophets but not found in the Bible version of their books. We are reminded of Nephi's declaration that "plain and precious things" would be removed from the Bible (see 1 Nephi 13:25–35, 40; 14:23).

44. See ibid., 1:424–25.

45. Sir Ernest A. Wallis Budge, *The Queen of Sheba and Her Only Son Menyelek* (London: Medici Society, 1922), 10. *Kebra Nagast* means "glory of the kings" of Ethiopia and is one of the most highly praised traditional stories among Ethiopian Christians.

46. Ibid., 200.

47. For a discussion of scientific research into glowing stones, see Nicholas Read, Jae R. Ballif, John W. Welch, Bill Evenson, Kathleen Reynolds Gee, and Matthew Roper, "New Light on the Shining Stones of the Jaredites," FARMS Update, *Insights* (July 1992): 2; reprinted in *Pressing Forward with the Book of Mormon,*

ed. Welch and Thorne, 253–55; and John A. Tvedtnes, "More on Glowing Stones," FARMS Update, *Insights* (July 1999): 2.

48. See Hugh Nibley, *Lehi in the Desert; The World of the Jaredites; There Were Jaredites* (Salt Lake City: Deseret Book and FARMS, 1988), 359–79; *An Approach to the Book of Mormon,* 3rd ed. (Salt Lake City: Deseret Book and FARMS, 1988), 337–58; *Since Cumorah,* 2nd ed. (Salt Lake City: Deseret Book and FARMS, 1988), 209–10; *The Prophetic Book of Mormon* (Salt Lake City: Deseret Book and FARMS, 1989), 243–44; *Teachings of the Book of Mormon, Semester 4* (Provo, Utah: FARMS, 1993), 268–70; and John A. Tvedtnes, "Glowing Stones in Ancient and Medieval Lore," *Journal of Book of Mormon Studies* 6/2 (1997): 99–123. A revised version of the latter work was published as an appendix in John A. Tvedtnes, *The Book of Mormon and Other Hidden Books: "Out of Darkness unto Light."* In most of his discussion of this topic, Nibley also compares the Jaredite barges to the vessel described in the Mesopotamian versions of the flood story.

49. See TB *Sanhedrin* 108b, TY *Pesahim* 1.1, *Targum Pseudo-Jonathan* on Genesis 6:16, *Midrash Bereshit Rabbah* 31.11, *Pirqe de Rabbi Eliezer* 23, and Rashi on Genesis 6:16. For a recap of the story, see Louis Ginzberg, ed., *The Legends of the Jews* (Philadelphia: Jewish Publication Society, 1937), 1:162–63. The first person to bring the Jewish tradition to the attention of Latter-day Saints was Janne M. Sjodahl, in his *An Introduction to the Study of the Book of Mormon* (Salt Lake City: Deseret News Press, 1927), 248. The tradition was discussed at length by Hugh Nibley, "There Were Jaredites: The Shining Stones," *Improvement Era,* September 1956, 630–32, 672–75.

50. The idea of a "window" came from the Latin Vulgate translation and is also found in the Greek translation by Aquila. The Aramaic *Targum Onkelos* renders it "light."

51. See Thackston Jr., trans., *Tales of the Prophets of al-Kisaʾi,* 2:98.

52. See the discussion in John A. Tvedtnes, "The Jaredite Ocean Voyage," in his *Most Correct Book,* 285–90. Hugh Nibley

discusses the so-called wind-flood in his *The Ancient State* (Salt Lake City: Deseret Book and FARMS, 1991), 33–34, and in *Teachings of the Book of Mormon, Semester 4,* 244–45.

53. S. C. Malan, trans., *The Book of Adam and Eve, also called The Conflict of Adam and Eve with Satan* (London: Williams and Norgate, 1882), 155.

54. The translation used here was prepared by William Whiston in the seventeenth century and has been frequently reprinted since.

55. Translation by James L. Kugel, *Traditions of the Bible: A Guide to the Bible as It Was at the Start of the Common Era* (Cambridge: Harvard University Press, 1998), 887.

56. See Jacob Neusner, *Sifre to Deuteronomy* (Atlanta: Scholars Press, 1987), 2:457.

57. For a discussion of the Jewish sources, see Samuel E. Loewenstamm, "The Death of Moses," in *Studies on the Testament of Abraham,* ed. George W. E. Nickelsberg Jr. (Atlanta: Scholars Press, 1976).

58. See also chapter 5 of John Whitmer's unpublished *History of the Church,* in which it is recorded that in the early part of June 1831 "the Spirit of the Lord fell upon Joseph in an unusual manner, and he prophesied that John the Revelator was then among the Ten Tribes of Israel who had been led away by Shalmaneser king of Assyria to prepare them for their return from their long dispersion to again possess the land of their fathers." That this is John's role was subsequently confirmed in a revelation given in March 1832 (see D&C 77:9, 14).

59. Sir Ernest A. Wallis Budge, *Coptic Martyrdoms* (London: British Museum, 1914), 475.

60. Ibid., 492–93. I am grateful to Matthew Roper for bringing this passage to my attention.

61. See John W. Welch, "Legal Perspectives on the Slaying of Laban," *Journal of Book of Mormon Studies* 1/1 (1992): 119–41; John W. Welch and Heidi Harkness Parker, "Better That One Man Perish," FARMS Update, *Insights* (June 1998): 2; reprinted

in *Pressing Forward with the Book of Mormon,* ed. Welch and Thorne, 17–19; and Fred Essig and Dan Fuller, "Nephi's Slaying of Laban: A Legal Perspective" (Provo, Utah: FARMS, 1981).

62. See John A. Tvedtnes, "The Slaying of Laban," in his *Most Correct Book,* 110–12.

63. *Targum Pseudo-Jonathan* on Exodus 2:12 notes that Moses knew that no proselyte would come from the Egyptian's posterity, something also mentioned in *Zohar* Exodus 12b.

64. Eveline van Staalduine-Sulman, "The Aramaic Song of the Lamb," in *Verse in Ancient Near Eastern Prose,* ed. Johannes C. de Moor and Wilfred G. E. Watson (Netherlands: Verlag Butzon and Bercker Kevelaer, 1993), 272.

65. See John W. Welch, "The Execution of Zemnarihah," in *Reexploring the Book of Mormon,* ed. John W. Welch (Salt Lake City: Deseret Book and FARMS, 1992), 250–52.

66. See John A. Tvedtnes, "More on the Hanging of Zemnarihah," FARMS Update, *Insights* (April 1997): 2; reprinted in *Pressing Forward with the Book of Mormon,* ed. Welch and Thorne, 208–10.

67. *Temple Scroll* (11Q19), col. LXIV, lines 6–13, in García Martínez, *Dead Sea Scrolls Translated,* 178.

68. See, for example, John A. Tvedtnes, "The Messiah, the Book of Mormon, and the Dead Sea Scrolls," in his *Most Correct Book,* 328–43.

How Could Joseph Smith Write So Accurately about Ancient American Civilization?

John L. Sorenson

Level of Civilization

Some statements in the Book of Mormon about ancient Near Eastern lands, concepts, and activities might have been incorporated into the Nephite text because a nineteenth-century writer, such as Joseph Smith Jr. or Sidney Rigdon, knew about ancient lifeways through reading the Bible or secular sources accessible before 1830. But once the Book of Mormon story claims to be taking place in an American setting, such an argument makes no sense, for nobody knew enough by 1830 to get so many facts right. At point after point the scripture accurately reflects the culture and history of ancient Mesoamerica (southern Mexico and northern Central America). Where did such information come from if not through Joseph in the manner he claimed? Literally no person in Joseph Smith's day knew or could have known enough facts about exotic Central America to depict the subtle and accurate picture of ancient life that we find as background for the Book of Mormon. In this paper a look at a dozen or so characteristics of Mesoamerican civilization that are mirrored in the Book of Mormon will illustrate why this question is appropriate.

LEVEL OF
CIVILIZATION

Joseph Smith could not have known in 1830 from published books or his contemporaries that an ancient civilization had existed anywhere in the Americas. To all settlers of the western New York frontier, an "Indian" was just a savage. If young Joseph took his ideas for the Book of Mormon from his neighbors and their cultural milieu, as many critics maintain, we would expect him to have rather similar notions of America's indigenous peoples. Yet the Book of Mormon characterizes itself as a record from a real civilization (which included not only "the Nephites" but also "the Lamanites," as shown by Mosiah 24:1–7 and Alma 21:2). New York frontier dwellers did not attribute civilization to the native American peoples they knew anything about. Joseph Smith himself was surprised to learn in 1842 from reading the sensational book by John Lloyd Stephens, *Incidents of Travel in Central America, Chiapas, and Yucatán* (published in 1839), that there had once been a spectacular ancient civilization in Central America and that, at least in superficial terms, it agreed with the cultural pattern characterized in the Book of Mormon.

In the early nineteenth century, knowledge of the geography, history, and cultures of most of the world, and particularly of the Western Hemisphere, was very limited on the U.S. frontier and only somewhat better in the cities along the eastern seaboard.[1] Orson Pratt, an early leader in the Church of Jesus Christ of Latter-day Saints, is accurate in his recollection in 1849 that "no one will dispute the fact that the existence of antique remains in different

The sacred precinct of the urban core of the Aztec capital, Tenochtitlán. This reconstruction, based on Spanish eyewitness accounts and archaeological findings, depicts the impressive scale of the Aztec civilization.

I. Marquina, Arquitectura prehispánica, 1951.

parts of America was known long before Mr. Smith was born. But every well-informed person knows that . . . most of the discoveries made by Catherwood and Stephens were original—that most of the forty-four cities described by [Stephens's book] had not been described by previous travelers."[2] Stephens's biographer makes the same point: "The acceptance of an 'Indian civilization' demanded, to an American living in 1839, an entire reorientation, for to him, an Indian was one of those barbaric, tepee dwellers against whom wars were constantly waged. . . . Nor did one ever think of calling the other indigenous inhabitants of the continent [e.g., of Central America] 'civilized.' In the universally accepted opinion [of that day], they were like their North American counterparts—savages."[3] So Joseph Smith was surprised when, in 1842 in Nauvoo, he and his associates read Stephens's book. A comment in the *Times and Seasons,* the newspaper that Smith edited, clearly reflects that fact: "Mr. Stephens' great developments of antiquities are made bare to the eyes of all . . . by reading the history of the Nephites in the Book of Mormon. . . . Who could have dreamed that twelve years could have developed such incontrovertible testimony to the Book of Mormon?"[4]

What evidence does the Book of Mormon give that what it records for early America took place within the context of an actual ancient civilization?[5] First we need to ask what constitutes a civilization. Definitions differ, but most historians and archaeologists would agree on the following essential features of a civilization: (1) multiple cities (implying well-developed agriculture) with a population of corresponding scale, (2) complex social structure (numerous specialists and at least three levels of social rank), (3) major public structures of high symbolic significance to those who use them, (4) state-level government (that is, a ruling apparatus in which coercive power is centralized), (5) mass warfare, and (6) writing.[6] The Book of Mormon reports all of these key features for the peoples who kept that record.

Of course, in the pioneering stages of settlement Book of Mormon societies operated at a less-than-civilized level, while later periods covered in the record reflect more advanced levels of civilization. By far the larger proportion of information in the Book of Mormon concerns full-blown Nephite and Lamanite societies. Much less is recorded about the Jaredites.

The book reports a population that reached at least into the hundreds of thousands and perhaps millions. At the final battle of the Nephites, some 230,000 on the Nephite side alone are said to have been killed (see Mormon 6:10–15), and the winning side must have suffered casualties of the same order while leaving safe a sizable supporting population. The societies involved were spread over an area of something like 100,000 square miles, about the same order of size as Mesopotamia and larger than the territory encompassed by the Greeks. At one point leaders in the city of Zarahemla were said to live among "thousands" and even "tens of thousands" of people in or near the capital city. Those masses were in large measure specialists, not just farmers, of whom it was charged that they "sit in idleness" (Alma 60:22). Such a socioeconomic structure could only occur in a civilized society.

By the time Mormon was a youth, after A.D. 300, the Nephites had built or rebuilt so many cities and towns that "the whole land," he reported, "had become covered with buildings" (Mormon 1:7). The crowning class of Nephite urban settlements was the "great city." Five Nephite centers are so named, and other "great and notable cities" also existed, although their names are not recorded in the scriptures (see 3 Nephi 8:14). The absolute size of "great cities" is suggested by mention of the city of Jerusalem in the land of Israel, which was also called a "great city" (1 Nephi 11:13).[7] Furthermore, shortly before the time of Christ the area inhabited by the Nephites and Lamanites was characterized as an interrelated trade zone in which "they did have free intercourse one with another, to buy and to sell" (Helaman 6:8). "There was all manner of gold . . . and of silver, and of precious ore of every kind" (v. 11). Their craftspeople also "did make all manner of cloth" (v. 13). Many books and records of all kinds were produced (see Helaman 3:15), an additional characteristic of civilized status. Thus the marks of civilization were there, although none were evident among the traditions or the material remains left by the Indians of the northeastern United States, where Joseph Smith dwelled in his formative years.

Not only was the level of civilization depicted in Mormon's volume impressively like that which archaeologists have since found in Central America, but the chronology also agrees generally. The heyday of the Nephites and civilized Lamanites was from the first century B.C. to the fourth century A.D. (the earlier Nephites and Lamanites alike were smaller in numbers). According to the Nephite historians, not until around 100 B.C. did the growth of political, economic, and cultural elements crystallize into extensive and intensive societies.[8] Especially in the third and fourth centuries A.D., the Nephites and Lamanites built cities and impressive public buildings (see 4 Nephi 1), as well as engaged in extensive trade and large-scale war (see Mormon 1–6).

Archaeological and other historical research carried out over the past half century has demonstrated a striking external correspondence to this picture in southern Mexico and northern Central America. Ruins of even the Classic period of Mesoamerican civilization, from A.D. 300 to 900, were still unknown when Joseph Smith published the Book of Mormon. Only within recent decades have archaeologists determined that during the centuries even before Cumorah—before the Classic period—civilized people had built and left ruins as impressive as anything ever constructed in this heartland of ancient American civilization.⁹

Geographical Consistency

The Book of Mormon contains hundreds of statements related to the geography of the Nephites' "land of promise." When all of them are collated, a picture of the physical setting emerges that is highly consistent. Inconsistencies that might be expected of the author of a fraudulent work (such as locating a particular named city in different spots at different points in the story) are notably absent in the Book of Mormon. Yet Joseph Smith himself later made statements by way of commentary that contradict what the text says of its geography. That is, when Smith freshly dictated the text of the scripture, the geography came out fine; but his private interpretations of the geography could err.

COMPLEX GEOGRAPHICAL CONSISTENCY

A prime example occurs in a statement recorded in a journal dated to 1838. A group of travelers passing through Randolph County, Indiana, was given to understand by local members of the Church of Jesus Christ of Latter-day Saints that "the ancient site of the [Nephite] city of Manti" was thereabouts.¹⁰ No direct attribution to Joseph Smith is made, but it is doubtful that anyone would have drawn this conclusion unless the Prophet, who had traveled the route, had said something like this. Actually, when all the statements about Manti that appear in the Nephite account are examined together, they can only be interpreted to show that the city of Manti lay south of "the narrow neck of land" and the city of Zarahemla and was near the headwaters of the northward-flowing Sidon River. A very neat fit for the relationships of the land and city of Manti as reported in the scriptural text is found in southernmost Mexico, and city ruins in the vicinity date to Book of Mormon times.¹¹ But the suggested correlation in Indiana completely fails to fit the statements in the Nephite account. It would appear that Joseph Smith and his close associates had not personally grasped the geographical scheme that the book itself consistently reveals.

To recapitulate, when Joseph Smith-as-translator dictated the text of the Book of Mormon to his scribes, he produced a seamless, plausible geography of limited scale, but when Smith-as-mere-Joseph later commented on geography, the picture he communicated is that all South and North America were involved. This inconsistency is not what the author of a work of fiction—as naysayers often suppose Joseph to have been—would show. Were Joseph the sly schemer he is accused of being, he surely would have done two things differently in this regard: (1) inevitably he would have let geographical inconsistencies slip in during his hasty dictation of the text, and (2) thereafter he would have kept his mouth shut about matters of location lest the problems he knew could be present in the book he had created should be exposed by his offhand comments. He did neither.

There is a corollary to this point. The statements in the Book of Mormon describe a land of limited extent (a few hundred miles long) that had certain specific physical features (in configuration, topography, bodies of water, climate, and geology). Analyses of the text of the scripture in the last six decades have made this clear. Those characteristics fit remarkably well with the geography of Mesoamerica. Yet later statements by Joseph and his early associates reveal that he supposed that the entire Western Hemisphere had been occupied by Nephites and Lamanites. In other words, his personal interpretation of the book's geography differed in some respects from what the record itself stipulates. If we were to suppose, with many of Smith's critics, that he somehow wrote the Book of Mormon out of his own mind and knowledge, it is difficult to see how he would have interpreted this aspect of his "own literary work" inconsistently.

The Pattern of Culture History

The picture presented in the Book of Mormon of changes in peoples and cultures over time matches in major respects what we now know about the course of history in Mesoamerica. But this picture, which scientists and scholars have slowly built up from archaeology and related fields of expert study, was totally unknown in 1830. Not even the best-informed scholars in the world at that time, let alone Joseph Smith, had any notion of a pattern behind ancient American history that would come to light over a century later.

MESO-
AMERICAN
LINEAGE
HISTORY

An 1833 book by Josiah Priest, who was as much an expert on American prehistory as anyone at the time (which isn't saying much), expressed the opinion that not only "Asiatic nations" but also "Polynesians, Malays, Australasians, Phoenicians, Egyptians, Greeks, Romans, Israelites, Tartars, Scandinavians, Danes, Norwegians, Welch, and Scotch" groups had reached the Americas.[12] Dr. Samuel L. Mitchell, the savant to whom Martin Harris took his sample of Nephite writing before he carried it to Professor Charles Anthon in New York City, had published the opinion that at least Malay, Tartar, and Scandinavian voyagers had reached America.[13] But neither Mitchell nor Priest had any notion of history as it related to the random finds of ancient objects in America, the only "archaeological" evidence then known. After all, no systematic method existed at that time for dating this continent's "antiquities." Archaeologists would not be able to produce even an orderly guess about the structure of Amerindian history until nearly another century had passed.[14]

The Book of Mormon was not hesitant to give a history of peoples in the region known to Lehi as "the promised land." This history, however, was only an account of certain events involving particular groups; nowhere does the Book of Mormon claim to give a comprehensive sketch about what happened throughout the area of its concern. What we do have in the book that Mormon edited—most of today's Book of Mormon—is instead a "lineage history" of his ancestral line, with a short version of a lineage history of the earlier Jaredites. The latter group came from Mesopotamia at the time of "the great tower," apparently sometime in the third millennium B.C. Their record came through a prophet named Ether, the final record keeper of the traditional Jaredite ruling line. His ancestors had inhabited what the Nephites later called "the land northward." There they competed with other would-be ruling families over many generations. Centuries after Ether and his people became extinct in civil wars culminating before about 500 B.C., the final Nephite record keeper, Moroni, prepared a skeletal version of Ether's account, which he left to us as the book of Ether.

The Nephites, along with their rivalrous relatives, the Lamanites, inhabited the land after the Jaredites, between about 600 B.C. and A.D. 400. They traced their origin to the Near Eastern land of Judah. (Both of these "peoples" were actually sociopolitical factions composed of diverse ethnic and linguistic groups whose rulers usually traced their ancestry to one of two brothers in the original party of settlers from the Old World.)[15] The Nephite record shows that it too was only a partial history; it concentrated on events of significance to the line of royalty that descended from the founder, Nephi. A third group that had also emigrated from the Near East, the people of Zarahemla ("Mulekites"), became incorporated under the Nephite rulers, but their separate history is all but ignored. The Nephite segment of the population, like its Jaredite predecessors, became extinct at the end of the story (near the end of the fourth century A.D.), but a miscellany of groups under the labels "Lamanites" and "robbers" continued the basic civilizational tradition in which the Nephites had participated.

Summarized, the scriptural record portrays the following basic sequence:

- First, the long-lasting Jaredite ruling line participated in a cultural tradition that, after a pioneering struggle (see Ether 1–9), came to a level of precocious advancement in arts and technology but not in statecraft or religious organization. The civilization was located primarily in the land northward in the centuries preceding about 500 B.C.

- Later, Nephites (including "Mulekites") and Lamanites, who constituted adjacent rival but interdependent factions with much in common culturally,[16] inhabited the land southward from soon after 600 B.C. to about A.D. 400 (colonizing portions of the land northward starting in the first century B.C.).

Within this twofold pattern the text discusses or alludes to additional subgroups, major events, and societal trends. Especially notable are the overall growth of population and participation in a class-structured civilization that emphasized ritual activities.

The last half century of concentrated historical and archaeological research on ancient Mesoamerican societies has produced a picture that, while far more complex than the abbreviated lineage histories that constitute the Book of Mormon, plausibly accommodates the histories of the Nephite and Lamanite ruling lines. The culture sequence reconstructed by scholars can be summarized as follows:

- First, there was an early cultural tradition that is increasingly recognized as deserving to be called a civilization. Its best-known component is sometimes called the Olmec culture. This, however, was only the best-known manifestation of a wider tradition dating from perhaps 1400 B.C. to about 500 B.C.,[17] when it quite abruptly lost its identity. Its climax was located in Mexico in the vicinity of the Isthmus of Tehuantepec.

- Some elements of the tradition that followed derived from the Olmec and related predecessor cultures but had a different ethos and emphasis. It featured elaborate religious monuments, ceremonies, and myths. While this second tradition grew from roots in several regions, a core of its concepts originated in southern Mesoamerica, that is, Guatemala and southernmost Mexico, during the period from about 500 B.C. to near A.D. 300. This tradition spread quite widely throughout Mesoamerica in that period and provided primary ideas and energy behind the spectacular cultures of the Classic period (after A.D. 200), such as the Maya, Zapotec, and Teotihuacán manifestations.[18]

If we identify Book of Mormon lands with the isthmian part of Mesoamerica (the land southward comprising mainly Guatemala and the Mexican states of Chiapas and Tabasco, the narrow neck of land being the Isthmus of Tehuantepec, and the land northward being that portion of Mexico near the isthmus to the north and west),[19] as many now do, then substantial agreement between the scriptural and scholarly pictures of culture history is evident. Moreover, evidence has been brought forward that certain key beliefs, symbols, and other cultural elements that appear in this second Mesoamerican tradition (and are referred to in the Book of Mormon text) relate closely to the ancient Near East.[20]

A book-length discussion would be required to document the literally hundreds of points upon which the historical dimension in the Book of Mormon agrees with the known culture history of Mesoamerica. (The most serious attempt at such a publication so far is the book *Images of Ancient America: Visualizing Book of Mormon Life*.)[21] Only the broadest agreement could be communicated in the summary discussion above, but many comparisons at a detailed level could be presented if time and space allowed.[22]

Even the general sequence, which shows an early and precocious Mexican civilization, epitomized as Olmec (although that label is oversimplified), followed by a religiously oriented second tradition that culminated in the great Classic era cultures and sites so well known to tourists, was not recognized by most scholars until forty or fifty years ago. That Joseph Smith's translation of what may be termed the Book of Mormon "codex" already contained parallel historical facts in 1830 is remarkable.

The Book of Mormon as a Mesoamerican Record

Mesoamerican Codex

The Nephite account is a record that resembles in form, nature, and functions—in scores of characteristics, in fact—what we would expect in an ancient Mesoamerican codex, a type of document that was utterly unknown to Joseph Smith.

At the time Smith lived, the only Mesoamerican object anything like a codex that had been described in an English-language source was the Aztec "calendar stone." It was pictured in a book by Humboldt published in 1814 in London,[23] although nobody at that time could make much sense of it. Nothing suggested by Humboldt sheds any real light on native American written documents nor relates to the Book of Mormon. Besides, the chance is vanishingly small that the learned German's esoteric work would have been accessible anywhere in America except at a handful of the best libraries on the Atlantic seaboard, to which Joseph had no access before the Book of Mormon was published.

The very idea that large numbers of books were written and preserved in any ancient American culture was also contrary to the notion universally held by literate and rustic citizens of the United States that the "Indians" were only "savages." The writer in Helaman 3:15 tells of "many books and many records of every kind" among his people in the first century B.C., some kept by the Lamanites but a majority by Nephites. They had been "handed down from one generation to another" (v. 16). Spaniards noted (but only in documents that Joseph Smith could not have known about) that numerous native books—many held in great reverence as sacred records—were in use when they arrived in Mexico in the early sixteenth century. Archaeologist Michael Coe believes "there must have been thousands of such books in Classic times" (generally A.D. 300–900).[24] Only four have been preserved from the Maya zone. But in the 1820s not even the experts knew about these Mesoamerican books.

Our information about the form of the Book of Mormon originally comes from statements in two letters that Professor Charles Anthon wrote years after Martin Harris came to him with a sample of the exotic writing that Joseph Smith had copied off the "gold plates." What he was shown, Anthon said, was "singular characters... arranged and placed in perpendicular columns, and the whole ended in a rude delineation of a circle, divided into various compartments, arched with various strange marks."[25] Anthon compared this form in general terms to an Aztec manuscript, the only type of native book he knew about. But such Aztec books, dating from near the time of the Spanish conquest of Mexico, were not shaped as "books." The records most like those kept by Mormon and his predecessors were from the Maya language area, and none of those were made public until later in the nineteenth century. The "Anthon transcript" (the sample of characters copied from the plates) confirms their "singular" nature. The marks do not resemble writing familiar to any scholars in the 1830s. In fact, the clearest parallels to them are signs on a Mexican artifact that was not discovered until the 1960s.[26]

Interestingly, the Nephite records on metal plates were used anciently to record the same *kinds* of sources and information as were found in native Mesoamerican records. Little or no such content would have appeared in any book written by a New York farm boy: key events affecting the fate of ruling lineages, diplomatic communications, annals of events recorded at the end of each year, letters from correspondents, political history, detailed accounts of battles and wars, descriptions and history of sacred practices, calendar data, prophecies, the adventures of heroes, genealogies, and tribute lists, among others.[27] Moreover, those varied materials are ordered in an intricate manner unlike what is found in any other volume written in the nineteenth century, yet the very disparate parts of the Nephite record prove to be remarkably consistent in how they flow and interconnect.[28]

Scores of statements reflecting strange religious and mythic beliefs and exotic symbols are also found in the Book of Mormon text. Many of these are parallel to beliefs and meanings that we find in ancient Mesoamerican sacred books but that moderns do not recognize, such as notions of a subterranean ocean, sacred artificial mountains, a holy tree at the center of the earth, and ceremonial cannibalism.[29]

The Book of Mormon turns out to be a type of book that no New York farm boy in the nineteenth century (or today) would dream of writing or could have produced if he had. The information that would be required for even the most sophisticated scholar or writer anywhere to come close to the book we have in our hands was just not available to anybody in the 1820s. The Mesoamerican elements that we now know about would not come to light until the middle of the twentieth century or later.

Language

Statements in the Book of Mormon about the language in which it was written and the nature of the record from which it was translated went far beyond anything Joseph Smith could have known about ancient tongues and writing. Yet those statements agree with the picture of ancient scripts that modern scholarship now recognizes.

LANGUAGE SYSTEMS

References to the writing system employed by the Nephite scribes present a picture of a script very different from alphabetic English, which was all that Joseph Smith knew. Mormon lamented that "there are many things which, according to our language, we are not able to write" (3 Nephi 5:18). His son Moroni$_2$ echoed the point in the book of Ether: "Lord, the Gentiles will mock at these things, because of our weakness in writing; . . . thou hast not made us mighty in writing. . . . Thou hast made us that we could write but little, because of the awkwardness of our hands. . . . Thou hast also made our words powerful and great, even that we cannot write them; wherefore, when we write we behold our weakness, and stumble because of the placing of our words" (Ether 12:23–25). Jacob$_2$, son of the original Lehi, felt the same limitation: "I cannot write but a little of my words, because of the difficulty of engraving our words upon plates" (Jacob 4:1). What could these writers have meant by their complaint?

Oral phrasing was not the problem. They had superior conceptual and spiritual ability to speak powerfully, for Moroni$_2$ recorded, "Lord thou hast made us mighty in word by faith . . . ; thou hast made all this people that they could speak much, because of the Holy Ghost which thou hast given them" (Ether 12:23). Nor was the problem merely mechanical; when Moroni$_2$ spoke of "the awkwardness of our hands" (v. 24) and Jacob$_2$ mentioned "the difficulty of engraving our words upon plates," we can suppose that with practice they could have learned to manage their engraving tools precisely enough that they could represent such characters as they desired.

We learn the real problem from Moroni$_2$'s comment that "if our plates had been sufficiently large we should have written in Hebrew; . . . and if we could have written in Hebrew, behold, ye would have had no imperfection in our record" (Mormon 9:33). In other words, writing in a longer, fuller, alphabetic script would have solved the problem they sensed. Now Hebrew was written wholly alphabetically; the sounds of each word would be exactly and explicitly spelled out, so ambiguity would have been reduced to a minimum, but at the cost of using more space. The trouble is that the "reformed Egyptian" system that they did use, like the original hieroglyphic system in Egypt, could pack the linguistic information into fewer signs or glyphs, although that compromised clarity. Many Egyptian-style signs (of "logographic" type) signified broad concepts that lacked precision. So the lack of clarity in language that bothered Jacob$_2$ and Moroni$_2$ was inherent in the hieroglyphic-style script they felt obliged to use.

The glyphic writing of the Maya and surrounding peoples of Mesoamerica suffered ambiguity similar to that of the Egyptians. They too knew that most of the characters they used represented whole concepts, and sometimes more than one concept, so subtle distinctions in meaning could be missed by those who read only literally. Furthermore, their frequent use of nicknames, metaphors, wordplays or code terms, and obscure allusions to history and myth meant that one had to be schooled extensively in literary forms, mythic lore, and history to "get" precisely what the original writer intended. Anciently, certain priests and sons in noble families alone had the privilege of receiving the necessary depth of schooling. The subtleties of certain Mesoamerican tongues, combined with the ambiguous type of script, means that "often a dozen or more quite disparate meanings may legitimately be proposed for a particular monosyllabic root."[30] Another scholar has noted that "many Maya words . . . sometimes can be reconciled with totally different text interpretations. Intended ambiguity in meaning, enhanced by metaphorical expressions, seems to be one of the crucial features of the Maya texts . . . [that] severely restricts . . . attempts towards decipherment."[31] The difficulty was compounded by the fact that much of the language of the sacred texts was a form of poetry. As noted above, the solution to these problems when the cultures were still alive was for readers of the most important texts to be extensively instructed in idioms, allusions, and complex contexts. That learning involved memorizing extensive commentaries on the ancient texts passed on through "wise men" of the culture, that is, priestly text specialists.[32] Fluency in plain everyday speech was never enough.

This situation recalls King Benjamin's urgency in wanting his three sons to become "men of understanding." For that reason he "caused that they should be taught in *all* the language of his fathers that they might know concerning the prophecies" (Mosiah 1:2).³³ He insisted to the princes that learning "the mysteries of God" (vv. 4, 5) depended entirely upon being taught to pore over "these engravings" of their ancestors, which learning had been passed on within the nobility from generation to generation since Lehi's day (see v. 4). The process was intricate, time-consuming, and expensive; only those wealthy enough to enjoy much leisure time, particularly royalty, could afford to master the records (compare 3 Nephi 6:12). It must have been the complications of context surrounding the texts written in "reformed Egyptian" that caused Moroni$_2$ to worry about how his "imperfections" (Mormon 9:31) and "weakness in writing" (Ether 12:23) might be misconstrued by his later readers. Centuries before, his ancestor Nephi$_1$ knew that his people could not understand in context "the things of the Jews" on the brass plates without his interpreting the text of Isaiah for them (see 2 Nephi 25:4–5). Moroni$_2$ hoped that what he wrote would be clear in the absence of any surviving interpreter.

The expression Moroni$_2$ used to label the Nephite script, "reformed Egyptian," applies typologically to the glyphic writing used in Mesoamerica by the Maya and other peoples. (At least half a dozen distinct scripts of this kind, perhaps descended from a common ancestral form, were used at one time or another in that region.)³⁴ Scholars have shown that indeed the early Mesoamerican hieroglyphic writing shared its essential characteristics with Egyptian and other mainly logographic scripts of the Old World.³⁵

An additional note of interest concerns Moroni$_2$'s statements that contrast the Nephite "reformed Egyptian" system of script with that used by the Jaredites. To the Lord he observed, "Thou has not made us mighty in writing like unto the brother of Jared, for thou madest him that the things which he wrote were mighty . . . unto the overpowering of man to read them" (Ether 12:24). What in the records led him to speak of this strong contrast? One possible basis for a difference could be the scripts that were involved. The Jaredites came from "the great tower, at the time the Lord confounded the language of the people" (Ether 1:33), so it is plausible that they used a writing system derived from what we see on the clay tablets from ancient Mesopotamia, the location of "the great tower." That system spelled out words by syllables, each character standing for one syllable. Spelling via syllables was not quite as neat a way to represent the niceties of spoken language as the alphabet (which would not be invented until over a thousand years later), but it was superior in precision to any hieroglyphic system. The power Moroni$_2$ attributed to the words of the brother of Jared might have been due, in part at least, to the Jaredites' use of a writing system different from—that is, a clearer device for communicating actual speech than—Mormon and Moroni$_2$'s hieroglyphic system.

How remarkable that the record keepers of the Book of Mormon allude again and again to their writing systems and, even more remarkable, that the Book of Mormon statements fit so well with what we know about the primary type of script in use in early Mesoamerica, the core Book of Mormon area (the only region in ancient America where writing was regularly used and books existed). Neither

Professor Anthon nor any other savant in 1830 knew such details, yet unlearned young Smith managed to get them right and avoid any number of missteps along these lines that would have revealed him to be a deceiver.

Nephite Political Economy

DETAILS OF POLITICAL ECONOMY

The picture of Nephite and Lamanite societies presented in the Book of Mormon shows numerous political and economic features that we now know were characteristic of ancient civilizations, especially those in Mesoamerica. Careful study of the text makes clear to those who have studied ancient civilizations that no poorly educated resident of nineteenth-century New York like young Smith knew even the basic facts about the exotic modes of social and economic organization that prevailed in Mesoamerican civilization. Secular sources on history available to Joseph could not have acquainted him with either the overall pattern or specific details of the system described or implied in the Book of Mormon.

The political and economic structure of Nephite society was generally similar to what prevailed among the Israelites from King David's day to that of Zedekiah and Lehi, but it has taken scholars immense research on Old Testament Israel and on other Near Eastern societies to understand these aspects (casual readers of the Bible miss most of the picture). Agriculture was, of course, the fundamental source of wealth. Practical control of the land was in the hands of descent groups or tribes and subtribes; families received allotments of cultivable land from councils of elders that headed those broader, kin-constituted groups. (Note that the law of Moses, according to Leviticus 25 and Numbers

36, required that land sold outside the lineage to whom it had been originally assigned should be returned to that unit each half century, during jubilee years.)

Superimposed on that basic structure of the "political economy" was the monarchy. In a formal sense the king was considered to own all the land. As chief decision maker on behalf of the nation, he had a legitimate claim to public support of his royal house and his administrators and their retainers. This claim was anchored in the belief that a sovereign was also properly head of the religious system or cult. According to 1 Samuel 8, when the people of Israel asked the prophet Samuel to choose a king for them so they could be like all their neighbors, he warned them that they would regret it. They would have to pay onerous taxes or tribute, he said, to support the royal family and government establishment. Indeed, within three generations they found themselves burdened with supporting hundreds of Solomon's queens and functionaries, a military establishment, and elaborate royal building projects (see, for example, 1 Kings 10:14–27; 12:4).

The Book of Mormon presents a generally parallel picture. After kingship ended with Mosiah$_2$, the central government, located in Zarahemla (now headed by a chief judge who enjoyed many kinglike powers), featured rulers who "[sat] upon [their] thrones in a state of thoughtless stupor," "surrounded with thousands of those, yea, and tens of thousands, who do also sit in idleness" at or near the capital city (Alma 60:7, 22).

Those multitudes could only have been supported by a system of taxation or tribute that funneled resources up to the dominant class. Certain statements make clear that local rulers "possessed" cities (see, for example, Alma 8:7).

This means they were considered to be owners of the localities they administered, which legally and morally justified their receiving support by tribute that came ultimately from the peasant farmers and craftspeople in their domain (see, for example, Mosiah 11:3; 22:15; 32:5; 35:3). The ambition of would-be rulers like Amalickiah (see Alma 46:4–6) and those who "professed the blood of nobility" (Alma 51:21) was to gain access to power and wealth by getting control of the taxation apparatus. The Nephite dissenter Giddianhi put it bluntly: "I hope that ye [Nephite rulers] will deliver up your lands and your possessions . . . that this my people [of the elite] may recover their rights and government" (3 Nephi 3:10)—"rights," that is, to collect taxes from their subjects. Much of Nephite history is explainable in terms of the struggles of generation after generation of dissenters to control the government so they could live lavishly in the manner of the Zeniffite king Noah and his ancient model, King Solomon.[36] This whole scheme of "possession" and tribute payments matched in all essential ways what had been done by the kings of the Egyptians, Hittites, Assyrians, and Babylonians, among others, for many centuries before Lehi$_1$ and Nephi$_1$'s day.

As noted, a kin-group structure in Nephite society underlay the monarchy. When the central government collapsed shortly before the Savior's visit to the Nephites (see 3 Nephi 7), the process of governing fell into the hands of "tribes and leaders of tribes. Now behold, there was no man among them save he had much family and many kindreds and friends; therefore their tribes became exceeding great" (v. 4). The tribal and kinship structure had always been in place (see Jacob 1:13); in the moment of crisis when the regime in Zarahemla evaporated, additional functions fell on the kin-based tribal structure. What we see in 3 Nephi 7 is a default government, not centralized like that formerly headed by kings or chief judges, yet sufficiently capable to enact and administer "their laws, every one according to his tribe" (3 Nephi 7:11). A version of that dispersed political structure surely continued following the appearance of Jesus Christ, because nothing is said of any central government from then until possibly the time of Mormon (see Mormon 2:2).

This depiction of the authority structure is nowhere spelled out in Mormon's abridgment. Rather, we have to infer it from situations and intimations scattered throughout the record. The same is true of the history of Israel in the Old Testament, whose political and economic context we understand much more fully when we supplement the Bible with information from other Near Eastern societies.[37] The structure of political or governmental power, and justifications for it too, was so established, so generally understood, that it would have seemed foolish for the ancient writers to waste space formally explaining details of what was obvious to people of that time.

Virtually every institution or event involving government and wealth among the Nephites and Lamanites can be matched with parallels from descriptions of the political economy of societies in Mesoamerica. For example, the following occur in Mesoamerican history: (1) a seemingly autocratic ruler like King Noah ended up being overthrown and slain by his own people, who tolerated his excesses only up to a certain point; (2) disagreements and dissensions sapped the unity of political communities so that rivals could seize power; (3) alliances among the ruling elites in rival societies were forged, often by marriage (as in King Lamoni's offer of a bride to Ammon and Amalickiah's taking the widowed Lamanite queen as his wife), as a means to bolster local power and prestige and promote wealth-generating trade relations; and (4) when rebels made trouble, the only sure way for rulers to respond was for the upstarts to be "hewn down" with the sword (see Alma 51:19; compare Moroni$_1$'s dire threat in Alma 60:27–30). Practically every facet of political life (with its entwined economic, religious, and military connections)[38] described in the Book of Mormon account has close parallels in ancient Mesoamerican life.[39]

Nothing Joseph Smith could have known in his day about "the Indians" or the biblical Israelites would have prepared him to dictate such a consistent picture of Nephite and Lamanite government and society as he actually did. Only in recent decades have scholars learned enough to describe these ancient Mesoamerican power mechanisms that prove to have been so much like what the Book of Mormon portrays.

Elements of Material Culture

Various features of material culture mentioned in the Book of Mormon make sense in terms of ancient Mesoamerican civilization. But if, as some claim, Joseph Smith wrote the volume from his personal environment, New York's Amerindians could not have provided him with any hint or data about cement, "sheum," wine, and silk or linen, among other items, mentioned in the Book of Mormon.

Cement

Cement is specifically discussed in Helaman 3:7–11. Nephite colonists from the land of Zarahemla who settled in the land northward in the first century B.C. are credited with becoming expert "in the working of cement," from which they constructed "houses in the which they did dwell" and built "many cities ... of cement" (vv. 7, 9, 11). The Book of Mormon dates this significant technological advance to the year 46 B.C. Here we have several testable facts: the Book of Mormon tells us that people in ancient America became very skillful in the use of cement at a precise historical time. No one in the nineteenth century could have known that cement, in fact, was extensively used in Mesoamerica beginning at about this time, the middle of the first century B.C.[40]

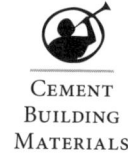

CEMENT BUILDING MATERIALS

A lime cement was in frequent use in southern Mesoamerica, especially in the lowland Maya area in the period after A.D. 200.[41] However, central and Gulf Coast Mexico was the scene of the culmination of concrete engineering. Particularly at the vast ruins of Teotihuacán, near Mexico City, large constructions of this material can still be seen.[42] (That area lies, of course, northward from the Isthmus of Tehuantepec, which most LDS scholars consider to be the dividing point between the Nephite lands southward and northward.) The earliest concrete known is from the Valley of Mexico and dates to perhaps two centuries B.C. Chemically, early Mexican concrete was "much the same as present-day concrete."[43] The fact that very little carbon is found in this cement "attests to the ability of these ancient peoples."[44] These constructions date a little earlier than the reference in the book of Helaman; we may assume that the Nephites' expertness in cement work was taught to them by people who were already living in the "land northward" and had earlier experience in that technology.

Sheum

Akkadian "She'um"

Zeniff, ruler over an enclave of Nephites who settled among the Lamanites in the land of Nephi around the beginning of the second century B.C., reported that among the crops they cultivated, which included corn, wheat, and barley, was one called *sheum,* a term for which Joseph Smith provided no translation (see Mosiah 9:9). Just in the last forty years we have learned that the most important cereal grain among the Akkadians (Babylonians) of Mesopotamia was called *she'um.*[45] The Jaredites of the Book of Mormon, who had originally lived in Mesopotamia, could have put the name on some cultivable plant they encountered in their new land; some of their undocumented descendants may well have passed the name and whatever grain it labeled down to the Zeniffites.

Wine

Fermented Drinks

Some scholars have faulted Joseph Smith for references in the Book of Mormon to wine in the New World promised land (as in Mosiah 11:15). These scholars assure us that wine produced from grapes—which is the usual meaning of the word *wine*—was never made nor used in the Americas. However, the Book of Mormon makes no reference to grapes, although it does mention "vineyards." Some other sort of wine could have been so labeled by the Nephites. When the Spaniards arrived in Mesoamerica, they spoke about several kinds of native "wines." An intoxicating drink was commonly manufactured by fermenting a mixture of water, a certain tree bark, and honey. Other groups fermented juices drawn from the agave plant, bananas, pineapples, or the heart of certain palm trees. To all of these the Europeans applied the term *wine*.⁴⁶ Further, the Spaniards spoke of native plantings of the agave cactus (from which the drink *balche* was made) as "vineyards."⁴⁷ So Joseph Smith's use of the terms *wine* and *vineyards* in the translation of the Book of Mormon has proved to be no mistake, whether some non-grape fruit was used or, as Joseph himself probably assumed, Nephite wine was made from grapes by a process like that used by European settlers in the early United States.⁴⁸

This fine ceramic sculpture from the Gulf Coast of Mexico at about A.D. 700 depicts a drunkard in a manner intended to condemn excessive drinking.

© Justin Kerr

Silk and Linen

The Book of Mormon, in Alma 4:6, refers to the "fine silks" and "fine-twined linen" of the Nephites in the early first century B.C. More than a thousand years earlier the Jaredites also had "silks, and fine-twined linen" (Ether 10:24). However, when European conquerors arrived in the Americas, they found neither Old World silkworms nor flax. Critics have charged Joseph Smith with arbitrarily inserting into the Book of Mormon text the names of those two textiles, and they say that the presence of the two fibers cannot be substantiated by the cultural record for pre-Columbian America. In recent years, however, several fabrics that have been identified in ancient Mesoamerica deserve to be called "silk" and "linen." The text of the Book of Mormon is now vindicated in this regard, although nobody in the nineteenth century, including Smith, could have known

NATIVE AMERICAN FABRICS

enough from secular learning to provide any historical basis for using the two words.

Normal usage today limits the term *silk* to the fabric made of thread exuded by the Japanese silkworm (actually the larva of an Asian moth, *Bombyx mori*). However, the term embraces meanings that extend beyond the Japanese reference. For instance, Aristotle and other classical Greek writers referred to "silk" in use in their world that had no entomological connection with the Far East, and two types of silkworm native to southeastern Europe yielded cocoons from which a fine thread comparable to Asian silk was obtained.[49] Thus a legitimate sense of the term *silk* is "a cloth having characteristics like [Japanese] silk," regardless of whether it originated from the Japanese insect.

Various fabrics in use among the inhabitants of Mexico and Central America when the Spaniards arrived were considered silk or its equivalent by the invaders. One of these fabrics was, indeed, made from cocoons that were gathered from trees in the wild in Mexico and spun into costly cloth. Although the insect involved is not the Japanese one, the procedure of gathering the fine thread is essentially the same as for Japanese silk.[50] There were also a number of other silk-like fabrics reported by the Spaniards. In Yucatán, fiber from inside the pod of the ceiba tree, called *kapok,* was gathered and spun. Bishop Diego de Landa compared the resulting cloth to imported silk,[51] while Father Clavigero described it as "soft and delicate, and perhaps more so, than [Japanese] silk."[52] Silky fiber from the wild pineapple plant was also used to weave a fine textile.[53] Moreover, a silk-like fabric was woven by the Aztecs from delicate rabbit hair.[54] Even cotton cloth could be woven so fine that specimens excavated at Teotihuacán, in central Mexico, and dating to the fourth century A.D. have been characterized as "exceedingly fine" and "of gossamer thinness."[55] These examples provide sufficient evidence that the Book of Mormon references to "silk" are plausible, even though Joseph Smith could not have known any of these historical facts on his own.

"Fine-twined linen" is mentioned three times and "fine linen" three more in the records of the Jaredites and Nephites (e.g., Mosiah 10:5). Yet the flax plant from which our familiar linen is made did not grow in America. On this count too the Book of Mormon has been charged with error. Actually, though, the word *linen* has a broad dictionary meaning in addition to the narrow meaning of cloth made from flax. A textile may be called linen if it has the characteristics of linen. Linen is prepared by soaking and pounding fibers from the flax or hemp plant until they congeal into a strong, solid sheet. In pre-Spanish America native peoples made two kinds of cloth by a similar process. The leaves of the ixtle, maguey, or agave plant were soaked and pounded in the same manner as flax was treated in Europe. The resulting thread and fabric, known as *henequen,* was the most commonly used cloth, especially among people of the lower economic classes in central Mexico. The Spanish conquistador Bernal Diaz explicitly described this cloth as "like linen."[56] Another cloth made of vegetable fiber is bark cloth. The bark of the fig tree was stripped off in large sheets, then soaked, pounded, and dried until the matted material was soft. (Details of the process, and even the same implements, are found in cultures all the way across the Pacific to Southeast Asia.)[57] The resulting "cloth" feels a good deal like *henequen* or linen.[58]

Joseph Smith had no way of knowing about the history of silk and linen, yet the record he translated, the Book of Mormon, turns out to agree with modern evidence that textiles with these labels were used in Mesoamerica.

Warfare

WARS AND WARFARE

The long descriptions of warfare in the Book of Mormon provide some of the most concrete data in the volume that may be compared with Mesoamerican archaeological remains. At several points in the narratives, statements are made about the aims, paraphernalia, and tactics of battle among the Nephites and Lamanites. These led critics in earlier days to claim that Joseph Smith had made repeated errors. They said that the archaeological and historical record about war, especially as it was fought in ancient Mesoamerica, failed to match statements in the Nephite record.

For many years experts claimed that wars played no major role in Mesoamerica's history.[59] They supposed that warfare did not arise there until around A.D. 1000. Before that, it was said, only docile peasants and peaceful chiefs and priests inhabited Mexico and Central America. If that had been so, this would have been the only civilized area in the world without a long military history and the Nephite record would have indeed been contrary to what archaeologists "knew." But in the last quarter century a tide of new studies has completely reversed the old image of social tranquility. It is now clear that armed conflict was as enduring and damaging in Mesoamerica as in any other part of the ancient world. The Book of Mormon record of frequent wars fits the new scholarly consensus.[60]

The forms and chronology of fortification mentioned in the scripture also coincide with what is known from

Mesoamerica. The earliest Nephite defensive walls surrounded the cities of Nephi (renamed by the Lamanites Lehi-Nephi) and Shilom, in the area first settled by Nephi's faction when they fled from his brothers (see Jarom 1:7; Mosiah 7:10; 9:8). We can suppose that they modeled those walls on those known from Old World Jerusalem, of which Nephi, Sam, and Zoram had firsthand knowledge. Mesoamerican examples are numerous, though probably cruder in finish than Jerusalem's wall.[61]

At the beginning of the wars started by Amalickiah, about 75 B.C., the Nephites adopted a different kind of fortification—something the Lamanites had never seen before (see Alma 49:5, 8), though this does not necessarily mean the Nephites invented it. It consisted of "a ridge of earth" formed by digging a ditch completely around a city (see Alma 50:1) and throwing up the excavated dirt to form the ridge; it was "so high" that the Lamanites could not get their missiles over it (Alma 49:4). Later, at lowland Bountiful where timber was probably more abundant, the Nephites built "a breastwork of timbers upon the inner bank of the ditch," then "cast up [more] dirt out of the ditch against the breastwork of timbers," forming together an even more daunting "wall of timbers and earth, to an exceeding height" (Alma 53:4). Attackers thus confronted a continuous steep slope that stretched from the bottom of the ditch to the top of the timber palisade. The defenders "could cast stones from the top thereof, according to their pleasure and their strength, and slay him who should attempt to approach" (Alma 50:5).

On the inside, of course, the timber retaining wall presented a sheer vertical face. Thus at the city of Nephihah, which the Lamanites had captured, Moroni$_1$ and his men at night climbed the outer earthen slope and "came upon the top of the wall" to spy out the sleeping Lamanites (Alma 62:20). Finding the enemy bedded down some distance away, Moroni and his men used "their strong cords and their ladders" to get down from the top of the wall on the inside (see vv. 21–23). Later that sheer inside face led to the death of the Nephite chief judge Pacumeni when an invading Lamanite army under one Coriantumr penetrated the city of Zarahemla; Pacumeni "did flee before Coriantumr, even to the walls of the city," where he could flee no farther, and "Coriantumr did smite him against the wall" (Helaman 1:21).

When members of Cortez's expedition crossed the base of the Yucatán Peninsula in the 1520s, they encountered fortifications very similar to those described in the book of Alma; other historical accounts also tell of fortified sites of the same nature.[62] Of greater interest, however, are earlier examples revealed by archaeology. One of the best-excavated so far is at Becan, in the center of the Yucatán Peninsula, where David L. Webster worked in 1970. He dates the erection of these fortifications to about A.D. 250–300, although the general design was probably much older.[63] His description recalls the wording in the book of Alma: "The vertical distance from the top of the embankment to the bottom of the ditch . . . would have averaged something over 11 m. [35 ft.], not counting any . . . wooden palisade. The steep angles of the inner ditch wall and parapet slope could not have been climbed without the aid of ladders; an enemy force caught in the bottom of the ditch would have been at the mercy of the defenders, whose most effective weapons under the circumstances would have been large rocks. . . . To throw 'uphill' from the outside is almost impossible. Defenders, possibly screened by a palisade, could have rained long-distance missiles on approaching enemies using spearthrowers and slings" [compare Alma 49:4]. The attackers' approach would have been spotted by watchmen on tall towers, for which there is evidence (see Alma 50:3–4), although decay and erosion have removed any evidence of the presumed wooden palisade.[64]

The Book of Mormon mentions another feature of warfare that no one in Joseph Smith's time would have known about. We read a puzzling statement in Alma 49:4 to the effect that Lamanite warriors attempted to "*cast . . . their arrows*" over the Nephite fortification walls. Surely the Indians of the northeastern United States that Joseph Smith knew about shot their arrows rather than "cast them." A primary war weapon among Mesoamerican peoples was the spear-thrower, or *atlatl* (the name of the device in Nahuatl, the language spoken by the Aztecs).[65] This implement consisted of a carved stick about eighteen inches long that was grasped at one end in the user's right hand as he extended his throwing arm behind him. The end of a relatively long, heavy arrow was placed with its blunt end against a notch at the far end of the atlatl, while two fingers of the user's hand held the projectile parallel to the throwing stick. When the user cast his arm and the weapon forward, the length of the atlatl served to increase the propelling power of the thrower's arm. That gave the thrower greater leverage to increase the velocity and range of the missile.

In Mesoamerican warfare and hunting both the regular bow and arrow and the atlatl were used. If we suppose that the Lamanites in the day of Moroni$_1$ used atlatls—and this is plausible on the basis of archaeology—the Nephite fortification barrier would indeed pose a problem for attackers if they attempted to "cast" their "arrows" into the stronghold, just as the wording in the account in Alma neatly states.

John Tvedtnes has pointed out that this expression in Alma 49:4 could also stem from use of the Hebrew root *YRH,* which means "to throw."[66] When that word is applied to arrows in Bible usage, the English translation is "to shoot," even though the Hebrew literally reads "to throw" (see, for example, 1 Samuel 20:20, 36–37).

Nothing in books available to Joseph Smith in 1830, be they books about Indians in the New World or about the Hebrew language, could have furnished him with information that would justify the translation "cast . . . their arrows." Nor could he have gleaned from any published source the details of ancient American warfare that fit so well within the Book of Mormon account and yet have only recently come to light.

Further "Hits"

Historical, geographical, and cultural statements made in the Book of Mormon hit targets both large and small. Here are three small cases—information in the scripture that matches what we now know of ancient Mesoamerica but that nobody in 1830 knew. Numerous other points of similar nature could be mentioned.

LOCATION FOR ZARAHEMLA

The archaeological site known forty years ago as Santa Rosa, which sat beside the Grijalva River in the Mexican state of Chiapas (the ruin now lies beneath waters impounded by a large dam), meets all the geographical requirements for the Nephite city of Zarahemla.[67] Test excavations in a limited portion of Santa Rosa were made in 1958. An exact chronology and full picture of life there could not be determined in detail, but it was concluded that a "tremendous amount of building activity" likely took place in about the first century B.C. In addition to earthen mound foundations up to more than 40 feet high, a huge platform built in the center of the place measured over 150 feet wide by 180 feet long and 22 feet high; this platform lay directly on the center line through the site. Presumably, various public buildings had once been built on top of the giant platform, although no search was made for evidence of such structures. At some point, likely in the first century B.C. (approximately when $Mosiah_2$ was alive), this platform was newly covered with a layer of gravel, and a plaster floor was laid over that. The gravel on either side of a line that ran exactly through the middle of this "temple" was found to be of distinct composition, half from one geological source, the other half of a different origin. The excavator suggested that the divided floor "may be taken to imply two separate groups, each working on its section" in a ceremonial context. The surrounding residential area was also divided into two sections that were separated along an extension of the line between the gravels. The archaeologist involved thought that a division of the community into two social groups had prevailed and that the gravel laying had been a ceremonial act acknowledging the social separation.[68]

This dual pattern recalls the situation in the city of Zarahemla at the time of King $Mosiah_2$ when his subjects, who spoke two different languages, assembled to hear him—"all the people of Nephi..., and also all the people of Zarahemla, and they were gathered together in two bodies" (Mosiah 25:4). At the least, Santa Rosa provides an example of the type of ethnically or linguistically divided Mesoamerican community reflected in Mosiah 25:4, whether or not it was the actual scene of the historical event reported there.

HAGOTH'S SHIPS

Hagoth is reported to have built ships and sent explorers northward from a spot on the coast of the west sea "by the narrow neck of land" (see Alma 63:5–6). The time was shortly before the birth of Christ. This is the only instance in Book of Mormon history when mention is made of shipbuilding and exploring by sea in the Nephites' promised land. It so happens that on the west-sea side (Pacific) of the Isthmus of Tehuantepec, which qualifies on many criteria as the narrow neck of land, there are a pair of large, placid lagoons, over thirty miles long. They could have provided a sheltered place not only to construct Hagoth's ships but also to master their use. In the mountains overlooking the lagoons, the Spaniards long afterward located timber that they found ideal for their own shipbuilding purposes. Also, it is generally agreed by Mesoamericanists that over a period of many centuries large seagoing rafts (de facto "ships") from Ecuador actually came up the Pacific coast to the Isthmus of Tehuantepec and beyond on trading expeditions.[69] No other spot north of Panama fits the Hagoth story as well as the Pacific coast "by the narrow neck of land."

HUMAN SACRIFICE

Near the end of the Nephite history, in the depths of that people's depravity, the Book of Mormon reports ceremonial human sacrifice being carried out by the Lamanites (see Mormon 4:11–15, 21), accompanied by cannibalism among both Lamanites and Nephites (see Moroni 9:8–10). Evidence for these heinous practices at about the same period of time have been revealed by archaeological excavations, but not until a long time after the Book of Mormon translation was published.[70]

Dozens of similarly provocative correlations could be documented. In the ones just sketched, as in the many left unmentioned, we are left to marvel at how Joseph Smith managed to dictate—in a few months and without significant editing—such a book that time and again matches up with life and events in ancient Mesoamerica. Not a single scholar in young Joseph's day knew enough to get any, let alone all, of these things right. One must ask, how then did he do it? The only choices available to answer the question seem to be (1) that he was an unbelievably creative writer, for which we have no other evidence, or (2) that he had access to an actual ancient Mesoamerican book.

Notes

1. For example, note a comment in 1835 by W. W. Phelps to Oliver Cowdery (who represent two of the better-educated early converts to the Church of Jesus Christ of Latter-day Saints): "There may be a continent at the North Pole, of more than 1300 square miles [he probably meant miles square], containing thousands of millions of Israelites [thousands of millions translates to billions!]." *Latter Day Saints' Messenger and Advocate,* October 1835, 194.

2. "Reply to a Pamphlet Printed in Glasgow, Entitled 'Remarks on Mormonism,'" part 3, *Millennial Star,* 15 April 1849, 115–16.

3. Victor W. Von Hagen, *Maya Explorer: John Lloyd Stephens and the Lost Cities of Central America and Yucatán* (Norman: University of Oklahoma Press, 1947), 75.

4. *Times and Seasons,* 15 September 1842, 915.

5. A broader treatment of this question than given here

appears in John L. Sorenson, *Mormon's Map* (Provo, Utah: FARMS, 2000), 93–105.

6. See Matthew Melko, *The Nature of Civilization* (Boston: Porter Sargent, 1969); Stephen K. Sanderson, ed., *Civilizations and World Systems: Studying World-Historical Change* (Walnut Creek, Calif.: AltaMira Press, 1995); and David Wilkinson, "Cities, Civilizations and Oikumenes," parts 1 and 2, *Comparative Civilizations Review* 27 (1992): 51–87 and 28 (1993): 41–72.

7. For a fuller discussion see John L. Sorenson, "The Settlements of Book of Mormon Peoples," in *Nephite Culture and Society: Collected Papers,* ed. Matthew R. Sorenson (Salt Lake City: New Sage Books, 1997), 131–54.

8. On the Lamanites see Alma 22:27. On the Nephites see John L. Sorenson, "Growing Pains," chap. 5 in his *An Ancient American Setting for the Book of Mormon* (Salt Lake City: Deseret Book and FARMS, 1985).

9. For example, see Ray T. Matheny, "An Early Maya Metropolis Uncovered: El Mirador," *National Geographic,* 3 September 1987, 317–39; and John L. Sorenson, *Images of Ancient America: Visualizing Book of Mormon Life* (Provo, Utah: Research Press, 1998), 103, 146–47.

10. Samuel D. Tyler Diary, 25 September 1838, Family and Church History Department Archives, The Church of Jesus Christ of Latter-day Saints.

11. See Sorenson, *Mormon's Map,* 35, 57; and Sorenson, *Ancient American Setting,* 254–59.

12. See Josiah Priest, *American Antiquities and Discoveries in the West . . .* (Albany: Hoffman and White, 1833), iv.

13. See John L. Sorenson, "The Book of Mormon as a Mesoamerican Record," in *Book of Mormon Authorship Revisited: The Evidence for Ancient Origins,* ed. Noel B. Reynolds (Provo, Utah: FARMS, 1997), 489–90 n. 9.

14. A convenient summary of developments is found in "History in the Trenches," *American Archaeology* 3/3 (1999): 26–32.

15. See John L. Sorenson, "When Lehi's Party Arrived in the

Land, Did They Find Others There?" *Journal of Book of Mormon Studies* 1/1 (1992): 1–34; and Sorenson, *Ancient American Setting,* 50–56, 81–91.

16. See Sorenson, *Mormon's Map,* 93–95, 102–3.

17. John L. Sorenson, "A Mesoamerican Chronology," 2001. Unpublished MS.

18. See Sorenson, *Ancient American Setting,* 108–37.

19. See Sorenson, "The Book of Mormon Mapped," chap. 1 in his *Ancient American Setting.*

20. See John L. Sorenson, "The Significance of an Apparent Relationship between the Ancient Near East and Mesoamerica," in *Man across the Sea: Problems of Pre-Columbian Contacts,* ed. C. L. Riley et al. (Austin: University of Texas Press, 1971), 219–41; and John L. Sorenson, "The Book of Mormon as a Mesoamerican Codex," *Newsletter and Proceedings of the Society for Early Historic Archaeology* 139 (December 1976): 1–9.

21. Sorenson, *Images of Ancient America.*

22. Many are sketched in preliminary fashion in chapters 4 through 8 of Sorenson, *Ancient American Setting.*

23. Alexander von Humboldt, *Researches concerning the Institutions and Monuments of the Ancient Inhabitants of America . . .* (London: Longmans, 1814).

24. Michael D. Coe, "Early Steps in the Evolution of Maya Writing," in *Origins of Religious Art and Iconography in Preclassic Mesoamerica,* ed. Henry B. Nicholson (Los Angeles: UCLA Latin American Center Publications, 1976), 110.

25. Quoted in B. H. Roberts, *A Comprehensive History of The Church of Jesus Christ of Latter-day Saints* (Salt Lake City: The Church of Jesus Christ of Latter-day Saints, 1930), 100–107; also in FARMS staff, "Martin Harris' Visit with Charles Anthon: Collected Documents on 'Shorthand Egyptian'" (Provo, Utah: FARMS, 1990), 16–18.

26. See David H. Kelley, "A Cylinder Seal from Tlatilco," *American Antiquity* 31/5 (1966): 744–45; and Carl Hugh Jones, "The 'Anthon Transcript' and Two Mesoamerican Cylinder

Seals," *Newsletter and Proceedings of the Society for Early Historic Archaeology* 122 (September 1970): 1–8.

27. See Sorenson, "Book of Mormon as a Mesoamerican Record," 391–522.

28. See, for example, Melvin J. Thorne, "Complexity, Consistency, Ignorance, and Probabilities," in *Book of Mormon Authorship Revisited*, ed. Reynolds, 179–94; and John W. Welch, "Textual Consistency," in *Reexploring the Book of Mormon*, ed. John W. Welch (Provo, Utah: FARMS, 1992), 21–23.

29. See Sorenson, "Book of Mormon as a Mesoamerican Codex," 1–9.

30. Munro S. Edmonson, *The Book of Counsel: The Popol Vuh of the Quiché Maya of Guatemala*, Middle American Research Institute, no. 35 (New Orleans: Tulane University, 1971), xii.

31. Dieter Dütting, "'Bats' in the Usumacinta Valley. Remarks on the Inscriptions of Bonampak and Neighboring Sites in Chiapas, Mexico," *Zeitschrift für Ethnologie* 103 (1978): 53.

32. The Aztec schools are best known. See Miguel León-Portilla, "Pre-Hispanic Literature," in *Archaeology of Northern Mesoamerica*, ed. Gordon F. Ekholm and Ignacio Bernal, vol. 10 of *Handbook of Middle American Indians*, ed. Robert Wauchope (Austin: University of Texas Press, 1971), 453. See also Clemency Coggins, "The Manikin Scepter: Emblem of Lineage," *Estudios de Cultura Maya* 17 (1988): 124–25, regarding the intentional and unintentional ambiguity in Maya sacred writings.

33. See fuller discussion in Sorenson, "Book of Mormon as a Mesoamerican Record," 435–62.

34. See ibid., 508–9 n. 135.

35. See Linda Miller Van Blerkom, "A Comparison of Maya and Egyptian Hieroglyphics," *Katunob* 11/3 (1979): 1–7; and C. F. and F. M. Voegelin, "Typological Classification of Systems with Included, Excluded and Self-Sufficient Alphabets," *Anthropological Linguistics* 3 (1961): 68–80.

36. This subject is treated in detail in John L. Sorenson, "The Political Economy of the Nephites," in *Nephite Culture and Society*, ed. Sorenson, 195–236.

37. For example, see Tomoo Ishida, "Solomon," in *The Anchor Bible Dictionary,* ed. David Noel Freedman (New York: Doubleday, 1992), 6:105–13.

38. For a military example, see John A. Tvedtnes, "Book of Mormon Tribal Affiliation and Military Castes," in *Warfare in the Book of Mormon,* ed. Stephen D. Ricks and William J. Hamblin (Salt Lake City: Deseret Book and FARMS, 1990), 296–326.

39. See Sorenson, "Political Economy of the Nephites," in comparison with, for example, Eva Hunt, "Irrigation and the Socio-Political Organization of Cuicatec Cacicazgos," in *Chronology and Irrigation,* ed. Frederick Johnson, vol. 4 of *The Prehistory of the Tehuacan Valley,* ed. Douglas S. Byers (Austin: University of Texas Press, 1972), 162–259, especially pp. 200–230. See also Sorenson, *Images of Ancient America,* especially pp. 102–23.

40. See Matthew G. Wells and John W. Welch, "Concrete Evidence for the Book of Mormon," in *Reexploring the Book of Mormon,* ed. Welch, 212–14.

41. See H. E. D. Pollock, "Architecture of the Maya Lowlands," in *Archaeology of Southern Mesoamerica,* ed. G. R. Willey, vol. 2 of *Handbook of Middle American Indians,* ed. Robert Wauchope (Austin: University of Texas Press, 1965), 378–44, especially p. 396.

42. See Carlos R. Margain, "Pre-Columbian Architecture of Central Mexico," *Archaeology of Northern Mesoamerica,* ed. Ekholm and Bernal, 45–91, especially p. 54.

43. David S. Hyman, *Precolumbian Cements: A Study of the Calcareous Cements in Prehispanic Mesoamerican Building Construction* (Baltimore: Johns Hopkins University, Department of Geography and Environmental Engineering, 1970), sec. 2, p. 3; Maurice Daumas, ed., *Histoire Générale des Techniques* (Paris: Presses Universitaires de France, 1962), 1:403, as cited by Hyman.

44. Hyman, *Precolumbian Cements,* sec. 6, p. 5.

45. See R. F. Smith, "Some 'Neologisms' from the Mormon Canon," in *1973 Conference on the Language of the Mormons* (Provo, Utah: BYU Language Research Center, 1973), 66. In

Akkadian the word meant "barley"; in Old Assyrian, a neighbor tongue, the term signified "wheat." Since both wheat and barley are separately listed in Mosiah 9:9, *she'um* did not mean either of those two grains, but it could have been transferred to another seed or even a non-seed plant. Regarding seven little-known grain crops from Mesoamerica to which the name *she'um* might have been applied, see John L. Sorenson, "Viva Zapato! Hurray for the Shoe!" *Review of Books on the Book of Mormon* 6 /1 (1994): 338–39.

46. See documentation in Sorenson, *Ancient American Setting,* 186–87.

47. See J. E. S. Thompson, ed., *Thomas Gage's Travels in the New World* (Norman: University of Oklahoma Press, 1958), 76.

48. The grape plant has now been identified from an archaeological site in the Mexican state of Chiapas that dates to the Nephite period. The archaeologist making the discovery presumed that the ancient people made wine from the fruit. See Alejandro Claudio Martínez Muriel, "Don Martín, Chiapas: inferencias económico-sociales de una comunidad arqueológica" (master's thesis, Escuela Nacional de Antropología e Historia, and Universidad Nacional Autónoma de México, 1978), 105, 120, 125.

49. See W. T. M. Forbes, "The Silkworm of Aristotle," *Classical Philology* 25 (1930): 22–26; and Gisela M. A. Richter, "Silk in Greece," *American Journal of Archaeology* 33 (1929): 27–33.

50. See Irmgard W. Johnson, "Basketry and Textiles," in *Archaeology of Northern Mesoamerica,* ed. Ekholm and Bernal, 312; and Matthew Wallrath, *Excavations in the Tehuantepec Region, Mexico,* Transactions of the American Philosophical Society, vol. 57, pt. 2 (Philadelphia: American Philosophical Society, 1967), 12.

51. Alfred M. Tozzer, ed., *Landa's Relación de las Cosas de Yucatán: A Translation,* Papers of the Peabody Museum of American Archaeology and Ethnology, Harvard University, vol. 18 (Cambridge, Mass.: Peabody Museum, 1941), 201, 205.

52. Francesco Saverino Clavigero, *History of Mexico 1,* trans. Charles Cullen (Philadelphia: Thomas Dobson, 1817), 41.

53. See William E. Safford, "Food Plants and Textiles of Ancient America," in *Proceedings of the 19th International Congress of Americanists* (Washington, 1917), 17.

54. Johnson, "Basketry and Textiles," 312.

55. Elisabeth Stromberg, quoted in *Mexican Highland Cultures: Archaeological Researches at Teotihuacán, Calpulalpan, and Chalchicomula*, ed. Sigvald Linné (Stockholm: H. Ohissons Boktryckeri, 1942), 157–60.

56. Bernal Diaz del Castillo, *The Discovery and Conquest of Mexico* (New York: Farrer, Straus, and Cudahy, 1956), 24.

57. Paul Tolstoy, "Cultural Parallels between Southeast Asia and Mesoamerica in the Manufacture of Bark Cloth," *Transactions of the New York Academy of Sciences*, no. 25 (1963): 646–62.

58. See Johnson, "Basketry and Textiles," 312.

59. See David L. Webster, *Defensive Earthworks at Becan, Campeche, Mexico: Implications for Maya Warfare*, Middle American Research Institute, no. 41 (New Orleans: Tulane University, 1976), 1, 3.

60. This history of thought is treated at greater length in John L. Sorenson, "Fortifications in the Book of Mormon Account Compared with Mesoamerican Fortifications," in *Warfare in the Book of Mormon*, ed. Ricks and Hamblin, 445–77.

61. For Yucatán, an example dating to late Nephite times is reported by Prudence M. Rice and Don S. Rice, "Topoxte, Macanche, and the Central Peten Post-Classic," in *The Lowland Maya Postclassic*, ed. A. F. Chase and Prudence M. Rice (Austin: University of Texas Press, 1985), 166–83, especially p. 176. Millions of tourists have seen similar walls at the site of Tulum near Cancún, Mexico.

62. See Hernán Cortés, *Letters from Mexico*, trans. A. R. Pagden (New York: Grossman, 1971), 371–72; compare in other areas Maurice Keatinge, *The True History of the Conquest of Mexico* (New York: Robert M. McBride, 1922), 426–27, 51–52.

63. See Webster, "Defensive Earthworks," 85. Webster suspects that this type of "defensive system is of great antiquity in the lowlands," 108.

64. Ibid., 95–96; compare Alma 49:18–20. For artists' reconstructions, see p. 91 of Webster's study and p. 133 of Sorenson, *Images of Ancient America*.

65. See illustrations and discussion in Sorenson, *Images of Ancient America*, 131–32. See also William J. Hamblin, "The Bow and Arrow in the Book of Mormon," in *Warfare in the Book of Mormon*, ed. Ricks and Hamblin, 365–99, especially 388–89.

66. Personal communication, February 2001.

67. See Sorenson, *Ancient American Setting*, 46–47, 153–57.

68. See Donald L. Brockington, *The Ceramic History of Santa Rosa, Chiapas, Mexico*, Papers of the New World Archaeological Foundation, BYU, no. 23 (1967), especially pp. 1, 2, 60, and 61. The archaeologists who produced these results were not Latter-day Saints.

69. See Sorenson, *Ancient American Setting*, 268–69; Robert C. West, "Aboriginal Sea Navigation between Middle and South America," *American Anthropologist* 63 (1961): 133–35; and Jorge G. Marcos, "Breve prehistoria del Ecuador," in *Arqueología de la costa ecuatoriana: Nuevos enfoques*, ed. Jorge G. Marcos (Guayaquíl: ESPOL y Corporación Editora Nacional, 1986).

70. See, for example, Sergio Gómez Chávez, "La función social del sacrificio humano en Teotihuacán: Un intento para formalizar su estudio e interpretación," in *La época clásica: Nuevos hallazgos, nuevas ideas*, ed. Amalia Cardós de Méndez (Mexico: Museo Nacional de Antropología, Instituto Nacional de Antropología e Historia, 1990), 147–62. On Olmec practices see Michael D. Coe, "San Lorenzo Tenochtitlán," *Archaeology*, ed. J. A. Sabloff, vol. 1 of *Supplement to the Handbook of Middle American Indians*, ed. Victoria R. Bricker (Austin: University of Texas Press, 1981), 117–46, especially 144. See also Sorenson, *Ancient American Setting*, 346.

The Wrong Type of Book

John Gee

Environmental explanations of the Book of Mormon have been popular among critics in the twentieth century as alternatives for Joseph Smith's explanation of the book's origins.[1] The environmentalists attempt to explain the Book of Mormon as a product of the cultural milieu of early-nineteenth-century America, a backdrop that presumably explains all the features of the book. They assume that Joseph Smith wanted to write a history of the ancient inhabitants of America. Although many people, including Latter-day Saints, have imprecisely described the Book of Mormon as a record of "the ancient inhabitants of the Americas,"[2] the book explains itself more narrowly—as "an abridgment of the record of the people of Nephi, and also of the Lamanites" (Book of Mormon title page).

Even so, environmentalists choose to place the Book of Mormon in "the broad contours of public discussion about the ancient inhabitants of America which had taken place or was taking place by 1830 when the Book of Mormon first appeared."[3] Presumably, for the environmentalists, the Book of Mormon was the sort of book that anyone in Joseph Smith's day could have or would have written as a history of the ancient inhabitants of the Americas. Unwittingly, these observers have provided good examples of exactly what the people of Joseph's day thought a "history" like the Book of Mormon should contain. Yet the book does not contain those things; it is simply not that sort of book. The environmentalists need to explain why, if the Book of Mormon is merely a typical product of Joseph Smith's environment, it differs so much—in subject matter, phraseology, and descriptions of particulars—from the kind of book that those who lived in Joseph's day expected.

Nineteenth-Century Expectations

DIVERGING NINETEENTH-CENTURY EXPECTATIONS

We know exactly what kind of book Joseph Smith's contemporaries expected the Book of Mormon to be like because we have two other works from that same period that are said to be of the same general sort. Within months of the publication of the Book of Mormon, Abner Cole, under the name of Obadiah Dogberry, published a satire entitled "The Book of Pukei."[4] The other work was an unfinished novel by Reverend Solomon Spaulding entitled "Manuscript Story" but which others have called "Manuscript Found." Throughout the nineteenth century this novel was put forward as the original of the Book of Mormon, though the manuscript itself was carefully concealed because it was obvious to those who had read the work that it bore only casual resemblance to the Book of Mormon.[5] In fact, when the manuscript was discovered, the Mormons were the first to publish it as a means of putting the weary rumors to rest. Cole's and Spaulding's works fit comfortably within their early-nineteenth-century milieu and provide a control against wild speculation about nineteenth-century origins for the Book of Mormon.

I will also discuss Ethan Smith's *View of the Hebrews*[6] because some people believe it inspired or influenced Joseph Smith in writing the Book of Mormon.[7] If people of the nineteenth century expected a record of the ancient inhabitants of the Americas to be a work like Ethan Smith's, it would be strange indeed, since Ethan Smith's work, unlike the Book of Mormon, is not a narrative but an essay. Environmentalists who argue that Joseph Smith somehow got the idea for the Book of Mormon by reading *View of the Hebrews* (there is no indication that Joseph had read that book) are no closer to explaining the Book of Mormon than if they were arguing that government technical manuals explain Tom Clancy's books.[8] This is because the germ of an idea is not the story or narrative itself, but merely the spark that can precede the tremendous creative effort that gives life to that idea through the writing process. Along these lines, one popular science fiction writer observed:

> It was a good idea. . . . But, having thought of [it], I hadn't the faintest idea of how to go about turning the idea into a story. It occurred to me then for the first time that the *idea* of the story is nothing compared to the importance of knowing how to find a character and a story to tell around that idea. Asimov, having had the idea of paralleling *The Decline and Fall*, still had no story; his genius—and the soul of the story—came when he personalized his history, making the psychohistorian Hari Seldon the god-figure, the planmaker, the apocalyptic prophet of the story. I had no such character, and no idea of how to make one.[9]

Beyond the issue of the unexplained narrative, environmentalists need to explain why Joseph Smith, if he had read Ethan Smith's work, got so many details wrong for his own day (as compared with Ethan Smith)—details that work out so well with the ancient setting of the Book of Mormon.

Subject Matter

The Book of Pukei tells in a mocking fashion about the sort of things that Joseph's neighbors in Palmyra expected to find in the Book of Mormon. Thus, because Joseph had been hired to dig for treasure,[10] almost all of Cole's account deals with digging for treasure.[11] Cole talks about "where the Nephites hid their treasure,"[12] which treasure included "a box of gold watches."[13] Yet hiding treasures takes up no more than 20 out of 6,604 verses in a book of more than five hundred pages, yielding no more than 0.3 percent of the Book of Mormon (see Helaman 12:18–20; 13:17–23, 30–37; Mormon 1:18–19). Such sparse coverage about hiding treasures can hardly be called a major theme. Furthermore, most of the Book of Mormon references to hiding treasures are contained in prophecy, not historical accounts, the one historical account being a very generalized statement that "the inhabitants thereof began to hide up their treasures in the earth; and they became slippery" (Mormon 1:18). Digging for treasure is mentioned in only one verse of the Book of Mormon, and that type of digging was a regular mining operation "to get ore, of gold, and of silver, and of iron, and of copper" (Ether 10:23).

Reverend Spaulding's manuscript is mainly a romance, devoting more than a quarter of its pages to the themes of romance, courtship, and marriage.[14] This is not surprising

DIGGING FOR TREASURE

in a document written about the same time that Jane Austen's novels appeared. The subject matter of Spaulding's work, however, is foreign to the Book of Mormon. Courtship, of a sort, does show up in the Book of Mormon, but not in a recognizable form for the nineteenth or even the twentieth century. The courtship of Nephi and his brothers, who were sent to Ishmael by Lehi "that his sons should take daughters to wife" (1 Nephi 7:1), is described in the following way:

COURTSHIP AND ROMANCE

> We went up unto the house of Ishmael, and we did gain favor in the sight of Ishmael, insomuch that we did speak unto him the words of the Lord.
>
> And it came to pass that the Lord did soften the heart of Ishmael, and also his household, insomuch that they took their journey with us down into the wilderness to the tent of our father. (1 Nephi 7:4–5)

The marriages are recorded later in a matter-of-fact style:

> And it came to pass that I, Nephi, took one of the daughters of Ishmael to wife; and also, my brethren took of the daughters of Ishmael to wife; and also Zoram took the eldest daughter of Ishmael to wife. (1 Nephi 16:7)

Thus the courtship of Lehi's sons is distinctly different from the courtship of Miles Standish. The courtship of the priests of Noah is even more abrupt and foreign to nineteenth-century-American tastes:

> And having tarried in the wilderness, and having discovered the daughters of the Lamanites, they laid and watched them;
>
> And when there were but few of them gathered together to dance, they came forth out of their secret places and took them and carried them into the wilderness. (Mosiah 20:4–5)

And what Jane Austen heroine, even the adulterous Lady Susan, would behave as did the daughter of Jared?

> Now the daughter of Jared was exceedingly fair. And it came to pass that she did talk with her father, and said unto him: Whereby hath my father so much sorrow?...
>
> ... Let my father send for Akish, the son of Kimnor; and behold, I am fair, and I will dance before him, and I will please him, that he will desire me to wife; wherefore if he shall desire of thee that ye shall give unto him me to wife, then shall ye say: I will give her if ye will bring unto me the head of my father, the king. (Ether 8:9–10)

Nineteenth-century-American notions of romantic love are far removed from the patterns of Nephite and Jaredite courtships mentioned in the Book of Mormon, clearly separating the book in that regard from the cultural milieu of Joseph Smith's day.

LOST TRIBES OF ISRAEL

Ethan Smith's work attempts to prove "that the American Indians are the ten tribes of Israel"[15] by various arguments and by citing several parallels between the ancient Israelites and the Native Americans. Rather than cite proofs or parallels, the Book of Mormon tells a long, involved story of Lehi's descendants. It asserts rather than argues the Israelite origin of some of the different peoples mentioned in the record. In opposition to the *View of the Hebrews*, it specifically claims that its peoples "are a remnant of the house of Joseph" (3 Nephi 15:12) and that "the other tribes of the house of Israel . . . are not of this land, neither of the land of Jerusalem, neither in any parts of that land round about" (3 Nephi 15:15–16:1).[16] Jesus tells the Nephites that he must leave them and go "also to show myself unto the lost tribes of Israel" (3 Nephi 17:4), which clearly means that the Nephites were not among those tribes. If Ethan Smith's work is any indication of nineteenth-century expectations that Native Americans were the lost ten tribes, the Book of Mormon clearly contradicts that paradigm.

The Cultural Setting

The cultural setting of the Book of Mormon is markedly different from that of the Book of Pukei, the Spaulding manuscript, and *View of the Hebrews*. Of these four works, it is the Book of Mormon that does not reflect a nineteenth-century milieu.

DIFFERENT CULTURAL SETTINGS

The setting of both the Book of Pukei and "Manuscript Found" is a world dominated by the cultural heritage of the Roman Empire, while the setting of the Book of Mormon is dominated by the ancient Near Eastern and Mesoamerican cultures. Thus when the Book of Pukei refers to "an old book in an unknown tongue," it turns out to be "Cicero's *Orations* in Latin."[17] Those orations constituted a common Latin school text in the nineteenth century, and mastery of it was required for university admission. Similarly, Reverend Spaulding set his novel as coming from "twenty eight *sheets* of parchment . . . written in an elegant [*sic*] hand with Roman Letters & in the Latin Language."[18] This manuscript was supposed to have been written by one Fabius at the time of Constantine, who, with a group of Romans, was blown off course on a sea voyage to Britain.[19] The heavy Roman bias is typical of nineteenth-century America, where the Roman Republic was consciously imitated.

Even *View of the Hebrews* shows the influence of Latin, for it begins with a discussion of the Roman destruction of Jerusalem based on the Bible and supplemented by Greek (Josephus) and Latin sources (Tacitus, Suetonius),[20] and it includes an appeal to Scaliger, the classical scholar.[21] The Book of Mormon, on the other hand, refers to the Babylonian destruction of Jerusalem six hundred years earlier.[22]

In contrast, the original cultural setting of the Book of Mormon is described in quite different terms. For example, the language is a mixture of "the learning of the Jews and the language of the Egyptians" (1 Nephi 1:2). We read, "I say Jew, because I mean them from whence I came" (2 Nephi 33:8). These Jews in Lehi's group became "a lonesome and a solemn people, wanderers, cast out from Jerusalem" (Jacob 7:26). After their arrival in the New World, they began to assimilate the local environment and customs, their previous cultural patterns having been "handed down and altered" (Mormon 9:30; compare Alma 49:11).

Stylistic Features

DISPARATE STYLISTIC FEATURES

The nineteenth-century concern with Latin and imitating its style in speech and writing is partly a product of the educational system of the time. Reverend Spaulding's manuscript reflects this penchant for Latinate expression. In Latin the term *inquit,* meaning "he said" or "she said," is placed after the first word of a quotation. Because Latin grammar was a model for English grammar, quotations that mimicked the *inquit* form became a point of good English style. Reverend Spaulding was trained in this, so it is not surprising that "Manuscript Found" typically introduces quotation in the following manner:

> "I am not[,] says he, my most excellent father, I am not mistaken."[23]

> "I am[,] quoth he to himself, honoured above all the other princes of the empire."[24]

The Book of Mormon, however, follows not the style esteemed in the nineteenth century but normal Hebrew syntax in introducing quotations. For example:

> And then Ammon said: Believest thou that there is a Great Spirit? (Alma 18:26)

It is remarkable that, even as a nineteenth-century translation, the Book of Mormon eschews certain syntactic features common in the language of Joseph Smith's day.

Like the Book of Mormon, *View of the Hebrews* contains some narrative portions with dialogue.[25] But any similarity between the two works in that regard ends on that general level. For example, while Ethan Smith did not use the *inquit* form as Spaulding did, he did follow Latin style by varying verbs when attributing quotations. Examples from *View of the Hebrews* include the following:

> Our Lord proceeds; "And ye shall hear of wars."[26]

> Our Saviour added; "And great earthquakes shall be in divers places."[27]

> "Pestilences" too, the Saviour adds.[28]

The Book of Mormon, however, never uses the verb *proceed* as a verb of speaking,[29] although to *proceed forth from the mouth* is used to refer to writing.[30] The verb *add* is used only five times in the Book of Mormon, but never as a verb of speaking.[31]

Another stylistic feature of the nineteenth century noticeably absent from the Book of Mormon is the penchant for pompous language. Spaulding's manuscript is replete with vocabulary without parallel in the Book of Mormon. A random sample of Reverend Spaulding's text shows that 10 percent of his vocabulary is foreign to the Book of Mormon.[32] Some of those words were commonly used in the nineteenth century and are found in the Doctrine and Covenants. A random sample of the vocabulary from Ethan Smith's text shows that about 14 percent of his vocabulary is not found in the Book of Mormon.[33]

If the Book of Mormon were a nineteenth-century book, we would expect it to contain passages like the following: "Dearest Helaman, I hardly know what I would write, but I have bad news for you, and it cannot be delayed. Imprudent as a marriage between Isabel and our poor Corianton would be, we are now anxious to be assured it has taken place, for there is but too much reason to fear they are not gone to Mulek."[34] However, nothing of the sort appears.

Conspicuous stylistic features of the Book of Mormon, such as the ubiquitous *it came to pass,* while at home in ancient Hebrew literature, are notably absent from nineteenth-century literature,[35] including Spaulding's manuscript.[36] Statements like that of Henry Lake—"I well recollect telling Mr. Spaulding, that the so frequent use of the words 'And it came to pass,' 'Now it came to pass,' rendered it [Spaulding's manuscript] ridiculous"[37]—show that this stylistic feature was thought absurd in Joseph's day. (Incidentally, the complete absence of the phrase *it came to pass* from Spaulding's manuscript also shows that Mr. Lake was lying.)

This sampling of linguistic differences between the English of Joseph's day and the English translation of the Book of Mormon shows that the Book of Mormon is not the type of book one would expect to come from a nineteenth-century milieu.

Writing Materials

The Book of Mormon describes its principal writing surface as being plates of metal, for "whatsoever things we write upon anything save it be upon plates must perish and vanish away" (Jacob 4:2). This is in direct contradiction to the view of Ethan Smith, who wrote that the Native Americans were "destitute of books and letters"[38] (probably an accurate assessment of the tribes in the area of New England and New York). The Reverend Spaulding, on the other hand, fancied, according to common nineteenth-century notions, that an ancient record would be written according to Western European conventions for Latin manuscripts upon "*sheets* of parchment."[39] Thus Spaulding's fictional Ohons tribe "generally wrote on parchment"[40] formed into "Roll[s]."[41]

PLATES VS. PARCHMENT

Like his contemporaries, Spaulding thought that an ancient manuscript from the Americas should be "written in an eligant [*sic*] hand with Roman Letters & in the Latin Language,"[42] while native languages were written with "characters which represent words—& all compound words had each part represented by its apropriate [*sic*] character. The variation of cases moods & tenses was designated by certain marks placed under the character."[43] The characters were written "beginning at the right . . . from the top to the bottom [*sic*], placing each character directly under the preceding one."[44] The Book of Mormon, on the other hand, describes itself as being engraved on plates (see Jacob 4:1–3; Mormon 1:4) and written "in the characters which are called among us the reformed Egyptian" (Mormon 9:32), although the language seems to have been based on Hebrew (see 1 Nephi 1:2; Mormon 9:33). Thus both the medium and the language of the Book of Mormon plates match the two earliest texts of biblical passages known, the oldest being written on metal plates and the next oldest being written in a form of the Egyptian script with the underlying language being Semitic.[45]

Describing the Natives

Views of the Natives

Compared with the view of the native inhabitants of the Americas set forth in the Book of Pukei, the Spaulding manuscript, and *View of the Hebrews,* the Book of Mormon again stands in marked contrast.

The Book of Pukei, mocking the Egyptian origin of the Book of Mormon, describes the Native Americans as "clad, as I supposed, in Egyptian raiment, except his Indian blanket, and moccasins—his beard of silver white, *hung far below his knees.* On his head was an old fashioned military half cocked hat, such as was worn in the days of the patriarch Moses."[46] In the description of the hat and the Egyptian raiment "as I supposed," Cole obviously intended to show that Joseph Smith would not know an anachronism when he saw one, for Cole elsewhere described Joseph as "the *Ignoramus*"[47] who "can neither read nor write."[48] Cole's description of the Native Americans agrees mainly with contemporary Native Americans in upstate New York. He notes familiar items and traits such as their blankets,[49] moccasins,[50] "bark canoes,"[51] internecine warfare,[52] and susceptibility to smallpox.[53]

With the exception of warfare, which is too ubiquitous among humans to serve as a cultural indicator, all of the other details that Cole mentions are absent from the Book of Mormon. The closest that the Book of Mormon comes to blankets are generic references to cloth.[54] The only references to any sort of footwear in that record pertain to the Old World.[55] Beards are mentioned in the Book of Mormon only in a quotation of Isaiah (2 Nephi 17:20). Boats in the Book of Mormon are either barges,[56] vessels,[57] or ships.[58] Far from being bark canoes designed for navigating rivers and lakes, Book of Mormon ships are ocean-going vessels made of unspecified materials. Diseases are mentioned in the Book of Mormon[59] as things that Christ would cure[60] or as a regular part of life,[61] being treatable with Nephite plant lore[62] or power from on high.[63] There is no mention of plagues of small pox or of any other disease that devastates the population; wars and famines do that.

Solomon Spaulding's extensive description of the Native Americans matches many of the characteristics familiar to nineteenth-century Americans. [64] The natives wear cotton garments,[65] headdresses "ornimented [sic] with feathers,"[66] and "shoes and long stockings."[67] Their buildings "exhibit no eligance [sic]—no appearans [sic] of wealth and grandure [sic]—all is plain—& nothing superfluous."[68] He also described the natives as having "wigwams."[69] This all accords with Yankee experience with the native peoples of North America in the 1800s.

Spaulding's descriptions stand in marked contrast to the Book of Mormon. Headgear in the Book of Mormon is limited to "head-plates,"[70] although headbands are mentioned in the book's biblical quotations.[71] Nothing is said about feathers, which were a prominent feature of Native American dress in the nineteenth century.[72] The same can be said for footwear, which has already been discussed. The Book of Mormon describes a variety of buildings, and, as opposed to the aesthetic sensibilities of Reverend

Spaulding, some of them are expressly mentioned as being elaborately decorated: "And it came to pass that king Noah built many elegant and spacious buildings; and he ornamented them with fine work of wood, and of all manner of precious things" (Mosiah 11:8). These were definitely not the sort of buildings that Joseph Smith's neighbors would have expected Native Americans to have. In fact, David Whitmer recounted:

> When we were first told to publish our statement, we felt sure the people would not believe it, for the Book told of a people who were refined and dwelt in large cities; but the Lord told us that He would make it known to the people, and people should discover the ruins of the lost cities and abundant evidence of the truth of what is written in the Book.[73]

"Wigwams" are not mentioned in the Book of Mormon, although "tents" are mentioned in the contexts of pilgrimage[74] and military excursions,[75] the latter use being parallel to that mentioned in the Conquistadores' accounts of the inhabitants of Central America.[76] In sum, nothing out of Spaulding's imagination could have prepared him for the later discovery of extensive, impressive ruins in Central America that demonstrate an advanced level of civilization.[77]

Ethan Smith attempted to prove "that the American Indians are the ten tribes of Israel"[78] by means of various arguments in which he cited supposed parallels between the ancient Israelites and the Native Americans. For example, in *View of the Hebrews* he argued that (1) the American natives had one origin, (2) their language appears to have been Hebrew, (3) they had their imitation of ancient Israel's ark of the covenant, (4) they practiced circumcision, (5) they acknowledged only one God, (6) the celebrated William Penn's accounts of the natives of Pennsylvania corroborate Ethan Smith's thesis, (7) the Indians had a tribe that answered in various respects to the tribe of Levi, (8) prophesied Hebrew character traits accurately apply to the aborigines of America, (9) the Indians belonged to tribes, each with its own name and leader, and (10) apparent parallels to the Israelites' ancient cities of refuge indicate the Indians' Israelite extraction.[79]

Each of Ethan Smith's ten claims deserves to be analyzed against any statements on the same subject from the Book of Mormon.

1. In opposition to Ethan Smith, the Book of Mormon does not claim that all the American natives had one origin. In fact, the Book of Mormon reports at least three different migrations from the Old World (Nephite, Mulekite, and Jaredite) and expressly allows that there were others "who should be led out of other countries by the hand of the Lord" (2 Nephi 1:5). Additionally, a careful reading of the Book of Mormon indicates that there may have been other peoples present in the land when the Nephites arrived.[80]

2. Ethan Smith argues that the original Native American language appears to have been Hebrew. Although the Book of Mormon started out, Nephi reports, as "a record in the language of my father, which consists of the learning of the Jews and the language of the Egyptians" (1 Nephi 1:2), nearly a thousand years later, Moroni writes, "We have written this record according to our knowledge, in the characters which are called among us [the Nephites] the reformed Egyptian, being handed down and altered by us, according to our manner of speech" (Mormon 9:32). Even though the language may have been based on Hebrew, Moroni acknowledges that "the Hebrew hath been altered by us also"

(Mormon 9:33). Book of Mormon writers also acknowledge, regarding other groups that presumably started out speaking Hebrew or a related language, that "their language had become corrupted; . . . and Mosiah, nor the people of Mosiah, could understand them" (Omni 1:17).

3. Although Ethan Smith claims that the Native Americans had an object resembling the ark of the covenant,[81] the Book of Mormon never mentions such a relic. The only ark mentioned in the Book of Mormon is the ark of Noah (see Ether 6:7).

4. Ethan Smith argues that circumcision was widespread among the Native Americans.[82] The Book of Mormon mentions it only once, in a letter of Mormon saying that the practice has been "done away" (Moroni 8:8).

5. Ethan Smith argues that the Native Americans were some sort of monotheists because "they have acknowledged one and only one God."[83] This trait is not diagnostic, because it has been argued that many disparate cultures are monotheistic (whether or not they technically are). Acknowledging one and only one God does not prove that Native Americans were part of the lost ten tribes any more than it proves that Muslims or Egypt under Akhenaten was part of the lost ten tribes.

6. The descriptions by William Penn that Ethan Smith refers to deal with "dress and trinkets" and ceremonies.[84] As we have seen, the Book of Mormon does not describe the dress, and ceremonies are mentioned only obliquely and without detail (see Mosiah 19:24).

7. Ethan Smith claims that the Native Americans had a tribe like the Levites, but the Book of Mormon has no such tribe. The only mention of the tribe of Levi in the Book of

Mormon is when Jesus quotes Malachi to the Nephites (see 3 Nephi 24:3).

8. What Ethan Smith means by seeing in the Native Americans "prophetic traits of character given of the Hebrews" is that the former were inclined to get drunk and they adorned themselves with "tinkling ornaments."[85] These two traits are too widespread to be diagnostic of any civilization.

9. Ethan Smith argues that the mention of various animals in Jacob's blessing of his sons (see Genesis 49) is a "trait of character . . . not wanting among the natives of this land."[86] The Book of Mormon, however, mentions no animals as "emblems of their tribes."[87]

10. Ethan Smith argues that the Native Americans had cities of refuge,[88] but such cities are not mentioned at all in the Book of Mormon.

Summary

Despite the efforts of critics to portray the Book of Mormon as a typical product of the nineteenth century, the book fails to conform to that mold. The easiest way to see the flaws in the environmentalist argument is to look at three clear products of the nineteenth century that were what folks of that period expected the Book of Mormon to be like: (1) the Book of Pukei, because as a satire of the Book of Mormon it exposes the elements that people of the nineteenth century thought would likely be included in the Book of Mormon; (2) Solomon Spaulding's "Manuscript Found," because many people in the nineteenth century, and even some today, claim it is the source of the Book of Mormon; and (3) Ethan Smith's *View of the Hebrews,* because many critics in the twentieth century have argued that therein lies the origin of the Book of Mormon. All three accounts show bias towards Latin in phraseology and cultural background and discuss subjects that were common at the time: satire, romance, money digging, and speculation about the lost ten tribes. All three also depict the inhabitants of the New World as resembling the Native American tribes in the vicinity of New York and New England. As has been shown, the natives described in the Book of Mormon are not the Native Americans of the world of Joseph Smith. Further, the Book of Mormon scarcely mentions the major subjects of the Book of Pukei or "Manuscript Found," and it treats the subject of *View of the Hebrews* very differently. Moreover, rather than reflecting Latin influences, the Book of Mormon bears trademark features of having come from an ancient Near Eastern background—all the more remarkable because it was translated half a dozen years before Joseph Smith started studying Hebrew.[89]

Nineteenth-century accounts purported to be similar to the Book of Mormon all clearly betray their American cultural background in ways that significantly differ from what we find in the Book of Mormon. Why then, if the Book of Mormon is said to be a nineteenth-century book, does it not read like one?

NOTES

1. For an overview, see Terryl L. Givens, *By the Hand of Mormon: The American Scripture That Launched a New World Religion* (Oxford: Oxford University Press, 2002), 155–84; and Louis C. Midgley, "Who Really Wrote the Book of Mormon? The Critics and Their Theories," in *Book of Mormon Authorship*

Revisited: The Evidence for Ancient Origins, ed. Noel B. Reynolds (Provo, Utah: FARMS, 1997), 101–39. An earlier overview with the same conclusions is Hugh Nibley, "Just Another Book?" in *The Prophetic Book of Mormon* (Salt Lake City: Deseret Book and FARMS, 1989), 148–69.

2. For example, see the introduction (written by Bruce R. McConkie) to the 1981 edition of the Book of Mormon.

3. Dan Vogel, *Indian Origins and the Book of Mormon* (Salt Lake City: Signature Books, 1986), 5.

4. Obadiah Dogberry [Abner Cole], "The Book of Pukei, Chapter I," Palmyra *Reflector,* June 1830, in Francis W. Kirkham, *A New Witness for Christ in America: The Book of Mormon,* 4th ed. (Salt Lake City: Utah Printing Co., 1960), 1:273–75; and Obadiah Dogberry [Abner Cole], "The Book of Pukei, Chapter II," Palmyra *Reflector,* 7 July 1830, in Kirkham, *New Witness for Christ in America,* 1:275–77. See Andrew H. Hedges, "The Refractory Abner Cole," in *Revelation, Reason, and Faith,* ed. Donald W. Parry, Daniel C. Peterson, and Stephen D. Ricks (Provo, Utah: FARMS, 2002), 447–75. For convenience, references to Cole's work will be "Book of Pukei," followed by chapter and verse.

5. See the introduction to Solomon Spaulding, *The "Manuscript Found." Manuscript Story* (Salt Lake City: Deseret News Company, 1886), iii–iv. See also Givens, *By the Hand of Mormon,* 160–61.

6. Ethan Smith, *View of the Hebrews; or the Tribes of Israel in America* (Poultney, Vt.: Smith and Shute, 1825).

7. See Givens, *By the Hand of Mormon,* 161–62, and sources.

8. I have used this argument before in John Gee and Daniel C. Peterson, "Graft and Corruption: On Olives and Olive Culture in the Pre-Modern Mediterranean," in *The Allegory of the Olive Tree: The Olive, the Bible, and Jacob 5,* ed. Stephen D. Ricks and John W. Welch (Salt Lake City: Deseret Book and FARMS, 1994), 224–25.

9. Orson Scott Card, introduction to *Ender's Game*, rev. ed. (New York: Tor, 1994), xv.

10. Joseph Smith—History 1:55–56.

11. "Book of Pukei" 1:1–2:8.

12. Ibid., 2:2.

13. Ibid., 2:7.

14. Spaulding, *"Manuscript Found,"* 8–10, 14–15, 49–52, 55–77, 86–87.

15. Smith, *View of the Hebrews*, 85.

16. "It should be pointed out that in contradistinction to the many preceding versions, the Book of Mormon maintains that its peoples descended from Manasseh and Judah, *not* the ten lost tribes" (Givens, *By the Hand of Mormon*, 161–62).

17. "Book of Pukei" 1:2.

18. Spaulding, *"Manuscript Found,"* 2.

19. Ibid., 4–5.

20. Smith, *View of the Hebrews*, 23–43.

21. Ibid., 26.

22. See 1 Nephi 1:4, 13, 18; 3:17; 5:4; 7:13–15; 10:3–4; 2 Nephi 1:4; 6:8; 25:14; Helaman 8:20–22.

23. Spaulding, *"Manuscript Found,"* 66.

24. Ibid., 67.

25. Smith, *View of the Hebrews*, 13–46.

26. Ibid., 21.

27. Ibid., 22.

28. Ibid., 23.

29. The verb *proceed* appears in an altogether different sense in 1 Nephi 10:1; 13:23–24, 38; 14:23; 19:5; 22:8, 11; 2 Nephi 3:21; 8:4; 25:7, 17; 27:14, 26; 29:1–2, 4; 33:14; Words of Mormon 1:9; Alma 20:28; Helaman 5:20; 3 Nephi 5:19; 26:12; Ether 1:1; 2:13; 6:1; 9:1; 13:1; and Moroni 7:25; 10:28.

30. See 1 Nephi 13:23–24, 38; 14:23; 2 Nephi 3:21; 29:2; 33:14; Moroni 7:25; 10:28.

31. See Mosiah 18:17; Alma 17:2; Helaman 15:6; 3 Nephi 13:27, 33.

32. I randomly analyzed p. 43 of Spaulding, *"Manuscript Found,"* and found 39 words of 375 that were never used in the Book of Mormon.

33. I randomly analyzed p. 113 of Smith, *View of the Hebrews,* and found 50 words of 352 that were never used in the Book of Mormon.

34. After Jane Austen, *Pride and Prejudice,* chap. 46.

35. A computerized search of several prominent nineteenth-century titles failed to detect a single instance of the phrase *and it came to pass.*

36. Since the Book of Pukei appeared after the Book of Mormon, imitating and mocking its style, it is not useful as a guide to early-nineteenth-century literary style.

37. Henry Lake, affidavit, September 1833, in E. D. Howe, *History of Mormonism* (Painseville, Ohio: E. D. Howe, 1840), 282.

38. Smith, *View of the Hebrews,* 113, emphasis in original.

39. Spaulding, *"Manuscript Found,"* 2.

40. Ibid., 25.

41. Ibid., 26.

42. Ibid., 2.

43. Ibid., 25.

44. Ibid., 25.

45. See John Gee and John A. Tvedtnes, "Ancient Manuscripts Fit Book of Mormon Pattern," *Insights* (February 1999): 3–4. (*Insights* is the newsletter of the Foundation for Ancient Research and Mormon Studies.)

46. "Book of Pukei" 2:4.

47. Ibid., 2:5.

48. Ibid., 2:8.

49. Ibid., 2:4.

50. Ibid., 2:4.

51. Ibid., 2:6.

52. Ibid., 2:6.

53. Ibid., 2:6.

54. See 1 Nephi 13:7–8; 2 Nephi 13:23; 14:1; Mosiah 10:5; Alma 1:6, 27, 29, 32; 4:6; 5:53; Helaman 6:13; 3 Nephi 13:28; 4 Nephi 1:24; Mormon 8:36; Ether 9:17; 10:24.

55. See 1 Nephi 10:8; 2 Nephi 15:27; 21:15.

56. See Ether 2:6, 16–18; 6:4.

57. See Mormon 5:18; Ether 2:2, 23; 3:1, 4; 6:2–7.

58. See 1 Nephi 17:8–9, 17–19, 49, 51; 18:1–22; 2 Nephi 12:16; Alma 63:5–10; Helaman 3:10–14.

59. See 1 Nephi 11:31; Mosiah 3:5; 17:16; Alma 9:22; 46:40.

60. See 1 Nephi 11:31; Mosiah 3:5; 3 Nephi 17:7–9; 26:15.

61. See Jacob 2:19; Mosiah 4:26; 17:16; Alma 1:27–30; 4:12; 9:22; 15:3–5; 34:28; 46:40; 3 Nephi 17:7–9; 26:15; Mormon 8:37–39; 9:24; Moroni 8:8.

62. See Alma 46:40.

63. See Alma 15:3–11.

64. See Spaulding, *"Manuscript Found,"* 20–31.

65. See ibid., 21.

66. Ibid., 21.

67. Ibid.

68. Ibid., 23.

69. Ibid., 7.

70. See Alma 43:38, 44; 46:13; 49:24; Helaman 1:14; 3 Nephi 4:7; Ether 15:15.

71. See 2 Nephi 13:20, which quotes Isaiah 3:20.

72. As they were in Central American civilizations.

73. David Whitmer in James H. Hart interview, 21 August 1883, in *David Whitmer Interviews: A Restoration Witness,* ed. Lyndon W. Cook (Orem, Utah: Grandin Book, 1991), 96.

74. See Mosiah 2:6.

75. See Alma 51:34; 52:1; Ether 9:3.

76. Some of these have been gathered by John L. Sorenson, "Viva Zapato! Hurray for the Shoe!" *Review of Books on the Book of Mormon* 6/1 (1994): 331–35.

77. In making this comparison I am not arguing for the identification of any Book of Mormon location with any specific ruin, site, or general area in Central America.

78. Smith, *View of the Hebrews,* 85.

79. See ibid., 85. Smith has an eleventh point, a hodgepodge about Native American traditions that I am deliberately omitting in the interest of space.

80. See John L. Sorenson, "When Lehi's Party Arrived in the Land, Did They Find Others There?" *Journal of Book of Mormon Studies* 1/1 (1992): 1–34; and Brant A. Gardner, "The Other Stuff: Reading the Book of Mormon for Cultural Information," *FARMS Review of Books* 13/2 (2001): 29–37.

81. See Smith, *View of the Hebrews,* 95–96.

82. See ibid., 96–98.

83. Ibid., 85.

84. See ibid., 107–8.

85. See ibid., 109–11.

86. Ibid., 111–12.

87. Quotation from ibid., 111.

88. Smith, *View of the Hebrews,* 112–13. Compare p. 427 in this volume.

89. See Joseph Smith, Ohio Journal 1835–1836, 20 November–7 December 1835, in *The Papers of Joseph Smith,* ed. Dean C. Jessee (Salt Lake City: Deseret Book, 1992), 2:87–97.

A Steady Stream of Significant Recognitions

John W. Welch

People of all kinds have read the Book of Mormon over and over, from various points of view and in many different times and places. The words of this timeless record speak to people in numerous ways, even from one reading to the next. The search for significant archaic details embedded in this record that were in all probability unknown and most likely even unknowable to Joseph Smith or anyone else in the early nineteenth century is not intended to detract from other kinds of readings, but rather to bring to light a stream of significant and interesting details that are part of the fabric of this complex and yet simple book. It is especially intriguing to me how these nuances have often caught my attention when I was least expecting to find them.

For example, in reading the Book of Mormon with a class of honors students at Brigham Young University recently, I was rewarded with yet another round of ideas that I had not previously noticed. Several years ago I had noticed that the word *Lord* appears in an expanded form ten times (seven times as "Lord God," three times as "Lord Omnipotent") in King Benjamin's speech, perhaps reflecting an old liturgical requirement for showing respect and tenfold perfection in calling upon the divine name, especially when seeking atonement.[1] Thus I was impressed to notice that the word *Lord* also appears exactly ten times in the psalm of Nephi, which also deals with the atoning embrace of God (see 2 Nephi 4:16–35), and that the words *Lord* and *Son* are both mentioned precisely ten times in Alma's powerfully articulate speech on the plan of redemption and atonement in Alma 12–13. Remarkably, the phrase *O Lord* is found exactly ten times in Alma's prayer in Antionum, when he called upon God for strength in bringing souls to Christ (see Alma 31:26–35). Standing behind this tenfold repetitive practice may be the ancient poem of Zenos quoted in Alma 33:4–11 (which Alma apparently knew well enough to recite spontaneously from memory), for it contains ten times the word *hear,* in various tenses, affirming that the Lord has heard and will hear the prayers of those who call upon his name. Could all this have something to do with the ten commandments, which date to preexilic Israel, or with the need for ten men to form a Jewish minyan for prayer or marriage, a practice traceable to the time of Ruth 4:2?

TENFOLD
REPETITIONS

My reason for mentioning this particular case is not so much to draw attention to this single phenomenon but rather to illustrate the steady flow of new ideas that has come forth from the text of the Book of Mormon in recent years. We cannot be sure that Zenos, Nephi, Benjamin, or Alma were aware of this numerological character of their texts, and we cannot conclude with certainty that all preexilic Israelites placed religious importance on counting to ten, especially in connection with prayer and atonement (even though several textual and liturgical factors point in that direction), but elements such as these raise interesting questions and open doors for detailed examination and reexamination of the text itself. Moreover, I doubt that Joseph Smith was aware of the these tenfold occurrences in the Book of Mormon or that anyone in 1829 would have sensed the significant place that the number ten may have held in ancient minds or would have been able to work them so subtly into the text of the Book of Mormon.

What follows are a few similar examples of details that I have spotted in researching the language, law, and literature of the Book of Mormon. This selection focuses on easily overlooked details that both specialists and nonspecialists will readily understand. In each case the significance of the details involved could hardly have been recognized, let alone fully appreciated, in the early nineteenth century, when the Book of Mormon was translated and published.

The Absence of *Without a Cause* from the Savior's Words in 3 Nephi 12:22

While studying at Oxford in the early 1970s, I became aware of an interesting textual variant in the New Testament. In a well-known passage in the Sermon on the Mount, the King James translation of Matthew 5:22 reads, "Whosoever is angry with his brother *without a cause [eikēi]* shall be in danger of the judgment" (emphasis added). Yet the phrase *without a cause* is absent in most of the best and earliest Greek manuscripts of the New Testament.² Joseph Smith could hardly have guessed that this phrase did not originally belong in this passage, because textual criticism of the Bible was scarcely in its infancy in America in 1829. And yet,

"Without a Cause"
3 Nephi 12:22

significantly, the parallel text in the Sermon at the Temple in the Book of Mormon agrees with those early manuscripts, precisely lacking the phrase *without a cause* (3 Nephi 12:22).[3]

While lacking unanimous consensus among the manuscripts of the Sermon on the Mount (a situation not unusual), the absence of the phrase *without a cause* is notably evidenced by the following manuscripts of Matthew: the papyrus fragment known as *p67*, Codex Sinaiticus (original hand), Codex Vaticanus, some Greek minuscules (scriptural texts written in lowercase Greek letters), the Latin Vulgate (Jerome mentions that the phrase was not found in the oldest manuscripts known to him), the Ethiopic texts, and the Gospel of the Nazarenes. Moreover, the phrase is missing in writings of Justin, Tertullian, Origen, and other early church fathers who quoted the New Testament scriptures as they knew them. In the field of New Testament textual criticism, one may generally count as compelling any reading that is supported by "the best Greek MSS—by the A.D. 200 *p64* (where it is extant) and by at least the two oldest uncials, as well as some minuscules, [especially if] it also has some Latin, Syriac, Coptic, and early patristic support."[4] A survey of the manuscripts supporting the original absence of the phrase *without a cause* in Matthew 5:22 shows that the shorter reading meets that criterion. Yet Sinaiticus and the most important manuscripts of the New Testament were not discovered until after Joseph Smith was dead.

I also find it interesting that this textual difference in the Greek manuscripts of the Sermon on the Mount has a significant impact on this verse's meaning. It is much more severe to say, "*Whoever is angry* is in danger of the judgment," than to say, "Whoever is angry *without a cause* is in danger of the judgment." The first discourages all anger; the second permits anger as long as it is justifiable. The former is more like the demanding sayings of Jesus regarding committing adultery in one's heart (see Matthew 5:28) and loving one's enemies (see v. 44), neither of which offers the disciple a convenient loophole of self-justification or rationalization. Indeed, as Wernberg-Møller points out, the word *eikēi* may have been added to Matthew 5:22 in an effort to reflect a Semitic idiom that does not invite allowance for "just" anger in certain circumstances at all, but actually "echoes some Aramaic phrase, condemning anger as sinful in any case" and "alluding to . . . the harbouring of angry feelings for any length of time."[5] If correct, Wernberg-Møller's interpretation offers a second reason supporting the claim that the Book of Mormon accurately reflects the original sense of Matthew 5:22.

In my estimation, this original reading preserved in the Book of Mormon since 1830 is very meaningful. The absence of *without a cause* has important moral, behavioral, psychological, and religious ramifications. Moreover, 3 Nephi 12:22 is the main place in the account of the Sermon at the Temple (3 Nephi 12–14) where a significant textual change from the parallel account in the King James Version of Matthew 5–7 was needed and delivered by Joseph Smith. As far as I have been able to determine, no copy of the Greek New Testament present in the United States before 1830 made any reference to this variant reading. No scholars in the world of Joseph Smith seem to have been even remotely aware of this apparently late insertion in the Greek that actually weakens the text of the Bible. Yet in the Book of Mormon, Joseph Smith offered the world this stronger wording, reflecting the original meaning of the Savior.

The Lord's Requirement of Secrecy in Matthew 7 and 3 Nephi 14

SACRED SECRECY

In the Sermon on the Mount, the Lord required his hearers to keep some holy things secret: "Give not that which is holy unto the dogs, neither cast ye your pearls before swine, lest they trample them under their feet, and turn again and rend you" (Matthew 7:6; 3 Nephi 14:6). For most readers "the original meaning [of this saying] is puzzling."[6] One renowned scholar has concluded in frustration, "The logion [saying of Jesus] is a riddle."[7] For virtually all interpreters of the Sermon on the Mount, this requirement of secrecy seems badly out of place in the narrative or is hard to explain.[8]

The emphasis in these parallel passages is clearly on withholding and protecting certain things because of their sacred nature. Drawing on Logion 93 in the *Gospel of Thomas,* which was first discovered in 1945 at Nag Hammadi, Egypt, Georg Strecker identifies the holy thing in Matthew 7:6 as "gnostic secret knowledge."[9] If this is correct, the implication is that Jesus gave his hearers something that he required them to keep sacred and confidential—an implication consistent with some other interesting conclusions of Joachim Jeremias regarding the existence of sacred, secret teachings and practices in primitive Christianity.[10] Similarly, Professor Hans Dieter Betz finds it most likely that Matthew 7:6 refers to

> an esoteric saying that the uninformed will never be able to figure out. Finding the explanation is not a matter of natural intelligence but of initiation into secrets. . . . In other words, we are dealing with some kind of secret *(arcanum).* Indeed, the language reminds us of arcane teaching *(Arkandisziplin)* as it was

used in the Greek mystery religions and in philosophy.... Originally, then, the [Sermon on the Mount] was meant to be insiders' literature, not to be divulged to the uninitiated outsiders.... Remarkably, Elchasai used the same language: "Inasmuch as he considers that it would be an insult to reason that these great and ineffable mysteries should be trampled under foot or that they should be handed down to many, he advises that they should be preserved as valuable pearls saying this: Do not read this word to all men and guard carefully these precepts because all men are not faithful nor are all women straightforward."[11]

Such a requirement of secrecy is a common feature of rituals and temple ordinances.[12] Indeed, the first-century Christian *Didache,* discovered in 1873, associates the saying in Matthew 7:6 with a requirement of exclusivity, specifically the prohibition not to let anyone "eat or drink of the Eucharist with you except for those baptized in the name of the Lord" (see *Didache* 9:5 and 14:1–2, which connect Matthew 5:23–25 and the observance of the sacrament). Accordingly, Betz concludes that "the 'holy' [mentioned in Matthew 7:6] could be a ritual."[13] Whenever sacred knowledge is given to recipients, it becomes a string of precious pearls of great price, revelations for which one will sell all that one has in order to obtain, and one keeps this knowledge hidden to protect it (see Matthew 13:44–46). Indeed, the Joseph Smith Translation of the Bible confirms that Matthew 7:6 is exactly concerned with the requirement of keeping certain sacred things secret. It adds: "The mysteries of the kingdom ye shall keep within yourselves.... For the world cannot receive that which ye, yourselves, are not able to bear" (Matthew 7:10–11 JST; on the plural, "holy things," compare the *Gospel of Thomas* 93).

It is significant that only in recent decades have biblical scholars begun to appreciate the likely setting of this cryptic saying in the Sermon on the Mount, seeing in it some reference to holy things imparted by Jesus to his faithful followers. Yet this is precisely the setting in which these words had already appeared in 1829 in 3 Nephi 14, namely, when the glorious Son of God appeared to a righteous body of saints, bestowed upon their leaders priesthood powers, taught the people exalting principles, gave them commandments, and put them under covenant to keep those commandments, all of which was conducted in a sacred temple precinct.[14] A sense of awe and holy silence surrounds much of the account of the glorious events on these occasions (see, for example, 3 Nephi 28:14). Thus the new understanding of the ancient meaning of Matthew 7:6 makes its explicit appearance in a temple context in the Book of Mormon perfectly but unexpectedly appropriate.

The Words of Benjamin as a Classic Ancient Farewell Address

CLASSIC
FAREWELL
ADDRESS

Scholars have recently taken an interest in similarities in the farewell speeches of many ancient religious and political leaders. Certain themes appear consistently in these addresses given by people such as Moses and Socrates at the end of their lives. It almost seems as if these ancient speakers were following a customary pattern. Interestingly, these themes are found to an equal or greater extent in the farewell speeches of the Book of Mormon.

William S. Kurz has published a detailed study comparing twenty-two addresses from the classical and biblical traditions.[15] He has identified twenty elements common to farewell addresses in general. Of course, no single speech contains all twenty, and some contain more than others. Moses' farewell speech, for example, contains sixteen such elements (see Deuteronomy 31–34); Paul's, fourteen (see Acts 20); and Socrates', eleven.

It is remarkable that King Benjamin's oration contains at least as many elements of the ancient farewell address as any of Kurz's examples do. Fortunately, Benjamin's speech was recorded in full and was precisely preserved, and the report of his final address is even more detailed than such addresses in the Bible, allowing for rigorous scrutiny. Sixteen elements of the ideal ancient farewell address appear directly in Benjamin's speech, and others may be implied.

Kurz has also found that in Greek or Roman writings, the dying speaker, usually a philosopher or statesman, was concerned with suicide, the meaning of death, and life after death. However, in biblical farewell addresses, the speaker, typically a man of God, focused on God's plan, his people, and covenants, or on theological interpretations of history. Kurz signals four of the elements as particularly common to Hebrew farewell addresses: the speaker (1) proposes tasks for successors, (2) reviews theological history, (3) reveals future events, and (4) declares his innocence and fulfillment of his mission. These elements all appear in the Benjamin account. Furthermore, the emphasis in Benjamin's address, as in the Israelite tradition, is on God's relationship to man, the speech ending with a covenant renewal. At the same time, no trace of the prominent Greek or Roman preoccupation with death occurs in Benjamin's remarks. Benjamin's speech thus fits illustriously into the Israelite tradition of farewell addresses. Indeed, it is the most complete example of this speech typology yet found anywhere in world literature. Yet the profile of this ancient Hebrew literary genre remained unrecognized and unanalyzed until only a few years ago.

Chiasmus in Alma 36 and Helaman 6:7–13

Chiasmus

Chiasmus is a style of writing known in antiquity and used by many ancient and some modern writers. It consists of arranging a series of words or ideas in one order and then repeating it in reverse order. In the hands of a skillful writer, this literary form can serve several literary and structural purposes. In the 1820s, two British scholars (John Jebb in 1820 and Thomas Boys in 1824 and 1825) published books about their new recognition of this form of parallelism in the Bible, and the 1825 edition of Horne's encyclopedic guide to the critical study of the Bible, printed in London and Philadelphia, discussed the main arguments and gave a few examples from Jebb.[16] But I see little reason to believe that the young and unlettered Joseph Smith was aware of these books or, even if he were, that he would have been sufficiently equipped to create elaborate and meaningful passages utilizing a form rather foreign to his own culture's way of thinking and writing.

Not all chiasms, of course, are created equal. They differ in significance, precision, and artistic achievement. Some are very clear; others are not. Some are very long; others are short. Of all the examples of chiasmus I have studied in world literature, I wish to highlight two:

1. Alma 36 is, in my opinion, the very best chiasm in the Book of Mormon, if not in all of world literature. Alma 36 was one of the first chiasms I discovered while serving as a missionary in Regensburg, Germany, in 1967.[17] Many

years later, it still remains my favorite. It is a masterpiece of composition on several levels.

Level 1: The overall structure. This text features at least seventeen key elements, each repeated twice (italics identify repeated elements, and verse numbers are indicated in parentheses):

a My son, give ear to my *words* (1)
 b Keep the commandments and ye shall prosper in the land (1)
  c Do *as I* have done (2)
   d *Remember the captivity* of our fathers (2)
    e They were in *bondage* (2)
     f He surely did *deliver* them (2)
      g *Trust* in God (3)
       h Supported in *trials, troubles, and afflictions* (3)
        i Lifted up at the *last day* (3)
         j *I know* this not of myself but *of God* (4)
          k *Born of God* (5)
           l I sought to destroy the church (6)
            m My *limbs* were paralyzed (7–11)
             n Fear of being in the *presence of God* (14–15)
              o *Pains* of a damned soul (16)
               p *Harrowed up by the memory of sins* (17)
                q I remembered *Jesus Christ, a Son of God* (17)
                q' I cried, *Jesus, Son of God* (18)
               p' *Harrowed up by the memory of sins* no more (19)
              o' Joy as exceeding as was the *pain* (20)
             n' Long to be in the *presence of God* (22)
            m' My *limbs* received strength again (23)
           l' I labored to bring souls to repentance (24)
          k' *Born of God* (26)
         j' Therefore *my knowledge is of God* (26)
        h' Supported under *trials, troubles, and afflictions* (27)

    g' *Trust* in him (27)

   f' He will *deliver* me (27)

     i' and *raise me up at the last day* (28)

  e' As God brought our fathers out of *bondage* and captivity (28–29)

  d' Retain in *remembrance their captivity* (28–29)

 c' Know *as I* do know (30)

b' *Keep the commandments* and ye shall *prosper in the land* (30)

a' This according to his *word* (30)

    The structural design of this text is amazing. I am especially impressed with the repetition of Jesus Christ as the Son of God at the precise center of the chapter.

    Level 2: The full text. At a more detailed, literary level, we are able to detect how individual panels of text fill in the gaps between the main elements. There is no simple way to display these segments here, but they have been discussed in previous publications noted above. As has been shown, virtually every word serves to enhance the chapter's overall structure. Sometimes they skillfully bridge from one section to the next. Other times they strengthen individual segments. Altogether, they work in masterful harmony.

    Level 3: Detailed relations between the paired sections. The impressive overall structure of the full text of this complex passage becomes even more evident as pairs of sections are examined. For example, elements *a* and *a'* introduce and conclude the chapter by referring to Alma's "words" and the "word" of God (see 36:1, 30), and *d-e-f* and *f'-e'-d'* speak reciprocally of bondage and deliverance. Indeed, the elements in *d-e* themselves constitute a small chiasm:

for they were *in bondage,*

  and none could *deliver them*

    except it was the God of Abraham,

and the God of Isaac,
and the God of Jacob;
and he surely did *deliver them
in their afflictions* (36:2; see 36:29)

Elements *h* and *h'* are both marked by the same triplet "supported under trials, troubles, and afflictions" (36:3, 27). In *h'* the third member is stressed ("yea, and in all manner of afflictions") to make the repetition clear (36:27).

Sections *l* and *l'* draw the contrast between Alma's persecution of the church on the one hand and his work to bring souls to repentance on the other. In *m* and *m'* the comparison is between being stricken by the angel of the Lord and then recovering and regaining strength; both of these sections speak of "limbs," "feet," and falling down or standing up (36:7–11, 23).

Most dramatically, *n* and *n'* contrast the agony of Alma's suffering (36:12) with his joy following his conversion (36:20). Indeed, the contrast is made explicit: "Yea, my soul was filled with joy *as exceeding as was my pain*" (Alma 36:20, emphasis added). This overt comparison strongly supports the idea that Alma consciously created the chiastic structure of this chapter in order to strengthen these linkages.

A remarkable thing about Alma 36:22 is that Lehi's words are not just summarized but precisely quoted. These twenty-one words are a verbatim quote of 1 Nephi 1:8. Such exactness cannot be explained by thinking that Joseph turned to 1 Nephi and copied the words of Lehi from what Oliver Cowdery had already recorded from Joseph's dictation, for 1 Nephi may not yet even have been translated at the time when Joseph and Oliver were translating Alma 36.[18] Evidently, Alma was very meticulous in quoting

Lehi's words from the small plates of Nephi when he composed Alma 36, and Joseph Smith's dictated translation preserved that exactitude.

Elements q and q' stand at the epicenter of this composition, twice mentioning the Savior by name: "Jesus Christ, a Son of God," and "Jesus, thou Son of God" (36:17, 18). Only when Alma called upon Jesus Christ after remembering that his father had spoken of the atonement of Christ did his tormented condition change. At the absolute center stand the words *atone, mind,* and *heart,* bordered by the name of Jesus Christ (36:18, 19). The message is clear: Christ's atonement and man's responding sacrifice of a broken heart and willing mind are central to receiving forgiveness from God.

Level 4: Weaving factors. The fact that each segment flows smoothly into the next adds another dimension to the textual complexity of this chapter. No awkwardness, no sharp breaks are found here. Bridges connect each section to the one that follows it. These linkages are accomplished largely by introducing a minor item in one section that anticipates ideas in the next. For example, the phrase *my words,* which appears at the end of the first section, blends into the beginning of the next, which begins with the phrase *for I swear* (36:1). *Captivity* at the end of the third compositional section blends directly into *bondage* at the beginning of the fourth (36:2). These weaving links are subtle but effective. They make the transitions from section to section smooth and flowing. This reflects a highly polished literary product. If an author uses chiasmus mechanically, it can produce rigid, stilted writing (a poor result from misusing or poorly implementing any artistic device). Alma, however, does not simply stick a list of ideas together in one order and then awkwardly and slavishly retrace his steps through that list in the opposite order. His work has the markings of a skillful, painstaking writer, one completely comfortable with using this difficult mode of expression well.

Degree of chiasticity. Overall, the degree of chiasmus in this text is exceptionally high. Chiasmus can occur in any literature, but it only becomes meaningful when its degree of chiasticity, to coin a phrase, is high. When the chiastic format is truly complex and concise, we are most justified in supposing that the author intentionally followed the pattern. At least fifteen criteria, including objectivity, purposefulness, climax, centrality, boundaries, length, density, and balance, as described here, demonstrate that the chiasmus in Alma 36 can best be explained only if Alma learned it as part of a long literary tradition extending back to Old Testament prophets.

2. Another fine example of chiasmus is found in Helaman 6:7–13, the annual record for the sixty-fourth year of the reign of the judges. Its main features are as follows:

a "And behold, there was *peace* in all the land" (7).
  b [Freedom of travel and trade in *both lands* is discussed (7–8)]
    c "And it came to pass that they became exceedingly *rich,* both the Lamanites and the Nephites;
      d and they did have an exceeding *plenty* of . . . *precious metals,* both in the *land* south and in the *land* north" (9).
        e 1 "Now the land *south*
          2 was called *Lehi,* and
            3 the land *north*
              4 was called *Mulek,*
                5 which was after the son of Zedek*iah;*
                5 for the *Lord*[19]

    4 did bring *Mulek*
    3 into the land *north,*
    2 and *Lehi*
    1 into the land *south"* (10).
 d' "And behold, there was *all manner* of *gold* in *both* these
   lands, and of *silver,* and of *precious ore* of *every kind;*
 c' and there were also curious workmen, who did
   work all kinds of ore and did refine it; and thus
   they did become *rich"* (11).
 b' [Economic prosperity in *both lands* is discussed (12–13)]
a' "And thus the sixty and fourth year did pass away in
 peace" (13).

  This composition is remarkable in several ways. First, the report itself is beautifully executed. The overall structure is concentrically organized, and individual words, phrases, and ideas that appear in the first half are repeated with precision and balance in the second half. This entry exhibits both fine quality and admirable length.

  Second, since the chiasm encompasses the entire report for the year, this unifying structure strongly suggests that the account was written as a single literary unit that Mormon found on the large plates of Nephi. If the contemporary historian used chiasmus to record the events of the sixty-fourth year of the reign of the judges, the form draws attention to the fact that it was an extraordinary year in the annals of his people. Indeed, this report documents the great changes that occurred during that year involving prosperity, free travel, and peace between the Nephites and Lamanites. Significant trade and peace treaties must have been entered into in order for this kind of peace and prosperity to occur, since before this time, limited travel was the norm in Nephite society, as is evidenced by Mosiah 7:1; 8:7; 28:1; Alma 23:2; 50:25; and Helaman 4:12. In addition to marking an unprecedented turning point in Nephite history, using chiasmus would insure against additions to or deletions from the text, since any alteration would be strikingly apparent.

Third, and most remarkable, is the way in which the center of this chiasm involves two individual words. Just as divine names often appear at the center of biblical chiasms, at the very apex of this passage in Helaman 6, the words *Zedekiah* and *Lord* stand parallel to each other. The parallelism between these two names is intriguing not only because Zedekiah was the king and adoptive royal son of Yahweh, the Lord, but also because the Hebrew word for *Lord (YHWH)* constitutes the final syllable, or theophoric suffix, *-yah,* at the end of the name *Zedekiah*. Thus the central chiastic structure in Helaman 6:10 actually would have worked better and would have been more obvious in Hebrew (or its related Nephite dialect) than in the English translation. Joseph Smith would have had no way of consciously concocting this parallelism on his own.

Finally, it may be that other reports from antiquity were written in chiastic form. The Mesoamerican *Chilam Balam of Chumayel*, like Helaman 6, not only focuses chiastically on the migration of the people into the land they now occupy, but also similarly features, at the center, a wordplay on the land's name, as J. E. S. Thompson has noted.[20]

Helaman 6:7–13 deserves to take its place among the finest examples of chiasmus found in the Book of Mormon. Through understanding this masterful composition, we can better appreciate the precision and richness of an Old World literary legacy in the Nephite records.

Ancient Parallels for Mosiah's System of Weights and Measures

COMPARABLE
WEIGHTS
AND
MEASURES

In 1981 I began teaching a course in BYU's J. Reuben Clark Law School on ancient Near Eastern law in the world of the Bible and Book of Mormon. One of the earliest collections of laws that we study is the Code of Eshnunna. In order for ancient economies to work effectively, kings had to spell out the value of various commodities and establish exchange ratios, especially between consumable goods and precious metals. Thus, the laws of Eshnunna, promulgated in Babylonia probably during the early eighteenth century B.C. but not discovered until the mid-twentieth century A.D., instituted an elaborate system of weights and measures. The following initial provisions stand at the head of this ancient law code:

> 1 kor of barley *[she'um]* is (priced) at *[ana]* 1 shekel of silver;
>
> 3 *qa* of "best oil" are (priced) at 1 shekel of silver;
>
> 1 seah (and) 2 *qa* of sesame oil are (priced) at 1 shekel of silver [and so on]. . . .
>
> The hire for a wagon together with its oxen and its driver is 1 *massiktum* (and) 4 seah of barley. If it is (paid in) silver, the hire is one third of a shekel. He shall drive it the whole day.[21]

On their first reading of this text, my law students are readily impressed with several parallels between these laws and the economic system decreed by King Mosiah and found in Alma 11:3–19, especially since any evidence of this ancient pattern of establishing a commercial economy was unknown in Joseph Smith's day. Consider these parallels:

First, the basic legal form of these two texts is consistent. The standard phrasing "1 kor of barley is (priced) at 1 shekel of silver" resembles that in the Book of Mormon, "A senum of silver was equal to a senine of gold" (Alma 11:7).

Second, the primary conversion in Babylonia was between barley and silver. Nine other Babylonian provisions converted various additional commodities into silver values, followed by three more provisions that converted others into measures of barley. Thus, precious metal and grain measures were convertible into each other. The law of Mosiah featured precisely the same conversion capability: the basic measure for either gold or silver was equated with "a measure of barley" (Alma 11:7).

Third, in Babylonia the basic commodity valuation system allowed traders to deal in a variety of items, all convertible into silver or barley. Similarly, Mosiah's system covered transactions from silver into "a measure of every kind of grain" (Alma 11:7).

Fourth, both economic systems were announced by kings to have been instituted for similar reasons. The laws of Eshnunna began with a royal superscription that proclaimed this standardization as instrumental in establishing justice, eliminating enmity, and protecting the weak. Likewise, King Mosiah enacted his laws expressly to establish peace and equality in the land (see Mosiah 29:38, 40).

Fifth, the ideal, practical motivation behind the laws of Eshnunna seems to have been to undergird the rental market and to standardize values on daily wages and the computation of various damages and penalties. Similarly, a motivation for the economic part of King Mosiah's reforms was to provide a standard system under the new reign of judges for the payment of judges on a daily basis: "a senine of gold for a day, or a senum of silver" (Alma 11:3).

In enacting his law, as the Book of Mormon takes pains to tell us, King Mosiah "did not reckon after the manner of the Jews who were at Jerusalem" (Alma 11:4). Evidently he drew on some other system of weights and measures. Perhaps Mosiah obtained the legal form of his economic decree from the Mulekites, who had had contact with the Jaredites, who had left from Mesopotamia not long before the time of Eshnunna.

Moreover, Mosiah's system is distinctively binary: each unit of measure is half the size of the next larger unit. Perhaps Mosiah found this binary manner of reckoning somewhere on the plates of brass, which, after all, were written in a type of Egyptian text. Indeed, as became known in the early twentieth century, the units in the ancient Egyptian grain measure were also binary in ratio.[22]

Of course, we cannot be sure how to explain the similarities between the laws of Mosiah and Eshnunna or between the Nephite and Egyptian grain measures, but this much can be said: Such similarities between the laws of Mosiah and Eshnunna and the Egyptian mathematical papyri (which were unknown in Joseph Smith's day) show yet another way in which the Book of Mormon presents specific details whose roots run unexpectedly deep in ancient societies.

LEGAL CURSE OF SPEECHLESSNESS

Cursing an Opposing Litigant with Speechlessness

While browsing through the BYU Bookstore a few years ago, I came across a book that described the ancient legal practice of invoking a curse on one's opponents. This study was based on recently discovered Greek epigrams and inscriptions. I was intrigued. While I read these texts, it dawned on me that Alma's curse on Korihor in Alma 30:49—"In the name of God, ye shall be struck dumb, that ye shall no more have utterance"—closely resembles an ancient Greek practice of cursing a litigant with speechlessness. When Alma's curse materialized, God's disapproval of Korihor was so clearly manifested that he was compelled to yield the case and concede legal defeat.

Such curses were common in the ancient Mediterranean world, especially in the legal sphere. In recent decades more than a hundred ancient Greek and Roman binding spells—curses inscribed on small lead sheets that were folded up and pierced with a nail—have been recovered from tombs, temples, and especially wells near the law courts, where they were placed in hopes that a deity from the underworld would receive and act upon them. These spells are known as *defixiones* because their words and powers were intended to "defix" (restrain or hinder) an opponent. In ancient Greece those targeted by these spells could be commercial, athletic, or romantic rivals, or adversaries in litigation.[23]

The largest body of Greek binding spells deals with litigation, with sixty-seven different *defixiones* invoking curses on legal opponents. The earliest of these date to the fifth century B.C., not far from the time of Lehi. Eleven of them ask the gods to bind the tongue of a legal opponent so the opponent would lose the lawsuit.[24] One third-century B.C. inscribed stone slab from the Greek island of Delos expresses the gratitude of a victorious litigant who believed he had been helped in court by a god: "For you bound the sinful men who had prepared the lawsuit, secretly making the tongue silent in the mouth, from which [tongue] no one heard a word or an accusation, which is the helpmate in a trial. But as it turned out by divine providence, they confessed themselves to be like god-stricken statues or stones."[25]

The speechlessness of Korihor, and the stunning of Sherem, was precisely the kind of sign or restraint that people in the ancient Mediterranean world expected a god to manifest in a judicial setting when false accusations or unfair ploys placed an innocent party at a distinct disadvantage. The stricken litigant would sometimes then confess his guilt, exposed by a god through "illness or accident."[26] In hopes of appeasing the offended god, a punished litigant would inscribe in stone a clear profession of his newly admitted faith and would warn others not to disdain the gods.

Similarly, God was seen as an active participant in the courts of Hebrew law in biblical times,[27] and the trials of Sherem and Korihor show the same use of confession. Sherem recanted his public teachings, confessed the truth of the god who had intervened against him, admitted his error, and expressed concern that he would never be able to appease that god (see Jacob 7:17–19). Korihor's confession acknowledged the power of God, probably to assure those concerned in Zarahemla that the curse would not afflict any others, as well as to terminate the dispute (see Alma 30:51). Such reactions are very similar to the responses of others in the ancient world whose judicial perfidy had been exposed by the intervention of a god responding to the restraining curse of a beleaguered litigant.

Although not mentioning the curse of speechlessness explicitly (and thus leaving it unknown to Joseph Smith), Hebrew law in Lehi's day made frequent use of other curses to anathematize and to invoke divine punishment upon those who transgressed the law. In Deuteronomy 27:15–26 one finds a string of twelve curses, and in Numbers 5:21–22 one encounters the curse imposed in the trial of a suspected adulteress. Yet until recent archaeological discoveries were made, one would not have suspected that placing a curse of speechlessness upon an opposing litigant was common practice not far from Lehi's world itself and, by implication, perhaps right in Jerusalem as well.

Hebrew Terms for *Law, Statutes, Judgments, Ordinances,* and *Commandments*

In 2 Nephi 5:10, Nephi records that his people were strict to observe "the judgments, and the statutes, and the commandments of the Lord in all things, according to the law of Moses." Why did he use so many words to convey what seems to us the simple idea that they kept the law? Part of the answer comes from Hebrew, which uses several words to express different semantic aspects and subtle nuances of our word *law*.[28] Those Hebrew words appear to match the Book of Mormon usage of comparable English terms.[29]

FIVE HEBREW TERMS

Torah. In Hebrew the law of Moses is always referred to as the *torah* of Moses. It means more than "law" in any modern sense. *Torah* derives from the verb *yarah,* whose many meanings include "to show, to instruct, to teach." The *torah* thus embodies all God's instructions given to his people, implemented and taught through his priests. Only a rebellious people would fail to listen to the *torah* of the Lord (see Isaiah 30:9). These ideas fit the frequently mentioned priestly function of teaching in the Book of Mormon (see, for example, Jacob 1:17–19; Jarom 1:11; Mosiah 6:3; 12:25; Alma 8:24; Moroni 3:3).

Mishpat. Usually translated "judgment," this Hebrew word not only means "to pronounce a verdict," but it also embraces most phases of a legal trial. It usually has something to do with the rules of governing properly. Likewise, in the Book of Mormon, when the term *judgments* appears by itself, it is in the context of judges who "judge righteous judgments" (Mosiah 29:29, 43), or it refers to the outcome of a court procedure (see Alma 30:57) or to God's judgments upon his people.

Mitzvah. This broad term has no technical meaning and is usually translated "commandment" or "precept." It is found frequently in Deuteronomy to signify divine commandments in general. Similarly, the use of the word *commandments* in relation to God is extensive in the Book of Mormon (see, for example, 1 Nephi 3:7; Jacob 1:12).

Edut. Less common is this word, meaning "testimony, witness, or monument." Especially in the early biblical period, the law was thought of as a testimony or witness that God had established. The book of the "law" (*edut*, Deuteronomy 31:26) witnessed that God had established his law, by which mankind will be judged (see Psalm 78:5). In the Book of Mormon similar ideas are found, for example, in Benjamin's farewell speech (see Mosiah 3:23–24) and in Moroni's words concluding the monumental Nephite record (see Moroni 10:27).

Most interesting are the words *ḥoq* and *ḥuqqah*. In this pair, the first is masculine, the second feminine, though both have substantially the same meanings, basically "custom, manner, decree, portion, order, prescription, limit," and so on. Thus when the word *ordinance* is used to translate these terms from an ancient text, we should understand that it includes more than priesthood rites, ceremonies, or sacra-

How Do You Say "Law" in Hebrew?

HEBREW	USUAL TRANSLATION	MEANINGS AND CONTEXTS
torah	law, law of Moses	teachings, instructions
mishpat	judgment	pronouncement of a verdict, standards of behavior
ḥuqqah or ḥoq	statute, ordinance	custom, manner, decree, portion, order, prescription, limit
mitzvah	commandment	frequently signifies divine commandments, *bar mitzvah* = "son of the commandment"
edut	testimony, witness	often a monument, stela, or book of the law

ments. Indeed, when the Book of Mormon speaks of ordinances in a priesthood sense, the term *performances* is often included (see 2 Nephi 25:30; Mosiah 13:30).

Moreover, Hebrew usage of *ḥoq* and *ḥuqqah* may correspond quite precisely with the Book of Mormon terms *ordinances* and *statutes*. Due to the near identity of these two Hebrew words, finding them both in the same pleonastic list would be odd. In fact, no Hebrew pleonastic list has been found containing both *ḥoq* and *ḥuqqah* (when the English words *statute* and *ordinance* occur together in such a list in the King James translation, the Hebrew word translated as *statute* is either *ḥoq* or *ḥuqqah*, but the word for *ordinance* is *mishpat*).³⁰ Thus I find it quite significant that the English words *ordinance* and *statute* never appear as companions in the pleonastic lists in the Book of Mormon. Indeed, they are the only two English equivalents of the Hebrew terms for "law" that never appear in the Book of Mormon in combination with each other.

"Better That One Man Should Perish"

SLAYING OF
LABAN

For many years I have studied Nephi's slaying of Laban from a legal point of view based on the law as it existed around 600 B.C. In directing Nephi to slay Laban, the Spirit gave the sober justification that "it is better that one man should perish than that a nation should dwindle and perish in unbelief" (1 Nephi 4:13). Five hundred years later, Alma would invoke this same justification in reluctantly subjecting Korihor to divine punishment (see Alma 30:47).

This principle, of course, runs sharply contrary to American jurisprudence. But because a similar sentiment was expressed by Caiaphas in John 11:50, I once asked a prominent biblical scholar at Duke University, while I was there receiving my legal education, if he knew where this idea had originated. That scholar, who should have known if anyone did, was at a loss to give an answer. Thus, twenty years later, as I was updating my *Biblical Law Bibliography*, I was immediately drawn to a recent article by David Aus entitled "The Death of One for All in John 11:45–54 in Light of Judaic Traditions."³¹ Aus demonstrates that this principle prevailed in certain cases under biblical law, and more than coincidentally, around 600 B.C.³²

A pivotal precedent was found by the ancients in 2 Samuel 20, which recounts how King David had sought the life of Sheba, a rebel guilty of treason. When Sheba took refuge in the city of Abel, Joab, the leader of David's army, demanded that Sheba be released to him or he would destroy the city. The people of Abel beheaded Sheba instead, and Joab retreated. This episode became an important legal precedent justifying the killing of one person in order to preserve an entire group.

Most strikingly, another Old Testament case, one preserved more fully only in oral Jewish traditions, involved Jehoiakim, the king of Judah.[33] He rebelled against Nebuchadnezzar at the very time of Lehi and Nephi. In response, Nebuchadnezzar went to Antioch and demanded that the great Jewish council surrender Jehoiakim or the nation would be destroyed. Jehoiakim protested, "Can ye sacrifice one life for another?" Unmoved, the council replied, "Thus did your ancestors do to Sheba the son of Bichri." Based on this legal ruling, Jehoiakim was released to Nebuchadnezzar, who took him to Babylon (see 2 Chronicles 36:6), where presumably he was executed. Because Zedekiah became king less than four months later (see vv. 9–10), at the time the Book of Mormon account begins (see 1 Nephi 1:4), Nephi was probably keenly aware of how the "one for many" principle was used to justify Jehoiakim's death. Clearly, the cases of Laban and Korihor fit within this tradition, although even the best of scholars have not been aware of this obscure principle of Jewish law until recently.

A Legal Exemption from Military Duty

The only Book of Mormon group given an exemption from military service were the famous converts of Ammon. In repenting of their previous shedding of blood, they swore an oath that they would never again take up

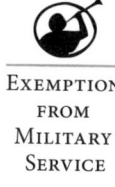

EXEMPTION FROM MILITARY SERVICE

arms (see Alma 24:11–13). After arriving in Zarahemla, they were granted an extraordinary exemption from active military duty if they would help to sustain the Nephite armies with provisions (see Alma 27:23–24). Surprisingly, this grant of exceptional privilege was consistent with ancient Israelite law.[34]

Normally, ancient peoples were absolutely obligated to take up arms in defense of their tribe or nation: "Among nomads there is no distinction between the army and the people: every able-bodied man can join in a raid and must be prepared to defend the tribe's property and rights against an enemy. . . . This was probably true of Israel also."[35] Saul called upon "all Israel" to take up arms against the Ammonites and the Amalekites (see 1 Samuel 11:1–11; 15:4). Threats and curses were pronounced upon anyone who would not join in the battle. Saul once sent messengers to marshal the troops after he symbolically cut a yoke of oxen into pieces in view of the people and proclaimed, "Whosoever cometh not forth after Saul and after Samuel, so shall it be done unto his oxen" (1 Samuel 11:7). Yaqim-Addu, governor of Sagaratum, executed a criminal in prison and paraded his head among the villages in a similar type of warning of what would happen if the men did not assemble quickly for battle.[36]

The same basic duty to serve in the army existed in Nephite law and society. Indeed, Moroni had power to punish any person in the land of Zarahemla who would not "defend [his] country" (Alma 51:15; see 46:35). Like Saul and Yaqim-Addu, he symbolically portrayed the brutal fate of those who would not fight (see Alma 46:21–22). Under extreme and desperate circumstances, this duty fell even upon old men, women, and children (see Mosiah 10:9; Alma 54:12).

How, then, could the able-bodied Ammonites be granted exemption? There may be several reasons. Their reasons for not fighting were obviously righteous and bona fide. But beyond that, the justification of their military exemption may have been based on four specific provisions in the law of Moses, especially as they were interpreted in an obscure section of Jewish law.

1. The absolute duty to go to war applied only in fighting against an *enemy*. Deuteronomy 20:1–2, which instructs the Israelite leader to speak to his troops in a holy tongue when they go up to battle against an *enemy*, was interpreted in the Talmud as not applying in a conflict against other Israelites, for as the scripture says, "'Against your enemies' but *not against your brethren*, not Judah against Simeon nor Simeon against Benjamin."[37] A similar understanding may be reflected in the Ammonites' reluctance to "take up arms against their *brethren*" (see Alma 24:6, 18; 27:23). Of course, the Talmud was written long after Lehi's departure from Jerusalem, yet it often reflected older oral material, especially from Deuteronomy. Although the wars reported in Judges 12 and 19–20 clearly show Israelite tribes fighting against each other, the book of Deuteronomy was not followed assiduously until the reign of Josiah, precisely during the time of Lehi. Thus it seems that the Nephites interpreted Deuteronomy 20:1–2 (which was known to them on the plates of brass) the same way the rabbis did, even though this interpretation would not have been obvious from a casual reading of the Old Testament. And it almost goes without saying that the Talmud was not translated into English until long after the Book of Mormon was in print.

2. The laws of Deuteronomy also afforded humanitarian exemptions for those who had recently married, built a new house, planted a new vineyard, or were "fearful and fainthearted" (see Deuteronomy 20:5–9; 24:5; compare Judges 7:3). Since everyone going into battle was likely "fearful and fainthearted," the exemption undoubtedly had a narrower meaning in actual practice; otherwise nearly everyone would have been exempt. Indeed, as the Talmud explains, this expression in Deuteronomy "alludes to one who is afraid *because of the transgressions he had committed.*"[38] If a soldier would cower in the face of enemy battle because of his previous sins (fearing that his sins prevented God from defending him or that he might die a sinner), he was deemed unfit for battle. Certainly the Nephites would have recognized that the profound fears of the Ammonites who were afraid to break their oath rendered them unsuitable for military duty under such a rule.

3. The rabbis further limited the exemption for the fearful and fainthearted to voluntary exploits of the king. In a compulsory war of national defense, however, even the fainthearted were obligated to go into battle. A similar distinction may have contributed to the Ammonites' feeling, several years later, that they could no longer claim their exemption in the face of the extreme compulsory war then threatening the Nephites' entire existence. Moved by compassion and no longer afraid, they were willing to take up arms (see Alma 53:13). Only Helaman's fear that they might lose their souls if they were to violate their oath stopped them. So they sent their sons into battle instead (see vv. 15–17).

4. The men who remained at home, however, continued to support the war behind the lines. Their exemption was granted only "on condition that they will give us [the

Nephites] a portion of their substance to assist us that we may maintain our armies" (Alma 27:24). This arrangement is especially noteworthy because the Talmud likewise holds that those who are exempted from military service under the law of Moses are *"only* released from actual fighting, *but not from serving in the rear:* 'They must furnish water and food and repair the roads.'"[39]

The rare exemption granted to the Ammonites was logical, religiously motivated, and consistent with ancient Israelite law, as embedded in Deuteronomy and elsewhere, which placed a high civic obligation on all citizens to contribute, as appropriate, to the defense of their country, their God, their religion, and their people.

Handling a Case of an Unobserved Murder

The account of the obscure trial of Seantum in Helaman 7–8 raises some interesting points of Nephite and Israelite law, details that only an ancient lawyer or judge could fully appreciate. The Book of Mormon story describes how Nephi spoke from his garden tower (see Helaman 7:10), was threatened with a lawsuit for "reviling" against the government, but in the end revealed that the chief judge had been "murdered, and he [lay] in his blood; and he [had] been murdered by his brother, who [sought] to sit in the judgment-seat" (Helaman 8:27). Five men ran and found things to be as Nephi had said. A public proclamation was then sent out by heralds announcing the murder and calling a day of fasting, mourning, and burial (see Helaman 9:10). Incidentally, in ancient Israel the day after the death of a political leader was traditionally a day of fasting, mourning, and burial (see 1 Samuel 31:13; 2 Samuel 1:12).

Rule of Evidence in an Unobserved Murder

Following the burial, five suspects (the men who had been sent to investigate) were brought to the judges. They could not be convicted, however, on circumstantial evidence, for such was ruled out under Israelite law, which required every fact to be substantiated by the testimony of two eyewitnesses (see Deuteronomy 19:15). This presented a serious legal problem in this particular case, for no one had witnessed the killing of the chief judge. Seantum had killed his brother "by a garb of secrecy" (Helaman 9:6).

Cases of unwitnessed murders presented special problems under the law of Moses. While the two-witness rule would seem to stand insurmountably in the way of ever obtaining a conviction in these cases, such slayings could not simply be ignored. If a person was found slain in the land and the murderer could not be found, solemn rituals, oaths of innocence, and special purification of all the men in the village had to be performed (see Deuteronomy 21:1–9). Things turned out differently in Seantum's case, however, for he was soon exposed in a way that opened the door to an exceptional rule of evidence that justified his conviction.

Nephi first revealed to the people that Seantum was the murderer, that they would find blood on the skirts of his cloak, and that he would say certain things to them when they told him, "We know that thou are guilty" (Helaman 9:34). Indeed, Seantum was soon detected and immediately confessed his guilt (see vv. 37–38).

Seantum's self-incriminating admission would not normally be admissible in a Jewish court of law. Under the Talmud, no man could be put to death on his own testimony: "No man may call himself a wrongdoer," especially in a capital case.[40] But from earlier times came four episodes that gave rise to a narrow exception to that policy.

Those four precedents, each of which involved convictions or punishments based on confessions, were the executions of Achan (see Joshua 7), of the man who admitted that he had killed Saul (see 2 Samuel 1:10–16), and of the two assassins of Ishbosheth, the son of Saul (see 2 Samuel 4:8–12), as well as the voluntary confession of Micah, the son who stole from his mother (see Judges 17:1–4).

The ancients reconciled these four cases with their normally rigid two-witness rule by explaining that these episodes involved confessions *before* trial (or else were proceedings before kings or rulers instead of judges).[41] In addition, an exception was especially granted when the confession was "corroborated [1] by an ordeal as well as [2] by the production of the *corpus delicti* [the material substance or evidence upon which or by which a crime is committed]."[42] This occurred in the case of Achan, who was detected (1) through the divine ordeal of casting lots and whose confession (2) was corroborated when the illegal goods were found under his tent floor (Joshua 7:22).

Thus one can conclude with reasonable confidence that in the biblical period the normal two-witness rule could be overridden in the special case of a self-incriminating confession if the confession occurred outside of court; if God's will was evidenced in the matter by ordeal, lots, or otherwise in the detection of the offender; and if corroborating physical evidence of the crime could be produced.

Seantum's self-incriminating confession satisfies all three of these requirements completely and precisely, and thus his conviction was ensured. His confession was spontaneous and before trial. The evidence of God's will was supplied through Nephi's prophecy. Tangible evidence was present in the blood found on Seantum's cloak. These factors, under biblical law, would override the normal Jewish concerns about the use of self-incriminating confessions to obtain a conviction.

Given the complicated and important ancient legal issues uniquely presented by the case of Seantum (the two-witness rule would easily have been satisfied in the cases of Abinadi, Nehor, and others, whose actions were witnessed by many people who arrested them; see Mosiah 12:9; Alma 1:10), it is little wonder that the Book of Mormon makes special note of the fact that Seantum himself was legitimately "brought to prove that he himself was the very murderer" (Helaman 9:38). No further evidence was legally needed to convict him under these circumstances.[43]

Legal Terminology for Theft and Robbery

DISTINCTION BETWEEN THEFT AND ROBBERY

Although there is only little difference between a thief and a robber in most modern minds, there were considerable differences between the two under ancient Near Eastern and biblical law. A thief *(ganab)* was usually a local person who stole from his neighbor. He was dealt with judicially, and he was tried and punished civilly, most often by a court composed of his fellow townspeople. A robber *(gedud)*, on the other hand, was treated as an outsider, as a brigand or highwayman. He was dealt with militarily, and he could be executed summarily.

The legal distinctions between theft and robbery, especially under the laws of ancient Israel, have been analyzed thoroughly by Bernard S. Jackson, an English barrister, professor of law, and former editor of the *Jewish Law Annual*. In his treatise *Theft in Early Jewish Law*, Jackson shows, for example, how robbers usually acted in organized groups rivaling local governments and attacking towns and how they swore oaths and extorted ransom, a menace worse than outright war. Thieves, however, were a much less serious threat to society.[44] Precisely the same thing can be said of the Gadiation robbers.

In my own research, I have shown in detail how these ancient legal and linguistic distinctions are also observable in the Book of Mormon.[45] For example, this ancient factor explains how Laban could call the sons of Lehi "robbers" and threaten to execute them on the spot without a trial, for that is how a military officer like Laban no doubt would have dealt with a robber. It also explains why the Lamanites are always said to "rob" from the Nephites but never from their own brethren—that would be *theft,* not *robbery.* Furthermore, it explains the rise and fearful menace of the Gadianton society, whose members are always called "robbers" in the Book of Mormon, never "thieves."

Other significant details also emerge. It is probably no coincidence that the Hebrew word for "band" or "bandits" is *gedud,* and the most famous Book of Mormon robbers were known as Gadianton's "band."

The importance of this ancient legal tradition in the Book of Mormon is further enhanced by the fact that Anglo-American common law would have provided Joseph Smith with quite a different understanding of the legal definitions of the terms *theft* and *robbery,* inconsistent in many ways with the dominant usages found in the Book of Mormon. In ordinary American usage, the two terms are nearly synonymous.

Moreover, if Joseph Smith had relied on the language of his King James Bible for legal definitions of these terms, he would have stumbled into error, for that translation uses the English words *thief* and *robber* indiscriminately. For example, the same phrase is translated inconsistently from the Hebrew or Greek of Jeremiah 7:11 as "den of robbers" and yet from the identical Greek in Matthew 21:13 as "den of thieves," even though Jesus was quoting Jeremiah on that occasion, to say nothing of the fact that thieves do not have dens. In addition, the same word for robbers in the Greek New Testament *(lestai)* is sometimes translated as "thieves" (crucified next to Jesus in Matthew 27:38) and other times as "robber" (describing Barabbas in John 18:40). Nevertheless, there was indeed an important ancient distinction between thieves and robbers that no translator should neglect, and over which Joseph Smith did not blunder.[46]

The Execution of Zemnarihah

In 3 Nephi 4:28–33 we find a detailed account of the execution of Zemnarihah, the captured leader of the defeated Gadianton robbers. This public execution followed ancient ceremony and law in a way that is out of character in European law. The Book of Mormon text reads:

PROCEDURE IN ZEMNARIHAH'S EXECUTION

> Their leader, Zemnarihah, was taken and hanged upon a tree, yea, even upon the top thereof until he was dead. And when they had hanged him until he was dead they did fell the tree to the earth, and did cry with a loud voice, saying: May the Lord preserve his people in righteousness and in holiness of heart, that they may cause to be felled to the earth all who shall seek to slay them because of power and secret combinations, even as this man hath been felled to the earth. (3 Nephi 4:28–29)

After the Nephites chopped down the tree on which Zemnarihah was hanged, they all cried out "with one voice" for God to protect them. Then they sang out "all as one" in praise of God (see 3 Nephi 4:30–33). It certainly appears that some kind of ritual or legal procedure was involved here, and several evidences point to an ancient and previously unknown background for this form of execution.⁴⁷ Consider the following points.

First, notice that the tree used in carrying out the execution was felled. Was this ever done in antiquity? Apparently it was. For one thing, Jewish practice required that the tree upon which the culprit was hanged should be buried with the body, so the tree had to be chopped down. Since the rabbis understood that this burial should take place immediately, the Talmud recommended hanging the culprit on a precut tree or post so that, in the words of Maimonides, "no felling is needed."⁴⁸

Second, consider why the tree was chopped down and buried. As Maimonides explains: "In order that it should not serve as a sad reminder, people saying: 'This is the tree on which so-and-so was hanged.'"⁴⁹ In this way the tree became associated with the person being executed; it came to symbolize the culprit and the desire to forget him or her. By way of comparison, the Nephites identified the tree with Zemnarihah and all those like him, that his infamy might not be forgotten, when they cried out: "May [the Lord] cause to be felled to the earth all who shall seek to slay them, . . . even as this man hath been felled to the earth."

Third, the text suggests that the Nephites understood Deuteronomy 21:22 as allowing execution by hanging—a reading that the rabbis saw as possible. While they generally viewed hanging as a means only of exposing the dead body after a person was stoned, the rabbis were aware of a Jewish penalty of "hanging until death occurs." For example, there were rare Jewish instances of hanging: Seventy women were "hung" in Ashkelon.⁵⁰ Eight hundred

Pharisees were crucified by Alexander Jannaeus the High Priest,[51] but the rabbis rejected that means of execution because it was "as the government does"[52] and the rabbis at that time wanted to keep as much distance as possible between Jewish and Roman practices.

Fourth, observe that the ancient idea of fashioning a punishment that fits the crime was carried out in the execution of Zemnarihah. For example, if a thief broke into a house, he was to be put to death and "hung in front of the place where he broke in."[53] Under both biblical and ancient Near Eastern law, ancient punishments called "talionic punishments" were often related symbolically to the offense. Thus the punishment for a false accuser was to make him suffer whatever would have happened to the person he had falsely accused (see Deuteronomy 19:19). In Zemnarihah's case this widely recognized principle of ancient jurisprudence was followed when he was hanged in front of the very nation he had tried to destroy and when he was felled to the earth just as he had tried to bring that nation down.

Finally, the people all chanted loudly, proclaiming the wickedness of Zemnarihah, which may be reminiscent of the ancient practice of heralding a notorious execution. Deuteronomy 19:20 says that "those which remain shall hear, and fear, and shall henceforth commit no more any such evil among you." How was this to be accomplished? Rabbi Jehudah explained: "I say that he is executed immediately and messengers are sent out to notify the people."[54] Indeed, public matters, such as the execution of a rebelling judge (see 3 Nephi 6:22–28), had to be heralded.[55] An even clearer example of heralding in the Book of Mormon is found in Alma 30:57, where the results in Korihor's case were heralded abroad. In both these cases, the apparent requirement of publishing the wickedness of the culprit was satisfied, so that all who remained would "hear and fear" and the evil would be removed from among God's people.

The Destruction of Ammonihah and the Law of Apostate Cities

Alma 16:9–11 records the utter destruction of the wicked city of Ammonihah by Lamanite soldiers following Alma's stern warning and call to repentance. Once while I was reading the account of Alma's daring mission into Nehorite territory, it dawned on me why Alma had to go to Ammonihah, as unpleasant as that surely would have been. Several striking but obscure affinities exist between that account and the ancient Israelite law regarding the annihilation of apostate cities.[56] That law is found in Deuteronomy 13:12–16, which would have been well known to Alma, the chief judge over the land of Zarahemla and keeper of the plates of brass on which this law was found:

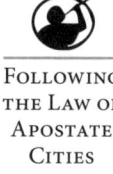

FOLLOWING THE LAW OF APOSTATE CITIES

> If thou shalt hear say in one of thy cities, . . . Certain men, the children of Belial, are gone out from among you, and have withdrawn the inhabitants of their city, saying, Let us go and serve other gods, which we have not known; then shalt thou enquire, and make search, and ask diligently; and, behold, if it be truth, and the thing certain, that such abomination is wrought among you; thou shalt surely smite the inhabitants of that city with the edge of the sword, destroying it utterly. . . . And thou shalt gather all the spoil of it into the midst of the street thereof, and shalt burn with fire the city, and all the spoil thereof every whit . . . : and it shall be an heap for ever; it shall not be built again.

Because Alma would have known this law (after all, he had served for eight years as the Nephite chief judge, and he was the custodian of the plates of brass, which contained this text), his concept of justice would have included the idea that an apostate city should be destroyed and anathematized in the specific way set forth in the governing law.

Alma clearly lacked both the desire and the power to have the city of Ammonihah destroyed by a Nephite military force (and certainly no legal decree was ever issued calling for the extermination of the city), but he did carefully record and document the fact that the city's inhabitants had satisfied every element of the crime of being an apostate city. When the justice of God destroyed that city, Alma effectively showed in the record that this fate befell them in accordance with divine law. Consider the following elements:

1. The deuteronomic law pertains to "certain men [who] are gone out from among you." Alma clearly states that the leaders in Ammonihah were Nephite apostates: "If this people, who have received so many blessings from the hand of the Lord, should transgress contrary to the light and knowledge which they do have, . . . it would be far more tolerable for the Lamanites than for them" (Alma 9:23).

2. The law applies when men have led a city to withdraw from God to serve other gods. Alma explains that certain men in Ammonihah, the followers of Nehor, had undertaken to pervert their people, to turn them away from the statutes, judgments, and commandments of the Lord (see Alma 8:17).

3. Deuteronomy describes the offenders as "the children of Belial." Likewise, Alma made it a matter of record

that "Satan had gotten great hold upon the hearts of the people of the city of Ammonihah" (Alma 8:9).

4. The law required officers to investigate the situation thoroughly, to inquire, search, and ask, to be sure that the offensive condition in fact existed. Alma did this too. After being rejected, Alma was instructed to return to preach in the city, to give the inhabitants the necessary warning that they would be destroyed if they did not repent (see Alma 8:16). Then, acting as the two required eyewitnesses (see Deuteronomy 17:6), Alma and Amulek stood and witnessed the abominable scene of the burning of the faithful, innocent wives and children of their followers (see Alma 14:9). This was a revolting experience, but it completed the case against the city and sealed its fate (see Alma 14:11).

5. The prescribed mode of execution for an apostate city was by "the sword, destroying it utterly." This is the only place in the law of Moses where slaying by the sword is required. When the day of judgment came upon Ammonihah, the Lamanites did "slay the people and destroy the city" (Alma 16:2), presumably by the sword, their primary weapon of hand-to-hand combat (see, for example, Alma 44:12, 17; 58:18).

6. The law demanded that the city should be destroyed completely by fire, "and it shall be a heap for ever." Alma records, "Every living soul of the Ammonihahites was destroyed, and also their great city, . . . [and] their dead bodies were heaped up upon the face of the earth" (Alma 16:9, 11). Alma does not say how Ammonihah was destroyed, but that fire was involved would have been normal.

7. Finally, the law stated that the ruins "shall not be built again." In the case of Ammonihah, "the people did not go in to possess the land of Ammonihah for many years.

... And their lands remained desolate" (Alma 16:11). What Joseph Smith probably never realized is that the land of Ammonihah was deemed untouchable for just over seven years, a likely ritual cleansing period in the Israelite or Nephite worlds (notice that there are eight years, nine months, and five days between Alma 16:1 and Alma 49:1). Apparently, the Nephites understood that the deuteronomic prohibition against reinhabitation could expire or be revoked. In a similar fashion, an early Christian synod removed a ban on the resettlement of Cypress, which had remained unoccupied for seven years following the annihilation of its inhabitants.[57]

Thus the destruction of Ammonihah conforms quite thoroughly with the legal provision of Deuteronomy 13, making this a remarkable case of the falling of the vengeful sword of God's justice (see Alma 54:6; compare Joshua 6:26).

Concrete Evidence for the Book of Mormon

Mesoamerican Structural Cement

Evidence for the Nephite record extends tangibly beyond the words in the record itself. Helaman 3:7–11 reports that Nephite dissenters moved from the land of Zarahemla into the land northward and began building with cement: "The people ... who went forth became exceedingly expert in the working of cement; therefore they did build houses of cement," "all manner of their buildings," and many cities "both of wood and of cement." The Book of Mormon dates this significant technological advance to the year 46 B.C.

Here we have several testable facts: the Book of Mormon tells us that people in ancient America became very skillful in the use of cement at a precise historical time. No one in the nineteenth century could have known that cement, in fact, was extensively used in Mesoamerica beginning largely at this time, the middle of the first century B.C.[58]

One of the most notable uses of cement is in the temple complex at Teotihuacán, north of present-day Mexico City. According to David S. Hyman, the structural use of cement appears suddenly in the archaeological record. And yet its earliest sample "is a fully developed product." The cement floor slabs at this site "were remarkably high in structural quality." Although exposed to the elements for nearly two thousand years, they still "exceed many present-day building code requirements."[59] This is consistent with the Book of Mormon record, which treats this invention as an important new development involving great skill and becoming something of a sensation.

After this important technological breakthrough, cement was used at many sites in the Valley of Mexico and in the Maya regions of southern Mexico, Guatemala, and Honduras, which very well may have been close to the Nephite heartlands. Cement was used in the later construction of buildings at such sites as Cerro de Texcotzingo, Tula, Palenque, Tikal, Copán, Uxmal, and Chichen Itza. Further, the use of cement is "a Maya habit, *absent* from non-Maya examples of corbelled vaulting from the southeastern United States to southern South America."[60]

Mesoamerican cement was almost exclusively lime cement. The limestone was purified on a "cylindrical pile of timber, which requires a vast amount of labor to cut and considerable skill to construct in such a way that combustion of the stone and wood is complete and a minimum of impurities remains in the product."[61] The fact that very little carbon is found in this cement once again "attests to the ability of these ancient peoples."[62]

John Sorenson has further noted the expert sophistication in the use of cement at El Tajín, east of Mexico City, in the centuries following Book of Mormon times. Cement roofs covered sizable areas: "Sometimes the builders filled a room with stones and mud, smoothed the surface on top to receive the concrete, then removed the interior fill when the [slab] on top had dried."⁶³

The presence of expert cement technology in pre-Hispanic Mesoamerica is a noteworthy archaeological fact inviting further research. Cement seems to take on significant new roles in Mesoamerican architecture close to the time when the Book of Mormon mentions the importance of this apparently new mode of building. The dating by archaeologists of this technological advance to the precise time mentioned in the book of Helaman seems far from knowable to anyone in the world in 1829.

Doubled, Sealed, Witnessed Documents

FORM OF
IMPORTANT
DOCUMENTS

A final example of an archaic practice employed in Israel around 600 B.C. and only recently understood through archaeological discoveries was the use of doubled, sealed, and witnessed documents. These documents had two parts: one was left open for ready access while the other was sealed up for later consultation by the parties or for the conclusive use of a judge in court. This widespread practice may illuminate the way in which the plates of Mormon themselves were constructed.

In an intriguing but opaque Old Testament passage, the prophet Jeremiah relates an event that occurred about 590 B.C. Pursuant to his right of redemption within the family and with prophetic foreknowledge of the transaction, Jeremiah bought from his cousin a field located at

Anathoth in the lands of Benjamin. His willingness to make this long-term investment was supportive of God's enduring promise that "houses and fields and vineyards shall be possessed again in this land" (Jeremiah 32:15), notwithstanding the prophecy that Jerusalem would also soon fall to the invading Babylonians (see v. 3). In order to memorialize his purchase as impressively and as permanently as possible, Jeremiah as purchaser drafted and executed not just a single document but a two-part deed. One part of its text "was sealed according to the law *[mitzvah]* and custom *[ḥuqqim],*" and the other part of the document "was open" (v. 11; compare v. 14). Jeremiah signed this double document and sealed it, as did several other people who witnessed the transaction and subscribed the text (see vv. 10, 12). Moreover, in order to preserve this evidence of his purchase, Jeremiah took his doubled, sealed document and, in the presence of his witnesses, securely deposited it with both of its parts in a clay jar, "that they may continue many days" (v. 14).

Jeremiah's detailed account reflects many interesting legal technicalities that were evidently well known and customary in his day.[64] As John Bright says of Jeremiah's text, "Technical legal terminology is no doubt involved," even though the precise nature of this practice cannot be ascertained from the Hebrew text alone, let alone the ordinary English translations.[65] Only because of several archaeological discoveries in the twentieth century can we now understand this interesting form of ancient legal documentation.[66]

When written on parchment or papyrus, legal documents were written on a single sheet, but the text was written twice, once at the top and again at the bottom of the sheet. The repeated text could be either a verbatim copy

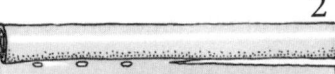

Depicted here are the stages in folding a typical double document used by Hellenistic scribes in Egypt. The text of the document was stated (A) and then repeated or abridged (B), with one version remaining open, the other being sealed. Drawing by Michael Lyon.

or an abridgment of the full text. The document was then folded so that one part was open for inspection and use, while the other part was protected and sealed.

A similar procedure was followed when important records were written on metal. In that case two or more metal plates were used. For example, two bronze tablets of the Roman emperor Trajan, with a Roman date equivalent to A.D. October 103, present the full text of an official decree neatly lettered on the open side of the first bronze plate and then repeated exactly in more hurried lettering on the inside faces of the two plates.[67] Having an open version and also a sealed iteration of important documents served several purposes, and in some cases following this convention was legally mandated.

Sealing (closing) the document was also essential, and the manner of sealing papyrus or parchment documents was relatively standard. Typically, these documents have a horizontal slit from the edge of the papyrus to the middle, between the two texts. The top half was rolled to the middle and then folded across the slit. Three holes were punched from the slit to the other side, thin papyrus bands were threaded through these holes and wrapped around the rolled-up and folded-over upper portion of the document, and on these bands the seals (wax or clay impressions) of the participants were affixed.[68] The manner of sealing metal documents was functionally the same.

Witnesses were necessary, and their number could vary. In one Assyrian agreement on a clay tablet from 651 B.C. that documented the sale of a property, twelve witnesses were listed.[69] The Babylonian Talmud stipulated that "at least three witnesses were required by law."[70] Accordingly, in most Jewish texts three witnesses were common, and it appears that normally not more than seven were used,[71] although in principle one witness was required to sign on each fold and "if there are more than three folds more witnesses must be added, one for each fold."[72]

When and by whom could these seals be opened? It appears that only a judge or some other duly authorized official could break the seals and open the document. In Babylonia, if a dispute ever arose concerning the correct wording of the contract, a judge could remove the outer envelope and reveal the original tablet.[73] John the Revelator, seeing the book sealed with seven seals, "wept much, because no man was found worthy to open and to read the book" that he beheld, until "the Lion of the tribe of Judah . . . prevailed to open the book, and to loose the seven seals thereof" (Revelation 5:4–5; compare Isaiah 29:11).

The legal use of doubled, sealed, witnessed documents during Jeremiah's (and Lehi's) lifetime in Jerusalem, together with the secular use of such instruments throughout much of the ancient world and the religious utilization of this formalism in biblical and intertestamental literature, raises the distinct possibility that Lehi knew of this practice and that Nephi and his successors had this form of double documentation in mind when they contemplated the preservation of their own records, constructed and assembled their written texts, and ultimately sealed and deposited the Book of Mormon plates (see 1 Nephi 1:17; 19:1; 3 Nephi 5:18). The Book of Mormon prophets, like Jeremiah, saw the final Nephite record as having two parts, one sealed and the other not (see Mormon 6:6; Words of Mormon 1:3, 6). Consistent with the ancient practices and requirements, witnesses were promised; in particular, at least three witnesses were stipulated. Others would be provided for, according to God's will: "as many witnesses as seemeth him good" (2 Nephi 27:14) to "testify to the truth of the book and the things therein" (v. 12).

Yet this widespread ancient legal practice was unknown until long after the Book of Mormon was published. In the summer of 1995, I visited several curators in famous museums in London and Oxford in an effort to locate examples of such doubled documents, but none of those curators had taken notice of these artifacts. Soon I found myself at a seminar in the library of the Papyrological Institute in Leiden, Holland, where quite by good fortune a large collection of sources on this very subject stood right before me.

From this research I conclude that Nephi was familiar with the Israelite legal practice of using double documents or deeds and that he instructed his posterity to construct the Nephite record in a fashion that would comply with that tradition.[74] In conformance with the concepts of the double deed, the sealed portion of the Book of Mormon will confirm the truth of the open and available portion. Moroni himself indicated that the final judgment will have legal elements, that we will see him "at the bar of God," and that God will verify the truth of the words "declare[d] . . . unto you" and "written by this man" (Moroni 10:27).

Nothing could reflect the ancient form of doubled legal documentation more genuinely.

Conclusion

Many other points of a similar nature could readily be added to this steadily growing list of impressive details about the Book of Mormon. I hope that the foregoing selection of previous recognitions draws together an interesting and convenient sample of facts about ancient language, law, and literature that were unknown to Joseph Smith and, in all likelihood, were completely unknowable to the young prophet or any of his peers as he set to work in bringing forth the text of the Book of Mormon in 1829. I present these points simply as evidence that the Book of Mormon is what it claims to be. People may make of this evidence what they will,[75] but at a minimum these points show how dismissing that book as a clever forgery leaves much of it unexplained and inexplicable.

People may not be able to account for the existence of the Book of Mormon on normal, rational grounds. But then neither could they account for Elijah's miraculous victory over the priests of Baal or Jesus' healing of the ten lepers or his feeding of the five thousand. The main purpose of those miracles was to invite or even impel people to ask God if those wonders came from him or from some other source. For Latter-day Saints the Book of Mormon serves a similar function. This book is seen as the miraculous, wondrous work foreseen in Isaiah 29. And just as were the miracles in ages past, so it is a manifestation to the world of God's continuing power and love in the world today, inviting all to come unto Christ and to ask God with a sincere heart whether the book is true. The promise is that its truth will be manifest through the power of the Holy Ghost as a living stream that will continuously gush forth in many good and unexpected ways.

Notes

1. See Terrence L. Szink and John W. Welch, "An Ancient Israelite Festival Context," in *King Benjamin's Speech: "That Ye May Learn Wisdom,"* ed. John W. Welch and Stephen D. Ricks (Provo, Utah: FARMS, 1998), 179.

2. For a discussion of this text, see David A. Black, "Jesus on Anger: The Text of Matthew 5:22a Revisited," *Novum Testamentum* 30/1 (1988): 1–8. While arguing that the longer reading "should at least be reconsidered in scholarly discussions of this passage," Black acknowledges that "the shorter text undoubtedly has impressive manuscript support," and scholarly opinion clearly favors excluding the word *eikēi*. See Hans Dieter Betz, *The Sermon on the Mount* (Minneapolis: Fortress, 1995), 219.

3. This point was first published in John W. Welch, "A Book You Can Respect," *Ensign*, September 1977, 45–48. See further discussion in John W. Welch, *Illuminating the Sermon at the Temple and Sermon on the Mount* (Provo, Utah: FARMS, 1999), 200–201.

4. Stanley R. Larson, "The Sermon on the Mount: What Its Textual Transformation Discloses concerning the Historicity of the Book of Mormon," *Trinity Journal* 7 (spring 1986): 43.

5. P. Wernberg-Møller, "A Semitic Idiom in Matt. v. 22," *New Testament Studies* 3 (1956): 72–73; italics omitted.

6. Georg Strecker, *The Sermon on the Mount: An Exegetical Commentary*, trans. O. C. Dean Jr. (Nashville: Abingdon, 1988), 146; and Betz, *Sermon on the Mount*, 494–95.

7. Ulrich Luz, *Matthew 1–7: A Continental Commentary*, trans. Wilhelm C. Linss (Minneapolis: Fortress, 1989), 418.

8. H. C. van Zyl, in "'N Moontlike Verklaring vir Matteus 7:6" (A Possible Explanation of Matthew 7:6), *Theologia*

Evangelica 15 (1982): 67–82, collapses this saying into Matthew 7:1–5 as a possible solution to the problem.

9. Strecker, *Sermon on the Mount*, 147.

10. Joachim Jeremias, *The Eucharistic Words of Jesus* (New York: Scribner's Sons, 1966), 125–37. P. G. Maxwell-Stuart, in "Do Not Give What Is Holy to the Dogs," *Expository Times* 90 (1979): 341, argues that *dogs* has a nonliteral, metaphorical sense of "those who are unbaptized and therefore impure, . . . without shame," and that *holy* might originally have meant "what is precious, what is valuable."

11. Betz, *Sermon on the Mount*, 495–96; citations and footnotes omitted.

12. See Stephen D. Ricks, "Temples through the Ages," in *Encyclopedia of Mormonism*, ed. Daniel H. Ludlow (New York: Macmillan, 1992), 4:1463–65; and Hugh W. Nibley, "On the Sacred and the Symbolic," in *Temples of the Ancient World: Ritual and Symbolism*, ed. Donald W. Parry (Salt Lake City: Deseret Book and FARMS, 1994), 553–54, 569–72.

13. Betz, *Sermon on the Mount*, 496.

14. A discussion of the temple context of the Sermon on the Mount first appeared in a FARMS Update, "The Sermon at the Temple," March 1988; also in John W. Welch, ed., *Reexploring the Book of Mormon* (Salt Lake City: Deseret Book and FARMS, 1992), 253–56.

15. See William S. Kurz, "Luke 22:14–38 and Greco-Roman and Biblical Farewell Addresses," *Journal of Biblical Literature* 104 (1985): 251–68. A discussion of the relevance of this study to King Benjamin's speech was first published as a FARMS Update, "Benjamin's Speech: A Classic Ancient Farewell Address," in June 1987 and later included in Welch, ed., *Reexploring the Book of Mormon*, 120–22, and in a fully developed form in *King Benjamin's Speech*, ed. Welch and Ricks, 88–117.

16. See John Jebb, *Sacred Literature* (London: T. Cadell and W. Davies, 1820), cited in John W. Welch, "Chiasmus in the Book of Mormon," *BYU Studies* 10/1 (1969): 72 n. 3; Thomas

Boys, *Tactica Sacra* (London: Seely, 1824) and *Key to the Book of Psalms* (London: Seely, 1825); and Thomas H. Horne, *An Introduction to the Critical Study and Knowledge of the Holy Scriptures* (Philadelphia: Littell, 1825), 2:446–73.

17. First published in Welch, "Chiasmus in the Book of Mormon," 83. For the most extensive published discussions, see John W. Welch, "Chiasmus in Alma 36," FARMS Paper 1989, and "Alma 36: A Masterpiece," in *Rediscovering the Book of Mormon,* ed. John L. Sorenson and Melvin J. Thorne (Salt Lake City: Deseret Book and FARMS, 1991), 114.

18. See John W. Welch, "How long did it take Joseph Smith to translate the Book of Mormon?" I Have a Question, *Ensign,* January 1988, 46–47.

19. In Hebrew the theophoric suffix (the use of God's name as the last syllable of a human personal name) is *yah* = *iah*. Hence, the name *Zedekiah* parallels the name *Yahweh* (Lord). This analysis was first detected by John W. Welch and published as "Was Helaman 7–8 an Allegorical Sermon?" FARMS Update, May 1986; and reprinted in Welch, ed., *Reexploring the Book of Mormon,* 232.

20. Personal correspondence to John L. Sorenson, 13 June 1970, referring to pp. 4–6 of Ralph Roys's translation of *Chilam Balam of Chumayel* (Norman: University of Oklahoma Press, 1973).

21. James B. Pritchard, ed., *Ancient Near Eastern Texts Relating to the Old Testament* (Princeton: Princeton University Press, 1950), 161; see Martha T. Roth, *Law Collections from Mesopotamia and Asia Minor* (Atlanta: Scholars Press, 1995), 59. This analysis was first published by John W. Welch as "The Laws of Eshnunna and Nephite Economics," FARMS Update, *Insights* (December 1998): 2; also in John W. Welch and Melvin J. Thorne, eds., *Pressing Forward with the Book of Mormon* (Provo, Utah: FARMS, 1999), 147–49.

22. See John W. Welch and J. Gregory Welch, *Charting the Book of Mormon* (Provo, Utah: FARMS, 1999), chart 113.

23. See Christopher A. Faraone, "The Agonistic Context of Early Greek Binding Spells," in *Magika Hiera: Ancient Greek Magic and Religion,* ed. Christopher A. Faraone and Dirk Obbink (New York: Oxford University Press, 1991), 11.

24. See A. Audollent, *Defixionum Tabellae* (Paris: n.p., 1904), nos. 22–24, 26–29, 31, 33–34, 37.

25. Faraone, "Early Greek Binding Spells," 19. First reported as "Cursing a Litigant with Speechlessness," FARMS Update, *Insights* (October 1998): 2; also in Welch and Thorne, eds., *Pressing Forward with the Book of Mormon,* 154–56.

26. H. S. Versnel, "Beyond Cursing: The Appeal to Justice in Judicial Prayers," in *Magika Hiera,* 75.

27. See Ze'ev W. Falk, *Hebrew Law in Biblical Times* (Jerusalem: Wahrmann, 1964; reprint, Provo, Utah: BYU Press, 2001), 50–56.

28. See J. van der Ploeg, "Studies in Hebrew Law: The Terms," *Catholic Biblical Quarterly* 12 (1950): 248–59; and Falk, *Hebrew Law in Biblical Times,* 8.

29. First published as a FARMS Update, "Statutes, Judgment, Ordinances, and Commandments," in June 1988; reprinted in Welch, ed., *Reexploring the Book of Mormon,* 62–65.

30. In Leviticus 18:4–5, which does not involve a pleonastic list, an a-b-b-a chiasm (mishpatim-ḥuqqot-ḥuqqot-mishpatim) has been translated as judgments-ordinances-statutes-judgments. This does not pose a counterexample.

31. In his volume *Barabbas and Esther and Other Studies in the Judaic Illumination of Earliest Christianity* (Atlanta: Scholars Press, 1992), 29–63.

32. This point was first observed by John W. Welch and law student assistant Heidi Harkness Parker in an article originally published as "Better That One Man Perish," FARMS Update, *Insights* (June 1998): 2; also in Welch and Thorne, eds., *Pressing Forward with the Book of Mormon,* 17–19.

33. *Genesis Rabbah* 94:9, vol. 2 of *Midrash Rabbah,* ed. and trans. H. Freedman and Maurice Simon (London: Soncino, 1939), 879.

34. As first observed in a FARMS Update, "Exemption from Military Duty," in June 1989; reprinted with minor changes in Welch, ed., *Reexploring the Book of Mormon,* 189–92.

35. Roland de Vaux, *Ancient Israel* (New York: McGraw Hill, 1965), 1:2.

36. From the royal archive in Mari, II, 48:15–20; cited in Victor H. Matthews, "Legal Aspects of Military Service in Ancient Mesopotamia," *Military Law Review* 94 (1981): 143.

37. Babylonian Talmud, *Sotah* VIII, 1, 42a.

38. Ibid., 3, 4a, emphasis added.

39. Ibid., 2, 43a, emphasis added.

40. Babylonian Talmud, *Sanhedrin* 9b.

41. See Menachem Elom, *The Principles of Jewish Law* (Jerusalem: Keter, 1975), 614.

42. Falk, *Hebrew Law in Biblical Times,* 60.

43. This point was first explained in a FARMS Update, "The Case of an Unobserved Murder," February 1990; also in an edited form in Welch, ed., *Reexploring the Book of Mormon,* 242–44.

44. See Bernard S. Jackson, *Theft in Early Jewish Law* (Oxford: Oxford University Press, 1972).

45. See John W. Welch, "Theft and Robbery in the Book of Mormon and in Ancient Near Eastern Law" (Provo, Utah: FARMS, 1985); "Thieves and Robbers," *Insights* (July 1985): 2; and Welch, ed., *Reexploring the Book of Mormon,* 248–49. See also my "Legal and Social Perspectives on Robbers in First-Century Judea," in *Masada and the World of the New Testament,* ed. John F. Hall and John W. Welch (Provo, Utah: BYU Studies, 1997), 141–53.

46. This point was explained in a FARMS Update, February 1990; also in Welch, ed., *Reexploring the Book of Mormon,* 248–49.

47. As first observed in "The Execution of Zemnarihah," FARMS Update, November 1984; reprinted in Welch, ed., *Reexploring the Book of Mormon,* 250–52.

48. Maimonides, *Sanhedrin* XV, 9; see also Babylonian Talmud, *Sanhedrin* VI, 6.

49. Maimonides, *Sanhedrin* XV, 9.
50. Babylonian Talmud, *Sanhedrin* 45b–46a.
51. See Josephus, *War* 1.97.
52. Babylonian Talmud, *Sanhedrin* 45b–46a.
53. Code of Hammurabi, sec. 21.
54. Babylonian Talmud, *Sanhedrin* X.6.
55. Ibid.
56. See FARMS Update, July 1987.
57. Constantinus Prophyrogenitus, *De Administrando Imperio* 47, in *Patrologia Graeca* 113:366.
58. See Matthew G. Wells and John W. Welch, "Concrete Evidence for the Book of Mormon," *Insights* (May 1991): 2.
59. David S. Hyman, *A Study of the Calcareous Cements in Prehispanic Mesoamerican Building Construction* (Baltimore: Johns Hopkins University, 1970), ii, sec. 6, p. 7.
60. George Kubler, *The Art and Architecture of Ancient America,* 2nd ed. (Baltimore: Penguin, 1975), 201, emphasis added.
61. Tatiana Proskouriakoff, *An Album of Maya Architecture* (Norman: University of Oklahoma Press, 1963), xv.
62. Hyman, *A Study of the Calcareous Cements,* sec. 6, p. 5.
63. John L. Sorenson, "Digging into the Book of Mormon," *Ensign,* October 1984, 19.
64. See Leopold Wenger, "Über Stempel und Siegel," *Zeitschrift der Savigny-Stiftung* 42 (1921): 626, in which Wenger correlates Jeremiah's double deed to Assyrian double deeds while noting the difference in material.
65. John Bright, ed., *Jeremiah,* The Anchor Bible, vol. 21 (Garden City, N.Y.: Doubleday, 1965), 237 n. 11.
66. See especially Leopold Fischer, "Die Urkunden in Jer 32 11–14 nach den Ausgrabungen und dem Talmud," *Zeitschrift der Altertums Wissenschaft* 30 (1910): 136–42; and Wenger, "Über Stempel und Siegel," 611–38.
67. See Alfred v. Domaszewski, "Ein neues Militärdiplom," in *Die Altertümer unserer heidnischen Vorzeit* (Mainz: Römisch-Germanisches Zentralmuseum, 1911), 5:181.

68. See Otto B. Rubensohn, *Elephantine-Papyri* (Berlin: Weidmann, 1907), 6–8; Fischer, "Die Urkunden in Jer 32 11–14," 138; and Friedrich Preisigke, *Griechische Papyrus* (Leipzig: Hinrichs, 1912), 1:221.

69. See E. Hammershaimb, "Some Observations on the Aramaic Elephantine Papyri," *Vetus Testamentum* 7 (January 1957): 24.

70. Elizabeth Koffmahn, *Die Doppelurkunden aus der Wüste Juda: Recht und Praxis der jüdischen Papyri des 1. und 2. Jahrhunderts n. chr. samt Übertragung der Texte und deutscher Übersetzung* (Leiden: Brill, 1968), 12.

71. See Fischer, "Die Urkunden in Jer 32 11–14," 139; Hans J. Wolff, "Die hellenistische Zeugen-Hüterurkunde," in *Das Recht der griechischen Papyri Ägyptens* (Munich: Beck, 1978), 2:63 n. 39.

72. Babylonian Talmud, *Gittin* 81b.

73. See ibid.

74. This point was initially developed in John W. Welch, "Doubled, Sealed, Witnessed Documents: From the Ancient World to the Book of Mormon," in *Mormons, Scripture, and the Ancient World,* ed. Davis Bitton (Provo, Utah: FARMS, 1998), 391–444.

75. For a discussion of what counts as evidence and how evidence is relevant to faith, see my chapter on "The Power of Evidence in the Nurturing of Faith," in *Nurturing Faith through the Book of Mormon: The Twenty-Fourth Annual Sidney B. Sperry Symposium* (Salt Lake City: Deseret Book, 1995), 149–86; reprinted in condensed form in chapter 2 herein.

Converging Paths: Language and Cultural Notes on the Ancient Near Eastern Background of the Book of Mormon

Stephen D. Ricks

In the past half generation, Book of Mormon study has come into its own. The accumulated efforts of scholars in examining the results of major finds, in reassessing reports of other discoveries, and in rethinking the geography of Book of Mormon events have all combined to place the historical plausibility of the Book of Mormon on a very sure footing. In what follows I review nine aspects of Book of Mormon language, history, and culture that were unknown or unexamined at the time of the publication of the Book of Mormon but have since entered the forefront of scholarly discussion.

Treaty and Covenant in King Benjamin's Address

There is an amazing ritual density in King Benjamin's address and its related events, which included a covenant making/covenant renewal ceremony as well as a coronation ceremony in which Benjamin's son Mosiah acceded to

Treaty/
Covenant
Pattern

the throne.¹ The series of events outlined in Mosiah 1–6 reflects what biblical scholars call the "treaty/covenant pattern" in ancient Israelite literature—a literary feature that was completely unknown when the Book of Mormon was published in 1830 and was not identified and studied until the past two generations. In 1931 Viktor Korosec identified the treaty pattern from ancient Hittite treaties,² and in 1950 Elias Bickerman tentatively connected this Hittite treaty pattern with Israelite covenant making.³ It was not until 1954, however, that George Mendenhall set out in detail that connection, identifying the specific elements of the treaty/covenant pattern: (1) the king/prophet gives a preamble that introduces God as the one making the covenant or that introduces his prophet as a spokesman for God; (2) the king/prophet gives a brief review of God's dealings with Israel in the past; (3) the king/prophet notes the terms of the covenant, listing specific commandments and obligations that God expects Israel to keep; (4) the people bear witness in formal statements that they accept the covenant; (5) the king/prophet lists the blessings and curses for obedience or disobedience to the covenant; and (6) the king/prophet makes provisions for depositing a written copy of the covenant in a safe and sacred place and for reading its contents to the people in the future.⁴

Among its other connections with ancient Israelite religious practice, the assembly recorded in Mosiah 1–6 mentions three interesting features: the pilgrimage of whole families to the temple site, the sacrifice of animals, and the people's dwelling in tents. These elements are so typical of the Israelite Feast of Tabernacles that they strongly suggest that the events recorded in these chapters took place during a Nephite observance of that festival. The Old Testament indicates that the Feast of Tabernacles most likely took place when the Israelites renewed their covenant with God, and that appears to be what the Nephites were doing in the assembly reported in Mosiah 1–6.[5]

The six elements of covenant renewal mentioned above can be found in Exodus, Deuteronomy, and Joshua. In addition, the new king would ideally take office before the death of the old one, and this transfer of power was connected with the ceremony in which the people made or renewed their covenant with God. Interestingly, each of these features is found in Mosiah 1–6.

1. *Preamble.* The passages in the Bible dealing with the renewal of the covenant sometimes introduce God as the maker of the covenant: "God spake all these words saying . . ." (Exodus 20:1). At other times a prophet is introduced to act for God: "Joshua said unto all the people, Thus saith the Lord God of Israel . . ." (Joshua 24:2). Similarly, Benjamin's covenant assembly in the book of Mosiah begins: "These are the words which [Benjamin] spake and caused to be written, saying . . ." (Mosiah 2:9). Although Benjamin is speaking, he is clearly acting as the mouthpiece of God. In fact, a sizable part of his address consists of words that had been made known to him "by an angel from God" (Mosiah 3:2).

2. *Review of God's Relations with Israel.* At this point in the covenant renewal ceremony, according to the Bible, the people hear of God's mighty acts on behalf of his people, Israel. For example, Jehovah says through Moses, "Ye have seen what I did unto the Egyptians, and how I bare you on eagles' wings, and brought you unto myself" (Exodus 19:4; compare Exodus 20:2; Joshua 24:11–23). The Mosiah passage includes a long account of the past relations between

King Benjamin and his people as an *a fortiori* argument for the people's obligation to God (see Mosiah 2:19).

3. *Terms of the Covenant.* Each of the biblical covenant passages states the commandments that God expects his people, Israel, to keep. A prime example is in Exodus 20–23, where God first briefly lists the Ten Commandments (see Exodus 20:3–17) and then spells out in greater detail what the people are to obey (see Exodus 21:1–23:19). Benjamin's address also contains numerous commandments; for example: "Believe in God. . . . Believe that ye must repent of your sins and forsake them, and humble yourselves before God; and ask in sincerity of heart that he would forgive you" (Mosiah 4:9–10).

4. *Formal Witness.* Once in the Old Testament, an object—a particular stone—was made witness to the covenant: "for it hath heard all the words of the Lord which he spake unto us: it shall be therefore a witness unto you, lest ye deny your God" (Joshua 24:27). In general, though, the people themselves were the witnesses, stating, for instance, "All that the Lord hath spoken we will do" (Exodus 19:8). Following King Benjamin's address, the people express a similar desire "to enter into a covenant with [their] God to do his will, and to be obedient to his commandments" (Mosiah 5:5). They further witness their willingness to obey by allowing their names to be listed among those who have "entered into a covenant with God to keep his commandments" (Mosiah 6:1).

5. *Blessings and Curses.* Biblical covenants often end with a list of curses and blessings for those who enter into the covenant: "Cursed be the man that maketh any graven or molten image. . . . And all the people shall answer and say, Amen. Cursed be he that setteth light by his father or

his mother. And all the people shall say, Amen" (Deuteronomy 27:15–16). "Blessed shalt thou be in the city, and blessed shalt thou be in the field. Blessed shall be the fruit of thy body, and the fruit of thy ground, and the fruit of thy cattle" (Deuteronomy 28:3–4).

More often in the Old Testament, however, such curses and blessings are merely implied: "Joshua said unto the people, . . . If ye forsake the Lord, and serve strange gods, then he will turn and do you hurt, and consume you, after that he hath done you good" (Joshua 24:19–20). Similarly, the curses and blessings in Benjamin's speech are implied rather than stated outright: "Whosoever doeth this shall be found at the right hand of God. . . . Whosoever shall not take upon him the name of Christ must be called by some other name; therefore, he findeth himself on the left hand of God" (Mosiah 5:9–10).

6. *Reciting and Depositing the Covenant.* The Bible frequently mentions that the covenant was read aloud. For example, we read that "[Moses] took the books of the covenant, and read in the audience of the people" (Exodus 24:7). Other passages mention that the covenant was written and put in a safe and sacred place: "Joshua wrote these words in the book of the law of God, and took a great stone, and set it up there under an oak, that was by the sanctuary of the Lord" (Joshua 24:26). The words of King Benjamin were written and sent out among the people, not only so they could be studied and understood but also, it can be surmised, so they could serve as a permanent record of the assembly (see Mosiah 2:8–9). At the end of Benjamin's address, when all of the people expressed a willingness to take upon themselves Christ's name, their names were

recorded and presumably preserved as a memorial of the covenant (see Mosiah 6:1).

Kingship and Coronation

Mosiah's Coronation Ceremony

Mosiah 1–6 is also a coronation ceremony for Benjamin's son Mosiah, a ceremony not unlike those associated with ancient Near Eastern and Mediterranean coronations. Kingship in ancient Israel and in the ancient Near East and the various steps of the coronation ceremony remained unexamined until the first decades of the twentieth century, when they became the subject of systematic investigation.[6] The account of Mosiah's coronation contains the following four key elements of ancient Israelite coronations: the sanctuary as the coronation site, installation in office with insignia, anointing, and receiving a throne name.

The Sanctuary as the Coronation Site

A society's most sacred spot is the location where the sacred act of coronation takes place. For Israel, the temple was that site. Thus we read that, during his coronation, Joash stood "by a pillar [of the temple], as the manner was" (2 Kings 11:14). However, the temple had not been built when Solomon became king, so he was crowned at Gihon (see 1 Kings 1:45), a site made sacred by the presence of the ark of the covenant (which contained the sacred objects from Moses' day) within the special tabernacle that David had made to shelter it. The priest Zadok took "out of the tabernacle" the horn containing oil, from which he anointed Solomon (see 1 Kings 1:39). In the Nephite case, the temple at Zarahemla was the sacred site chosen for

Benjamin's address to the people and for Mosiah's consecration as king (see Mosiah 1:18).

Installation in Office with Insignia

At the coronation of Joash, Jehoiada the priest conferred upon him two objects, called the *nēzer* and the *ʿēdût*. The meaning of the first term is "crown" (see 2 Kings 11:12). The meaning of *ʿēdût* is far less certain. It may have been a piece of writing that affirmed the king's adoption by God and promised the new king victory over his enemies, as Psalm 2:7–9 suggests, or it may have been a document, one the ruler was to wear, containing the basic terms of Yahweh's covenant with the house of David (Israel's line of the kings).

The transfer of power to Mosiah involved something similar. Benjamin gave him certain objects, passing on the official records of the people (the plates of brass and the plates of Nephi), the sword of Laban, and the miraculous ball, also called the director or Liahona (see Mosiah 1:15–16). Of course, the royal documents were the most important records in the kingdoms of the ancient world, and a sword was a frequent sign of kingship in Europe and Asia.[7] In addition, from the sixteenth century at least back to the Roman Empire, rulers in the Old World commonly held in one hand an orb or ball.[8] Although the Bible does not mention such an object, it still might have been part of the Israelite coronation paraphernalia.

Anointing

To anoint the king with oil was a significant part of coronation ceremonies in ancient Israel and in the ancient Near East generally. The Bible records the anointing of six kings: Saul, David, Solomon, Jehu, Joash, and Jehoahaz.

Indeed, the name-title *Messiah*, which was used to refer to several of the kings of Israel, means "anointed," no doubt referring to the rite of anointing the king during his installation in office.

The Hittites, northern neighbors of the Israelites, also had a ceremony that included anointing the king with oil. Moreover, although there is no clear evidence that the Egyptian king was anointed when he became king, he was apparently anointed every morning before entering the temple to perform daily chants.

Following his address and the people's renewal of the covenant, Benjamin "consecrated his son Mosiah to be a ruler and a king over his people" (Mosiah 6:3). The context does not indicate whether this "consecration" included anointing. However, some ritual act was evidently involved since almost the beginning of Nephite history, for Jacob mentioned a coronation that included anointing. He reported that his brother Nephi, the first king, "began to be old, and he saw that he must soon die; wherefore, he anointed a man to be a king and a ruler over his people now, according to the reigns of the kings" (Jacob 1:9). "According to the reigns of the kings" clearly refers to the pattern of kingship in Judah, with which Nephi was personally familiar.

Receiving a Throne Name

In many ancient societies a king received a new name or throne name when he was crowned king. Several Israelite kings had two names, a birth name and a throne name. It may be that all the kings of Judah received a new name when they came to the throne. During the Middle Kingdom period (approximately 2000–1800 B.C.), each king of Egypt had no fewer than five names and received a throne name at the time he became king. Kings in Mesopotamia also received a new name. Each Parthian king (in ancient Iran) assumed the same throne name, Arsak, at his crowning, an act that has made it hard for historians to distinguish one ruler from another.

Similarly, use of a single royal title marked the early Nephite kings. Jacob wrote, "The people having loved Nephi exceedingly, . . . wherefore, the people were desirous to retain in remembrance his name. And whoso should reign in his stead were called by the people, second Nephi, third Nephi, and so forth, according to the reigns of the kings; and thus they were called by the people, let them be of whatever name they would" (Jacob 1:10–11). While we do not know that this new name was given to the Nephite rulers as part of the coronation rite, there is every reason to expect that it was.

The Tree and Waters of Life

Given the Semitic background of the Book of Mormon, it is not surprising that an ancient Near Eastern symbol such as the tree of life should appear in the Book of Mormon and be supported by many other evidences from other ancient Near Eastern cultures, including Mesopotamia and Egypt.⁹ The tree of life is first mentioned in the account of Lehi's dream, where Lehi states that "it came to pass that I beheld a tree, whose fruit was desirable to make one happy" (1 Nephi 8:10). In Nephi's similar vision the tree of life is associated with the waters of life: "And it came to pass that I beheld that the rod of iron . . . led to the fountain of living waters, or to the tree of life; which waters are a representation of the love of God" (1 Nephi 11:25).¹⁰

Symbolism of the Tree of Life

Though not expressly named as such, the Semitic *kiškānu*-tree (like the Sumerian *giš-kin*) of Mesopotamia "is identical with the tree of Life."[11] As in the Book of Mormon, this tree of life is closely linked to the waters of life, since "the tree of Life constantly needs the Water of Life near which it is growing in the garden of paradise."[12] This is also reminiscent of an ancient Jewish tradition that "the tree of life is planted near the source of the water of life."[13]

The ancient Mesopotamian legend of the hero Gilgamesh gives further insight into the "plant of Life" that, according to Geo Widengren, is like the "tree of Life."[14] In the legend, Gilgamesh, exhausted from his search for the very aged Utnapishtim, who lived on an island at the edge of the world, is taken by Utnapishtim "to the washing place" in order to "wash off his grime in water clean as snow." Gilgamesh is then clothed in "a cloak to clothe his nakedness" with a band placed on his head.[15] Utnapishtim later tells him where to get the "plant of Life." Gilgamesh does find the plant, but it is spirited away by a snake, thereby allowing the snake to shed its skin periodically but causing Gilgamesh to fail in his quest.

The tree of life and its connection with the waters of life also occur in ancient Egyptian religion and literature: "From the age of the Pyramid texts the word *ḥt n ꜥankh*, 'Tree of Life,' appears."[16] There is a miniature statue of Rameses II stretched out on the leaves of the *ished* (i.e., persea) tree, the Egyptian tree of life. The inscription on the statue indicates that Rameses' name was written on the leaves of the *ished* tree, which served as a kind of book of life or book of remembrance.[17] The sacred tree and water are found together in many Egyptian temple complexes.

Hebraisms in the Book of Mormon

We do not know what language was written on the plates of the Book of Mormon.[18] Nephi described the writing as consisting of "the learning of the Jews and the language of the Egyptians" (1 Nephi 1:2), while Moroni, writing at the end of Nephite history, described it as "reformed Egyptian" (Moroni 9:32). The language of the plates may have been Egyptian symbols to represent Egyptian words, Egyptian symbols to represent Hebrew words, or Egyptian and Hebrew signs to represent Hebrew words or Hebrew and Egyptian words. In any event, the day-to-day speech of the Nephites was some form of Hebrew. Even in its English translation, the Book of Mormon reflects Hebrew speech and thought patterns. Of the many such Hebraisms discoverable in the Book of Mormon, I will briefly discuss the construct state, adverbials, the cognate accusative, and relative clauses.

HEBREW FORMS

Word Order of the Construct State

The "construct state" in Hebrew indicates possession or relationship of one noun to another. This relationship is conveyed in English by the possessive case, by use of the preposition *of,* or by an adjective modifying a noun. For example, in English the phrase *the king's house* or *house of the king* would read *house the king* in Hebrew. Similarly, an adjective-noun pair in English such as *brass plates* would read *plates brass* in Hebrew or, in translation, *plates of brass,* which is precisely what we find in the Book of Mormon. A number of other phrases in the English translation of the Book of Mormon preserve this underlying Hebrew word order. Here are a few examples:

words of plainness (Jacob 4:14) instead of *plain words*

skin of blackness (2 Nephi 5:21) instead of *black skin*

night of darkness (Alma 34:33) instead of *dark night*

Adverbials

Hebrew is decidedly lacking in adverbs. Instead of adverbs, it frequently uses the prepositions meaning "in" or "with." Two examples will suffice to illustrate how the Book of Mormon conforms with Hebrew syntax in this regard:

with patience (Mosiah 24:15) instead of *patiently*

with much harshness (1 Nephi 18:11) instead of *very harshly*

The Cognate Accusative of "Possess" and "Inheritance"

It is well known that Hebrew frequently uses a verb and an object using a related word: "she vowed a vow" (1 Samuel 1:11). This feature of Hebrew style is viewed as attractive if not elegant, though English stylists view it as infelicitous phrasing to be avoided. The Book of Mormon contains many examples of the cognate accusative, such as, "I have dreamed a dream [Hebrew *ḥālamtî ḥālôm*]; or, in other words, I have seen a vision [*ḥāzîtî ḥāzôn*]" (1 Nephi 8:2). Other examples include "work all manner of fine work" (Ether 10:23), and "taxed with a tax" (Mosiah 7:15).

Much more difficult to notice, however, are cognate accusatives obscured by the English translation. Consider, for example, the construction that arises from the similarity between the related Hebrew words for *Jershon, inheritance,* and *possession* in Alma 27: "And they went down into the land of Jershon, and took *possession* [Hebrew *YRŠ] of the land of *Jershon*" (Hebrew *yaršôn,* Alma 27:26) "for an *inheritance*" (Hebrew *yaršôn*, Alma 27:22). This is a remarkable instance of the cognate accusative in the underlying Hebrew text.

Relative Clause

In biblical Hebrew the relative clause (usually introduced by *who* or *which*) does not always closely follow the word or phrase to which it refers. This unique aspect of the Hebrew language is seen in the Book of Mormon as well. Consider two examples:

> *Then shall they confess, who live without God in the world* (Mosiah 27:31) instead of *Then shall they who live without God in the world confess.*

> *The Egyptians were drowned in the Red Sea, who were the armies of Pharaoh* (1 Nephi 17:27) instead of *The Egyptians, who were the armies of Pharaoh, were drowned in the Red Sea.*

Names in the Book of Mormon

In the Book of Mormon, many personal names and place-names reflect the book's Israelite and Egyptian background.[19] In this section I will discuss two personal names of Egyptian origin—*Paanchi* and *Nephi*—and three names of Hebrew origin—the personal name *Sariah* and the place-names *Jershon* and *Cumorah*.

EGYPTIAN AND HEBREW NAMES

Egyptian Names: Paanchi, Nephi

Paanchi. Among those who contended unsuccessfully for the judgment seat was Paanchi (see Helaman 1:3, 7, 8). Egyptologist Günther Vittmann, in an article on the name *Pꜣ-ꜥnkhi* (pronounced "Piꜥankhi" or "Paꜥankhi"), indicates that it is a Twenty-Fifth-Dynasty royal name of Meroitic origin.[20] Even critics of the Book of Mormon concede that this name is indisputably Egyptian in provenance.

Nephi. In his study *Personal Names in the Phoenician and Punic Inscriptions,* Frank Benz cites a Phoenician name, *KNPY,* found at Elephantine, in Upper Egypt. Benz sees the name as a Canaanite form of the Egyptian personal name *Kȝ-nfr.w.*[21] In Phoenician, a Semitic language closely related to Hebrew, the medial *P* in *NPY* would be pronounced /f/, making the name essentially congruent with the name *Nephi.* In addition, in the late Egyptian period (approximately 1000–300 B.C.) the *r* in the personal name *nfr* was pronounced /y/ ("ee"), again recalling the name *Nephi.* (In Coptic, the successor language to late Egyptian, *nfr* was rendered *noufi,* pronounced "noo-fee").[22] The name *Nephi* is thus "an attested Syro-Palestinian Semitic form of an attested Egyptian man's name dating from the Late Period of Egypt."[23]

Hebrew Names: Sariah, Jershon, Cumorah

Sariah. Sariah is introduced in the Book of Mormon as the wife of the prophet Lehi and the mother of Laman, Lemuel, Sam, Nephi, Jacob, and Joseph (see 1 Nephi 2:5). Her name, which would be *śryh* in Hebrew spelling, has been found in an Aramaic papyrus dating to the fifth century B.C.[24] In line 4 of this text (denominated Papyrus 22) the name is given as *śry[h br]t hwšʿ br ḥrmn,* which may be vocalized as *Śariah barat Hoshea bar Ḥarman,* "Sariah the daughter of Hoshea son of Harman." According to Jeffery R. Chadwick, who has studied this text, "Cowley had to reconstruct part of the text, supplying the final *h* of *Sariah* and the initial *b-r* of *barat,* but the spacing is adequate, and the comparative context of the papyrus leaves little doubt that the reconstruction is accurate."²⁵ Papyrus 22 belongs to the Elephantine Papyri, discovered at the beginning of the twentieth century, more than seventy years after the first publication of the Book of Mormon.

Cumorah. *Cumorah* is the name of the hill in which Mormon buried the Nephite records before turning his abridgment of it over to his son Moroni (see Mormon 6:6). Suggested etymologies range from a corruption of the biblical place-name *Gomorrah* to a comparison with *Qumran*, the name of the site near the caves where the Dead Sea Scrolls were found. The most plausible etymology for *Cumorah*, however, is the Hebrew *kəmôrāh*, "priesthood," an abstract noun based on the word *kōmer*, "priest." *Kōmer/ kômer* and *kəmôrāh* may be compared in both form and meaning with the Hebrew nouns *kōhēn*, "priest," and *kəhunnāh*, "priesthood."

Some have privately objected that this explanation is unlikely because the term *kōmer* is always used in the Old Testament in reference to false priests (see 2 Kings 23:5; Hosea 10:5; Zephaniah 1:4), while the word *kōhēn* is used to denote Israelite priests. It seems more likely that the term *kōmer* was simply used to denote a priest who was not of the tribe of Levi, while *kōhēn* in all cases refers to a Levitical priest. Since Lehi's party did not include descendants of Levi, they probably used *kōmer* wherever the Book of Mormon speaks of priests.

Jershon. When the Lamanites converted by the sons of Mosiah fled their homeland to escape persecution, the Nephites allowed them to settle in the land of Jershon. The name *Jershon*, though not found in the Bible, has an authentic Hebrew origin, the root *YRŠ* meaning "to inherit" and the suffix *-ôn* denoting a place-name. Three passages in the Book of Mormon present *Jershon* in context with the idea of inheritance: Alma 27:22 ("and this land Jershon is the land which we will give unto our brethren for an inheritance"), Alma 27:24 ("that they may inherit the land Jershon"), and Alma 35:14 ("they have lands for their inheritance in the land of Jershon").

The *-ôn* ending of *Jershon* is typical of other place-names belonging to the ancient Near East. Wilhelm Borée, in his outstanding study *Die alten Ortsnamen Palästinas* (The ancient place-names of Palestine), cites fully eighty-four ancient Canaanite place-names with the ending *-ôn* in biblical and extrabiblical sources (e.g., Egyptian and Mesopotamian writings, the El-Amarna letters, ostraca), including *Ayyalon* (spelled *Ajalon* in KJV Joshua 19:42), *Ashkelon* (spelled *Asklon* in KJV Judges 1:18), *Gibeon* (Joshua 9:3), *Hebron* (Joshua 10:36), *Dibon* (Numbers 21:30), and *Heshbon* (Numbers 21:30). The Book of Mormon place-name *Jershon*, then, is right at home with a number of other biblical and extrabiblical place-names.

"The Place Which Was Called Nahom"

GEOGRAPHIC
CORRELATION
OF NAHOM

Nephi recounted that at one point in his family's travels "in the borders near the Red Sea . . . we did pitch our tents again, that we might tarry for the space of a time. And it came to pass that Ishmael died, and was buried in the place *which was called* Nahom" (1 Nephi 16:14, 33–34). It is striking that in this instance Lehi did not follow desert practice and name the locale himself, as he did with "the valley which he called Lemuel" (1 Nephi 16:6), "the place [they called] Shazer" (1 Nephi 16:13), "the land which we called Bountiful," and "the sea, which we called Irreantum" (1 Nephi 17:5). Instead, the name *Nahom* predated the group's arrival and was adopted by them.

In his book *Lehi in the Desert,* Hugh Nibley makes the linguistic point that the name *Nahom* derived from the Semitic triliteral roots NHM and NḤM that mean "lament" or "grieve" (in Arabic *nahama* means "to sigh, groan, moan" and *naḥama* signifies "to groan, roar, complain," while in Hebrew the root NḤM means "to mourn").[26]

Lynn and Hope Hilton traveled the presumed route of Lehi in the Arabian Peninsula and proposed that the place called Nahom was by al-Kunfidah in the southwest corner of Saudi Arabia.[27] The late Brigham Young University archaeologist Ross T. Christensen cites the instance of a site named Nehhm in an eighteenth-century map drawn by the German explorer Carsten Niebuhr, in a valley to the north of Sanaʾa, the modern capital of the Arab Yemen Republic.[28] Warren and Michaela Knoth Aston have followed Christensen's lead in seeking Islamic and early modern sources for *Nahom*. They found a 1976 map at the University of Sanaʾa in the Yemen Arab Republic that indicated a site called Nehem about thirty-five miles northeast of Sanaʾa, about the same place cited by Christensen. Nehem is the site of numerous tombs dating back centuries, quite possibly suggesting that it served as a cemetery since antiquity. The Astons also note that the medieval Arab authors Ibn al-Kalbi and al-Hamdani "refer variously to a pagan god known as Nuhum (Ibn al-Kalbi), a tribal ancestor named Nuham (Ibn al-Kalbi), and a region and a tribe called Nihm (al-Hamdani), all in southwest Arabia."[29] Despite the venerable age of these intriguing references, all of them were "1,400 or more years after Lehi's party passed through the area."[30]

A few years ago, however, Professor S. Kent Brown of Brigham Young University learned that Burkhard Vogt and a German archaeological team excavating the Barʾan temple in Marib, Yemen, had found an inscribed altar dating from the seventh to sixth centuries B.C., "generally the time of Lehi and his family."[31] The inscription on the altar indicates that one "Biᶜathar, son of Sawād, son of Nawᶜān, the Nihmite," dedicated the altar to the temple.[32] The discovery of this altar is astonishing since, according to Brown, "it predates by almost 1,500 years the Arabic sources cited by the Astons which refer to [a place-name corresponding to *Nahom*]."[33]

Writing on and Burying Metal Plates

ANCIENT
TEXTS ON
METAL PLATES

On 21 September 1823, when the angel Moroni appeared to Joseph Smith, "he said there was a book deposited, written upon gold plates, giving an account of the former inhabitants of this continent" (Joseph Smith—History 1:34). Following Moroni's appearance, Joseph went to what was later called the Hill Cumorah and reported: "On the west side of this hill, not far from the top, under a stone of considerable size, lay the plates, deposited in a stone box. This stone was thick and rounding in the middle on the upper side, and thinner towards the edges, so that the middle part of it was visible above the ground, but the edge all around was covered with earth" (Joseph Smith—History 1:51).

A striking parallel to Joseph Smith's receiving the gold plates from a stone box occurred in September 1933, when the German archaeologist Ernst Herzfeld discovered in Persepolis that "two shallow, neatly made stone boxes with [sealed] lids, each containing two square plates of gold and silver, had been sunk into the bedrock beneath the walls at the corners of . . . the apadana," the multicolumned audience hall of the palace at Persepolis."[34] These plates "were laid down, probably in the presence of Darius, in 516–515 B.C." and were recovered in perfect condition, "the metal shining as the day it was incised."[35] According to Herzfeld:

> All these tablets—one gold and one silver from Hamadan, two gold and two silver from Persepolis—were discovered in situ. . . . The texts of the gold tablets from Hamadan and Persepolis vary only in the line arrangements imposed by different formats. The Persepolis tablets underlie the issuance of this "edition," whose unconventional writing [of a particular word] . . . shows that all of its copies were created from one and the same Urtext in a central office. Darius had undertaken simultaneous building projects in Persepolis, Susa, and Ecbatana, and the administration of these buildings was a unified thing.[36]

This is only one example, among many that could be cited, of the burial of metal documents in stone boxes,[37] providing evidence not only of the format of the Book of Mormon record but also of the manner in which it was concealed for some fourteen hundred years.

Eyewitnesses of the Translation of the Book of Mormon

In addition to the Three and Eight Witnesses to the Book of Mormon, a steady stream of individuals viewed the plates, observed the translation process, and consistently described that process: members of Joseph's family, members of Emma's family, even newcomers and strangers. The following statements come from these participants in

TRANSLATION PROCESS CONSISTENTLY DESCRIBED

408 • *Echoes and Evidences of the Book of Mormon*

the translation process—Joseph Smith Jr.; his wife, Emma; and Martin Harris. Significant passages are indicated with italics.

Joseph Smith

One of the best descriptions of the plates themselves was given by Joseph Smith in his 1842 letter to John Wentworth, editor of the Chicago *Democrat:*

> These records were engraven on plates which had the appearance of gold, each plate was six inches wide and eight inches long, and not quite so thick as common tin. They were filled with engravings, in Egyptian characters, and bound together in a volume as the leaves of a book, with three rings running through the whole.

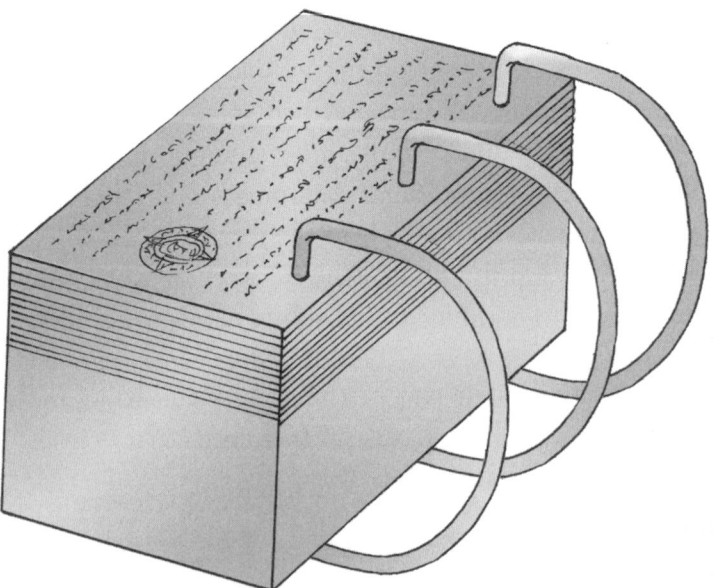

Based on descriptions by eyewitnesses such as Joseph Smith and David Whitmer, this conjectural reconstruction of the Book of Mormon plates shows how the title page, the last plate written on in the Book of Mormon, could also appear as the first plate in the record. Drawing by Michael Lyon.

The volume was something near six inches in thickness, a part of which was sealed. The characters on the unsealed part were small, and beautifully engraved. The whole book exhibited many marks of antiquity in its construction, and much skill in the art of engraving. With the records was found a curious instrument, which the ancients called "Urim and Thummim," which consisted of two transparent stones set in the rim of a bow fastened to a breastplate. Through the medium of the Urim and Thummim I translated the record by the gift and power of God.[38]

Emma Smith

In the latter part of 1827 and the early part of 1828, when the book of Lehi was being translated and Emma was acting as scribe, Joseph translated a passage describing Jerusalem as a walled city and stopped to ask Emma if Jerusalem indeed had walls. In 1856 Emma recalled this incident (which, incidentally, reflects how poorly equipped educationally Joseph Smith was to produce the Book of Mormon on his own):

> When my husband was translating the Book of Mormon, I wrote a part of it, as he dictated each sentence, word for word, and when he came to proper names he could not pronounce, or long words, he spelled them out, and while I was writing them, if I made any mistake in spelling, he would stop me and correct my spelling, although it was impossible for him to see how I was writing them down at the time. Even the word Sarah [sic!] he could not pronounce at first, but had to spell it, and I would pronounce it for him. When he stopped for any purpose at any time he would, when he commenced again, begin where he left off without any hesitation.[39]

In early 1879 Emma was interviewed by her son Joseph III; her second husband, Major Bidamon; and others. She responded to a number of questions concerning events in the early history of the church:

Q. What of the truth of Mormonism?

A. I know Mormonism to be the truth; and believe the Church to have been established by divine direction. I have complete faith in it. *In writing for your father I frequently wrote day after day, often sitting at the table close by him, he . . . dictating hour after hour with nothing between us.*

Q. *Had he not a book or manuscript from which he read, or dictated to you?*

A. He had neither manuscript nor book to read from.

Q. *Could he not have had, and you not know it?*

A. If he had had anything of the kind he could not have concealed it from me.

Q. *Are you sure that he had the plates at the time you were writing for him?*

A. The plates often lay on the table without any attempt at concealment, wrapped in a small linen table cloth, which I had given him to fold them in. *I once felt of the plates, as they thus lay on the table, tracing their outline and shape. They seemed to be pliable like thick paper, and would rustle with a metallic sound when the edges were moved by the thumb, as one does sometimes thumb the edges of a book.*

Q. *Where did father and Oliver Cowdery write?*

A. Oliver Cowdery and your father wrote in the room where I was at work.

Q. *Could not father have dictated the Book of Mormon to you, Oliver Cowdery and the others who wrote for him, after having first written it, or having first read it out of some book?*

A. Joseph Smith . . . could neither write nor dictate a coherent and well-worded letter; let alone dictating a book like the Book of Mormon. And, though I was an active participant in the scenes that transpired, and was present during the translation of the plates, and had cognizance of things as they transpired, it is marvelous to me, "a marvel and a wonder," as much so as to any one else.

Q. *I should suppose that you would have uncovered the plates and examined them?*

A. I did not attempt to handle the plates, other than I have told you, nor uncover them to look at them. I was satisfied that it was the work of God, and therefore did not feel it to be necessary to do so.

Q. *(from Major Bidamon): Did Mr. Smith forbid your examining the plates?*

A. I do not think he did. I knew that he had them, and was not specially curious about them. I moved them from place to place on the table, as it was necessary in doing my work.[40]

Martin Harris

Martin Harris aided in the translation of the book of Lehi. Edward Stevenson reported about him:

After continued translation they would become weary, and would go down to the river and exercise by throwing stones out on the river, etc. While so doing on one occasion, Martin found a stone very much resembling the one used for translating, and on resuming their labor of translation, Martin put in [its] place the stone that he had found. He said that the Prophet remained silent, unusually and intently gazing in darkness, no traces of the usual sentences appearing. Much surprised, Joseph exclaimed, "Martin! What is the matter? All is as dark as Egypt!" Martin's countenance betrayed him, and the Prophet asked Martin why he had done so. Martin said, to stop the mouths of fools, who had told him that the Prophet had learned those sentences and was merely repeating them, etc.[41]

These and other independent witnesses to the translation provide modern researchers with significant information about the Book of Mormon plates. These firsthand witnesses are an indigestible lump in the throats of those who deny that the plates existed and try to explain the experience as an example of "collective hysteria."

The "Garment of Joseph" and Parallels from the Ancient World

The great Nephite leader Moroni, when attempting to rouse his brethren to defend themselves against Amalickiah and the Lamanites, reminded them of their link to Joseph of Egypt when he said: "Behold, we are a remnant of the seed of Jacob; yea, we are a remnant of the seed of Joseph, whose coat was rent by his brethren into many pieces. . . . Yea, let us preserve our liberty as a remnant of Joseph; yea, let us remember the words of Jacob, before his death, for behold, he saw that a part of the remnant of the coat of Joseph was preserved and had not decayed. And he said—Even as this remnant of garment of my son hath been preserved, so shall a remnant of the seed of my son be preserved by the hand of God, and be taken unto himself, while the remainder of the seed of Joseph shall perish, even as the remnant of his garment" (Alma 46:23–24).[42]

"Coat of Joseph" in Ancient Tradition

The "coat of Joseph" had a venerable legendary "history." It was first given by God to Adam in the Garden of Eden, who passed it on through the generations from Seth to Noah. Noah wore it when he sacrificed on an altar, and he carried with him in the ark. But the garment was also seen as having power that might be misused by those into whose hands it fell. Ham stole it and gave it to his son Cush, who later gave it to Nimrod. Nimrod used this garment to obtain power and glory among men and as a means to deceive people and to gain unconquerable strength. He also used the garment while hunting, thereby causing all the birds and other animals to fall down in honor and respect before him. As a result, the people made him king over them. He first became king of Babylon and "was soon able through skillful and subtle speeches to bring the whole of mankind to the point of accepting him as the absolute ruler of the earth."[43] Appropriately, it was the garment that finally cost Nimrod his life. According to one account, Nimrod went forth with his people on a hunt at a time when he was jealous of the great hunter Esau. As Nimrod and two attendants approached Esau, Esau hid, cut off Nimrod's head, and killed the two attendants.

Having obtained the garment, Esau either buried it or sold it to Jacob along with his birthright. Numbers *Rabbah* relates that Jacob desired to offer sacrifice but could not because he was not the firstborn and did not have the birthright, part of which consisted of Adam's garment. It was for this reason that Jacob bought the birthright from Esau, who said, "There is no afterlife, death ends everything, and the inheritance will do me no good," and willingly let Jacob have the garment, along with his birthright. Here Muslim and Jewish traditions overlap. In the *Rasāʾil Ikhwān al-Ṣafā* (Epistles of the brethren of purity), Esau's sale of the birthright to Jacob was symbolized by the transfer of the sacred garment. Again, according to the Jewish scholar Micha Josef bin Gorion, "Esau's garment in which Rebekah clothed him, namely those made by God for Adam and Eve, had now rightfully become Jacob's, and Isaac recognized their paradisiacal fragrance."[44]

In a parallel tradition the early church father Hippolytus says that when Isaac laid his hands on Jacob, at the same time feeling Esau's skin garment, Isaac knew that Jacob was the legitimate heir to the blessing—the garment proved that, for Esau would hardly have parted with the garment if he had been worthy of it. Jacob later gave this garment to Joseph. This garment, a Jewish commentary on Genesis 37:3 informs us, was the high priest's tunic.[45] Louis Ginzberg observes that, in the original Hebrew of that passage, "*pargud mesuyyar* is a paraphrase of *passim,* which accordingly is not to be translated 'a coat of many colors,' but 'an upper garment in which figures are woven.'"[46]

According to legendary traditions collected by the Muslim theologian al-Thaʿlabī, Jacob recognized the same fragrance in the garment of Joseph when it was brought to him by Joseph's brothers and at the same time knew by the marks in it that it was the identical garment that he had received from his brother and that Adam had received from God in the garden of Eden. Earlier, when the jealous brothers took the garment away and lowered Joseph into the cistern, Gabriel immediately appeared and brought him a garment so he would never be without protection. The *Testament of Zebulon* says that Joseph's brothers took from Joseph his garment of honor and put on him the garment of the slave,[47] a reminder of traditions about two portions of Joseph's garment, one that decayed and the other that was miraculously preserved.[48]

Why is the story of Joseph and the covenant-making ceremony in Alma 46:21–24 significant? Because it squares with the ancient Near Eastern stories of sacred garments of the patriarchs and patterns of covenant making. Notably, the use of simile curses in that passage (e.g., "he [God] may cast us at the feet of our enemies, even as we have cast our garments at thy [Moroni's] feet to be trodden under foot, if we shall fall into transgression," v. 22) follows a venerable tradition in the ancient Near East.[49] Further, in mentioning Joseph's garment the Book of Mormon alludes to an ancient tradition in which a patriarch passed on to his successor garments symbolic of his patriarchal authority. Both traditions had a heritage going back to the earliest times, a heritage unknown to Joseph Smith at the time of the translation of the Book of Mormon but with which we have subsequently become well acquainted.

NOTES

1. I have drawn materials for this and the following section from my study, "King, Coronation, and Covenant in Mosiah 1–6," in *Rediscovering the Book of Mormon,* ed. John L. Sorenson and Melvin J. Thorne (Salt Lake City: Deseret Book and FARMS, 1991), 209–19.

2. See Viktor Korosec, *Hethitische Staatsverträge: Ein Beitrag zu ihrer juristischen Wertung* (Leipzig: Weicher, 1931).

3. See Elias Bickerman, "Couper une alliance," *Archives d'histoire du droit oriental* 5 (1950–51): 26–54; reprinted in his *Studies in Jewish and Christian History* (Leiden: Brill, 1976), 1:1–32.

4. See George Mendenhall, "Covenant Forms in Israelite Tradition," *Biblical Archaeologist* 17 (1954): 66; and George Mendenhall, "Puppy and Lettuce in Northwest-Semitic Covenant Making," *Bulletin of the American Schools of Oriental Research* 133 (February 1954): 26–30.

5. See John A. Tvedtnes, "King Benjamin and the Feast of Tabernacles," in *By Study and Also by Faith: Essays in Honor of Hugh W. Nibley,* ed. John M. Lundquist and Stephen D. Ricks (Salt Lake City: Deseret Book and FARMS, 1990), 2:197–237.

6. Arthur Hocart's *Kingship* (London: Oxford University Press, 1927) is one of the pioneering cross-cultural investigations of the ideology of kingship and of coronation ceremonies.

7. Brett L. Holbrook describes the symbolic aspects of the sword in ancient Israel and among the Nephites in "The Sword of Laban as a Symbol of Divine Authority and Kingship," *Journal of Book of Mormon Studies* 2/1 (1993): 39–72.

8. On the symbolism of the orb, or *Reichsapfel,* in the ancient, medieval, and modern world, see Percy E. Schramm, *Sphaira, Globus, Reichsapfel: Wanderung und Wandlung eines Herrschaftszeichens von Caesar zu Elisabeth II: Ein Beitrag zum "Nachleben" der Antike* (Stuttgart: Hiersemann, 1958).

9. I have been assisted in the preparation of this section by C. Wilfred Griggs's excellent article "The Tree of Life in Ancient Cultures," *Ensign,* June 1988, 26–31; also published as a FARMS reprint.

10. The tree of life is frequently mentioned elsewhere in the Book of Mormon, including 1 Nephi 15:22, 28, 36; 2 Nephi 2:15; Alma 5:34, 62; 12:21, 23, 26; 32:40; 42:2, 3, 5, 6.

11. Geo Widengren, *The King and the Tree of Life in Ancient Near Eastern Religion* (Uppsala: Lundequistka Bokhandeln, 1951), 6.

12. Ibid., 15.

13. Bernard Chapira, "Légendes bibliques," *Revue des études juives* 69 (1919): 105 n. 4.

14. Widengren, *The King and the Tree of Life,* 7.

15. Ephraim A. Speiser, ed. and trans., "Epic of Gilgamesh," in *Ancient Near Eastern Texts Relating to the Old Testament,* ed. James B. Pritchard (Princeton: Princeton University Press, 1969), 96, tablet XI, lines 239–44.

16. Edmund Hermsen, *Lebensbaumsymbolik im alten Ägypten* (Cologne: Brill, 1981), 3.

17. See Griggs, "Tree of Life," 28–29.

18. I have been greatly aided in the preparation of this section by the material in John A. Tvedtnes, "The Hebrew Back-

ground of the Book of Mormon," in *Rediscovering the Book of Mormon,* ed. John L. Sorenson and Melvin J. Thorne (Salt Lake City: Deseret Books and FARMS, 1991), 77–91.

19. For this section I have made use of materials from John Gee, "A Note on the Name *Nephi,*" *Journal of Book of Mormon Studies* 1/1 (1992): 189–92; and Stephen D. Ricks and John A. Tvedtnes, "The Hebrew Origin of Some Book of Mormon Place Names," *Journal of Book of Mormon Studies* 6/2 (1997): 255–59.

20. Günther Vittmann, "Zur Lesung des Königsnamens Pʾnkhj" (On the reading of the royal name Pʾ-ʿnkhj), *Orientalia* 43 (1974): 12–16. In a personal communication, John Gee informs me that the reading of the royal name as Pʾ-ʿnkhj is disputed—Vittmann's article itself is part of that dispute—but that the name is clearly attested in nonroyal contexts at an earlier period.

21. Frank L. Benz, *Personal Names in the Phoenician and Punic Inscriptions: A Catalog, Grammatical Study, and Glossary of Elements* (Rome: Biblical Institute, 1972), 192; compare Hermann Ranke, *Die ägyptischen Personennamen* (Glückstadt: Augustin, 1935–77), 1:390. Günther Vittmann, "Zu den in den phönikischen Inschriften enthaltenen ägyptischen Personnamen," *Göttinger Miszellen* 113 (1989): 95.

22. Walter E. Crum, *A Coptic Dictionary* (Oxford: Clarendon, 1939), 240.

23. Gee, "Note on the Name *Nephi,*" 191. For further discussion of the name *Nephi,* see John Gee, "Four Suggestions on the Origin of the Name *Nephi,*" in *Pressing Forward with the Book of Mormon: The FARMS Updates of the 1990s,* ed. John W. Welch and Melvin J. Thorne (Provo, Utah: FARMS, 1999), 1–5; and Paul Y. Hoskisson, "Nephi," *Journal of Book of Mormon Studies* 9/2 (2000): 64–65.

24. See Arthur E. Cowley, ed. and trans., *Aramaic Papyri of the Fifth Century B.C.* (Oxford: Clarendon, 1923).

25. Jeffery R. Chadwick, "Sariah in the Elephantine Papyri," *Journal of Book of Mormon Studies* 2/2 (1993): 196. For further discussion of the name *Sariah,* see "Seeking Agreement on the

Meaning of Book of Mormon Names" and John A. Tvedtnes, John Gee, and Matthew Roper, "Book of Mormon Names Attested in Ancient Hebrew Inscriptions," *Journal of Book of Mormon Studies* 9/1 (2000): 28–39, 43.

26. Hugh Nibley, "Lehi in the Desert," *Improvement Era*, June 1950, 517; compare *Lehi in the Desert and the World of the Jaredites* (Salt Lake City: Bookcraft, 1952), 90–91; also in *Lehi in the Desert; The World of the Jaredites; There Were Jaredites* (Salt Lake City: Deseret Book and FARMS, 1988), 79.

27. See Lynn M. Hilton and Hope Hilton, *In Search of Lehi's Trail* (Salt Lake City: Deseret Book, 1976), 94; also in *Ensign*, September 1976, 33–54, and October 1976, 34–63.

28. See Ross T. Christensen, "The Place Called Nahom," *Ensign*, August 1978, 73.

29. S. Kent Brown, "'The Place Which Was Called Nahom': New Light from Ancient Yemen," *Journal of Book of Mormon Studies* 8/1 (1999): 67; compare Warren P. Aston and Michaela Knoth Aston, *In the Footsteps of Lehi* (Salt Lake City: Deseret Book, 1994); and Warren P. and Michaela Knoth Aston, "'The Place Which Was Called Nahom': The Validation of an Ancient Reference to Southern Arabia" (Provo, Utah: FARMS, 1991).

30. Brown, "Nahom," 67.

31. Ibid., 68.

32. Ibid.

33. Ibid.

34. See Richard S. Ellis, *Foundation Deposits in Ancient Mesopotamia* (New Haven: Yale University Press, 1968), 104.

35. J. P. Barden, "Xerxes a Doughty Warrior until He Met the Greeks," *University of Chicago Magazine*, February 1936, 25.

36. Ernst E. Herzfeld, *Altpersische Inschriften*, Erster Ergänzungsband zu den archäologischen Mitteilungen aus Iran (Berlin: Reimer, 1938), 18–19, cited in English translation in H. Curtis Wright, "Ancient Burials of Metal Documents in Stone Boxes," in *By Study and Also by Faith*, ed. Lundquist and Ricks, 2:282.

37. For a full treatment see Wright, "Metal Documents in Stone Boxes," 273–334.

38. Joseph Smith, *History of the Church of Jesus Christ of Latter-day Saints,* ed. B. H. Roberts (Salt Lake City: Deseret Book, 1996), 4:537.

39. As quoted in Edmund C. Briggs, "A Visit to Nauvoo in 1856," *Journal of History* 9 (January 1916): 454.

40. *Saints' Herald* 26 (1 October 1879): 289–90, emphasis added.

41. Edward Stevenson's account of Harris's Sunday morning lecture in Salt Lake City, 4 September 1870, published in the *Deseret News* of 30 November 1881 and in the *LDS Millennial Star* 44 (6 February 1882): 86–87.

42. I have drawn materials for this section from my study "The Garment of Adam in Jewish, Muslim, and Christian Tradition," in *Temples of the Ancient World,* ed. Donald W. Parry (Salt Lake City: Deseret Book and FARMS, 1994), 704–39.

43. Bernhard Beer, *Das Leben Abraham's nach Auffassung der jüdischen Sage* (Leipzig: Leiner, 1859), 7.

44. Micha Josef bin Gorion, *Die sagen der Juden* (Frankfurt: Rütten and Loening, 1914), 2:371.

45. *Keli Yaqar* on Genesis 37:3.

46. Louis Ginzberg, *The Legends of the Jews* (Philadelphia: Jewish Publication Society of America, 1967–68), 5:329 n. 43.

47. *Testament of Zebulon* 4:11.

48. Al-Thaʿlabī, *Qiṣaṣ al-Anbiyāʾ* (Cairo: Muṣṭafā al-Bābī al-Ḥalabī wa-Awlāduhu, A.H. 1345), 80.

49. Mark Morrise, "Simile Curses in the Ancient Near East, Old Testament, and Book of Mormon," *Journal of Book of Mormon Studies* 2/1 (1993): 124–38.

From a Convert's Viewpoint

Alison V. P. Coutts

It would be fair to say that my upbringing on the Isle of Wight was in a Church of England environment. The religion at my schools was also predominantly Church of England. I was a fairly faithful churchgoer—especially once I was confirmed at age thirteen—up until the time I left for college. (College in London in the 1960s was not precisely conducive to the pursuit of a religious life.) Although my heritage was not a secret in my family, it was not until my early teens that I became truly aware that my mother's family was Jewish. Once at college in London, I had more exposure to the Jewish religion through increased contact with my uncle and cousins. This set me on a pursuit that has as a milestone my conversion to the Church of Jesus Christ of Latter-day Saints and continues with my interest in ancient Near Eastern studies. The following selection of issues on which the Book of Mormon and Joseph Smith give particularly relevant clarification is thus biased, on the one hand, toward those teachings that had a strong impact on me as I strove to learn about the church and, on the other, toward those that I have come across in my studies and work at Brigham Young University. I will begin with two of the latter issues.

Smiting Off Arms

SMITING OFF ARMS

During Ammon's mission to the Lamanites, a fairly gruesome incident occurred that seemed to me completely out of character with this exemplary missionary. Ammon and his fellow servants were out tending King Lamoni's flocks when they were set upon by a group of Lamanites and Ammon performed a stunning feat of strength and skill—smiting off the arms of those who were trying to scatter the flocks (see Alma 17). This violent episode puzzled me, but I rationalized that it gave Ammon sufficient credence to gain the willing ears of King Lamoni, who as a result was converted to Christ. Hugh Nibley, however, gave this passage a lot more thought and research.

In *The Prophetic Book of Mormon,* Nibley likens the seemingly common play between the two groups of Lamanites in Alma 17 to ancient games such as "the bloody fun of the famous basketball games played in the great ball courts of the ceremonial complexes of Mesoamerica," where "either the captain of the losing team or the whole team lost their heads."[1] From even more ancient sources, Nibley cites the games of chivalry depicted on Egyptian monuments showing "the first 'pharaohs' bashing the heads of rival rulers with the ceremonial mace" and the "famous scenes of the battles of Megiddo and Carchemish [displaying] the piles of severed hands and arms brought as trophies to the king."[2]

Nibley's views helped explain for me why King Lamoni executed his servants for their failure to protect the flocks, but I still wondered why Ammon went to far as to cut off the ruffians' arms.

In 1999 Bruce Yerman published an article that sheds light on this episode, with especial reference to the severed arms.[3] Beginning his research with a wonderful, if graphic, mural by Diego Rivera that currently hangs in the National Palace in Mexico City, Yerman shows that as a war trophy, an arm "was considered comparable to . . . fine jewelry." He cites the conquistador author Bernal Díaz, whose comrades in battle were sacrificed, after which "Aztec warriors held aloft the severed arms of the victims as they taunted and threatened the Spanish and their native allies who were within earshot."[4]

Staying with Mesoamerica, Yerman brings our attention to the Popol Vuh, the highland Maya historical and mythological text, in which the hero twins, Hunahpu and Xbalanque, battle the god Seven Macaw. At one point "Hunahpu shoots Seven Macaw with his blowgun. As the twin seeks to escape, Seven Macaw twists and tears an arm off Hunahpu's body." Later, Seven Macaw takes the arm home and hangs it over the fire.[5]

Book of Mormon scholars John Lundquist and John Welch provide further confirmation of the antiquity and authenticity of this practice. "On the extreme left of band 4 on the decorated Gates of Salmaneser III (858–824 B.C.), Assyrian troops are shown cutting off the heads, feet, and hands of vanquished enemies. 'In other reliefs, the artists of the Assyrian kings depict the military scribes recording the number of enemy dead in accordance with the number

La Gran Tenochtitlán, by Diego Rivera. © 2002 Banco de México Diego Rivera & Frida Kahlo Museums Trust, Av. Cinco de Mayo No. 2, Col. Centro, Del. Cuauhtémoc 06059, Mexico, D. F.

of severed heads, hands and feet which Assyrian soldiers hold up before them.'"⁶

The Egyptian, Assyrian, and Mesoamerican evidences for the practice of smiting off arms not only resolved for me this episode in the life of an exemplary missionary but also, since it was highly unlikely that Joseph Smith would have had access to the relevant sources, provided further confirmation of the Book of Mormon as an ancient record.

Asylum

Bible study was not a priority in my formative years. Although I did study the Bible in Sunday School as well as in religion classes at school, I do not remember spending much time in the Old Testament, and I certainly spent no time at all in Leviticus, Numbers, and Deuteronomy (with the exception of the story of Balaam and his donkey). My recollections of what I learned about Joshua back then are limited to visions of the walls "tumblin' down." So it was of great interest to me when my later studies revealed the establishment of six cities of refuge that, if nothing else, led to the asylum that Victor Hugo offered his eponymous hero in *The Hunchback of Notre Dame*.

ASYLUM

One of the provisions of the law of Moses was blood vengeance, or "an eye for an eye." It is generally accepted that this practice was to recompense the family of the victim for the loss of a faculty or limb. In practice, that compensation would not be monetary but in kind: the perpetrator would perform whatever tasks his victim could no longer perform. This idealistic law was designed to obviate the need for incarceration. However, inadvertent manslaughter had its own set of laws.

Asylum was prescribed to take the form of escape to a city of refuge. Moses established at least six cities as places of refuge for those who committed inadvertent manslaughter (see Deuteronomy 19:4; compare vv. 1–13; Numbers 35:6–34; Joshua 20).[7] The law provided that the refugee would request a trial, either by the elders of the city of refuge or by the elders of his own city, to determine the inadvertent nature of his offense. If his innocence from murder was established, he would be able to stay in the city, free from the blood vengeance of the victim's family, until the death of the current high priest, after which he was presumably free to leave the city.

The law of Moses made provision for atonement for inadvertent sin. During Yom Kippur, the high priest sacrificed two goats—one designated as the Lord's goat and the other as the *scapegoat,* or the Azazel goat (see Leviticus 16:7–10). According to biblical scholar Jacob Milgrom, when the purified high priest laid his hand on the live scapegoat, he transferred to it the ʿāwōnōt, "iniquities"—"the causes of the sanctuary's impurities, all of Israel's sins, ritual and moral alike, of priests and laity alike."[8]

The conditions of asylum can be summarized as follows:

1. Some kind of injustice is about to be perpetrated (see Deuteronomy 19:4).
2. The cause must be declared in the ears of the elders (see Joshua 20:4).
3. The seeker of asylum must be judged by the congregation (see Numbers 35:12, 24).
4. The seeker will either be delivered from those from whom refuge is sought (see Numbers 35:25; Joshua 20:5) or be delivered into the hands of the avenger of blood, that he may die.

5. The seeker will be released from asylum after the death of the high priest (see Numbers 35:25).

The Nephites were aware of the seriousness of premeditated murder, as evidenced by Jacob's imprecation "Wo unto the murderer who deliberately killeth, for he shall die" (2 Nephi 9:35). So it might follow that they were also aware of the stipulations in the law of Moses regarding inadvertent manslaughter. In his study of blood vengeance in the Old Testament and in the Book of Mormon, James Rasmussen comments: "There is no indication that the punishment is required to be administered by man. Indeed, the context suggests that the death referred to is a spiritual death. . . . 'Remember, to be carnally-minded is death, and to be spiritually-minded is life eternal.' [2 Nephi 9:39] This makes it clear that spiritual death is discussed and not criminal law. . . . Jacob's teaching is notable for making explicit that it is intentional killing which is forbidden. In the Old Testament the requirement of intention is implicit in the contrasting provisions for accidental homicide."[9]

A case has been made for Jershon, the land ceded to the Anti-Nephi-Lehies, as a city of refuge.[10] While there are certain similarities between Jershon and the biblical cities of refuge, I do not believe that we can go so far as to classify it as a city of refuge; but we can categorize it as an area of asylum.

When Ammon successfully converted Lamoni and his people, it was necessary for them, and the Lamanites converted by the other sons of Mosiah, to make significant changes in their lives. The first step for the converted Lamanites was to call themselves Anti-Nephi-Lehies, a name chosen after Lamoni's father, the king over all the land, consulted with "Aaron and many of their priests" regarding a name whereby "they might be distinguished from their brethren" (see Alma 23:16–17). To strengthen this separation further, on his deathbed Lamoni's father conferred the kingdom upon his other son and changed that son's name to Anti-Nephi-Lehi (see Alma 24:2–3, 5).

To save the Anti-Nephi-Lehies from destruction at the hands of their unconverted brethren, Ammon, with the Lord's blessing, conducted them to the land of Zarahemla (see Alma 27:11–26). The converted Lamanites' manner of atoning for the perceived murders was to present themselves for voluntary bondage: "We will go down unto our brethren, and we will be their slaves until we repair unto them the many murders and sins which we have committed against them" (Alma 27:8). Ammon, however, cited the law that Mosiah, his father, implemented after the example of his father, Benjamin: "It is against the law of our brethren . . . that there should be any slaves among them" (Alma 27:9).

We can look at what followed in light of the conditions of asylum given above:

1. Some kind of injustice was about to be perpetrated (see Deuteronomy 19:4). The Lamanites were going to exact vengeance on the Anti-Nephi-Lehies (see Alma 27:3).

2. The cause must be declared in the ears of the elders (see Joshua 20:4). Alma pled their case before the chief judge, who then sent out a proclamation to hear the voice of the people regarding the fate of the converted Lamanites (see Alma 27:20–21).

3. The seeker of asylum must be judged by the congregation (see Numbers 35:12, 24). The decision was to give the Anti-Nephi-Lehies a fertile land, Jershon, "on the east by the sea," as "an inheritance." The reasons for this generosity were *(a)* to enable the Nephites to set armies between

the lands of Jershon and Nephi, *(b)* to answer their "fear to take up arms against their brethren lest they should commit sin," and *(c)* to facilitate "their sore repentance . . . on account of their many murders and their awful wickedness." The only condition was that "they will give us a portion of their substance to assist us that we may maintain our armies" (see Alma 27:22–24).

4. The seeker will be delivered from those from whom refuge is sought (see Numbers 35:25; Joshua 20:5). The Anti-Nephi-Lehies joyfully accepted the offer of asylum in Jershon, but apparently another transition was necessary, for "they were called by the Nephites the people of Ammon; therefore they were distinguished by that name ever after" (Alma 27:26). It is interesting to note that, according to Hebrew scholars Stephen Ricks and John Tvedtnes, the name *Jershon* has an "authentic Hebrew origin" in the root ירש, "meaning 'to inherit,' with the suffix *-ôn* that denotes place-names." Each mention of Jershon is accompanied by some reference to inheritance (see Alma 27:22–24; 35:14).[11] In addition, from the Book of Abraham we learn that Abraham built an altar, a traditional place of asylum as well as of worship and sacrifice, at Jershon, which was between Haran and Sechem (Shechem) on the way to Canaan (see Abraham 2:16–18). Jershon is identified with ancient Jerash in the footnote to Abraham 2:16. *Jerash*, of course, has the same root as *Jershon*.

5. The seeker will be released after the death of the high priest (see Numbers 35:25). As mentioned earlier, an inadvertent manslayer was required to remain in a city of refuge until the death of the current high priest. Although no such stipulation is mentioned in the account of the people of Ammon, it is interesting to note that (1) Ammon

was appointed high priest over them (see Alma 30:20), and (2) the only reason they left Jershon was for their safety. After the converted Zoramites joined their ranks, the vengeful Zoramite chief made an alliance with the Lamanites in order to destroy the people of Ammon and the Nephites (see Alma 35:10–11). As a result, Ammon took his people to Melek so that Jershon might become a defense outpost (see Alma 35:13). Some thirty years later, well beyond Ammon's life expectancy, some of the people of Ammon formed part of the exodus to the land northward (see Helaman 3:12).

Having the opportunity to do this research into the minutiae of the transfer of the converted Lamanites to Jershon has given me greater insight into the biblical asylum tradition and has also strengthened my belief that the people of the Book of Mormon possessed and carried on the traditions brought with them by Lehi and Nephi from Jerusalem. Considering Joseph Smith's educational background and his very limited knowledge of the Bible at that time, as well as the short time it took him to translate the Book of Mormon, it is very doubtful that he could have extrapolated the details of asylum from the Bible and incorporated them into the story of the people of Ammon.

Plan of Salvation—Eternal Asylum

Hugh Nibley has frequently referred to the terrible questions that Clement formulated and that are universally avoided: "Is there a preexistence? Is there life after death? If we live after, will we remember this life? Why don't we remember the premortal existence? When was the world created? What existed before that? If the world was created, will it pass away? And then what? Will we feel things we cannot feel now?"¹² I remember as a child making myself dizzy lying in bed at night trying to imagine the scope of the universe, its boundaries, and then wondering what was outside those boundaries, since for me an endless universe was inconceivable. Later in life I struggled to understand the philosophies of Teilhard de Chardin, R. D. Laing, and others in an effort to determine if I was more than a mote in that incomprehensible expanse, if someone had a plan for me. The lack of credible answers to these questions can lead to a sense of futility culminating in despair. I was delighted to discover that the Book of Mormon provides logical, comprehensible answers to these questions and thus brings hope to the seeker after purpose and progression.

A Premortal Existence

A concept that had never really occurred to me was that there could be an existence before this one. My upbringing led me to believe that my life had a defined beginning (birth) and would have a defined end (death), with a smoky possibility of some kind of afterlife. I was intrigued with the possibility that I had a whole new breadth of life that stretched back before birth. As I studied the Book of Mormon, I found confirmation of this concept in its pages.

Although the most cogent descriptions of the premortal existence are found in scriptures other than the Book of Mormon that were revealed through or translated by Joseph Smith (see Moses 6:51; Abraham 3:22–23; D&C 93:29; 138:53, 56), it is obvious that a knowledge of the premortal existence was common among the Book of Mormon prophets. Alma, in his preaching to an audience in Ammonihah who exhibited apathy if not outright animosity, gives this informative passage on priests ordained after the order of the Son:

> And this is the manner after which they were ordained—being called and prepared from the foundation of the world according to the foreknowledge of God, on account of their exceeding faith and good works; in the first place being left to choose good or evil; therefore they having chosen good, and exercising exceedingly great faith, are called with a holy calling which was prepared with, and according to, a preparatory redemption for such. (Alma 13:3)

From this passage we learn that ordinations to the priesthood in mortality are a result of (1) preparation of the individual in premortality (given that the "world" was "founded" before it was physically created), (2) faith and good works, (3) choices of good over evil, (4) the opportunity to exercise faith, and (5) the provision of redemption. It follows that these stipulations are part of a plan that was conceived before the earth was created, even a plan to direct the creation of the earth and the course of its inhabitants. This gave me hope that I too was part of a plan; I mattered, and my being here on earth was not just a convergence of biological events.

The Plan of Redemption

Having learned that my existence extended into premortality, I realized that I was accountable for my actions. My parents had taught me well the value of obedience, selflessness, and virtue; but without the conviction of a need to account for my actions to a higher authority, in my adult life I was more concerned with keeping out of trouble than living a higher law. I knew nothing of the interrelationship of justice and mercy in regard to my accountability for my actions as a child of God. Thus my becoming aware of the ramifications of disobedience to God's law brought a trepidation that was immediately alleviated by the teachings of the plan of salvation. In the Book of Mormon Alma describes the conception and function of this plan that comes into effect as a result of Adam's fall:

> There was a space granted unto man in which he might repent; therefore this life became a probationary state; a time to prepare to meet God; a time to prepare for that endless state which . . . is after the resurrection of the dead. Now, if it had not been for the plan of redemption, which was laid from the foundation of the world, there could have been no resurrection of the dead. (Alma 12:24–25)

Lehi elaborates:

> And the Messiah cometh in the fulness of time, that he may redeem the children of men from the fall. And because that they are redeemed from the fall they have become free forever, knowing good from evil; to act for themselves and not be acted upon, save it be by the punishment of the law at the great and last day, according to the commandments which God hath given. (2 Nephi 2:26)

So the plan provides not only commandments that we can choose to follow but also, because we will inevitably make wrong choices, a Messiah with power to redeem us from the consequences of our disobedience, if we repent. This concept seems so integral to me now, but when I first was introduced to it, I marveled at its flawless logic. It awakened in me the beginnings of an understanding of the atonement and a continuing quest to be worthy of that atonement.

The Reality of the Other World

While I was living in Germany, I had limited access to LDS literature. The small ward library was helpful, and we did have a roving bookstore that had titles from General Authorities. While I was on vacation in the United States in 1990, the drive from Virginia to Utah with friends afforded me time to read. I had with me two *Ensign* magazines that contained installments of a multipart article by Hugh Nibley on the atonement.[13] This was my first exposure to this great scholar, and it began a relationship with his works that has essentially culminated in my living permanently in Utah and working at Brigham Young University. Shortly after returning to Germany, I subscribed to FARMS (the Foundation for Ancient Research and Mormon Studies) and began assembling my own library of Nibley's collected works. A tape set of Nibley's 1954 radio lectures under the title "Time Vindicates the Prophets" introduced me to the early Christian fathers and gave me further insight into the plan of salvation.

Essential to such a plan is a way to know how we are progressing; in other words, we need contact with the author of the plan. The early church fathers, specifically Anselm, redefined revelation: "It is the rationally endowed mind alone that has the capacity to achieve a concept of the Divine. At the same time the rational mind is the image of God: therefore the more it contemplates its own nature the better it understands God."[14] However, Augustine, in his last conversation with his mother, yearned "that we may hear his word *not* through any tongue of flesh; . . . but we may hear the very One whom we only love, . . . that we might hear his very self."[15] As the church fathers determined the course of the Christian church through the use of their "rational minds," and in the absence of revelation, prophets on the American continent were relying on revelation to direct the course of their people.

The Book of Mormon is full of references to mortals interacting with the other world. The opening chapters describe a vision given to both Lehi and Nephi. Angels appeared to the recalcitrant Laman and Lemuel. Visits from the other world do not stop with Christ's visit to the Nephites or with the death of the last apostle in Israel.

Certainly the Three Nephites are a link between the two worlds, as is John the Beloved. The Book of Mormon gives us insight into the transformation that these four followers of Christ underwent:

> And whether they were in the body or out of the body, they could not tell; for it did seem unto them like a transfiguration of them, that they were changed from this body of flesh into an immortal state, that they could behold the things of God. (3 Nephi 28:15)

> I have seen them, and they have ministered unto me. And behold they will be among the Gentiles, and the Gentiles shall know them not.... And it shall come to pass, when the Lord seeth fit in his wisdom that they shall minister unto all the scattered tribes of Israel, and unto all nations, kindreds, tongues and people. (3 Nephi 28:26–27, 29)

> And they are as the angels of God, and if they shall pray unto the Father in the name of Jesus they can show themselves unto whatsoever man it seemeth them good. (3 Nephi 28:30)

> There was a change wrought upon their bodies, that they might not suffer pain nor sorrow save it were for the sins of the world. Now this change was not equal to

that which shall take place at the last day; but there was a change wrought upon them. . . . They were sanctified in the flesh, that they were holy, and that the powers of the earth could not hold them. And in this state they were to remain until the judgment day of Christ. (3 Nephi 28:38–40)

Although the three "beloved disciples" were taken away from the Nephites in about A.D. 327, Mormon later testifies that he was "visited of the Lord" and these disciples (see Mormon 1:15–16; 3:16; 8:11).

The other world is indeed a reality, and the Book of Mormon shows us that, when it is necessary, the veil between that world and ours becomes very thin.

Judgment

Other than the natural guilt at disobedience to a parental figure, what are the far-reaching consequences of flouting commandments? Seen from a finite, mortal viewpoint, the matter resolves itself into simply getting caught or getting away with it. The former can bring punishment, usually commutable; and the latter, gain. The inference is that the more cunning and skillful one is at taking advantage of a neighbor, the more likely that person's worldly success. Far from condemning such ill-gotten success, society seems to grudgingly admire it. Indeed, it might be considered a prerequisite for high public office. So what incentive is there to obey? The Book of Mormon is extremely clear in putting disobedience in an eternal context.

First, Lehi, in his great discourse to Jacob on opposition and the power of the atonement, explains the necessity of freedom of choice (see 2 Nephi 2:21–26) and sets forth the consequences of willful disobedience in mortality: "Men are . . . free to choose liberty and eternal life, through the great Mediator of all men, or to choose captivity and death, according to the captivity and power of the devil" (2 Nephi 2:27). The latter choice, one apparently preferred by those whom we perceive as "getting away with it," brings an eternal consequence that perhaps those who deserve it hope to avoid, just as they apparently avoided mortal consequences: "eternal death, according to the will of the flesh and the evil which is therein, which giveth the spirit of the devil power to captivate, to bring you down to hell, that he may reign over you in his own kingdom" (2 Nephi 2:29).

King Benjamin expands on the character of those who would willfully "list to obey the evil spirit" (Mosiah 2:32):[16] "The same drinketh damnation to his own soul; for he receiveth for his wages an everlasting punishment, having transgressed the law of God contrary to his own knowledge. . . . The Lord has no place in him, for he dwelleth not in unholy temples" (Mosiah 2:33, 37). Carnal satisfaction may be the reward for such behavior, but the absence of any kind of light is in itself a dire punishment.

These statements lead up to what might be called the definition of judgment delivered first by Amulek and then by Alma:

> And he shall come into the world to redeem his people; and he shall take upon him the transgressions of those who believe on his name; and these are they that shall have eternal life, and salvation cometh to none else. Therefore the wicked remain as though there had been no redemption made, except it be the loosing of the bands of death; for behold, the day cometh that all shall rise from the dead and stand before God, and be judged according to their works. . . . The spirit and the body shall be reunited again in its perfect form; both limb and joint shall be restored . . . ; and we shall be brought

to stand before God, knowing even as we know now, and have a bright recollection of all our guilt. Now this restoration shall come to all, both old and young, both bond and free, both male and female, both the wicked and the righteous; and even there shall not so much as a hair of their heads be lost; but every thing shall be restored to its perfect frame, as it is now, . . . and shall be brought and be arraigned before the bar of Christ the Son, and God the Father, and the Holy Spirit, . . . to be judged according to their works, whether they be good or whether they be evil. (Alma 11:40–41, 43–44)

Small wonder that Zeezrom, who up until that point in time was firmly in the camp of those who profited from wrongdoing, "began to tremble" when he heard this discourse. Alma gives a second witness to Amulek's teachings:

If our hearts have been hardened, yea, if we have hardened our hearts against the word, insomuch that it has not been found in us, then will our state be awful, for then we shall be condemned. For our words will condemn us, yea, all our works will condemn us; we shall not be found spotless; and our thoughts will also condemn us; and in this awful state we shall not dare to look up to our God. . . . [W]e must come forth and stand before him in his glory, and in his power, and in his might, majesty, and dominion, and acknowledge to our everlasting shame that all his judgments are just; that he is just in all his works, and that he is merciful unto the children of men. (Alma 12:13–15)

Alma then goes further in explaining the ultimate consequence of willful disobedience:

Whosoever dieth in his sins, as to a temporal death, shall also die a spiritual death; yea he shall die as to things pertaining unto righteousness. Then is the time when their torments shall be as a lake of fire and brimstone, . . . that they shall be chained down to an everlasting destruction. . . . They shall be as though there had been no redemption made; for they cannot be redeemed according to God's justice; and they cannot die, seeing there is no more corruption. (Alma 12:16–18)

The Book of Mormon provides clear and precise answers to questions that have troubled thinking people since the beginning of time. Its teachings continually inspired and enlightened me as I sought increased understanding and guidance on the new path I had embarked on.

Eternal Judgment

The foregoing, especially the section on judgment, might at first seem to support the popular view of the vengeful God who thunders down his wrath upon the small, insignificant inhabitants of the earth. But here again, the Book of Mormon corrects that view, affording refreshing clarification that gives hope to all, even the most recalcitrant sinner.

I was never very comfortable with negative reinforcement. From an early age I had a horror of horror, and although I now realize that the works of the adversary are very real and effective, I do not believe that my contemplation of a Dantesque hell where pain and burning are the preferred methods of punishment would have been effective in my case. Such excruciating tortures were too terrible to admit into my thoughts, and my natural compassion would not accept that such would be the fate of anyone, regardless of his or her behavior on earth. Thankfully, judgment is not our call.

However, the Book of Mormon explains why some degree of negative reinforcement is necessary. As Enos was out in the woods undergoing his conversion and pleading with the Lord on behalf of the Lamanites, he made this poignant statement:

> And there was nothing save it was exceeding harshness, preaching and prophesying of wars, and contentions, and destructions, and continually reminding them of death, and the duration of eternity, and the judgments and the power of God, and all these things—stirring them up continually to keep them in the fear of the Lord. I say there was nothing short of these things, and exceedingly great plainness of speech, would keep them from going down speedily to destruction. (Enos 1:23)

Thus, when dealing with the natural man—apparently the spiritual level of the Lamanites at that time—it is necessary to use visceral language containing explicit punishments. As one's spiritual progression moves away from darkness and toward light, then, accordingly, the incentives of eternal life and exaltation become more of a pull forward by a loving, compassionate God and there is less need for the threat of the Inferno in order to halt a downward spiral.

The Concept of Opposition

In this modern world where "win-win" is a sought-after solution to problems, I had long thought that the Garden of Eden was a no-win situation for Adam and Eve. I longed for some kind of evidence of a contingency plan for the unlikely event that both Adam and Eve rebuked the tempter and that Satan was lying when he presented the fruit to Eve on the basis that this was the only way she would be able to know good from evil (see Genesis 3:3–6). Satan was, after all, "the father of all lies" whose self-appointed mission was to "deceive and to blind men, and to lead them captive at his will" (Moses 4:4).

The same feelings accompanied my reading of Job's terrible trials, permitted seemingly as a kind of a celestial game with Job's salvation at stake. Although I believe that Job's story is a true one, it is nevertheless easier to view it as an allegory for man's mortal probation. This insight came to me as a result of contemplating Lehi's discourse to Jacob in 2 Nephi.

Job, like Adam and Eve, had paradise taken from him, and his triumph against the advice of all those around him to "curse God, and die" (Job 2:9) is the triumph over opposition, for "when he hath tried me, I shall come forth as gold" (Job 23:10). Lehi explains that God "shall consecrate thine afflictions for thy gain" (2 Nephi 2:2). Satan had leave to tempt and to try Job; this is his permitted task as regards God's children in their mortal state because "it must needs be, that there is an opposition in all things. If not so . . . righteousness could not be brought to pass, neither wickedness, neither holiness nor misery, neither good nor bad" (2 Nephi 2:11).

S. Kent Brown, director of the Ancient Studies Center at BYU, explained Lehi's counsel as it pertains to the experience of Adam and Eve in the garden: "Lehi insisted that two ingredients were essential in our first parents' situation—a choice, along with freedom to choose. There had to be an 'opposition; even the forbidden fruit in opposition to the tree of life. . . . Wherefore, the Lord God gave unto man that he should act for himself' (2 Nephi 2:15–16). For Lehi, the opposition facing Adam and Eve was necessary so that they could make the choice that could bring about mankind's mortal existence."[17]

An Enlightened Understanding of Eve's Choice

THE ROLE OF EVE

While studying at BYU, I had a natural predilection for English literature and became interested in what was written around the time the King James Version of the Bible was first published, specifically works by Milton and Shakespeare. My encounter with Milton surprisingly brought me a view of Eve that argued against what I had gleaned before my conversion to the church—namely, that it was all Eve's fault; that she was the tempted and the temptress, weak and little able to withstand the serpent's guile; and that out of pity for her, Adam abandoned his ideals and left the Garden of Eden. The pseudepigraphical *Life of Adam and Eve* has Eve saying to her children of her confrontation with Adam after eating the fruit, "When your father came, I spoke to him unlawful words of transgression such as brought us down from great glory."[18]

This unflattering role has been attributed to women through such biblical models as Delilah; even Ruth and Esther supposedly used their feminine wiles to obtain their goals. It needs no feminist conviction to propose that women have not been portrayed fairly in history, starting with the very first woman. Much of literature would have us believe that desire for Eve prompted Adam's symbolic partaking of the apple. Milton's seventeenth-century *Paradise Lost*, however, portrays Eve with a mind—not just a body—able to reason out the consequences of not partaking of the fruit. Her explanation to Adam was compelling, and their decision to enter mortality was one born of logic and reason, not hormones.

> For us alone was death invented? or to us denied
> This intellectual food . . . ?
> What fear I then? rather what know to fear
> Under this ignorance of good and evil,
> Of God or death, of law or penalty?
>
> . . . .
>
> Were it I thought death menaced would ensue
> This my attempt, I would sustain alone
> The worst, and not persuade thee, rather die
> Deserted, than oblige thee with a fact
> Pernicious to thy peace; chiefly assured
> Remarkably so late of thy so true,
> So faithful, love unequalled: but I feel
> Far otherwise the event; not death, but life
> Augmented. . . .
>
> (Milton, *Paradise Lost,* Book 9, lines 766–68, 773–75, 977–85)

Although *Paradise Lost* was the one book, along with the Bible and Shakespeare, that emigrants from the United Kingdom purportedly brought with them to America, Joseph's upbringing hardly telegraphs familiarity with the classics. Therefore this passage from the Book of Mormon is revealing:

> If Adam [and Eve] had not transgressed [they] would . . . have remained in the garden of Eden. And all things which were created must have remained in the same state in which they were after they were created; and they must have remained forever, and had no end. And they would have had no children; wherefore they would have remained in a state of innocence, having no joy, for they knew no misery; doing no good, for they knew no sin. . . . Adam fell that men might be; and men are, that they might have joy. (2 Nephi 2:22–23, 25)

Milton's Eve maintained that the consequence of her decision was life, not death; and the perpetuation of life is contained in Lehi's words "Adam fell that men might be."

No discussion of Eve in modern revelation should pass over her own comments in Joseph Smith's translation of Genesis: "Were it not for our transgression we never should have had seed, and never should have known good and evil, and the joy of our redemption, and the eternal life which God giveth unto all the obedient" (Moses 5:11).

An indication that Joseph Smith's and Milton's general view of Eve was not false is aided by a study of the Hebrew word ʿezer, "help," as used in the KJV Genesis account: "I will make him an help meet for him" (Genesis 2:18). Hebrew scholar Donald W. Parry has pointed out that ʿezer usually applies to the Lord (see, for example, Exodus 18:4; Deuteronomy 33:26, 29; Psalm 20:1–2; 33:20; 121:1–2; 124:8). Because of the divine connotation of this term, Parry concludes that "Eve is emulating God himself when she becomes a help. She is working with Adam in a work that Adam cannot complete without her. Certainly the term *help* does not denote a lesser status or subordinating role, but an equal, or perhaps even superior, role. Eve is an enabling help."[19]

In the recently published Rabbinical Assembly commentary on Genesis 2:18, the editors remark that "the Hebrew for 'a fitting helper' *(eizer k'negdo)* can be understood to mean 'a helpmate equivalent to him.' It need not imply that the female is to be subordinate or that her role would be only as a facilitator."[20]

Further morphological evidence on this point is found in the form of the verb used for seeing in the sense of evaluation. When God created the earth he "saw every thing that he had made" (Genesis 1:31; see also 1:4, 10, 12, 18, 21, 25, 31; 6:5, 12). This form of the verb *to see,* Hebrew *yarʾa,* is the apocopated third-person masculine singular imperfect and is always used for the sense in which God sees. When, as recorded in Genesis 3:6, Eve *"saw that the tree was good for food, and that it was pleasant to the eyes, and a tree to be desired to make one wise,"* the same form of the Hebrew verb *to see* (only in its feminine form) is used. Parry, who has made an extensive study of the Garden of Eden pericope, believes that this also shows the importance of Eve to the narrative.[21]

The change in my view of Eve began with my first years at BYU and continued as I moved into ancient Near Eastern studies and learned to read the Hebrew text of the Bible.

Choosing Baptism

My brothers and I were all christened soon after birth. Pictures of these events figure prominently in the photographic record of our early years, and since we frequently looked at those albums and entreated our parents to rehearse stories associated with our christenings, we relived those snapshots. It appeared to be a very joyous time, but more a celebration of our birth, our parents' great love for each other and for us, and their close friendships rather than a religious ceremony. Certainly love and relationships rightly belong in such an ordinance, but was the ordinance of eternal significance? My adult feeling was that christening was somewhat of a superstition—an instant warding off of evil—compounded by the belief that the unbaptized cannot be buried in hallowed ground. That I was sprinkled with holy water for the remission of sins before I could even begin to contemplate sinning was a

INFANT BAPTISM

puzzling concept. Were my sins to be forgiven before the event? If so, then adherence to laws and acceptance of a moral standard seemed to be more a question of obedience to my elders and betters than they were a question of obedience to God.

The prophet Mormon had strong words to say along these lines:

> Behold I say unto you that this thing shall ye teach—repentance and baptism unto those who are accountable and capable of committing sin; yea, teach parents that they must repent and be baptized, and humble themselves as their little children, and they shall all be saved with their little children. And their little children need no repentance, neither baptism. Behold, baptism is unto repentance to the fulfilling the commandments unto the remission of sins. But little children are alive in Christ, even from the foundation of the world; if not so, God is a partial God, and also a changeable God, and a respecter to persons; for how many little children have died without baptism! . . . For awful is the wickedness to suppose that God saveth one child because of baptism, and the other must perish because he hath no baptism. (Moroni 8:10–12, 15)

There is no record of infant baptism in the New Testament, so when did the practice begin and for what reason? As is often the case, we find the roots of what has become common practice in Catholic and Protestant churches in the debates between the early church fathers. It is likely that infant baptism evolved from the rejection of the possibility of proxy baptism for the dead. This rejection caused a dilemma for St. Augustine, who in his younger days, according to Hugh Nibley,

> dared promise not only paradise but also the kingdom of the heavens to unbaptized children, since he

could find *no other escape* from being forced to say that God damns innocent spirits to eternal death.... But when he realized that he had spoken ill in saying that the spirits of children would be redeemed without the grace of Christ into eternal life and the kingdom of heaven, and that they could be delivered from the original sin without the baptism of Christ by which comes remission of sins—realizing into what a deep and tumultuous shipwreck he had thrown himself... he saw that there was *no other escape* than to repent of what he had said.[22]

Thus once the doctrine of original sin was established and the efficacy of proxy baptism was rejected, what course of action—in a time of high infant mortality—was there for the salvation of infants other than to baptize them as soon as possible after birth?

However, not all the early church fathers were in agreement. Tertullian, a North African theologian writing in about A.D. 200, believed that baptism should be delayed "according to the circumstances and disposition... of each individual." He was not convinced that baptism was indispensably necessary for salvation and especially not for little children. Baptizing little children would, according to Tertullian, thrust those performing such rites "into danger."[23] In the third century, Cyprian, Bishop of Carthage, in reply to a statement by Fidus that "the aspect of an infant in the first days after its birth is not pure, so that any one of us would still shudder at kissing it," countered, "Nor ought any of us to shudder at that which God hath condescended to make;... in the kiss of an infant" is implicit "the still recent hands of God," and "an infant, being lately born, has not sinned."[24]

Augustine, in politically correct fashion, commented on Cyprian's apparent rejection of infant baptism: "Cyprian, indeed, said, in order to correct those who thought that an infant should not be baptized before the eighth day, that it was not the body but the soul which behoved to be saved from perdition—in which statement he was not inventing any new doctrine, but preserving the firmly established faith of the Church; and he, along with some of his colleagues in the episcopal office, held that a child may be properly baptized immediately after its birth."[25]

Finally, with the last word on the subject for many centuries to come, Augustine, in around A.D. 400, wrote to the Donatist Petilian, "Do you not hear the words of Scripture saying, 'No one is clean from sin in Thy sight, not even the infant whose life is but of a single day upon the earth?'[26] 'For whence else is it that one hastens even with infants to seek remission of their sins?'"[27]

The transition by the early church fathers from rejection to acceptance of infant baptism compared with the clarity of Mormon's epistle only strengthens my earlier conviction that Mormon was correct, that infants have no need of repentance, and that baptism is a decision to be made consciously by one who has reached an age of accountability.

These are just a few of the questions that I raised during my years growing up in the Church of England, as I became aware of my Jewish heritage, as I joined the Church of Jesus Christ, and as I studied at Brigham Young University. In every case, the Book of Mormon provides clear, logical answers whose verity I have been able to satisfactorily test.

I am grateful for my many teachers, starting with my parents and extending through to my association with BYU and the Institute for the Study and Preservation of Ancient Religious Texts. I am also grateful for the knowledge that the Book of Mormon has given me. As Marilyn

Arnold said, "With each reading it almost magically expands to meet my increased ability to comprehend it."[28]

NOTES

1. Hugh Nibley, *The Prophetic Book of Mormon*, ed. John W. Welch (Salt Lake City: Deseret Book and FARMS, 1989), 541. More on this ball game can be found in Allen J. Christenson, trans. and ed., *Popol Vuh: The Mythic Sections—Tales of the First Beginnings from the Ancient K'iche'-Maya* (Provo, Utah: FARMS, 2000), esp. 106–15.

2. Nibley, *Prophetic Book of Mormon*, 541. John Tvedtnes pointed out to me that "the Medinet Habu reliefs of Ramses III also show piles of amputated arms and phalli"; see Uvo Hölscher, *Medinet Habu Studies 1928/29* (Chicago: Oriental Institute, 1930), 1:14–15 and pl. 2. Even the Bible mentions the practice in passing, in Jeremiah 48:25 and 1 Samuel 2:31. In the latter, the word for "arm" can also mean "seed," so we have a wordplay (personal communication, 5 September 2001).

3. Bruce H. Yerman, "Ammon and the Mesoamerican Custom of Smiting Off Arms," *Journal of Book of Mormon Studies* 8/1 (1999): 46–47.

4. Ibid., 46, citing Bernal Díaz del Castillo, *The Discovery and Conquest of Mexico, 1517–1521*, trans. A. P. Maudslay (London: Broadway House, 1928), 570.

5. See Yerman, "Ammon," 47; and Christenson, *Popol Vuh*, 58–61.

6. John M. Lundquist and John W. Welch, "Ammon and Cutting Off the Arms of Enemies," in *Reexploring the Book of Mormon*, ed. John W. Welch (Salt Lake City: Deseret Book and FARMS, 1992), 180–81, citing Yigael Yadin, *The Art of Warfare in Biblical Lands* (New York: McGraw Hill, 1963), 2:399. See also note 1 above.

7. These cities were Kedesh, Shechem, and Hebron on the west of the Jordan, and Golan, Ramoth-Gilead, and Bezer on the east of the Jordan.

8. Jacob Milgrom, *Leviticus 1–16* (New York: Doubleday, 1991), 1044.

9. James Rasmussen, "Blood Vengeance in the Old Testament and the Book of Mormon" (Provo, Utah: FARMS, 1981), 14.

10. Sarah Dee Nelson, unpublished paper in my possession, 13–15.

11. Stephen D. Ricks and John A. Tvedtnes, "Book of Mormon Place-Names," *Journal of Book of Mormon Studies* 6/2 (1997): 257–58.

12. Hugh W. Nibley, *Temple and Cosmos* (Salt Lake City: Deseret Book and FARMS, 1992), 523, citing *Clementine Recognitions* I, 2, in J.-P. Migne, ed., *Patrologiae Latinae* (Paris: Migne, 1844–64; hereinafter *PL*); see also pp. 336–78 in Nibley, *Temple and Cosmos*.

13. Hugh W. Nibley, "The Atonement of Jesus Christ," *Ensign*, July–October, 1990.

14. Quoted in Hugh Nibley, *The World and the Prophets* (Salt Lake City: Deseret Book and FARMS, 1987), 292, citing Martin Grabmann, *Geschichte der scholastischen Methoden* (Graz: Akademische Druck, 1957), 1:275–78, on Anselm and Augustine.

15. Quoted in Nibley, *World and the Prophets,* 91, citing Augustine, *Confessions* IX, 10, in *PL* 32:774–75, emphasis added.

16. For further insight on the phrase *list to obey,* see the appendix of John W. Welch and Stephen D. Ricks, eds., *King Benjamin's Speech: "That Ye May Learn Wisdom"* (Provo, Utah: FARMS, 1998), 533.

17. S. Kent Brown, "Nephi's Use of Lehi's Record," in *Rediscovering the Book of Mormon,* ed. John L. Sorenson and Melvin J. Thorne (Salt Lake City: Deseret Book and FARMS, 1991), 13.

18. M. D. Johnson, trans., *Life of Adam and Eve,* 21:3a, in

The Old Testament Pseudepigrapha, ed. James H. Charlesworth (Garden City, N.Y.: Doubleday, 1985), 2:281.

19. Donald W. Parry, "Notes on Eden," unpublished manuscript. I am grateful to Professor Parry for bringing this to my attention.

20. David L. Lieber, ed., *Etz Hayim: Torah and Commentary* (New York: Jewish Publication Society, 2001), 16. It is interesting that this commentary also mentions Milton's *Paradise Lost* and comments, "A modern reader can easily see Eve as the heroine of the story, bravely crossing the boundary from animal to human and willingly sharing her newfound wisdom with her mate" (p. 20).

21. Personal communication, 18 February 2000. I am grateful to S. Kent Brown for informing me of this morphological evidence.

22. Hugh W. Nibley, *Mormonism and Early Christianity* (Salt Lake City: Deseret Book and FARMS, 1987), 141, 165 n. 212, citing Augustine, *On the Soul and Its Origin* 9, in *PL* 44:480–81.

23. Tertullian, *De Baptismo,* 18, in *Ante-Nicene Fathers,* ed. Alexander Roberts and James Donaldson (Peabody, Mass.: Hendrickson, 1995), 3:678 (hereinafter *ANF*); see Keith E. Norman, "Infant Baptism," in *Encyclopedia of Mormonism,* ed. Daniel H. Ludlow (New York: Macmillan, 1992), 2:682–83.

24. Cyprian, *The Epistles of Cyprian,* 53 (*ANF* 5:354).

25. Augustine, *Letters,* 166.8.23, in *Nicene and Post-Nicene Fathers,* ed. Philip Schaff (Peabody, Mass.: Hendrickson, 1995), 1:530–31 (hereinafter *PNF*).

26. Augustine is here citing LXX Job 14:4–5, a complex passage that the KJV renders "Who can bring a clean thing out of an unclean? not one. Seeing his days are determined, the number of his months are with thee." The NIV translates the passage as "Who can bring what is pure from the impure? No one! Man's days are determined; you have decreed the number of his months and have set limits he cannot exceed."

27. Augustine, *The Letters of Petilian, the Donatist,* chaps. 102–233 (*PNF* 4:589).

28. Marilyn Arnold, "Unlocking the Sacred Text," *Journal of Book of Mormon Studies* 8/1 (1999): 50.

Appendix

Echoes and Evidences from the Writings of Hugh Nibley

Compiled by Daniel McKinlay
Edited by Alison V. P. Coutts and Donald W. Parry

Scrolls and the Other Israel

"From the Book of Mormon we learn that through the centuries the Jews have had as it were a double history. Along with the conventional story of the nation as recorded in the official accounts kept closely under the control of the schoolmen, there has coexisted in enforced obscurity another Israel, a society of righteous seekers zealously devoting their lives to the preservation of the law of their fathers in all its purity and considering the bulk of their nation to have fallen into sin and transgression.... Often they took to the desert and lived in family groups or communities there, teaching the law and the prophets to each other and looking forward prayerfully to the coming of the Messiah. There were many dreamers among them and real prophets as well, for they believed—unlike the scribes and doctors of official Jewry—in continued prophecy. Also they practiced rites rejected by the majority of the nation and talked constantly of such things as the resurrection of the flesh and the eternities to come—things which though they figure prominently enough in the apocryphal writings and also the Talmud, are hardly found at all in the official canon of Jewish scripture. They were a sober, watchful, industrious people, sorely distressed by the wickedness of their nation as a whole; and that nation would have nothing to do with them and did all it could to obscure the fact that they even existed. This briefly is the picture the Book of Mormon paints of Lehi and his ancestors, who had from time to time been driven out of Jerusalem for looking forward too eagerly for the Messiah. It is also the picture that now meets us in the abundant and ever-increasing documents which have come forth from the caves in Palestine almost in a steady stream since the first find was made in 1947. For some years the best scholars, Jewish and Christian, fought strenuously against accepting any of the so-called Dead Sea Scrolls as genuine—they must be medieval forgeries, it was argued, since the picture they presented was one totally at variance with the picture which had been delineated by the meticulous labors of generations of devoted scholars. . . . And as new scrolls are unrolled, the picture itself is unrolling—the picture of that other Israel that lived in obscurity and hope, first sketched out for us in the Book of Mormon and now for the first time emerging into the light of history."[1]

Epic Milieu

"The Book of Mormon draws us the picture of another and totally different type of society which has become a historical reality only within the last thirty years or so. It was once thought that the world which Homer described was purely the product of his own inventive genius. Toward the end of the eighteenth century, however, the shrewd and observant English scholar and traveler Robert Wood had the idea of writing 'a detailed work in which similarities of the cultures exhibited in the Old Testament, in Homer, and in the Near East of his own day should be collected, and prove that a "Heroic Age" is a real and recurrent type in human society.' Wood died before he could produce the work, and it was not until the 1930s that Milman Parry showed that what is called a heroic poetry is necessarily 'created by a people who are living in a certain way, and so have a certain outlook on life, and our understanding of the heroic will come only as we learn what that way of living is and grasp that outlook.' Then Chadwick showed that epic poetry cannot possibly be produced except in and by a genuine epic milieu, as he called it—a highly developed, complex, very peculiar but firmly established and very ancient cultural structure. How ancient may be guessed from Kramer's recent and confident attempt to describe the culture of the earliest Sumerians in detail simply on the basis of the knowledge that they produced a typical epic literature. Knowing that, one may be sure that theirs was the same culture that is described in epic poetry throughout the world, for epic cannot be faked: innumerable attempts to produce convincing epics by the creative imagination are almost pitifully transparent. Now one of the books of the Book of Mormon, the book of Ether, comes right out of that epic milieu, which it faithfully reproduces, though of course the world of Joseph Smith had never heard of such a thing as an epic milieu. Here is a good test for the Book of Mormon. It is but one of many—all awaiting fuller treatment, and none as yet settled with any degree of finality. But the mere fact that there are such tests is a most astonishing thing. That one can actually talk about the Book of Mormon seriously and with growing respect after all that has been discovered in the last 125 years is, considering the nature of its publication, as far as I am concerned, in itself ample proof of its genuineness."[2]

LAND OF
JERUSALEM

"When we speak of Jerusalem, it is important to notice Nephi's preference for a nonbiblical expression, 'the land of Jerusalem' (1 Nephi 3:10), in designating his homeland. While he and his brothers always regard 'the land of Jerusalem' as their home, it is perfectly clear from a number of passages that 'the land of our father's inheritance' (1 Nephi 3:16) cannot possibly be within, or even very near, the city, even though Lehi had 'dwelt at Jerusalem in all his days' (1 Nephi 1:4). The terms seem confused, but they correctly reflect actual conditions, for in the Amarna letters we read of 'the land of Jerusalem' as an area larger than the city itself, and even learn in one instance that 'a city of the land of Jerusalem, Bet-Ninib, has been captured.' It was the rule in Palestine and Syria, as the same letters show, for a large area around a city and all the inhabitants of that area to bear the name of the city. This was a holdover from the times when the city and the land were a single political unit, comprising a city-state; when this was absorbed into a larger empire, the original identity was preserved, though it had lost its original political significance. The same conservatism made it possible for Socrates to be an Athenian, and nothing else, even though he came from the village of Alopeke, at some distance from the city. This arrangement deserves mention because many have pointed to the statement of Alma 7:10 that the Savior would be born 'at Jerusalem which is the *land* of our forefathers' as sure proof of fraud. It is rather the opposite, faithfully preserving the ancient terminology to describe a system which has only been recently rediscovered."³

"While the Book of Mormon refers to the city of Jerusalem plainly and unmistakably over sixty times, it refers over forty times to another and entirely different geographical entity which is always designated as 'the land of Jerusalem.' In the New World also every major Book of Mormon city is surrounded by a *land of the same name*."⁴

"At the end of the last century scholars were mystified to find that a demotic prophecy datable to the time of Bocchoris (718–712 B.C.), in which coming destructions were predicted with the promise of a Messiah to follow, was put into the mouth of 'the Lamb' *(pa-hib)*. Greek sources inform us that this prophecy enjoyed very great circulation in ancient times. The strange wording of Lehi's great prophecy, uttered by 'the Lamb' (1 Nephi 13:34, 41), is thus seen to be no anachronism, taken from Hellenistic or Christian times, as was once maintained."⁵

PROPHECY OF THE LAMB

"Whether or not *Nehi* and *Nehri* are in any way related to the name *Nephi* (there are other Egyptian names that come nearer) remains to be investigated. But no philologist will refuse to acknowledge the possible identity of the Book of Mormon *Korihor* with the Egyptian *Kherihor,* and none may deny, philologist or not, a close resemblance between *Sam* and *Sam* (the brother of Nephi)."⁶

PERSONAL NAMES

"[In the Book of Mormon] the experiment with government by priestly judges collapsed, largely due to a rivalry for the chief judgeship among three candidates, all sons of the great chief judge, *Pahoran*. Their names are *Pahoran, Paanchi,* and *Pacumeni* (Helaman 1:1–3). . . . The name of *Pahoran* reflects the Palestinian *Pahura* (for the Egyptian Pa-her-an; cf. Pa-her-y, 'the Syrian'), which is 'reformed' Egyptian, i.e., a true Egyptian title, but altered in such a way as to adapt it to the Canaanite speech. *Pahura* (also written *Puhuru*) was in Amarna times an Egyptian governor *(rabu)* of Syria. The same man, or another man with the same name, was placed by Pharaoh as governor of the Ube district, with his headquarters at *Kumedi* (cf. the element *-kumen* in the Book of Mormon place-names). *Paanchi* is simply the well-known Egyptian *Paiankh* (also rendered *Pianchi, Paankh,* etc.). . . . *Pacumeni,* the name of the third son, resembles that borne by some of the last priest governors of Egypt, whose names are rendered *Pamenech, Pa-mnkh, Pamenches,* etc."[7]

"Another Book of Mormon judge, *Cezoram,* has a name that suggests that of an Egyptian governor of a Syrian city: *Chi-zi-ri.*"[8]

"Paanchi, the son of Pahoran, and pretender to the chief-judgeship, has the same name as one of the best-known kings in Egyptian history, a contemporary of Isaiah and chief actor in the drama of Egyptian history at a time in which the history was intimately involved in the affairs of Palestine. Yet his name, not mentioned in the Bible, remained unknown to scholars until the end of the nineteenth century."[9]

"The name of Lemuel is not a conventional Hebrew one, for it occurs only in one chapter of the Old Testament (Proverbs 31:1, 4), where it is commonly supposed to be a rather mysterious poetic substitute for Solomon. It is, however, like Lehi, at home in the south desert, where an Edomite text from 'a place occupied by tribes descended from Ishmael' bears the title 'The Words of Lemuel, King of Massa.' These people, though speaking a language that was almost Arabic, were yet well within the sphere of Jewish religion, for 'we have nowhere else any evidence for saying that the Edomites used any other peculiar name for their deity' than 'Yahweh, the God of Hebrews.'"[10]

"My Father Dwelt in a Tent"

"The editors of the Book of Mormon have given a whole verse to Nephi's laconic statement 'And my father dwelt in a tent' (1 Nephi 2:15), and rightly so, since Nephi himself finds the fact very significant and refers constantly to his father's tent as the center of his universe. To an Arab, 'My father dwelt in a tent' says everything. . . . So with the announcement that his 'father dwelt in a tent,' Nephi serves notice that he had assumed the desert way of life, as perforce he must for his journey. Any easterner would appreciate the significance and importance of the statement, which to us seems almost trivial. If Nephi seems to think of his father's tent as the hub of everything, he is simply expressing the view of any normal Bedouin, to whom the tent of the *sheikh* is the sheet anchor of existence."[11]

"It is most significant how Nephi speaks of his father's tent; it is the official center of all administration and authority. First the dogged instance of Nephi on telling us again and again that 'my father dwelt in a tent' (1 Nephi 2:15; 9:1; 10:16; 16:6). So what? we ask, but to an Oriental that statement says everything. Since time immemorial the whole population of the Near East have been either tent-dwellers or house-dwellers, the people of the *bait ash-sha'r* or the *bait at-tin,* 'houses of hair or houses of clay.' It was Harmer who first pointed out that one and the same person may well alternate between the one way of life and the other, and he cites the case of Laban in Genesis 31, where 'one is surprised to find both parties so suddenly equipped with tents for their accommodation in traveling,' though they had all along been living in houses. Not only has it been the custom for herdsmen and traders to spend part of the year in tents and part in houses, but 'persons of distinction' in the East have always enjoyed spending part of the year in tents for the pure pleasure of a complete change. It is clear from 1 Nephi 3:1; 4:38; 5:7; 7:5, 21–22; 15:1; 16:10 that Lehi's tent is the headquarters for all activities, all discussion and decisions."[12]

Smiting with a Rod

"Is it any wonder that Laman and Lemuel worked off their pent-up frustration by beating their youngest brother with a stick when they were once hiding in a cave? Every free man in the East carries a stick, the immemorial badge of independence and of authority, and every man asserts his authority over his inferiors by his stick, 'which shows that the holder is a man of position, superior to the workman or day-labourers. The government officials, superior officers, tax-gatherers, and schoolmasters use this short rod to threaten—or if necessary to beat—their inferiors, whoever they may be.' The usage is very ancient. 'A blow for a slave' is the ancient maxim in Ahikar, and the proper designation of an underling is *abida-l'asa,* 'stick-servant.' This is exactly the sense in which Laman and Lemuel intended their little lesson to Nephi, for when the angel turned the tables he said to them, 'Why do ye smite your younger brother with a rod? Know ye not that the Lord hath chosen *him* to be a ruler over *you?*' (1 Nephi 3:29)."[13]

PLACE-NAME "SHAZER"

"The first important stop after Lehi's party had left their base camp was at a place they called *Shazer* (1 Nephi 16:13–14). The name is intriguing. The combination *shajer* is quite common in Palestinian place-names; it is a collective meaning 'trees,' and many Arabs (especially in Egypt) pronounce it *shazher*. It appears in *Thoghret-as-Sajur* (the Pass of Trees), which is the ancient *Shaghur*, written *Segor* in the sixth century. It may be confused with Shaghur 'seepage,' which is held to be identical with Shihor, the 'black river' of Joshua 19:36. This last takes in western Palestine the form *Sozura*, suggesting the name of a famous water hole in South Arabia, called *Shisur* by Thomas and *Shisar* by Philby. It is a 'tiny copse' and one of the loneliest spots in all the world. So we have *Shihor, Shaghur, Sajur, Saghir, Segor* (even *Zoar*), *Shajar, Sozura, Shisur,* and *Shisar,* all connected somehow or other and denoting either seepage—a weak but reliable water supply—or a clump of trees. Whichever one prefers, Lehi's people could hardly have picked a better name for their first suitable stopping place than *Shazer*."[14]

LEHI'S POETRY

"Speaking of Lehi's poetry, we should not overlook the latest study on the *qasida*, that of Alfred Bloch, who distinguishes four types of verse in the earliest desert poetry:

(1) the *ragaz*-utterances to accompany any rhythmical work; (2) verses for instruction or information; (3) elegies, specializing in sage reflections on the meaning of life; and (4) *Reiselieder,* recited on a journey to make the experience more pleasant and edifying. Lehi's *qasida* (1 Nephi 2:9–10), as we described it in *Lehi in the Desert,* conforms neatly to any of the last three of these types, thus vindicating its claims to be genuine."[15]

"One of the most revealing things about Lehi is the nature of his great eloquence. It must not be judged by modern or western standards, as people are prone to judge the Book of Mormon as literature. In this lesson we take the case of a bit of poetry recited extempore by Lehi to his two sons to illustrate certain peculiarities of the Oriental idiom and especially to serve as a test-case in which a number of very strange and exacting conditions are most rigorously observed in the Book of Mormon account. Those are the conditions under which ancient desert poetry was composed. Some things that appear at first glance to be most damning to the Book of Mormon, such as the famous passage in 2 Nephi 1:14 about no traveler returning from the grave, turn out on closer inspection to provide striking confirmation of its correctness."[16]

DESERET

"By all odds the most interesting and attractive passenger in Jared's company is *deseret,* the honeybee. We cannot pass this creature by without a glance at its name and possible significance, for our text betrays an interest in *deseret* that goes far beyond respect for the feat of transporting insects, remarkable though that is. The word *deseret,* we are told (Ether 2:3), 'by interpretation is a honeybee,' the word plainly coming from the Jaredite language, since Ether (or Moroni) must interpret it. Now it is a remarkable coincidence that the word *deseret,* or something very close to it, enjoyed a position of ritual prominence among the founders of the classical Egyptian civilization, who associated it very closely with the symbol of the bee."[17]

"There is one tale of intrigue in the book of Ether that presents very ancient and widespread (though but recently discovered) parallels. That is the story of Jared's daughter.... This is indeed a strange and terrible tradition of throne succession, yet there is no better attested tradition in the early world than the ritual of the dancing princess (represented by the *salme* priestess of the Babylonians, hence the name *Salome*) who wins the heart of a stranger and induces him to marry her, behead the old king, and mount the throne. I once collected a huge dossier on this awful woman and even read a paper on her at an annual meeting of the American Historical Association. You find out all about the sordid triangle of the old king, the challenger, and the dancing beauty from Frazer, Jane Harrison, Altheim, B. Schweitzer, Farnell, and any number of folklorists. The thing to note especially is that there actually seems to have been a succession rite of great antiquity that followed this pattern. It is the story behind the rites at Olympia and the Ara Sacra and the wanton and shocking dances of the ritual hierodules throughout the ancient world. Though it is not without actual historical parallels, as when in A.D. 998 the sister of the khalif obtained as a gift the head of the ruler of Syria, the episode of the dancing princess is at all times essentially a ritual, and

SALOME'S
INTRIGUES

the name of Salome is perhaps no accident, for her story is anything but unique. Certainly the book of Ether is on the soundest possible ground in attributing the behavior of the daughter of Jared to the inspiration of ritual texts—secret directories on the art of deposing an aging king. The Jaredite version, incidentally, is quite different from the Salome story of the Bible, but is identical with many earlier accounts that have come down to us in the oldest records of civilization."[18]

LUMINOUS STONES

"But who gave the brother of Jared the idea about stones in the first place? It was not the Lord, who left him entirely on his own; and yet the man went right to work as if he knew exactly what he was doing. Who put him on to it? The answer is indicated in the fact that he was following the pattern of Noah's ark, for in the oldest records of the human race the ark seems to have been illuminated by just such shining stones. We have said that if the story of the luminous stones was lifted from any ancient source, that source was not the Talmud (with which the Book of Mormon account has only a distant relationship) but a much older and fuller tradition, with which the Ether story displays much closer affinities. The only trouble here is that these older and fuller traditions were entirely unknown to the world in the time of Joseph Smith, having been brought to light only in the last generation."[19]

"Nothing in the Book of Mormon itself has excited greater hilarity and derision than Joseph Smith's report that the original record was engraved on gold plates, the account being condensed from much fuller records on bronze plates. Today scores of examples of ancient historical and religious writings on sacred and profane plates of gold, silver, and bronze make this part of Joseph Smith's story seem rather commonplace. But it was anything but commonplace a hundred years ago, when the idea of sacred records being written on metal plates was thought just too funny for words."[20]

GOLD PLATES

"In the time of Jeremiah, or shortly before, a certain Jonadab ben Rechab had led a colony of permanent settlers from Jerusalem into the wilderness, where his descendants survived through all succeeding centuries as the strange and baffling nation of the Rekhabites. What makes them baffling is their Messianic religion, which is so much like primitive Christianity in many ways that it has led some scholars to argue that those people must have been of Christian origin, though the historical evidence for their great antiquity is unquestionable. When one considers that Jonadab's project was almost contemporary (perhaps slightly prior) to Lehi's, that his name, ending in -*adab,* is of a type peculiar to the period and to the Book of Mormon, and that the Book of Mormon specifically states that the Lord had led other people out of Jerusalem beside Lehi, and that the Rekhabite teachings are strangely like those in the Book of Mormon, one is forced to admit at very least the possibility that Lehi's exodus *could* have taken place in the manner described, and the certainty that other such migrations actually did take place."[21]

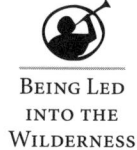

BEING LED INTO THE WILDERNESS

NAMING
VALLEYS AND
STREAMS

"Lehi's intimacy with desert practices becomes apparent right at the outset of his journey, not only in the skillful way he managed things but also in the quaint and peculiar practices he observed, such as those applying to the naming of places in the desert. The stream at which he made his first camp Lehi named after his eldest son; the valley, after his second son (1 Nephi 2:8). The oasis at which his party made their next important camp 'we did call . . . Shazer' (1 Nephi 16:13). The fruitful land by the sea 'we called Bountiful,' while the sea itself 'we called Irreantum' (1 Nephi 17:5). By what right do these people rename streams and valleys to suit themselves? By the immemorial custom of the desert, to be sure. Among the laws 'which no Bedouin would dream of transgressing,' the first, according to Jennings-Bramley, is that 'any water you may discover, either in your own or in the territory of another tribe, is named after you.' So it happens that in Arabia a great *wady* (valley) will have different names at different points along its course, a respectable number of names being 'all used for one and the same valley. . . . One and the same place may have several names, and the *wady* running close to the same, or the mountain connected with it, will naturally be called differently by different clans,' according to Canaan, who tells how the Arabs 'often coin a new name for a locality for which they have never used a proper name, or whose name they do not know,' the name given being usually that of some person."[22]

LAND OF
INHERITANCE

"Eduard Meyer says that all [Israel's] power and authority went back originally to the first land-allotments made among the leaders of the migratory host when they settled down in their land of promise. Regardless of wealth of influence or ability, no one could belong to the old aristocracy who did not still possess 'the land of his inheritance.' This institution—or attitude—plays a remarkably conspicuous role in the Book of Mormon. Not only does Lehi leave 'the land of his inheritance' (1 Nephi 2:4) but whenever his people wish to establish a new society they first of all make sure to allot and define the lands of their inheritance, which first allotment is regarded as inalienable. No matter where a group or family move to in later times, the *first* land allotted to them is always regarded as 'the land of their inheritance,' thus Alma 22:28; 54:12-13; Ether 7:16—in these cases the expression 'land of *first* inheritance' is used (Mormon 2:27-28; 1 Nephi 13:15; Alma 35:9, 14; 43:12; Jacob 3:4; Alma 62:42; Mormon 3:17). This is a powerful argument for the authenticity of the Book of Mormon both because the existence of such a system is largely the discovery of modern research and because it is set forth in the Book of Mormon very distinctly and yet quite casually."[23]

JUDGES AND JUDGMENT SEATS

"In Zedekiah's time the ancient and venerable council of elders had been thrust aside by the proud and haughty *judges*, the spoiled children of frustrated and ambitious princes, who made the sheet anchor of their policy a strong alliance with Egypt and preferred Tyre to Sidon, the old established emporium of the Egyptian trade, to which Lehi remained devoted. The institution of the judges deserves some attention. Since the king no longer sat in judgment, the ambitious climbers had taken over the powerful and dignified—and for them very profitable—'*judgment seats*,' and by systematic abuse of their power as judges made themselves obnoxious and oppressive to the nation as a whole while suppressing all criticism of themselves—especially from recalcitrant and subversive prophets. It was an old game. In 1085 B.C. one Korihor, the chief priest of Ammon, had actually seized the throne of Egypt, where for a long time the priests of Ammon ran the country to suit themselves in their capacity as judges of the priestly courts. These courts had at first competed with the king's courts and then by murder and intrigue quite forced them out of business. This story reads like a chapter out of the Book of Mormon. . . . The extreme prominence of judges and judgment seats in the Book of Mormon, apparent from a glance at the concordance, is a direct and authentic heritage of the Old World in Lehi's day."[24]

POWER OF OATHS

"What astonishes the western reader is the miraculous effect of Nephi's oath on Zoram. . . . The reactions of both parties make sense when one realizes that the oath is the one thing that is most sacred and inviolable among the desert people and their descendants. . . . But not every oath will do. To be most binding and solemn an oath should be by the *life* of something, even if it be but a blade of grass. The only oath more awful than 'by my life' or (less commonly) 'by the life of my head' is the *wa hayat Allah*, 'by the life of God' or 'as the Lord liveth.' . . . So we see that the only way that Nephi could possibly have pacified the struggling Zoram in an instant was to utter the one oath that no man would dream of breaking, the most solemn of all oaths to the Semite: 'As the Lord liveth, and as I live' (1 Nephi 4:32)."[25]

"An important part of [the War Scroll] is taken up with certain slogans and war cries which the army writes boldly upon its trumpets and banners . . . emphasizing as did Moroni's standard the program of deliverance from bondage and preservation of liberty. We are reminded of the great care the ancients took to establish the moral guilt of their enemies and thereby clear themselves of their blood by an inscription on a ritual dart. . . . The Romans also before making war on a nation would throw three darts in its direction, dedicating it to destruction in the archaic rite of the *feciales,* the great antiquity of which establishes both the age and the genuineness of the Jewish practice. . . . We have in the Title of Liberty episode a clear and independent parallel [to ancient Iranian tradition], for Moroni's banner is just like the 'Flag of Kawe' . . . , the legendary founder of the Magi. . . . To liberate the people there rose up in Isfahan a mighty man, a blacksmith named Kawe, who took the leather apron he wore at his work and placed it on the end of a pole; this became the symbol of liberation and remained for many centuries the national banner of the Persians as well as the sacred emblem of the Magi."²⁶

RAISING THE TITLE OF LIBERTY

"[Nephi] explicitly tells us that the hunting weapons he used were 'bows . . . arrows . . . stones, and . . . slings' (1 Nephi 16:15). That is another evidence for the Book of Mormon, for [Moritz] Mainzer found that those were indeed the hunting weapons of the early Hebrews, who never used the classic hunting weapons of their neighbors, the sword, lance, javelin, and club. . . . According to the ancient Arab writers, the only bow-wood obtainable in all Arabia was the *nab* wood that grew only . . . in the

NEPHI'S HUNTING WEAPONS

very region where, if we follow the Book of Mormon, the broken bow incident occurred. How many factors must be correctly conceived and correlated to make the apparently simple story of Nephi's bow ring true! The high mountain near the Red Sea at a considerable journey down the coast, the game on the peaks, hunting with a bow and sling, the finding of bow-wood viewed as something of a miracle by the party—what are the chances of reproducing such a situation by mere guesswork?"[27]

ALTAR OF STONES

"As his first act, once his tent had been pitched for his first important camp, Lehi 'built an altar of stones, and made an offering unto the Lord, and gave thanks to the Lord' (1 Nephi 2:7). It is for all the world as if he had been reading Robertson Smith. 'The ordinary . . . mark of a Semitic sanctuary [Hebrew as well as Arabic, that is] is the sacrificial pillar, cairn, or rude altar . . . upon which sacrifices are presented to the god. . . . In Arabia . . . we find no proper altar, but in its place a rude pillar or heap of stones.' . . . That Lehi's was such an altar would follow not only the ancient law demanding uncut stones, but also . . . the Book of Mormon expression 'an altar of stones,' which is not the same thing as a 'stone altar.'"[28]

DESERT IMAGERY

"In reporting his father's dreams, Nephi has handed us, as it were, over a dozen vivid little snapshots or colored slides of the desert country that show that somebody who had a hand in the writing of the Book of Mormon actually lived there: 1. The first is a picture of a lone traveler, Lehi himself, in 'a dark and dreary waste' (1 Nephi 8:4–7). . . . Of all the images that haunt the early Arab poets this is by all odds the most common. It is the standard nightmare of the Arab. . . . In the inscriptions a thousand lone wanderers send up, in desperation, prayers for help. . . . 2. In the next picture we see 'a large and spacious field' (1 Nephi 8:9). . . . This in Arabic is the symbol of release from fear and oppression. . . . The Arab poet describes the world as a . . . large and spacious field, an image borrowed by the earliest Christian writers, notably the Pastor of Hermes and the Pseudo-Clementines. . . . 3. The next picture is a close-up of a tree . . . (1 Nephi 8:10–12; 11:8). . . . Where would one find such a tree in the poets? Only in the gardens of kings. The Persian King, and in imitation of him, the Byzantine Emperor and the Great Khan, had such trees constructed artificially out of pure silver to stand beside their thrones and represent the Tree of Life. . . . In no land on earth is the sight of a real tree, and especially a fruit-bearing one, greeted with more joy and reverence than in treeless Arabia, where certain trees are regarded as holy because of their life-giving propensities. . . . 6. The next picture is largely a blur, for it represents a 'mist of darkness' . . . (1 Nephi 8:23). . . . In the many passages of Arabic poetry in which the hero boasts that he has traveled long distances through dark and dreary wastes all alone, . . . the culminating horror is almost always a 'mist of darkness,' a depressing mixture of dust, and clammy fog, which, added to the night, completes the confusion of any who wander in the waste. . . . 13. One of the most remarkable of our snapshots is that of a 'fountain of filthy water' (1 Nephi 12:16)—'the water which my father saw was filthiness' (1 Nephi 15:27). . . . This was a typical desert *sayl,* a raging torrent of liquid filth that sweeps whole camps to destruction.... Even a mounted rider, if he is careless, may be caught off guard and carried away by such a sudden spate of 'head water,' according to Doughty. One of the worst places for these gully-washing torrents of liquid mud is in 'the scarred and bare mountains which run parallel to the west coast of Arabia.'... This was the very region through which Lehi traveled on his great trek."²⁹

"From Whence No Traveler Can Return"

"This passage [2 Nephi 1:14] has inspired scathing descriptions of the Book of Mormon as a mass of stolen quotations.... A recent study of Sumerian and Akkadian names for the world of the dead lists prominently 'the hole, the earth, the land of no return, the path of no turning back, the road whose course never turns back, the distant land, etc.'... This is a good deal closer to Lehi's language than Shakespeare is.... Lehi... can hardly be denied the luxury of speaking as he was supposed to speak."³⁰

New Year Rites

"In the Book of Mormon we have an excellent description of a typical Great Assembly or year-rite.... Though everything takes place on a far higher spiritual plane than that implied in most of the Old World ritual texts, still not a single element of the primordial rites is missing, and nothing is added, in the Book of Mormon version."³¹

Sticks of Judah and Joseph

"Ezekiel is probably referring here to an institution which flourished among the ancient Hebrews but was completely lost sight of after the Middle Ages until its rediscovery in the [nineteenth] century. That is the institution of the tally-sticks. . . . When a contract was made, certain official marks were placed upon a stick of wood in the presence of a notary representing the king. . . . The stick was split down the middle, and each of the parties kept half as his claim-token. . . . When the time for settlement came and the king's magistrate placed the two sticks side by side to see that all was in order, the two would only fit together perfectly mark for mark and grain for grain to 'become one' in the king's hand if they had been one originally."[32]

JAREDITE BARGES

"An important clue is the statement in Ether 6:7 that Jared's boats were built on the same pattern as Noah's ark. . . . [But] the Bible is not the only ancient record that tells about the ark. . . . There are various versions of the Flood story floating about, all of which tell some of the story."[33]

"The oldest accounts of the ark of Noah, the Sumerian ones, describe it as a 'magur boat,' peaked at the ends, completely covered but for a door, without sails, and completely covered by the waters from time to time, as men and animals rode safe within."[34]

"The remarkable thing about Jared's boats was their illumination. . . . The Rabbis tell of a mysterious Zohar that illuminated the ark, but for further instruction we must go to much older sources: the Pyrophilus is traced back to the *Jalakanta* stone of India, which shines in the dark and enables its owner to pass unharmed beneath the waters; this in turn has been traced back through classical and Oriental sources to the Gilgamesh Epic, where Alexander's wonderful Pyrophilus stone turns up as the Plant of Life in the possession of the Babylonian Noah."[35]

474 • *Echoes and Evidences of the Book of Mormon*

Temple outside Jerusalem

"The Elephantine Papyri . . . show us a Jewish community living far up the Nile, whither they had fled for safety, possibly at the destruction of Jerusalem in Lehi's day. In 1954 some of these records, the Brooklyn Aramaic Papyri, were discovered. . . . Perhaps the most surprising discovery about these Jews settled so far from home was their program for building a temple in their new home. Not long ago, learned divines were fond of pointing out that Nephi's idea of building a temple in the New World was quite sufficient in itself to prove once and for all the fraudulence of the Book of Mormon, since, it was argued, no real Jew would ever dream of having a temple anywhere but in Jerusalem."³⁶

Colophons

"The major writings in the Book of Mormon are introduced and concluded by 'colophons,' which have the purpose of acquainting the reader with the source of the material given and informing him of the authorship of the particular manuscript. Such colophons are found at 1 Nephi 1:1–3; 22:30–31; Jacob 1:2; 7:27; Jarom 1:1–2; Omni 1:1, 3–4; Words of Mormon 1:9; Mosiah 1:4; 9:1; Helaman 16:25. . . . This complacent advertising of one's own virtues, in particular one's reliability, is a correct and indeed a required fixture of any properly composed Egyptian autobiography of Nephi's time."³⁷

Hermounts

"We have always thought that the oddest and most disturbing name in the Book of Mormon was Hermounts, since there is nothing either Classical or Oriental about it.

So we avoided it, until . . . a student from Saudi Arabia asked point blank what the funny word was. Well, what does the Book of Mormon say it is? Hermounts in the Book of Mormon is the wild country of the borderlands, the hunting grounds, 'that part of the wilderness which was infested by wild and ravenous beasts' (Alma 2:37). The equivalent of such a district in Egypt is Hermonthis, the land of Month, the Egyptian Pan—the god of wild places and things. *Hermounts* and *Hermonthis* are close enough to satisfy the most exacting philologist."³⁸

"Jacob's (or rather Zenos's) treatise on ancient olive culture (Jacob 5–6) is accurate in every detail: Olive trees do have to be pruned and cultivated diligently; the top branches are indeed the first to wither, and the new shoots do come right out of the trunk; . . . the ancient way of strengthening the old trees (especially in Greece) was to graft in the shoots of the oleaster or wild olive; also, shoots from valuable old trees were transplanted to keep the stock alive after the parent tree should perish; to a surprising degree the olive prefers poor and rocky ground, whereas rich soil produces inferior fruit; too much grafting produces a nondescript and cluttered yield of fruit; the top branches if allowed to grow as in Spain or France, while producing a good shade tree, will indeed sap the strength of the tree and give a poor crop; fertilizing with dung is very important, in spite of the preference for rocky ground, and has been practiced since ancient times; the thing to be most guarded against is bitterness in the fruit. All these points, taken from a treatise on ancient olive culture, are duly, though quite casually, noted in Zenos's Parable of the Olive Tree."³⁹

OLIVE CULTURE

DEATH OF
NEHOR AND
ZEMNARIHAH

"There is a peculiar rite of execution described in the Book of Mormon whose ancient background is clearly attested. When a notorious debunker of religion was convicted of murder, 'they carried him upon the top of the hill Manti, and there he was caused, or rather did acknowledge, between the heavens and the earth, that what he had taught to the people was contrary to the word of God; and there he suffered an ignominious death' (Alma 1:15). A like fate was suffered centuries later by the traitor Zemnarihah. This goes back to a very old tradition indeed, that of the first false preachers, Harut and Marut (fallen angels), who first corrupted the word of God and as a result hang to this day between heaven and earth confessing their sin. Their counterpart in Jewish tradition is the angel Shamhozai, who 'repented, and by way of penance hung himself up between heaven and earth.'"[40]

ELEPHANTS

"An interesting study on 'Men and Elephants in America'... in the *Scientific Monthly*... concludes: 'Archaeology has proved that the American Indian hunted and killed elephants; it has also strongly indicated that these elephants have been extinct for several thousand years. This means that the traditions of the Indians recalling these animals have retained their historical validity for great stretches of time.... Probably the minimum is three thousand years,' ... which would place [the elephant's] extinction about a thousand years B.C., when the Jaredite culture was already very old and Lehi's people were not to appear on the scene for some centuries.... Here, then, is a strong argument for Jaredite survivors among the Indians."[41]

"Another characteristic expression [in the Book of Mormon] is that of failing to heed 'the mark' set by prudence and tradition [see Jacob 4:14]. In the Zadokite Fragment the false teachers of the Jews are charged with having 'removed the mark which the forefathers had set up in their inheritance,' and there is a solemn warning to 'all those of the members of the covenant who have broken out of the boundary of the Law,' or stepped beyond the designated mark. The early Christian Gospel of Truth says Israel turns to error when they look for that which is beyond the mark."[42]

"Looking Beyond the Mark"

"A . . . study by an Arabic scholar has called attention to the long-forgotten custom of the ancient Arabs and Hebrews of consulting two headless arrows whenever they were about to undertake a journey; the usual thing was to consult the things at a special shrine, though it was common also to take such divination arrows along on the trip in a special container. The message of the arrows, which were mere sticks without heads or feathers, was conveyed by their pointing and especially by the inscriptions that were on them, giving detailed directions as to the journey."[43]

Liahona

"There is nothing in the Lachish Letters that in any way contradicts [the Book of Mormon's] story. . . . Both documents account for their existence by indicating specifically the techniques and usages of writing and recording in their day, telling of the same means of transmitting, editing, and storing records. . . . The proximity of Egypt

Lehi Account and Lachish Letters

and its influence on writing has a paramount place in both stories. . . . Both abound in proper names in which the *-yahu* ending is prominent in a number of forms. . . . The peculiar name of Jaush (Josh), since it is not found in the Bible, is remarkable as the name borne by a high-ranking field officer in both the Lachish Letters and the Book of Mormon. . . . The conflicting ideologies—practical vs. religious, materialist vs. spiritual—emerge in two views of the religious leader or prophet as a *piqqeah,* 'a visionary man,' a term either of praise or of contempt—an impractical dreamer. . . . For some unexplained reason, the anti-king parties both flee not towards Babylon but towards Egypt, 'the broken reed.' . . . Other parallels may be added to taste, but this should be enough to show that Joseph Smith was either extravagantly lucky in the opening episodes of his Book of Mormon—that should be demonstrated by computer—or else he had help from someone who knew a great deal."⁴⁴

LAMANITE GAMES AT THE WATERS OF SEBUS

"All the Lamanites would drive their flocks to a particular watering place (Alma 17:26). And when they got there, 'a certain number of Lamanites, who had been with their flocks to water, stood and scattered the . . . [king's] flocks.' After the flocks of the king 'scattered . . . and fled many ways,' the servants lamented that as a matter of course, 'now the king will slay us, as he has our brethren' (Alma 17:28). And they began to weep. What insanity is this, the king kills his own servants for losing a contest that had been acted out before? In fact, 'it was the *practice* of these Lamanites to stand by the waters of Sebus and scatter the flocks of the people,' keeping what they could for themselves, 'it being a *practice* of plunder among them' (Alma 18:7)... It should be clear that we are dealing with a sort of game; a regular practice, following certain rules. ... All this reminds us of those many ceremonial games in which the loser also lost his life, beginning with an Aztec duel in which one of the contestants was tethered by the ankle and bore only a wooden mace while his heavily armored opponent wielded a weapon with sharp obsidian edges. Then there were the age-old chariot races of the princes in which one was to be killed by the *Taraxippus,* and the equally ancient game of Nemi made famous by Frazer's *Golden Bough.* Add to these such vicious doings as the Platanista, the Krypteia, the old Norse brain-ball, the hanging games of the Celts, and so on. But the closest are those known to many of us here, namely the bloody fun of the famous basketball games played in the great ball courts of the ceremonial complexes of Mesoamerica. In these games either the captain of the losing team or the whole team lost their heads."⁴⁵

"From the days of the Jaredites to the final battle at Cumorah, we find our Book of Mormon warriors observing the correct chivalric rules of battle—enemies agreeing to the time and place of the slaughter, chiefs challenging each other to single combat for the kingdom, and so on."⁴⁶

"As to the army itself, the [War Scroll] specifies that 'they shall all be volunteers for war [as were Moroni's host], blameless in spirit and flesh, and ready for the day of vengeance, . . . for holy angels are together with their armies. . . . And no indecent, evil thing shall be seen in the vicinity of any of your camps.' Such ideal armies, consciously

CHIVALRY IN THE BOOK OF MORMON

dramatizing themselves as the righteous host, are also met with in the Book of Mormon, notably in the case of Helaman and his two thousand sons (Alma 53:17–19)."[47]

HARLOT
ISABEL

"One of the aspects of ancient American religion that archaeology is bringing increasingly to the fore is the dominance of the familiar Great Mother in religion: Where is she in the Book of Mormon? The Book of Mormon brands all non-Nephite cults as idolatry and does not go on to describe them. . . . But there is one broad hint. When Alma's youngest son wanted to misbehave with the harlot Isabel, he had to go into another country to do it (Alma 39:3). Parenthetically, Isabel was the name of the Patroness of Harlots in the religion of the Phoenicians."[48]

GADIANTON
ROBBERS

"These bands of robbers [in the Book of Mormon] are not some exotic invention of romantic fancy, but a major factor in world history. We think of the age-old traditions of Seth and his robber bands in the Egyptian literature (al-ʿArish, *Sieg über Seth*), of Pompey's Pirates or the Algerians, the Vikings, the Free Companies of the fourteenth century, the Kazaks, the Robber Barons, the Assassins, the Bagaudi, the Druze, the militant orders that imitated them (Templars, Knights of Rhodes, and so on), the Vitalian Brothers, the Riffs, and finally the Medellin drug lords of the south, whose long arm can constrain the leaders of nations. All of these operators were terrorists, and they held whole armies at bay and overthrew kingdoms. The best and perhaps the earliest description of such bands in action is from the Amarna Letters, where we find Lehi's own ancestors, the wandering, plundering Khabiru of the fourteenth century B.C., actually overthrowing city after city in Palestine and disrupting the lives of nations."[49]

"The word *atonement* appears only once in the New Testament, but 127 times in the Old Testament. . . . In the other Standard Works of the Church, *atonement* (including related terms *atone, atoned, atoneth, atoning*) appears 44 times, but only 3 times in the Doctrine and Covenants, and twice in the Pearl of Great Price. The other 39 times are all in the Book of Mormon. This puts the Book of Mormon in the milieu of the old Hebrew rites before the destruction of Solomon's Temple, for after that the Ark and the covering *(kapporeth)* no longer existed, but the Holy of Holies was still called the *bait ha-kapporeth*. . . . It has often been claimed that the Book of Mormon cannot contain the 'fullness of the gospel,' since it does not have temple ordinances. As a matter of fact, they are everywhere in the book if we know where to look for them, and the dozen or so discourses on the Atonement in the Book of Mormon are replete with temple imagery. From all the meanings of *kaphar* and *kippurim,* we concluded that the literal meaning of *kaphar* and *kippurim* is a close and intimate embrace, which took place at the *kapporeth,* or the front cover or flap of the tabernacle or tent. The Book of Mormon instances are quite clear, for example, 'Behold, he sendeth an invitation unto all men, for the arms of mercy are extended towards them, and he saith: Repent, and I will receive you' (Alma 5:33). 'But behold, the Lord hath redeemed my soul from hell; I have beheld his glory,

TEMPLE IMAGERY

and I am encircled about eternally in the arms of his love' (2 Nephi 1:15). To be redeemed is to be atoned. From this it should be clear what kind of *oneness* is meant by the Atonement—it is being received in a close embrace of the prodigal son."⁵⁰

Hiding Up Treasures

"In 2 *Baruch* we read an interesting thing. All the treasures of Israel, he says, must be hid up unto the Lord so that strangers may not get possession of them. And in Helaman, where people are rebuked for hiding their private treasures, we read, 'They shall hide up treasures unto [the Lord]' (Helaman 13:19). It's a commandment. . . . Later Baruch tells us how 'they hid all the vessels of the sanctuary, lest the enemy should get possession of them.' Though this writing was published only since Cumorah, a more recent find gives it solid historical dimensions—the famous *Copper Scroll,* found in Cave Four at Qumran. The significance of this, an important record written on copper alloy sheets and hidden up, is that it was in fact written and prepared with the express purpose of its being hidden up. That's why it was written, for it contains a record of all the other treasures hidden up to the Lord. Here we have a concrete and indisputable example of an ancient Israelite practice."⁵¹

More Desert Imagery

"Desert imagery has been shown to be vivid in the writings of the Jewish sectary. . . . In our civilization, the broadest roads are the safest; in the desert, they are the most confusing and dangerous. 'Walk in the strait path,' says good old Nephi—in true desert style—'which leads to life, and continue in the path until the end of the day of probation' (2 Nephi 33:9). It is not the geographical, but the apocryphal reference that interests us now. In the late Egyptian period [approximately 1000–300 B.C.], according to Grapow, it became a very common teaching that a man should never depart from the right road, but be righteous, not associate his heart with the wicked, nor walk in the path of unrighteousness. This had actually become a literary convention in Lehi's day; and in his culture, it is very closely connected with the Israelite use of it. . . . Another favorite desert image is the great castle in the desert, which, as Nephi tells us, represents 'the pride of the world; and it fell, and the fall thereof was exceeding great' (1 Nephi 11:36). Consider the castle of Agormi, from the time of Nectanebos the Second (from the time of Lehi); it was indeed a great and lofty building, with date trees growing at the foot of it and a big fruit tree in the courtyard— reminiscent of Lehi's description. The archetype of the great building that falls and slays its wicked owner is the house of Cain; we can trace this to the work called the al-Iklīl, the crown. The castle of Ghumdan is described by al-Hamdānī as the 'great and spacious building' which 'stood as it were in the air, high above the earth,' with the finely dressed people. . . . The Jewish legend goes back to the house of Cain, the first house to be built of stone. . . . The book of Jubilees reports that Cain was killed when his stone house fell on him: 'For with a stone he had killed Abel, and by a stone was he killed in righteous judgment.'"[52]

"One striking image that meets us in [the] account of Lehi's heavenly vision is that of a meeting breaking up. Lehi sees God on his throne, the people are singing the

LEHI'S VISION

hymn; but then the hymn stops, the meeting breaks up, and everyone goes about his business (1 Nephi 1). One of the newly discovered apocrypha, the so-called *Creation Apocryphon,* also describes such a situation. And what was decided on in the heavenly council is now being carried out by Gods, angels, and men. This concept of heaven is alien to conventional Judaism and Christianity, in which the chief characteristic of the heavenly order, conforming to the teachings of Athanasius, is absolutely motionless stability."[53]

APOCALYPTIC
IMAGERY

"Apocalyptic imagery is not missing from the Book of Mormon, though it's not nearly as prominent as one would expect if the book had actually been composed in the world of Joseph Smith, because this was the one kind of doctrine that did have popular reception—the apocalyptic destruction. End-of-the-world sects were very common in Joseph Smith's time; the forerunners of the Seventh-Day Adventists were expecting the end of the world in 1843 or 1844, as were many people. The Book of Mormon avoids this image. The fire and smoke of hell, and other apocalyptic images, are clearly stated to be types, rather than realities, as is the monster death and hell. This practice agrees with the old apocrypha. Typical is the phrase of Alma: 'I was in the darkest abyss; but now I behold the marvelous light of God' (Mosiah 27:29). 'He has freed us from the darkness to prepare himself a holy people,' says Barnabas [in his *Epistola Catholica*]. To the image of the diggers of the pit who themselves fall into it, there are many parallels. Nephi mentions it twice (cf. 1 Nephi 14:3; 22:14). [In Wisdom of Ben Sira 27:26], Ben Sira says, 'He that diggeth a pit shall fall into it; and he that setteth a snare shall be taken therein.'"⁵⁴

"Alma is obsessed with the image of the white garment: 'There can no man be saved except his garments are washed white' (Alma 5:21) [see Alma 13:11, 12; 7:25] ... Such expressions forcibly call to mind the work of Professor [Erwin] Goodenough, in which he shows that the white garment had a special significance for the early Jews. God himself may be represented in the earliest Jewish art as one of three men clothed in white.... This image [from the Dura Europos synagogue] wasn't even known to exist until 1958, but every time Goodenough goes back into the earliest Jewish pictorial representations he can find, there are the three men in white, or a single figure, the prophet in white. The symbol of the chosen prophet, an emissary from God, is always the white robe, which is reserved for heavenly beings. Nephi says that the righteous shall be 'clothed with purity, yea, even with the robe of righteousness' (2 Nephi 9:14)."⁵⁵

WHITE GARMENT

Notes

1. Hugh Nibley, *The World and the Prophets*, ed. John W. Welch, Gary P. Gillum, and Don E. Norton (Salt Lake City: Deseret Book and FARMS, 1987), 211–13.

2. Ibid., 213–14.

3. Hugh Nibley, *Lehi in the Desert; The World of the Jaredites; There Were Jaredites*, ed. John W. Welch, Darrell L. Matthews, and Stephen R. Callister (Salt Lake City: Deseret Book and FARMS, 1988), 6–7.

4. Hugh Nibley, *An Approach to the Book of Mormon*, ed. John W. Welch, 3rd ed. (Salt Lake City: Deseret Book and FARMS, 1988), 101.

5. Nibley, *Lehi in the Desert*, 18.

6. Ibid., 20–21.

7. Ibid., 22–23. See Hugh Nibley, *The Prophetic Book of Mormon*, ed. John W. Welch (Salt Lake City: Deseret Book and FARMS, 1989), 101.

8. Nibley, *Lehi in the Desert*, 23.

9. Nibley, *Approach to the Book of Mormon*, 283–84.

10. Nibley, *Lehi in the Desert*, 41.

11. Ibid., 51–52.

12. Nibley, *Approach to the Book of Mormon*, 243.

13. Ibid., 249; see pp. 246–47. See also Nibley, *Lehi in the Desert*, 67–71.

14. Nibley, *Lehi in the Desert*, 78–79.

15. Nibley, *Prophetic Book of Mormon*, 91.

16. Nibley, *Approach to the Book of Mormon*, 265–75. See Nibley, *Lehi in the Desert*, 84–92.

17. Nibley, *Lehi in the Desert*, 189.

18. Ibid., 210–13. See Nibley, *Prophetic Book of Mormon*, 248.

19. Nibley, *Approach to the Book of Mormon*, 352; see pp. 336–39. See also Nibley, *Lehi in the Desert*, 366–69.

20. Nibley, *Prophetic Book of Mormon*, 245. See Nibley, *Approach to the Book of Mormon*, 21–28.

21. Nibley, *Approach to the Book of Mormon*, 68–69.

22. Ibid., 81–82.

23. Ibid., 100.

24. Ibid., 102–4.

25. Ibid., 128–29.

26. Ibid., 214–17. See Hugh Nibley, *Since Cumorah*, 2nd ed. (Salt Lake City: Deseret Book and FARMS, 1988), 242; and Nibley, *Prophetic Book of Mormon*, 92–95.

27. Nibley, *Approach to the Book of Mormon*, 231–32.

28. Ibid., 245–46.

29. Ibid., 253–62. See Hugh Nibley, *Temple and Cosmos,* ed. Don E. Norton (Salt Lake City: Deseret Book and FARMS, 1992), 239–41.

30. Nibley, *Approach to the Book of Mormon,* 276–77. See Nibley, *Since Cumorah,* 162; and Nibley, *Prophetic Book of Mormon,* 90–91.

31. Nibley, *Approach to the Book of Mormon,* 297.

32. Ibid., 319–20. See Nibley, *Prophetic Book of Mormon,* 15–22, 286–87, 298.

33. Nibley, *Approach to the Book of Mormon,* 342–43.

34. Nibley, *Prophetic Book of Mormon,* 243.

35. Ibid., 243–44. See Nibley, *Approach to the Book of Mormon,* 348–58.

36. Nibley, *Since Cumorah,* 53.

37. Ibid., 151. See Nibley, *Lehi in the Desert,* 17.

38. Nibley, *Since Cumorah,* 169. See Nibley, *Prophetic Book of Mormon,* 246–47, 281.

39. Nibley, *Since Cumorah,* 238–39. See Nibley, *Temple and Cosmos,* 244–52.

40. Nibley, *Since Cumorah,* 244–45. See Nibley, *Prophetic Book of Mormon,* 250.

41. Nibley, *Prophetic Book of Mormon,* 111.

42. Nibley, *Since Cumorah,* 167. See Nibley, *Temple and Cosmos,* 241–42.

43. Nibley, *Prophetic Book of Mormon,* 244–45.

44. Ibid., 400–402.

45. Ibid., 539–41.

46. Ibid., 542.

47. Nibley, *Approach to the Book of Mormon,* 215.

48. Nibley, *Prophetic Book of Mormon,* 542.

49. Ibid., 556.

50. Hugh Nibley, *Approaching Zion,* ed. Don E. Norton (Salt Lake City: Deseret Book and FARMS, 1989), 566–67.

51. Nibley, *Temple and Cosmos,* 216–17.

52. Ibid., 219–23; see pp. 243–44.
53. Ibid., 227.
54. Ibid., 235–36.
55. Ibid., 238–39.

Scripture Citation Index

Old Testament

Genesis

1:11, p. 177
1:11–12, p. 241
1:31, p. 445
2:18, p. 444
3:3–6, p. 441
3:6, p. 445
4:10, p. 173
6:16, pp. 246, 258
6:17, p. 180
9:14, p. 177
10:20, p. 179
12:10, p. 97
15:4, p. 175
24:22, p. 174
27:38, p. 180
31, p. 460
37, p. 236
37:3, pp. 414, 419
37:23, p. 236
37:31, p. 236
37:33, p. 237
40:12, p. 238
45:22, p. 174
46:1–7, p. 97
49, p. 323
50, p. 240
50:24–25, p. 239
50:24–38, p. 238
50:25, p. 256
50:35, p. 238

Exodus

2:12, p. 260
10:9, p. 179
12:11, p. 179
17:9, p. 256
18:4, p. 444
19:4, p. 391
19:8, p. 392
20–23, p. 392
20:1, p. 391
20:2, p. 391
20:3–17, p. 392
21:1–23:19, p. 392
24:7, p. 393
24:12, p. 175

Leviticus

1:2–4, p. 63
3, p. 63
3:4–6, p. 63
3:19–30, p. 63
3:22, p. 63
16:7–10, p. 426
16:21–22, p. 23
18:4–5, p. 384
24, p. 51
25, p. 282
26:30, p. 179

Numbers

1:47–53, p. 104
2:34, p. 104
5:21–22, p. 353
6:24–26, p. 235
10:14–28, p. 104
10:33, p. 104
11:4, p. 177
15:22–29, p. 23
21:30, p. 404
23:9, p. 256
25:1–9, p. 251

35:6–34, p. 426
35:12, pp. 426, 428
35:24, pp. 426, 428
35:25, pp. 426, 427, 429
36, p. 283

Deuteronomy

13, p. 372
13:12–16, p. 369
17:6, p. 371
19:1–13, p. 426
19:4, pp. 426, 428
19:15, p. 362
19:19, p. 368
19:20, p. 368
20:1–2, 359
20:5–9, p. 360
21:1–9, p. 362
21:22, p. 367
24:5, p. 360
26:7, p. 179
27:15–16, p. 393
27:15–26, p. 353
28:3–4, p. 393
31–34, p. 339
31:26, p. 354
33:15, p. 256
33:26, p. 444
33:29, p. 444

Joshua

6:26, p. 372
7, p. 363
7:22, p. 363

9:3, p. 404
10:36, p. 404
11, p. 123
19:36, p. 461
19:42, p. 404
20, p. 426
20:4, pp. 426, 428
20:5, pp. 426, 429
24:2, p. 391
24:11–23, p. 391
24:19–20, p. 393
24:26, p. 393
24:27, p. 392

Judges

1:18, p. 404
7:3, p. 360
8:19, p. 170
11:23, p. 172
12, p. 359
17:1–4, p. 363
19–20, p. 359

Ruth

3:13, p. 170
3:15, p. 174
4:2, p. 332

1 Samuel

1:11, p. 400
2:39, p. 449
8, p. 283
11:1–11, p. 358
11:7, p. 358
15:4, p. 358
15:10, p. 170

17:34–35, p. 177
17:43, p. 250
20:20, p. 296
20:36–37, p. 296
31:13, p. 361

2 Samuel

1:10–16, p. 363
1:12, p. 361
4:8–12, p. 363
20, p. 356

1 Kings

1:39, p. 394
1:45, p. 394
10:1, p. 98
10:14–27, p. 283
11:26–40, p. 97
12:4, p. 283
14:7, p. 157
14:8, p. 157
14:10, p. 157
20:1, p. 175
22:19, p. 170

2 Kings

1:9, p. 174
9:18, p. 172
11:12, p. 395
11:14, p. 394
21:12–13, p. 157
23:5, p. 403

2 Chronicles

20:16, p. 57
36:6, p. 357

Nehemiah

9:19, p. 104
9:32, p. 179

Job

1:5, p. 101
2:9, p. 441
2:11, p. 98

4:1, p. 98
6:19, p. 98
14:4–5, p. 451
15:1, p. 98
21:30, p. 173
22:1, p. 98
23:10, p. 441
42:9, p. 98

Psalms

2:7–9, p. 395
14:5, p. 177
20:1–2, p. 444
20:2–6, pp. 234, 235, 253
33:20, p. 444
72:10, 15, p. 98
78:5, p. 354
82, p. 227
94:1, p. 173
107:4–6, p. 13
107:19–30, p. 13
107:22, p. 13
121:1–2, p. 444
124:8, p. 444
144:6, p. 177

Proverbs

1:20, p. 173
31:1, p. 459
31:4, p. 459

Isaiah

2:2, p. 201
3:20, p. 328
5:8, p. 170
5:11, p. 170
5:20, p. 170
19:1, p. 257
21:6–7, p. 98
21:13, p. 98
21:14, p. 98
29, p. 380
29:11, p. 378
29:14, p. 1

30:9, p. 353
33:6, p. 173
35:2, p. 177
42:1–4, p. 202
49:1, p. 170
52:7, p. 240
53, pp. 164–65
53:8, p. 241
53:10, p. 241
55:5, p. 202
57:18, p. 113
60:6, p. 98
61:2–3, p. 256

Jeremiah

6:20, p. 98
7:11, p. 366
25:23–24, p. 98
32:3, p. 375
32:10, p. 375
32:11, p. 375
32:14, p. 375
32:15, p. 375
43:1–7, p. 97
48:25, p. 449

Ezekiel

27:20, p. 98
27:21, p. 98
27:22, p. 98
27:23, p. 98

Daniel

9:24–26, p. 256

Hosea

10:5, p. 403
11:8, p. 113
14:8, p. 228

Joel

1:3–4, p. 166
3:1, p. 177

Amos

1:3, p. 169
1:6, p. 169
3:7, p. 227
4:2, p. 170
7:16, p. 170
8:7, p. 170

Habakkuk

2:9, p. 170
2:12, p. 170
2:15, p. 170

Zephaniah

1:4, p. 403

Zechariah

4:7, p. 241
7:1, p. 170

New Testament

Matthew

5:22, pp. 333, 334, 335
5:23–25, p. 337
5:28, p. 335
5:44, p. 335
7:1–5, p. 382
7:6, pp. 336, 337, 338
7:10–11, p. 337
7:20, p. 28
13:44–46, p. 337
21:13, p. 366
27:38, p. 366

Luke

4:18–19, p. 256
22:14–38, p. 382

John

3:18–19, p. 29
8:56, p. 245

Scripture Citation Index • 491

10:16, pp. 137, 200
11:45–54, p. 356
11:50, p. 356
18:40, p. 366
20:31, p. 11
21:20–23, p. 289

Acts
20, p. 339

Romans
10:17, p. 26
12:2, p. 46

1 Corinthians
3:5–9, p. 256
12:20–21, p. 19
13:12, p. 43
15:22, p. 168
15:45, p. 168

Galatians
3:8, p. 245

1 Peter
3:18–20, p. 257

Jude
1:9, p. 248

Revelation
5:4–5, p. 378

Book of Mormon

1 Nephi
1, p. 484
1:1–3, p. 474
1:2, pp. 314, 318, 321, 399
1:2–3, p. 233
1:4, pp. 155, 326, 357, 456
1:8, pp. 227, 343
1:13, p. 326
1:17, pp. 170, 378
1:18, p. 326
1:20, p. 72
2:4, pp. 68, 99, 467
2:4–6, p. 59
2:5, pp. 78, 402
2:6, p. 60
2:7, pp. 62, 470
2:8, pp. 78, 466
2:8–10, p. 61
2:9–10, p. 462
2:11, p. 174
2:15, p. 459
2:23, p. 177
3:1, p. 460
3:2, p. 177
3:10, p. 456
3:15, p. 170
3:16, p. 456
3:17, pp. 326, 354
3:24, p. 175
3:29, p. 461
3:31, p. 174
4:1–3, p. 193
4:10–12, p. 250
4:10–23, p. 249
4:13, p. 356
4:28, p. 172
4:32, pp. 170, 468
4:38, p. 460
5:4, p. 326
5:5, p. 165
5:7, p. 460
5:9, p. 63
7:1, p. 311
7:4–5, p. 311
7:5, p. 460
7:13–15, p. 326
7:21–22, p. 460
7:22, p. 63
8:2, pp. 177, 400
8:4, p. 66
8:4–7, p. 471
8:4–8, p. 65
8:5–7, p. 66
8:8, p. 66
8:9, pp. 66, 471
8:9–10, p. 87
8:9–13, pp. 65, 71
8:10, pp. 71, 397
8:10–12, p. 471
8:12–14, p. 66
8:13, p. 87
8:14, p. 67
8:17–18, p. 67
8:19, p. 175
8:20–21, p. 66
8:21, pp. 65, 67
8:22, p. 67
8:23, pp. 66, 471
8:24, pp. 65, 67
8:26, pp. 64, 67, 68, 69
8:27, pp. 64, 65, 67, 87
8:28, p. 66
8:30, pp. 65, 67
8:31, p. 67
8:32, p. 66
8:33, pp. 65, 68
9:1, p. 459
10:1, p. 326
10:3–4, p. 326
10:7–10, p. 242
10:8, p. 328
10:10, p. 67
10:16, p. 460
11:8, p. 471
11:8–11, p. 228
11:12, p. 172
11:12–21, p. 228
11:13, p. 266
11:22–23, p. 228
11:25, pp. 228, 397
11:27–33, p. 242
11:30–32, p. 178
11:31, p. 328
11:36, p. 483
12:2, p. 173
12:4, p. 178
12:16, pp. 65, 471
12:18, p. 65
13:5, p. 177
13:7–8, p. 328
13:12, pp. 199, 224
13:15, p. 467
13:23–24, p. 326
13:25–35, p. 257
13:34, p. 457
13:38, p. 326
13:40, p. 257
13:41, p. 457
14:3, p. 484
14:7, p. 177
14:23, pp. 257, 326
15:1, p. 460
15:5, p. 174
15:13–20, p. 187
15:22, p. 416
15:26–27, p. 65
15:27, p. 471
15:28, pp. 65, 416
15:33–35, p. 187
15:36, p. 416
16:6, p. 460
16:7, pp. 81, 311
16:10, p. 460
16:12, p. 61
16:13, pp. 77, 82, 466
16:13–14, p. 461
16:14, pp. 84, 111
16:15, pp. 77, 469
16:16, p. 84

16:17–32,
  pp. 84, 91
16:34, pp. 73, 76,
  77, 81, 99, 107
16:36, p. 84
16:39, pp. 84, 91
17:1, pp. 73, 77,
  81, 85, 89, 91
17:1–4, p. 92
17:4, pp. 88, 90
17:5, pp. 71, 79,
  466
17:5–6, pp. 92,
  93
17:6, p. 85
17:8, p. 79
17:8–9, p. 328
17:9–10, p. 96
17:12, pp. 92,
  121
17:16, p. 96
17:17–19, p. 328
17:23–44, p. 193
17:27, p. 401
17:33, p. 175
17:45, p. 161
17:49, p. 328
17:51, p. 328
18:1, p. 94
18:1–2, pp. 71,
  92, 94
18:1–22, p. 328
18:2, p. 128
18:6, pp. 71, 92,
  94
18:11, p. 400
19:1, p. 378
19:5, p. 326
19:10, pp. 162,
  242
20:17, p. 169
22:8, p. 326
22:11, p. 326
22:14, p. 484
22:30–31, p. 474

2 Nephi

1:4, p. 326
1:5, p. 321
1:12, p. 173
1:13, p. 187
1:14, pp. 462,
  472
1:15, p. 482
1:22, p. 177
2:2, p. 441
2:11, p. 441
2:15, p. 416
2:15–16, p. 441
2:21–26, p. 436
2:22–23, p. 443
2:25, p. 443
2:26, p. 433
2:27, p. 437
2:29, p. 437
3:5–15, p. 238
3:21, p. 326
4:16–35, pp. 164,
  332
5:10, pp. 176,
  353
5:14, p. 175
5:15, p. 177
5:16, pp. 130,
  175
5:19, p. 175
5:21, p. 400
6:8, p. 326
8:4, p. 326
9:8, p. 172
9:14, p. 485
9:27, p. 170
9:35, p. 427
9:39, p. 427
9:52, p. 160
10:3, p. 242
10:20–22, p. 202
11:3, p. 175
12:2, p. 201
12:16, p. 328
13:20, p. 328

13:23, p. 328
14:1, p. 328
15:21, p. 170
15:27, p. 328
17:20, p. 319
21:15, p. 328
25:2, pp. 161,
  175
25:4–5, p. 280
25:7, p. 326
25:14, p. 326
25:17, p. 326
25:19, p. 242
25:22, p. 2
25:30, p. 355
26:24, p. 2
27:11, p. 2
27:14, pp. 326,
  379
27:26, p. 326
29:1–2, p. 326
29:2, p. 326
29:4, p. 326
31, p. 140
31:8, p. 165
33:4, p. 142
33:8, p. 314
33:9, p. 483
33:10, p. 11
33:14, p. 326

Jacob

1:2, p. 474
1:7, p. 183
1:9, p. 396
1:10–11, p. 397
1:12, p. 354
1:13, p. 284
1:17–19, p. 353
2:11, p. 170
2:19, p. 328
2:27, p. 170
3:3, p. 177
3:4, p. 467
4:1, p. 277

4:1–3, p. 317
4:2, p. 317
4:5, p. 245
4:7, p. 173
4:14, pp. 400,
  477
5, pp. 36, 198
5–6, p. 475
5:72, p. 173
7:17–19, p. 352
7:26, pp. 221, 314
7:27, p. 474

Enos

1:13, p. 177
1:23, p. 440

Jarom

1:1–2, p. 474
1:7, p. 292
1:11, pp. 165, 353

Omni

1:1, p. 474
1:5, p. 175
1:6, p. 91
1:17, p. 322
1:26, p. 183

Words of Mormon

1:3, 6, p. 378
1:9, pp. 326, 474

Mosiah

1–6, pp. 390,
  391, 394
1:2, p. 280
1:4, p. 474
1:15–16, p. 395
1:17, pp. 85, 91
1:18, p. 395
2:6, p. 328
2:8–9, p. 393

Scripture Citation Index • 493

2:9, pp. 27, 391
2:14, p. 180
2:17–19, p. 187
2:19, p. 392
2:26, p. 180
2:32, p. 437
2:33, 37, p. 437
3:2, p. 391
3:5, p. 328
3:5–10, p. 242
3:11, p. 23
3:13, p. 166
3:19, p. 46
3:23–24, p. 354
3:24, p. 170
4:1, p. 11
4:9–10, p. 392
4:16, p. 177
4:26, p. 328
4:30, p. 180
5:5, p. 392
5:9–10, p. 393
5:10–12, p. 51
6:1, pp. 392, 394
6:3, pp. 353, 396
7:1, p. 347
7:10, p. 292
7:15, pp. 177, 400
7:19–20, p. 221
8:7, p. 347
8:20, p. 173
9:1, p. 474
9:8, p. 292
9:9, pp. 288, 304
10:5, pp. 291, 328
10:8, p. 178
10:9, p. 358
11:3, pp. 180, 284
11:8, p. 320
11:10, p. 177
11:15, p. 288
12:3, pp. 157, 158

12:9, p. 364
12:10, p. 158
12:11, p. 157
12:25, p. 353
13:30, p. 355
15:10–13, p. 241
15:13–15, p. 240
15:18, p. 240
16:6, p. 165
17:4, p. 172
17:6, p. 175
17:16, p. 328
18:17, p. 326
19:20, p. 158
19:24, p. 322
20:4–5, p. 311
22:15, p. 284
23:5, p. 177
24:1–7, p. 262
24:15, p. 400
24:20–23, p. 101
25:4, p. 297
27:29, p. 484
27:29–30, p. 33
27:31, p. 401
28:1, p. 347
29:29, pp. 177, 354
29:38, p. 349
29:40, p. 349
29:43, pp. 177, 354
32:5, p. 284
35:3, p. 284

Alma

1:6, p. 328
1:10, p. 364
1:15, p. 476
1:27, p. 328
1:27–30, p. 328
1:29, p. 328
1:32, p. 328
2:37, p. 475
4:6, pp. 289, 328

4:12, p. 328
5:21, p. 485
5:26, p. 177
5:33, p. 481
5:34, p. 416
5:40, p. 162
5:53, p. 328
5:62, p. 416
7:10, pp. 211, 456
7:10–12, p. 242
7:25, p. 485
8:3, p. 109
8:7, p. 283
8:9, p. 371
8:16, p. 371
8:17, pp. 170, 370
8:24, p. 353
9:10, p. 91
9:22, pp. 85, 91, 92, 328
9:23, p. 370
11:3, p. 350
11:3–19, p. 348
11:4, p. 350
11:7, p. 349
11:40–41, p. 438
11:43–44, p. 438
12–13, p. 332
12:13–15, p. 438
12:16–18, p. 438
12:21, p. 416
12:23, p. 416
12:24–25, p. 433
12:26, p. 416
13:3, p. 432
13:11, p. 485
13:12, p. 485
13:23, p. 221
14:9, p. 371
14:11, p. 371
15:3–5, p. 328
13:3–11, p. 328
16:1, p. 372
16:2, p. 371
16:9, p. 371

16:9–11, p. 369
16:11, p. 372
17, p. 422
17:2, p. 326
17:26, p. 478
17:28, p. 478
18:5, p. 177
18:7, p. 479
18:26, p. 315
20:13, p. 173
20:28, p. 326
21:1, p. 109
21:2, p. 262
22:6, p. 162
22:27, p. 300
22:28, p. 467
23:2, p. 347
23:16–17, p. 428
24:2–3, p. 428
24:5, p. 428
24:6, p. 359
24:11–13, p. 358
24:18, p. 359
27:3, p. 428
27:8, p. 428
27:9, p. 428
27:11–26, p. 428
27:20–21, p. 428
27:22, pp. 401, 404
27:22–24, p. 429
27:23, p. 359
27:23–24, p. 358
27:24, pp. 361, 404
27:26, pp. 400, 429
30:10, p. 163
30:20, p. 430
30:47, p. 47
30:49, p. 351
30:51, p. 352
30:57, pp. 354, 368
31:26–35, p. 332

32, p. 45
32:16, p. 22
32:21, p. 27
32:40, p. 416
32:42, p. 180
33:4–11, p. 332
34:28, p. 328
34:33, p. 401
35:9, p. 467
35:10–11, p. 430
35:13, p. 430
35:14, pp. 404, 467
36, pp. 33, 340–345
36:28–29, p. 221
37:42, p. 91
38:2, p. 180
39:3, p. 480
41:13–15, pp. 51, 52
42:2, p. 416
42:3, p. 416
42:5, p. 416
42:6, p. 416
42:17–20, p. 187
43:12, p. 467
43:24, p. 170
43:38, p. 328
43:44, p. 328
44:5, p. 180
44:12, pp. 172, 371
44:17, p. 371
45:18–19, p. 248
46:4–6, p. 284
46:12–13, p. 178
46:13, p. 328
46:21, pp. 158, 236, 237
46:21–22, p. 358
46:21–24, p. 414
46:22, pp. 157, 236, 237
46:23, pp. 236, 237
46:23–24, p. 412
46:24, p. 236
46:35, p. 358
46:40, p. 328
49:1, p. 372
49:4, pp. 293, 294, 295, 296
49:5, p. 293
49:8, p. 293
49:11, p. 314
49:19–20, p. 306
49:24, p. 328
50:1, p. 293
50:3–4, p. 295
50:5, p. 293
50:15, p. 109
50:25, p. 347
51:15, p. 358
51:19, p. 286
51:21, p. 284
51:22, p. 109
51:34, p. 328
52:1, p. 328
53:4, p. 293
53:13, p. 360
53:15–17, p. 360
53:17–19, p. 480
54:6, p. 372
54:12, p. 358
54:12–13, p. 467
57:19, p. 175
57:25, p. 175
58:18, p. 371
60:7, p. 283
60:22, pp. 265, 283
60:27–30, p. 286
62:20, p. 293
62:42, p. 467
63:5–6, p. 298
63:5–10, p. 328

Helaman

1:1–3, p. 458
1:3, p. 401
1:7, p. 401
1:8, p. 401
1:14, p. 328
1:21, p. 294
2:11, p. 251
3:7–11, pp. 286, 372
3:10–14, p. 328
3:12, p. 430
3:14, pp. 178, 180
3:15, pp. 266, 275
4:12, p. 346
5:6–8, p. 187
5:20, p. 326
6:7–13, pp. 345–47
6:8, p. 266
6:10, p. 34
6:13, p. 328
6:30, p. 175
7–8, p. 361
7:10, p. 361
8:13–20, p. 242
8:20, p. 243
8:20–22, p. 326
8:27, p. 361
9:6, p. 362
9:10, p. 361
9:34, p. 362
9:37–38, p. 362
9:38, p. 364
11:24–26, p. 251
12:13–21, p. 213
12:18–20, p. 310
13:3, p. 170
13:19, p. 482
13:21, p. 170
14:3–6, p. 242
14:20–27, p. 242
15:6, p. 326
16:25, p. 474

3 Nephi

1:27–28, p. 251
3:8, p. 251
3:9–11, p. 251
3:10, p. 284
4:7, p. 328
4:12, p. 172
4:28–29, p. 250
4:28–33, p. 366
5:18, pp. 277, 378
5:19, p. 326
6:12, p. 280
6:22–28, p. 368
7:4, p. 284
7:11, p. 285
8:14, p. 266
11, p. 141
11:32, p. 25
11:36, p. 25
12–14, p. 335
12:22, pp. 333, 334, 335
13:27, p. 326
13:28, p. 328
13:33, p. 326
14, pp. 336, 338
14:6, p. 336
15:12, p. 312
15:15–16, p. 312
15:16–17, p. 137
17:4, p. 312
17:7–9, p. 328
24:3, p. 323
26:11, p. 12
26:12, p. 326
26:15, pp. 328, 329
27, p. 141
28:6–9, p. 249
28:14, p. 338
28:15, p. 435
28:26–27, p. 435
28:29, p. 435
28:30, p. 435

28:38–40, p. 436
29:5, p. 161
30:1, p. 170
30:2, p. 179

4 Nephi

1, p. 266
1:24, p. 328

Mormon

1–6, p. 267
1:3, p. 378
1:6, p. 378
1:4, p. 317
1:7, p. 265
1:9, p. 474
1:15–16, p. 436
1:18–19, p. 310
1:19, pp. 173, 326
2:2, p. 285
2:9, p. 175
2:27–28, p. 467
3:16, p. 436
3:17, p. 467
4:11–15, p. 298
4:21, p. 298
5:18, p. 328
6:6, pp. 378, 403
6:10–15, p. 265
8:11, p. 436
8:35, p. 166
8:36, p. 328
8:37–39, p. 328
9:12–13, pp. 168, 187
9:24, p. 328
9:30, p. 314
9:31, p. 280
9:32, pp. 317, 321
9:32–33, p. 233
9:33, pp. 278, 318, 322

Ether

1:1, p. 326
1:33, pp. 247, 281
2:2, p. 328
2:3, p. 463
2:6, p. 328
2:13, p. 326
2:16–18, p. 328
2:23, p. 328
2:24, p. 247
3:1, p. 328
3:1–6, p. 246
3:4, p. 328
3:15–16, p. 187
6:1, p. 326
6:2–7, p. 328
6:4, p. 328
6:5–8, p. 247
6:6, p. 247
6:7, pp. 246, 322, 473
6:11, p. 20
6:23, p. 153
7:16, p. 467
8:9–10, p. 312
9:1, p. 326
9:3, p. 328
9:17, p. 328
10:23, pp. 177, 400
10:24, pp. 289, 328
12:23–25, p. 277
12:23, pp. 278, 280, 310
12:24, p. 281
13:1, p. 326
15:15, p. 328

Moroni

3:3, p. 353
7:25, p. 326
8:8, pp. 322, 328
8:10–12, p. 446
8:15, p. 446
8:25–26, p. 167
9:32, p. 399
9:32–33, p. 155
10:3–4, p. 25
10:4, pp. 182, 227
10:27, pp. 354, 379
10:28, p. 326
10:30, p. 183
10:32, p. 183

Doctrine and Covenants

1:21, p. 2
3:12, p. 4
7, p. 249
9:5, p. 5
9:7, p. 5
10:24, p. 3
33:8, p. 99
38:27, p. 48
46:13–14, p. 22
77:9, p. 259
77:14, p. 259
84:25, p. 248
88:118, p. 17
93:29, p. 431
121:7, p. 14
138, p. 257
138:53, p. 431
138:56, p. 431

Pearl of Great Price

Abraham

2:16–18, p. 429
2:21, p. 97
3:22–23, p. 431
3:22–28, p. 245

Joseph Smith— History

1:34, p. 406
1:51–52, p. 232
1:51, p. 406
1:55–56, p. 326
1:60, p. 3

Alphabetical Listing of Hits

Abinadi on Isaiah 52–53, p. 240
Akkadian "Sheʾum," p. 288
Altar of Stones, p. 470
Ancient Texts on Metal Plates, p. 406
Ancient Gold Plates, p. 138
Ancient Vessels, p. 246
Apocalyptic Imagery, p. 484
Asylum, p. 425
Being Led into the Wilderness, p. 465
Cement Building Materials, p. 287
Chiasmus, p. 340
Chivalry in the Book of Mormon, p. 479
Classic Farewell Address, p. 338
"Coat of Joseph" in Ancient Tradition, p. 412
Cognate Accusative, p. 176
Colophons, p. 474
Comparable Weights and Measures, p. 348
Complex Geographical Consistency, p. 267
Complexities of Actual Warfare, p. 143
Compound Prepositions, p. 172
Construct State, p. 175
Courtship and Romance, p. 311
Credible Demographics, p. 130
Death of Nehor and Zemnarihah, p. 476
Depth of Exodus Motif, p. 192
Deseret, p. 462
Desert Imagery, pp. 470, 482
Details about Bountiful, p. 92
Details of Political Economy, p. 282
Different Cultural Settings, p. 313
Digging for Treasure, p. 310
Disparate Stylistic Features, p. 314
Distinction between Theft and Robbery, p. 364
Distinctive Politics, p. 146
Diverging Nineteenth-Century Expectations, p. 308
Egyptian and Hebrew Names, p. 401
Elephants, p. 476
Epic Milieu, p. 454
Exemption from Military Service, p. 357
Fermented Drinks, p. 288
Five Hebrew Terms, p. 353
Following the Law of Apostate Cities, p. 369
Form of Important Documents, p. 374
"From Whence No Traveler Can Return," p. 472
Gadianton Robbers, p. 480
Geographic Correlation of Nahom, p. 404
Geology, p. 198
Gold Plates, p. 465
Guerrilla Warfare, p. 197
Hagoth's Ships, p. 298
Harlot Isabel, p. 480
Hebrew Conditional Sentences, p. 212
Hebrew Forms, p. 399
Hermounts, p. 474
Hiding Up Treasures, p. 482
Human Sacrifice, p. 298
Incense Trail, p. 83
Infant Baptism, p. 445
Inspiration of Christopher Columbus, p. 199
"It Came to Pass," p. 163
Jaredite Barges, p. 473
Joseph's Rent Garment, p. 236
Journey to Bountiful, p. 88

Journey to Nahom, p. 76
Judges and Judgment Seats, p. 467
Laban's and Zemnarihah's
  Executions, p. 249
Lamanite Games at the Waters of
  Sebus, p. 478
Land of Inheritance, p. 466
Land of Jerusalem, pp. 211, 456
Language Systems, p. 277
Legal Curse of Speechlessness, p. 350
Lehi Account and Lachish Letters,
  p. 477
Lehi's Appropriate Sacrifices, p. 62
Lehi's Dream in Ancient Context,
  p. 64
Lehi's Poetry, p. 461
Lehi's Route to First Camp, p. 56
Lehi's Vision, p. 483
Level of Civilization, p. 262
Liahona, p. 477
Location for Zarahemla, p. 296
Location of First Camp, p. 60
Location of Nahom, p. 81
"Looking beyond the Mark," p. 477
Lost Tribes of Israel, p. 312
Luminous Stones, p. 464
Many "Ands," p. 177
Marvelous Power to Translate, p. 4
Merismus, p. 142
Mesoamerican Lineage History,
  p. 269
Mesoamerican Structural Cement,
  p. 372
Mesoamerican Codex, p. 274
Moses' and John's Translation, p. 247
Mosiah's Coronation Ceremony,
  p. 394
Multiple Names of God, p. 171
"My Father Dwelt in a Tent," p. 459
The Name "Alma," p. 210
Name Peculiarities, p. 159
Naming Valleys and Streams, p. 466
Native American Fabrics, p. 289
Nephi and His Asherah, p. 214
Nephi's Hunting Weapons, p. 469

Nephi's Temple, p. 130
New Year Rites, p. 472
Number Usage, p. 174
Old Bible Texts, p. 235
Olive Culture, pp. 198, 475
Oliver's Firm Testimony, p. 11
Other Hidden Records, p. 232
Peoples of Arabia, p. 86
Personal Names, p. 457
Place-Name "Shazer," p. 461
Plates vs. Parchment, p. 317
Plural Amplification, p. 173
Poetic Gradation, p. 166
Poetic Parallelisms, p. 160
Power of Oaths, p. 468
Procedure in Zemnarihah's
  Execution, p. 366
Pronoun Emphasis, p. 180
Pronoun Repetition, p. 179
Prophecies of Christ, p. 242
Prophecy by Joseph of Old, p. 238
Prophecy of the Lamb, p. 457
Prophetic Call, p. 211
Prophetic Perfect, p. 164
Prophetic Speech Formulas, p. 169
Raising the Title of Liberty, p. 469
Reformed Egyptian, p. 233
Repetition of "The," p. 176
The Role of Eve, p. 442
Rule of Evidence in an Unobserved
  Murder, p. 361
Sacred Secrecy, p. 336
Sacrifices, p. 62
Salome's Intrigues, p. 463
Scrolls and the Other Israel, p. 453
Shipbuilding, p. 128
Short Translation Time, p. 5
Similar Early Christian Documents,
  p. 140
Simile Curses, p. 156
Slaying of Laban, p. 356
Smiting with a Rod, p. 460
Smiting Off Arms, p. 422
Sticks of Judah and Joseph, p. 472
Symbolism of the Tree of Life, p. 397

Temple Imagery, p. 481
Temple outside Jerusalem, p. 474
Tenfold Repetitions, p. 332
Translation Process Consistently Described, p. 407
Translation Process, p. 3
Treaty/Covenant Pattern, p. 389
Views of the Natives, p. 318
Wars and Warfare, p. 292

White Garment, p. 485
"Without a Cause" 3 Nephi 12:22, p. 333
The Witnesses, p. 203
Wordprinting Evidence of Multiple Authors, p. 132
Writings on Arabia, p. 69
Zosimus, p. 135

Contributors

S. Kent Brown (Ph.D., Brown University) has taught for thirty-one years at Brigham Young University, where he is Professor of Ancient Scripture and Director of Ancient Studies. He served as the director of the BYU Jerusalem Center for Near Eastern Studies from 1993 to 1996. In 1978–79 he was a fellow of the American Research Center in Egypt, where he worked on ostraca at the Coptic Museum in Old Cairo. He has also been a fellow of the David M. Kennedy Center in Provo. He received major grants from the National Endowment for the Humanities and the Mormon Archaeology and Research Foundation to microfilm more than fifteen hundred early Christian manuscripts in Cairo and Jerusalem. He was an editor for the *Encyclopedia of Mormonism* and a managing editor for the *Coptic Encyclopedia*. He currently serves as the editor of the *Journal of Book of Mormon Studies*.

Alison V. P. Coutts (M.A., Brigham Young University) is Director of Publications for the Institute for the Study and Preservation of Ancient Religious Texts at Brigham Young University. A native of the Isle of Wight in England, she came to BYU in 1994 after a successful career in administration in the United States, England, France, and Germany. She speaks fluent French and German and is studying modern Hebrew, having completed her M.A. in Ancient Near Eastern Studies with an emphasis in the asylum tradition. Her desire to pursue studies in this area was sparked by the works of Hugh Nibley and others. Prior to being appointed Director of Publications, she was the staff editor of the *Journal of Book of Mormon*

Studies. A longtime supporter of the Foundation for Ancient Research and Mormon Studies, she is coeditor of *Uncovering the Original Text of the Book of Mormon: History and Findings of the Critical Text Project.*

John Gee (Ph.D., Yale University) is William "Bill" Gay Assistant Research Professor of Egyptology at the Institute for the Study and Preservation of Ancient Religious Texts, where he is a series editor for Studies in the Book of Abraham and a member of the editorial board of the Eastern Christian Texts series. He is also on the board of directors for the Aziz S. Atiya Fund for Coptic Studies at the University of Utah. He is the author of several publications on the Book of Mormon and related subjects.

Elder Neal A. Maxwell (M.A., University of Utah) has served as a member of the Quorum of the Twelve Apostles of the Church of Jesus Christ of Latter-day Saints since July 1981. He was a member of the presidency of the First Quorum of the Seventy from 1976 to 1981 and an Assistant to the Twelve from 1974 to 1976. A lifelong educator, Elder Maxwell was Executive Vice President at the University of Utah at the time of his appointment as the Commissioner of Education for the Church Educational System, a position that he filled from 1970 to 1976. Before his full-time church callings, Elder Maxwell held a variety of administrative and teaching positions with the University of Utah. He has written twenty-nine books on religious topics, with one of the most recent receiving a literary prize for Latter-day Saint literature. Earlier he authored many articles on politics and government for national, professional, and local publications.

Donald W. Parry (Ph.D., University of Utah) is Associate Professor of Hebrew Language and Literature at Brigham Young University. As a member of the international team of translators of the Dead Sea Scrolls, he is assigned to translate the books of Samuel. He has published a new edition of the Great Isaiah Scroll. Among his research interests are the writings of Isaiah and ancient temples. He has published numerous articles and books on the Dead Sea Scrolls and the Old Testament, including several works on the book of Isaiah. He is a member of several professional societies, including the Princeton Dead Sea Scrolls Society, the Society for Biblical Literature, the International Organization for the Study of the Old Testament, and the National Association for Professors of Hebrew.

Daniel C. Peterson (Ph.D., University of California, Los Angeles) is Associate Professor of Islamic Studies and Arabic at Brigham Young University. He is Associate Executive Director and Codirector of Research for the Institute for the Study and Preservation of Ancient Religious Texts, where he is also Editor of the *FARMS Review of Books* and Executive Editor of the Middle Eastern Texts Initiative, which includes the Islamic Translation Series, Graeco-Arabic Sciences and Philosophy series, and Eastern Christian Texts series. He is the author of numerous articles on subjects related to the Book of Mormon.

Noel B. Reynolds (Ph.D., Harvard University) is Associate Academic Vice President for Undergraduate Studies and Professor of Political Science at Brigham Young University. He has also taught courses in philosophy, law, American heritage, and scripture at Brigham Young University and has been a visiting scholar at Harvard Law School, Edinburgh University, and the Hebrew University in Jerusalem. His scholarly interests include the philosophy of law, the founding of America, authorship studies, Plato, electronic religious texts, and the Book of Mormon. He is a member of the American Philosophical Association and the American Political Science Association. He served as president of the Foundation for Ancient Research and Mormon Studies and was an editor of Macmillan's *Encyclopedia of Mormonism*. He is the producer of the Dead Sea Scrolls Electronic Library on CD-ROM, which was released by BYU in collaboration with the academic publisher E. J. Brill.

Stephen D. Ricks (Ph.D., University of California, Berkeley, and Graduate Theological Union) is Professor of Hebrew and Cognate Learning in the Department of Asian and Near Eastern Languages at Brigham Young University. He served as president of the Foundation for Ancient Research and Mormon Studies from 1988 to 1991 and as chairman of the board from 1991 to 1997, as the founding editor of the *Journal of Book of Mormon Studies* from 1992 to 1997, and as Associate Dean of General Education and Honors at BYU from 1992 to 1996. His scholarly interests include temple-related texts, the Dead Sea Scrolls, the Book of Mormon, and early Christian literature. He has published eighty articles and authored or edited fifteen books in those areas.

John L. Sorenson (Ph.D., University of California, Los Angeles) is Professor Emeritus of Anthropology at Brigham Young University. He established the anthropology curriculum at BYU, serving on the faculty for twenty-three years before retiring in 1985. From 1964 to 1969 he was head social scientist at General Research Corporation in Santa Barbara, California. From 1969 to 1971 he founded and headed Bonneville Research Corporation in Provo, a subsidiary of GRC. He has been an officer or contributor to the Foundation for Ancient Research and Mormon Studies since its inception, most recently as editor of the *Journal of Book of Mormon Studies*. He has published more than two dozen articles, monographs, and books about archaeology, specializing in the Mesoamerican area. In addition, he has authored more than one hundred other works on sociocultural and applied anthropology.

John A. Tvedtnes (two M.A.'s, University of Utah) is a senior resident scholar at the Institute for the Study and Preservation of Ancient Religious Texts. He has taught at the University of Utah and at the BYU Jerusalem Center for Near Eastern Studies and has lectured in Israel and the United States. He has delivered papers at numerous symposia, including those sponsored by the University of Utah Middle East Center, the Society of Biblical Literature, the World Congress of Jewish Studies, the Israel Ministry of Education and Culture, the Society for Early Historic Archaeology, and the Institute for the Comparative Study of Civilizations. He has authored eight books and more than two hundred articles, many of them on the Book of Mormon, and has published with the University of Utah, Brigham Young University, the Hebrew University in Jerusalem, the Pontifical Biblical Institute, and the *Journal of Near Eastern Studies*.

John W. Welch (J.D., Duke University) is the Robert K. Thomas Professor of Law at Brigham Young University's J. Reuben Clark Law School, Editor in Chief of *BYU Studies*, and Director of Publications for the university's Joseph Fielding Smith Institute for LDS History. He is the founder of the Foundation for Ancient Research and Mormon Studies and has published books and articles on many scriptural subjects, including King Benjamin's speech, the Sermon at the Temple, and law and literature in the Book of Mormon. He serves on the executive committee of the Biblical Law Section of the Society of Biblical Literature. In addition to teaching contemporary legal subjects, he conducts research on law in the ancient Near East, Hebrew law in the Old Testament, and law in the world of the New Testament. His publications also cover the journals of William McLellin, the writings of B. H. Roberts, the Book of Mormon paintings of Minerva Teichert, and many other subjects of interest to Latter-day Saints. He was one of the editors of Macmillan's *Encyclopedia of Mormonism,* general editor of the Collected Works of Hugh Nibley, and codirector of the Masada and Dead Sea Scrolls Exhibition at BYU.

About FARMS

FARMS is part of Brigham Young University's Institute for the Study and Preservation of Ancient Religious Texts. As such, it encourages and supports research on the Book of Mormon, the Book of Abraham, the Bible, other ancient scripture, and related subjects. Under the FARMS imprint, the Institute publishes and distributes titles in these areas for the benefit of scholars and interested Latter-day Saint readers.

Primary research interests at FARMS include the history, language, literature, culture, geography, politics, and law relevant to ancient scripture. Although such subjects are of secondary importance when compared with the spiritual and eternal messages of scripture, solid research and academic perspectives can supply certain kinds of useful information, even if only tentatively, concerning many significant and interesting questions about scripture.

FARMS makes interim and final reports about this research available widely, promptly, and economically. These publications are peer reviewed to ensure that scholarly standards are met. The proceeds from the sale of these materials are used to support further research and publications. As a service to teachers and students of the scriptures, research results are distributed in both scholarly and popular formats.

It is hoped that this information will help all interested people to "come unto Christ" (Jacob 1:7) and to understand and appreciate more fully the scriptural witnesses of the divine mission of Jesus Christ, the Son of God.

Publication of this volume

is made possible by

a generous donation